THE REVELATION

THE EVOLUTION OF TRANSCENDENT PERCEPTION BY HUMANITY

An Esoteric Perspective Exploring the Principles Governing Humanity's Enlightenment and of Planetary Being

NEW REVISED EDITION

BODO BALSYS

UNIVERSAL DHARMA
PUBLICATIONS
SYDNEY, AUSTRALIA

ISBN 978-0-6487877-2-3

Edition 2, 2024
Revised Edition of 1989 publication

Front cover artwork by the author: 'The Crucified Christ'.
Front page artwork by the author: 'Orpheus'.

Dedication

Oṁ

Dedicated to the members of the School of Esoteric Sciences, and to the great Ones who have helped formulate the esoteric doctrine. A special thanks to Kylie Smith. Also to Robert MacDonald and Titania de Montaner, who helped to edit this edition

Oṁ

Contents

Preface ... xi

1. The Interpretation of Sacred Scriptures & the Question of 'God' 1
   - The current opportunity ... 3
   - What is the mind? ... 8
   - Trikāya - the three sheathes of a Buddha ... 11
   - Creation from Thought Substance ... 13
   - The nature of Mind ... 23
   - The planetary Logos ... 25
   - The seven keys of interpretation for understanding a sacred text ... 28

2. The Function of Energy and the Evolution of Consciousness ... 37
   - The etheric body, *prāṇa* and the *nāḍī* system ... 39
   - The Soul and the purpose of evolution ... 43
   - The three Outpourings and Individualisation ... 45
   - The ability to reason ... 51
   - The Hierarchy of Enlightened Being ... 59
   - The inevitability of change ... 65
   - The esoteric truth within the parables ... 67
   - Clarifying ancient history ... 71

3. The Nature of Karma and the Rebirth of Consciousness ... 76
   - Heaven and hell states ... 77
   - Individual and group *karma* ... 79
   - *Karma* and the conditions of rebirth ... 84
   - The evolution of a Christ ... 86
   - Life after death ... 87
   - Biblical references to rebirth ... 92
   - Jesus and the blind man ... 95
   - Achieving the perfection of the Christ ... 98
   - The censorship of reincarnation ... 101
   - Transmigration of Souls and lesser rebirths ... 102

4. The Development of an Enlightened Attitude ... 109
   - Societal progression from the 1950s onwards ... 111
   - Transforming conflict ... 116
   - Preparing for the return of the Christ ... 119
   - From Pisces to Aquarius ... 123
   - The Four Noble Truths and the Eightfold Path ... 125
   - The significance of death ... 130

The power to vision 138
The Seven Rays 142

5. The Function of Life and the use of the Physiological Key 146
Thoughts, energy, intelligence and will 148
The angelic *(deva)* kingdom 152
Esoteric physiology 157
The physiological key 160
The astral plane and the silver cord 169
The nature of multidimensional perception 174
Karma and the life after death 180

6. Instinct, Glamour and Thought-Forms 192
A. The question of instinct 194
The three Outpourings 201
Notes to figure six 202
B. The factor of desire *(kāma)*, auras 210
Glamour 214
The Atlantean epoch 217
C. The intellect and thought-forms 219

7. The Organs of Sensation and of Action 233
The five organs of action 239

8. The Question of Evil 259
The serpent and *kuṇḍalinī* 261
The ability to poison and to fly 266
The *chakras* 271
Other meanings of the serpent 274
Satan 282
References to Satan in the New Testament 284
References from ***St. John's Revelation*** 291
The Devil 295
Exorcism and obsession by entities 301
Symbolism of the sheep and the goats 302
The concept of hell 305
Accusations against Jesus 313
Conceptions of evil and related fears 316

9. The Five Vayūs (Prāṇas) and the Causative Process 334
The factor of *prāṇa* 334
Three fundamental energies 337
Further notes concerning the *chakras* 341

The *vayūs* 347
The five Stages of unfoldment of the *vayūs* 350
The *vayūs,* the Instincts and Initiation 358
Concluding explanations concerning the *vayūs* 365

10. The Nature of the Christ 374
Jesus' discourse with the Scribes and Pharisees 375
The Word 377
The significance of Abraham 381
I am That I am 387
Covenant with 'God' 392
The twelve apostles 399
Predestination 414
General summary 418

11. The Reappearance of the Christ 424
The doctrine of Avatars 424
The advent of Maitreya 427
The Aquarian epoch 432
Messianic sects and Christ's reappearance 437
Other erroneous Christian doctrines 442
The New Age 446
The twenty-fourth chapter of Matthew 450
General summary 461

Bibliography 470
Index 475

Figures

Figure 1: Mind as the mediator....9
Figure 2: The physical septenary....42
Figure 3: The pentagram....163
Figure 4: A group centre....164
Figure 5: Self-conscious (self-centred) individual....164
Figure 6: The evolution of instinct via the three Outpourings....203
Figure 7: The energy of thought....221
Figure 8: A compassionate thought....222
Figure 9: A sensual thought....223
Figure 10: The planes of perception & the constitution of Brahmā....249
Figure 11: The pentad governing a human unit....254
Figure 12: The serpent, the devil and Satan....260
Figure 13: The Caduceus....264
Figure 14: The cycle of time....275
Figure 15: Planetary and solar motion....275
Figure 16: The spinal column....276
Figure 17: The spiral of the time-space continuum....278
Figure 18: The cross-section of a *nāḍī*....279
Figure 19: The swastika....280
Figure 20: The Stages of *prāṇic* circulation....362
Figure 21: The Ray lines for the *vayūs*....364
Figure 22: The five Stages to liberation and the pentagram....367
Figure 23: The interrelated pentads....370
Figure 24: The summary of the *prāṇic* circulation....370
Figure 25: The attributes of Father-Son-Mother....381
Figure 26: I am That I am....388
Figure 27: The THAT....390
Figure 28: The twelve apostles....410
Figure 29: A line of planetary energisation....468

Tables

Table 1: The triune principles....19
Table 2: The triune aspects of Deity....23
Table 3: Discoverers and names of energy....41
Table 4. The five instincts and their relationships....209
Table 5: The five organs of sensation....234
Table 6: The evolved attributes of the senses....239
Table 7: The organs of action....240
Table 8: The mouth....242
Table 9: The hands....243
Table 10: The legs....244
Table 11: The genitals....246
Table 12: The anus....248
Table 13: The Rays and the planes of perception....251
Table 14: The position of *manas* *253*
Table 15: The *chakras*....274
Table 16: The five *vayūs*....349
Table 17: The five *vayūs* and the Initiations....358
Table 18: The Stages of Initiation and Breath....363
Table 19: Notes to figure 24....371

Preface

Most people have contemplated the purpose of human evolution. How did we come to be? What exactly constitutes humanity's real or fundamental nature? These are questions that few have had the ability to answer rightly. The nature of humanity was always enigmatic and communicated to us through riddles, such as that of the Sphinx or the analysis of the number of the 'beast', which is the 'number of a man'.[1] We were asked to solve the riddles by whatever means we had at our disposal. This necessarily required intense inner inquiry and self-analysis, intricately interwoven with the problem of pain and suffering. These became the impetus for self-discovery.

The resultant information, when related to the forces of the external universe, would enable a person to overcome the hindrances of the physical body and its pain-engendering qualities. They were overcome by means of certain knowledge concerning right meditative or ritualistic practices. One thereby could eventually master the entire life process and so evolve into the ranks of superhuman existence.

Those with advanced spiritual awareness were often worshipped by the devotional ones. They were known by such names as Prophet, Rishi, Guru, Adept, Arhat, Sage and Master (of wisdom). These enlightened ones could hold a covenant with 'God', and/or touch the highest sources of Truth, the 'fount of the Law' *(dharma)*. They thus wielded the most potent spiritual energies. By mastering life, the Sage came to realise

---

1 *Rev. 13:18.*

the interrelatedness of all beings. The law of cause and effect *(karma)* was observed. This law determines how each quality or act, though engendered by an individual, is really an effect of one's interrelation with the whole. The karmic conditionings thus need to be eliminated by the whole before an individual can become entirely freed from their effects.

Such freedom necessitates one's energies to be manifested in the form of compassionate understanding, to eliminate the root of all suffering and strife within and external to oneself. One can thus come to experience the Heart, the central animating Dynamo of all Being, which is the essential numinous essence of humanity itself. The information gleaned from such self-analysis is all that can be truly know. It is fundamental to our evolution as rational beings, as it rests on the edifice of our experiences in the realm of form, and awakens perception of the inner universe.

The question of 'what is human?' must be answered by each of us, with the conviction of our hearts and minds, united in common accord. This question concerns not only the cause and effect of human suffering, but also the survival of our civilisation. It is tied to the fabric of Nature, of which humanity is only a part. Answering this question is effectively a description of the nature of the enlightenment process, which is the concern of my books.

Many know by one means or another that a New Age is dawning. This arrival will increasingly affect all of our lives in both subjective and demonstratively objective ways. It is closely concerned with the imminent reappearance of the great Being (emanation, embodiment or type of energy) that is known as the Christ in the West. The concept of an imminent Messiah (the Bodhisattva Maitreya, the Imam Mahdi, or the Christ) expresses the worldwide expectancy by religious followers for a Saviour and Server to come in this age. His coming is prophesied to bring true lasting peace and prosperity to the earth.

Communistic and Democratic philosophies also aim for lasting peace and prosperity. However, their ideology of the means to obtain such prosperity differs. These concepts can, and must, change in such a way as to adapt to or incorporate a 'golden mean' for the desired goal of peace to be produced. A universal religion or order of being must arise and is arising. It will incorporate the best of all theologies, doctrines, philosophies, cultural activities and scientific research. Most people have begun to aspire (at least within their feeling-response or wish life) to engender this. We are thus in one of the most opportune and exciting times in world history. In general, what is strongly desired by the human kingdom has a real possibility of being achieved.

An understanding of the implications for the coming era creates a responsibility and opportunity for increasingly enlightened service. It necessitates each of us to perform works that will result in the rectification of some aspect of world suffering. We must loosen some of the chains that bind and limit human freedom, while engendering active peace and harmony in the world.

From a religious viewpoint this necessitates a re-examination of the information contained in the Bible, as the major religious dispensation of the West. My work hopes to explicate an esoteric level of knowledge that is little realised by the orthodox theologian. The philosophy presented here is drawn from many world religious systems as well as scientific discoveries. Religion and science are really facets of a universal embrace that seeks the enlightenment of humanity.

The major key is an understanding of meditation, based on increasingly perceptive awareness to the nature of intense energy reception, assimilation and retransmission. It relates to what for many aeons has been hidden from the eyes and ears of humanity – except for the relative few, who developed the capacity to 'see' in a real or deeply perceptive sense. It denotes the revelation of the nature of the Mysteries of Being, which concern an ancient and completely non-secular Wisdom Religion. This Religion has been in existence since time immemorial.

This book provides introductory postulates and lays a conceptual groundwork to succinctly deal with the basic philosophy to comprehend the nature of the Wisdom Religion. This concerns understanding the meaning of symbols used by the authors of the sacred texts and treatises of the past. These symbols veiled from the profane the true import of the profound revelations and multidimensional concept of the enlightened Ones. The profane would only produce mental-emotional distortions of what was incomprehensible to them. Without such explanatory grounding the true implications of such texts cannot be understood by the uninitiated. They are not based on the types of realisations associated with the intellect, although the methods of interpretation necessitate its complete use.

What is expounded is part of a continuum of Revelation that has been developing with increasing momentum in the past few centuries. This specifically concerns the depth of meaning in Gospel symbolism that Christ stated would be revealed to us.[2] Readers should however formulate their own opinions as to the context of any teaching by utilising their own unprejudiced, intuitive and discriminative faculties.

It matters relatively little whether one believes in this or that system of philosophy or creed, or if one knows the esoteric significance. What is truly of import is the expression of Love for humanity. Of specific concern are the capacity for good will and the concept of universality and cooperativeness. Through these traits, our capacity increases to intelligently respond to the many evolving ideas and ideals that are arising in the present age. The ability to demonstrate these traits automatically makes one a student of the divine or the esoteric lore (whether one reads books or not). As one's capacity to actively Love increases, the nature of, and purpose for, Love must eventually register within our consciousness.

The approach to the divine within and without the human system can only be self-initiated, self-perpetuated and self-realised. Spirituality is not the sacred possession of any one group, or a particular religious presentation. It never has been and never will be, except as arbitrary doctrines arising out of people's minds and desire natures. Seekers must follow their own innate code of ethics.

It is one's own conscience that dictates what is right for a person to do. What is right for one may not necessarily be right for another. The fact that people have a conscience is their hope for future glory, as it provides assurance of the 'Christ within'. Each must learn to listen to this subjective Voice, the 'voiceless inner Voice', or 'Voice of silence',[3] for it denotes the approach to our own salvation and immortality.

Much must be yet discovered and revealed concerning the ancient Mysteries. Much esoteric philosophy has been codified for us and preserved by the sages and wise men of old. This implicates

---

2 *Matthew 24:14* and *John 16:25.*

3 See also Helena P. Blavatsky, *The Voice of the Silence* (Pasadena: Theosophical University Press, [1889] 1992).

a vast expanse of knowledge and Revelation regarding the realms of enlightened perception, to which humanity is only at the portal. It is an immense quest, replete with a superabundance of the myriad qualities and interrelationships of lives contained within the One Life of the universe.

What is to manifest in the future has not been envisioned by present humanity. Most of the past has hardly even begun to be fathomed. We have only dimly started to comprehend all the subtleties concerning the present. Our present (materialistic) science is a rivulet travelling towards an ocean of discovery. That ocean is but a drop in the universe.

Every form in our solar system has the capacity to evolve sentience. Each form is sustained, and thus embodied, by a coherent animating principle or force. Every solar system, therefore, in the universe can be considered an embodied form that has its evolving Life and ordered Purpose. All these embodied forms answer to divine as well as to mundane law. Mundane law is essentially the effect of ritualistic endeavour of a greater Life upon lesser evolved forms within the body of manifestation of that greater Life. It becomes transcended when the forms within the greater Life consciously evolve to embrace the complete expression of that Life, whilst they actively express the results downwards into the realm of form.

Divine Law is the expression of that greater Life (or Divinity) in its own sphere of endeavour. Such statements need not be merely the expressions of articles of faith or belief – they can be ascertained as fact by direct experience or the transcendent awareness of consciousness. As science begins to fully explore the idea of inherent Divinity in all manifest Life, an entirely new era of realisation will manifest. This will produce a civilisation that incorporates the wise utilisation of subjective energies and qualities. Revelation of such qualities transcend all formulations of present empirical thought.

The information presented in the New Testament relates to the prophecy of the 'second coming' of the Christ and the revelation, which promises an unfoldment of such understanding. This work will endeavour to explain the details, to analyse and define all the implications of what is expressive of Divinity. Hopefully, readers will be assisted by such elucidation, thereby encouraging them to work with increasing effectiveness towards common beneficent aims within their own individual spheres and the greater whole. Enlightenment is the continually unfolding process that every unit of Life is undertaking, whether consciously realised or not.

Oṁ maṇi padme hūṁ!

To meet the Christ,
one needs a quiet
all-embracive mind
and an active heart
well versed in the art of
detached one-pointedness
answering the cry of all suffering.

Give your heart to That
which is the world's offering,
and rise
to greet the universal,
most vast and awesome Light
that is (His) Mind.

Grace be to the Guru,
inspiration of aspirational being
ineffable Love-Light Source.

Gift waves come
from That Light to you,
and through you
to all those that are you,
and from them
through you to the Guru.

He is your path to
the One and the other
that are separated
in time and space.

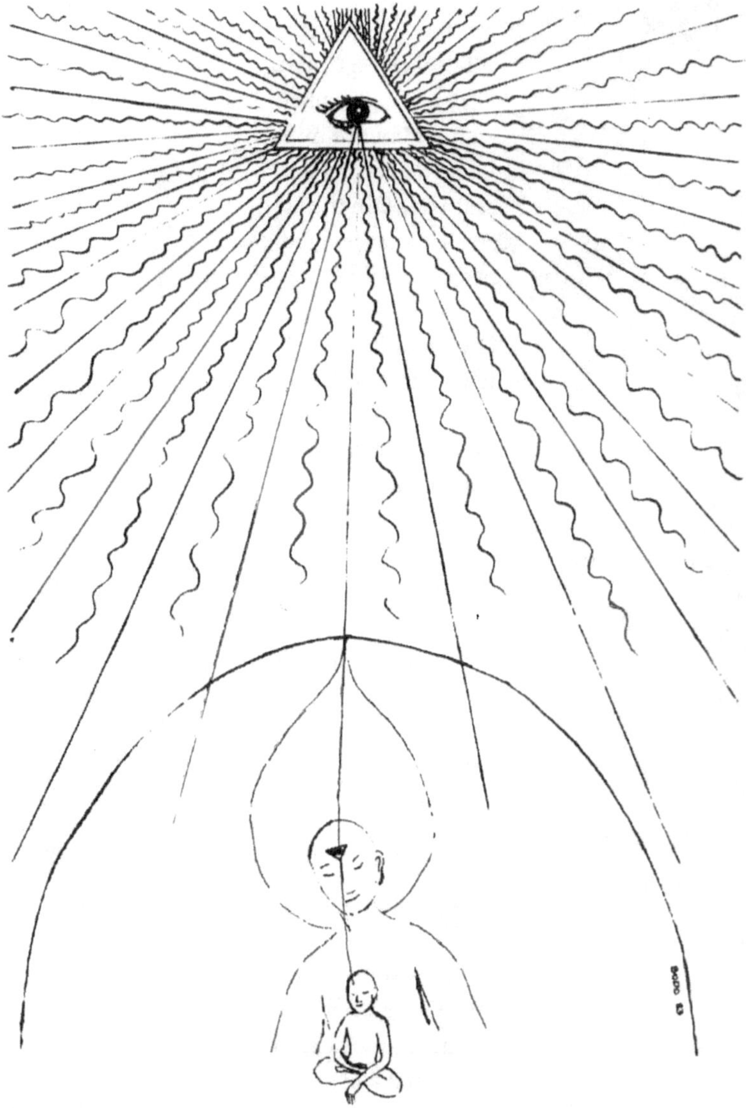

1

The Interpretation of Sacred Scriptures and the Question of 'God'

There are a bewildering plethora of teachings to confront the sincere seekers of enlightened perception. Many have fallen victim to short-sighted visionaries or to the assertions of those that claim a specific covenant with 'God' (or another such Divine personage). These teachings are associated with a myriad of different faiths, sects, and philosophic dispensations. The claims of a particular interpretation of Divine scripture as being the only delineation of truth are legion.

Each dogmatic claim to be 'correct' occurs despite conflict between the claims of various religious sects, philosophical groups, and personality cults. Thus, it is difficult for the sincere seeker to find a way to the source of all Love and Light (to enlightenment) and to have a clarified vision of what this implies. Yet somehow one must come triumphantly to that knowledge.

It is easy to see, therefore, that all aspirants on a serious quest for self-realisation of the Divine will be faced with the question of where or how to start. 'What is the course that will lead to right results?' The quest need not be as difficult as it appears at first. Positive results are gauged by the intensity of effort and integrity of motive that one expresses. If one is satisfied with short-sighted answers and quick goals, or an emotional salvation, so be it; a conventional formulation of spiritual teachings will likely suffice.

If, however, Truth and Divine Reality are above all the essence of one's quest, then the path will be more arduous. However, in the long run it bears greater fruit within an aspirant's field of perception, as well as in the results of their service work in the world. This necessitates a clear-headed resourcefulness to vigorously seek out the kernels of truth within each mountain of verbosity. To this, is added one's own storehouse of realisations until a complete picture is obtained.

A person's beliefs are often encouraged by a particular religious tradition, or the philosophic sect one is born into. Dogma is frequently followed by unquestioning faith due to tradition. Individuals have been led to believe that specific dogmatic interpretations must be condoned as the one explicit 'Word of God'.[1]

Most often, the rationalisations of the tenets of these doctrinal texts are misconstrued, distorted, or made to be misleading. This suits the objectives of those (either religious or secular) who are in power over masses of people. Such aberrations have gradually accumulated through the course of time. They garner widespread acceptance as 'Truth' when their interpolation first becomes obscured, and then forgotten. This gives the resulting distorted message a seeming agedness and thus a perceived sanctity.

In the past, the followers of distorted tenets from various religious and philosophic sects often warred against one another with unparalleled ferocity. Outright hatred or fear of opposing beliefs garnered no compromise, equanimity, or loving-kindness. Grievous historical examples of this include the Inquisitional period in Europe, however similar occurrences happen in modern times. People still commit mental, emotional and physical atrocities due to the bigoted attitudes and zealous intolerance stemming from biased interpretations of religious or philosophic scriptures. The much-bandied war cry of the religious, 'In the name of God', has led to countless millions suffering ruthless exploitation, cruelty and death. The progenitors of these actions ridicule

1 As firmly advocated by the state, a school of thought, or the society in which one lives.

and negate the example of Love as advocated by Jesus and many other respected theistic and ethical leaders.

Causes of wars are not necessarily theological, but also materialistic. They are still with humanity. The unprecedented threat of a nuclear holocaust could prevent the very survival of humanity. Therefore, rectifying the underlying causes of war has never been of greater necessity. The consequences are now so potently awful that people everywhere are rising up to challenge this threat, such as by endeavouring to promote international peace and harmonious co-operation. This activity is appearing in all fields, from the scientific to the artistic, educative, and religious. Hopefully, this will lead humanity towards a new era of peace and prosperity – however, the outcome is yet speculative.

Much depends upon the attitudes of the thinkers of the world. The thoughts of the average human being are rarely entirely their own. They are generally coloured by the massed weight of emotions, religious or philosophic beliefs, socio-political indoctrination, biased opinions, and selfishly motivated desire. Conflict results from the pursuit of unquestioning, prescribed, or regimented dogma; yet these conditionings encase the mental resources through which the interpretation of religious works or other presented philosophies must depend. The scope for manipulation of collective opinions by thinkers who feed the innate biases and selfishness of humanity is extensive. However, massed human manipulation is not the theme of this book.

The current opportunity

There is significant opportunity presenting itself at this time. Those qualities expressive of divinity are now able to be evoked by the human family, which is a development worthy of great optimism. The teachings are to be presented which may give seekers the keys leading to full comprehension of the symbolism in sacred scriptures and the Laws of Being. This appertains to large-scale human enlightenment. The presentation of these teachings allows further advancement towards the enlightening of the human family, via groups of self-determined individuals who are striving towards fulfilment in many fields of service. These are the individuals who clearly determine the right or wrong in any teaching or situation confronting them, and act accordingly.

It is obvious that one must clear one's mind of all adverse conditionings and erroneous beliefs to reveal the seeds of truth within any dogma. To obtain an enlightened mind, in essence, one must produce a tranquil state through which understanding may be intuited.[2] This 'tranquility' is an abstracted, perceptive, and intensely focused consciousness. It facilitates instantaneous analytical deduction and consequent realisation. For the duration of an abstraction, perception is experienced without the distinction of the self as perceiver, or awareness of separateness from the object being perceived.

A period of emotional, mental and ethical training is required to produce a state of mind in which no adverse conditionings exist. This will necessitate deep introspection and inner analysis of one's motivation. The goal is to distinguish the factors that produce illusion, glamour, distortion and muddled thinking, from those that produce clear unbiased results. Control must be instituted over unbridled emotional states and desires that provoke bias and conflict. This training has been advocated to varying degrees by many schools of the contemplative lifestyle. It has also been taught, in a less concise manner, by many scholastic disciplines that provide degrees at universities.

Only through tranquility can Christ-consciousness (enlightenment) speak. Only then, metaphorically, can the heart grow and expand into full compassionate understanding – to embrace the hearts of all sentient beings. Thus, the heart may come to know the secrets of life. One must embrace the tenets of one's findings while keeping the mind open for new information. Revelation may alter or extend one's previous interpretations to allow an enlightened mind to grow and flower.

The ability to live in the 'Heart of God' implies freedom to live in all realms of being – no bondage to ritual, nor subservience to dictates from mind-produced 'God' concepts, as many seem to think. True freedom is to love and be loved, with love that asks for naught from the beloved (whether the lover be human or 'God'). Love desires only the continued growth and prosperity of the beloved and the means to bring this about.

---

2 'The attributes of consciousness can be refined to the degree that it allows illumination and the intuition to manifest in the form of *bodhicitta* and wisdom.' See my book, *A Treatise on Mind,* Vol. 2, 45.

Conversely, separateness or segregation offers the limitations of friction, pain, suffering and disharmony. The sense of separateness in people's minds is the greatest 'evil' on earth today. Separateness fosters the blindness of sectarianism and leads to hatred, imprisonment and war. The energy of Love cannot manifest if truth is distorted in any way such that ignorance, in its many forms, may be fostered.

Love (magnetic attraction) is a blending together and fusion of all separative units into co-operative unity. It is harmony that produces prosperity, freedom and joy. It leads to an all-embracive open-mindedness, far-reaching inquiry and invites the understanding of all things within its scope. Eventually, Love produces identification with the emanating Source of all Being – the ever-present fount of wisdom from which 'all-knowledge' derives.

Separative beliefs are often fostered by a sense of inadequacy, complacency, distrust and fear of change. These states absolve us of the necessity to think and reason to conclusion. This provokes an emergence of the comforts of social convention, through arguing that certain beliefs that are traditionally accepted by the majority because they seem to be supported by scriptural passages should be followed. Of course, this is asserted by specialists who 'know' and are therefore apparently 100% right. It follows that many tenets are promulgated that lead to circumscribed and limiting ideals. Many of these ideals evolve to foster pride, selfishness, spite and vanity. For example, a religious doctrine of fear (in its many forms) condones the God of wrath, who imparts eternal retribution (hellfire) to all except the theologically faithful. Among non-religious doctrines, practices such as unbridled materialism are advocated.

All such concepts must be rectified or modified if the Christ is to reappear amongst humanity, and for that which He embodies to become part of the internal equipment of a seeker. Without an internalised expression, people will not be able to recognise the externalised embodiment.

Scriptures portray Christ as embodied Love. More precisely, He is portrayed as boundless Love, which cannot segregate, condemn, or distort. His presence will bring 'peace on earth' by fostering 'good will toward men'.[3] Such good will can only manifest through a sense of universality and oneness. This is all-embracive receptivity to the needs of others, regardless of another being's philosophy or religious differences. Love, of which good will is an expression, is an energy that necessitates knowledge to be applied as wisdom. Love's ability to rightly give and heal allows the rectification of what is disharmonious, malaised, and separative. Thereby, unity is produced and expressed as joy.

The word Christ is thus used in this text as: 'That which embodies and distributes the energy of Love, in a manner that allows people everywhere to utilise and express it'. The term Christ-consciousness[4] refers to the common experiences of mystics and sages from all religions who contact and express this energy. Translated into service, Love becomes good will. Good will is an emanatory quality of all those who endeavour to heal the suffering, diseased, and oppressed. It is effectively the right educational work for all who are becoming agents of the Christ; one automatically endeavours to dispel the darkness of ignorance in their particular spheres of activity by means of love.

The times are changing, and humanity has travelled far in the ability to rightly use the mind. The time has now come that people need no longer be spoken to 'in proverbs' subject to the interpretative faculty of the desire-mind. Instead, they can be plainly shown truths pertaining to the kingdom of 'God', and hence to the realm of enlightened Being. This was expressed by the Christ as: 'the time cometh, when I shall no more speak to you in proverbs, but I shall shew you plainly of the Father'.[5]

Following the 'dead letter' of one set of scriptures ('the proverbs') without making any allowance for the testimony from other traditions (or the emanations from the silent recesses of the heart) leads to pride, vanity and blindness. Only non-assertion of the personality and its views, along with attitudes of deep sincerity, humbleness and patience,

---

3 *Luke 2:14.* (All quotations from the Bible are from the authorised King James version.)

4 This Christ-consciousness is synonymous with the term *bodhicitta,* which has also been denoted in terms of the energy of *buddhi.* See my book, *Meditation and the Initiation Process,* 203. Compare this concept to Avalokiteśvara, Lord of compassion (the Buddhist equivalent of the personification of the Christ-consciousness). See my book, *The Constitution of Shambhala,* Vol. 7B & C, 458.

5 *John 16:25.*

can produce a true (intuited) understanding of sacred scriptures. When that happens, all religious friction ceases. The many paths of religious or doctrinal expression will all eventually be seen to lead to the one consummating goal. This realisation is becoming inevitable.

For all of humanity to have equal opportunity for realisation, the expression of universal Compassion and Love cannot possibly be limited to only one vehicle or religion. It must of necessity be clothed in the language of many different religions and national-cultural contexts. Emphasis must be on universally appealing approaches to divinity, such as compassion towards all sentient beings, service to humanity, and devotion to the Law of 'God'[6] as expressed in beneficent order. When these approaches are earnestly travelled upon, they will lead to similar realisations. The progression is upwards towards the One Divinity, no matter what names are given.

The concept of a Saviour of the world is common to the eschatology of most religious systems. The embodiment of Divine Love and Compassion as the vehicle or means of salvation[7] will be explained in the last chapter. The names differ, as does the symbology and method of presentation. Nevertheless, there is a central current of expectancy amongst the religious of the world.

The question of 'exactly when He is to appear?' is normally in doubt. It is the recipient of much spurious claim-making, as are many questions concerning the interpretation of prophetic scripture. In fact, an ability to derive Truth or Truths as found in the Bible (or other sacred texts) is entirely related to the methods of interpretation utilised. Results are always subject to the emotional, mental and psycho-spiritual nuances of an interpreter. Many have questioned whether a particular theologian's or sect's interpretations are necessarily correct, even when they have many followers.

To achieve true salvation (or enlightenment), interpretations must be asked and answered to the satisfaction of the Heart's Mind. Generally, the study of comparative religion or philosophy, understanding historical

---

6 The meaning of the term 'God' will be explained later in this chapter. See *John chapter 17* for Jesus' earnest prayer to his 'Father', which expresses the sentiment of such devotion.

7 From suffering, 'sin', or wrong actions.

developments of dogmatism within one's own sect, and examining one's personal religious-philosophic biases must be pursued for enlightenment to be obtained.

It is necessary to emphasise that only one's own efforts, interpretations, and experiences can produce true revelation of the nature of Deity, Satori, or union with 'God' (for the devotionally inclined). Within the realm of the mind these experiences are integrated and catalogued for further use. We must see that all concepts and interpretations (and effectively all things) exist only in the mind. The heart is, as can be seen from above, the 'mind's eye' – the organ of spiritual vision.

What is the mind?

As one creates an understanding of the deeply subjective workings and subconscious formulations within the realm of the mind, when united with the heart giving direction in space, the nature of oneself is understood. The how, why and whereto of one's being become known. As this is realised, one begins to cognise or identify with the eternal Presence of 'God', for 'man is built in the image of God'.[8]

The start of one's search for truth should therefore begin by endeavouring to understand exactly what the mind is. A basic eclectic framework of mind can be conceptualised by two understandings:

a. Mind is the cognised result of sense perception, and therefore of isolated units of perceived information. The principle that is termed the intellect can store, classify, and correlate that information.

b. As stated earlier, intellect is swayed or controlled by the emotional nature and the sense-desires of the body. The personality nearly always distorts and shapes units of perceived information into desired outcomes. Only mental processes that are tranquil, controlled, focussed and non-emotional can reason completely truthfully. When a person does this, enlightened aspects of mind manifest that defy classification. This enlightened 'awakened' Mind is the objective of all serious meditators.[9]

8 *Genesis 1:21.*

9 In my writings I use mind, with lower case 'm' to denote the empirical mind, and Mind to denote its enlightened attribute.

The enlightened Mind is not the result of sense-perceptive cognition; it is archetypal and abstract. It gives a person the ability to formulate deep ideals and expansive vistas of unbroken thought, without even being aware of the formulating process (or of any other mental process whatsoever).[10] It produces those aspects of thought which synthesise all related ideas intuitively known to be true. Mind is pure Reason manifesting as beauty, harmony and ordered purpose, thus it may evoke revelations or touches of genius. It has been called the higher Mind, an attribute of the Spirit-Soul. This is the subjective inner being that provides a purpose for existence, driving one on to the fulfilment of high achievement in the realms of form *(saṃsāra)* or in the domains of liberated existence.

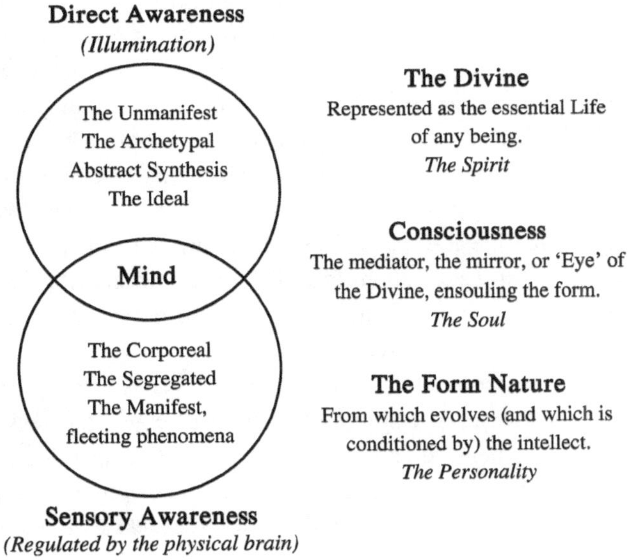

Figure 1: Mind as the mediator[11]

---

10 As stated in my *A Treatise on Mind,* Vol. 3, 179: 'A *yogin* later learns to detach from all conceptual thoughts and *saṃsāric* allurements, causing all bonds to ephemera to be broken by developing the Clear Light of Mind, whereby non-discursive thought manifests'.

11 See my *A Treatise on Mind,* Vol. 2, 6, for a similar figure adapted from a Buddhist perspective.

From Figure 1,[12] it is seen that mind/Mind incorporates:

a. *Direct Awareness* (the Divine, the Real). This is the source of all lasting values, into which one is ultimately resolved after the attainment of enlightenment.

b. *Sensory awareness* (the phenomenal, the unreal). This is impermanent and seen as the appearance of things. The Sanskrit term used throughout this book is *saṃsāra,* meaning 'that which goes on', or continues 'to come to be'. It signifies existence as conditioned being in the material cosmos. When phrased in terms of the continual cycles of death and rebirth of the phenomenal appearance of any form, it is then termed *māyā,* meaning illusion.

The Mind is the embodiment or what en-Souls the essential Life in such a way as to allow its experience of the material world. It is also the Causal Form, or Soul of a person,[13] in that it is the Eye of the Divine. In the form of mind/Mind it is the mediator or mirror between the abstract and the phenomenal. It embodies the essence of the past and is the seed of future divinity. This aspect of divinity relates to the evolving entity and incorporates it into an ideal form, as a continuum in time and space. This occurs throughout the births and deaths of successive generations of such entities. It is an embodied flux of Conscious receptivity, incorporated into a form that can relate the transcendental to the corporeal.

The Soul is a true cellular unit within the Ocean of Being. Within the Soul, the Ocean of Being and the unit of consciousness (that is the incarnate person) can interrelate without destruction of the latter, or abnegation of the purposes of existence emanating from above. In essence, the Soul is a radiant Sun that resides in the heart of manifest being.

---

12 This diagram is similar to one shown on p. 74 of *Foundations of Tibetan Mysticism* (E. P. Dutton & Co., New York, 1960) by Lama Anagarika Govinda, to which it can be related.

13 A technical term I often use for the Soul in my writings is the Sambhogakāya Flower.

Trikāya - the three sheathes of a Buddha

The Buddhist teachings of the three bodies of a Buddha (*trikāya*) find their application here. These are the three vestures or bodies of a Buddha (or liberated being). They are the *nirmāṇakāya, sambhogakāya and dharmakāya.* When perfectly expressed and embodied by an enlightened Being, the corporeal form becomes a *nirmāṇakāya* or the 'Divine Incarnation body'. It is the physical plane emanation, the outer or phenomenal appearance, the tangible something that can be contacted on the realms of illusion. (Such as occurred, for instance, in the physical form incarnation of the last Buddha, Gautama.) A Bodhisattva manifests in the guise of a *nirmāṇakāya* that can communicate with humans by means of writings and speech. The *nirmāṇakāya* acts as the focal point of the Will (bliss) of the *dharmakāya* and the conscious Love of the Sambhogakāya Flower. It integrates the personality via coordinating the activities of the *chakras* and directs the impressions.

The *sambhogakāya* (or 'Divine Body of Perfect Endowment') is the subtle body of a Buddha or an enlightened being. It is the form that such a Being takes in the higher realms. It is effectively the form of the Soul of a human unit, but for high Initiates it is a Mind-construct that allows interrelation with the world of form. In the form of the Sambhogakāya Flower it is the Buddha nature inherent within everyone, which is our destined fulfilment.[14]

What I have termed 'the Divine' compares well with the *dharmakāya,*[15] which W.Y. Evans-Wentz calls the 'Divine Body of Truth'. *Dharma*, means Truth, the fount of the law governing all Being. Concerning the *trikāya* W.Y. Evans-Wentz states:

> There is no place throughout the Universe where the Essentiality of a Buddha is not present....

---

14 For a complete explanation of the Sambhogakāya Flower refer to volume 3 of my *A Treatise on Mind* series.

15 The highest of the three bodies (*trikāya*) that empowers the Buddha, or any Initiate of the fourth degree or greater. It is the body of Bliss, identified with the Monad. *Dharma* is the fount of the universal Law of Being, and *kāya* is its vehicle. It has been defined as the primordial, eternally self-existing, essentiality of *bodhi* (transcendental insight, enlightenment).

> This Universal Essence manifests itself in three aspects, or modes, symbolised as the Three Divine Bodies (Skt. *Tri-Kāya).* The first aspect: the *Dharma-Kāya,* or Essential (or True) Body, is the Primordial, Unmodified, Formless, Eternally Self-Existing Essentiality of *Bodhi,* or Divine Beingness. The second is the *Sambhoga-Kāya,* or Reflected *Bodhi,* wherein, in heaven-worlds, dwell the Buddhas of Meditation (Skt. *Dhyānī-Buddhas)* and other Enlightened Ones while embodied in superhuman form. The third aspect is the *Nirmāṇa-Kāya,* or Body of Incarnation, or, from the standpoint of men, Practical *Bodhi,* in which exist Buddhas when on Earth.
>
> In the Chinese interpretation of the *Tri-Kāya,* the *Dharma-Kāya* is the immutable Buddha Essence, the Noumenal Source of the Cosmic whole. The *Sambhoga-Kāya* is, as phenomenal appearances, the first reflex of the *Dharma-Kāya* on the heavenly planes. In the *Nirmāṇa-Kāya* the Buddha Essence is associated with activity on the Earth plane; it incarnates among men, as suggested by the Gnostic Proem to the Gospel of St. John, which refers to the coming into the flesh of the 'Word', or 'Mind'...
>
> In its totality, the Universal Essence is the One Mind, manifest through the multitudinous myriads of minds throughout all states of *sangsāric* existence. It is called 'The Essence of the Buddhas', 'The Great Symbol', 'The Sole Seed', 'The Potentiality of Truth', 'The All-Foundation'. As our text teaches, it is the Source of all bliss of *Nirvāṇa* and all sorrow of the *Sangsāra'.*[16]

The Mind is the bridge between the involutionary (subhuman) and evolutionary (para-human) states of consciousness and is therefore a product, or combination, of characteristics mentioned below:

1. *Instinct* - Inherent in matter itself.
2. *Feeling* - Evolved in the plant kingdom.
3. *Desire* - Inherent within the animal kingdom.
4. *Imagination* - A combination of intellect and desire.
5. *Intellect* - An expression of the human kingdom.
6. *Pure Reason (Intuition)* - Implying the power to Vision.[17] Signifies the ability to visualise what is contained within the Mind of 'God',

---

16 W.Y. Evans-Wentz, *The Tibetan Book of the Great Liberation,* (Oxford University Press, London, 1968), 3-4.

17 This is not to be confused with the imagination.

for everything may be considered an aspect of 'His' Thought process. The key to the Revelation of the nature of the evolutionary process and the origination of the universe is found here.[18]

7. *Ineffable or Universal Mind* - the Divine.

A Seer (an enlightened being) is a vehicle through which the exalted consciousness of the Soul can manifest. This is due to the Seer's ability to broadcast the energy of Love, which is expressed through a purified, receptive, coordinated, and consecrated personality. Through intuition, the Seer receives the voiceless Voice that inspires all people of destiny who change aspects of civilisation in some beneficent way. The Seer's visions must be translated by means of the intellect into words or picture-images for people to understand. However, egotistic individuals interpret words according to what they imagine them to mean, as governed by their mental-emotional conditionings and reactions. Even when idealistic or inspirational, their imagination still emanates from the personality and related conditionings. The vision of the Seer is not thus conditioned. This is because the Seer's personality has been completely purified, therefore no emotion or desire are involved. The genuine true visions of the Seer thus always manifest to benefit the whole: a group or mass of beings or society in general. Only incidentally will personality considerations be involved.

Creation from Thought Substance

'God', it can be said, 'Created' the Universe out of His Thought-Substance. This was in order to express a yet unexpressed possibility, which is the objective of 'His Desire'.[19] The nature of Deity will always

---

18 This fleeting and phenomenal 'appearance of things', the entire physical world that we live in can be likened to images produced by 'His Imagination'. The 'cells' in the Brain of that Being can be visioned as great Angelic Beings that fashion the 'images' out of the substance of their Bodies. The lesser units of Mind (the hierarchy of *devas* within the bodies of the greater Angels) embody the various diversified aspects of the material world. See my *A Treatise on Mind,* Vol. 2, 64-7 for further detail concerning the above listing.

19 Predicated upon the possibility to relate such a quality as 'Desire' to an entity that is as inexplicably advanced to the present human mind, as humanity's developed consciousness would be to that of an amoeba.

remain inexplicable, unless one remembers that 'man is built in the image of God'. One can then fully utilise the concept of analogy as a tool towards understanding. 'As above so below, that which is within is also without' an ancient adage from the Emerald Tablets of Hermes Trismegistus reads, and indeed it is so. Although analogy is an invaluable aid for interpretation, we must take great care to not derive too literal of a meaning in our deductions, and when thinking of such concepts as 'God' we must conceptualise in terms of transmuted correspondences.

An object of human endeavour is to know all things. This knowledge must eventually give way to an understanding of 'God' – 'His' Nature and Qualities. This will make us 'sons of God....and joint-heirs with Christ'.[20] The basis for how this must come about is a necessary theme of this book, however it is only possible to give general, broad analogies (the thought-forms, or seeds, from which direct awareness may develop).

The process of Creation can be likened to that of meditation. The universe was not created out of nothing (unless that 'nothing' is energy that is ever-present and omnipotent). Energy, from another angle of expression, is substance. (For energy and matter are interchangeable.) From this, the energetic conception of a thought takes place, which then becomes a definite form as the meditator imbues it with the vitality of Fiery lives (atoms) that constitute all aspects of Being. All meditating entities are limited by the quality of the substance that they must work with, which relates to the quality and properties of their mental constitution. Therefore, it can also be inferred, that 'God' was similarly limited on 'His' exalted level of perception, for cause ever precedes effect. All substance (angelic or atomic) can in fact be considered tainted by the residue of past actions. If so, then the energy or substance that 'God' had to use must also have been imperfect.

The future is the effect of the past as it unfolds through the present. Since all of the entities on our earth system are evolving, they are also imperfect. The past is imperfect, whilst the present imperfection is evolving to a future perfection (or so it seems). For the concept of man being built in the image of 'God' to have any validity, 'God' may be

---

20 'For as many as are led by the Spirit of God, they are the sons of God. The Spirit itself beareth witness with our spirit, that we are the children of God. And if children, then heirs; heirs of God, and joint-heirs with Christ.' *Romans 8:14-17.*

said to be evolving towards That, which to 'Him' would represent a point of perfection.

Paul also hints at this in Corinthians by stating that when all things have been subjected to the Son, 'then shall the Son also himself be subject unto him that put all things under him, that God may be all in all'.[21] The phrase 'that God may be all in all' refers to the fact that He is not yet fully manifest 'in all'. This distinctly implies an objective of evolution, by means of the evolved Christ-principle. This is to allow Deity to fully embody the lowest as well as the highest realms of perception (or types of substance). The objective is to actually 'lift' or transmute substance, by infusing it with the highest spiritual energies.

In summary, it can be said that 'God, in deep meditation', formulated a sphere, or the 'limit' of possible attainment for His present Life Purpose. Within that 'limit' plays out the roles of the energetic interplay – the entire effect of action-reaction – that composes our lives and all other lives in the (local) universe. All proceeds towards the perfected fulfilment that already exists in 'His Mind'. This is concurrent with His Meditation process, as yet not fully manifested in form. The 'three times': of past, present and future are really an expression of present timelessness, visualised as one on an abstracted level. This is encompassed within the duration of the existence that is the Mind of Deity. (As will be explained in chapter four.) An implied objective of the practice of meditation is to provide one with necessary qualities and training that will eventually produce the ability to become a Creative Deity, concerned with the evolution of an immense number of entities. These entities are the higher correspondences of a person's corporeality: the body nature and thought-engendering equipment.

Even astronomers have likened our expanding universe to the effects of an enormous thought process. There are many differing conceptions concerning the question of 'God'.[22] Some have risen because of theological assertions, many of which are self-contradictory. Other philosophies such as Buddhism seem to negate such a concept. In other systems such as Hinduism, there may seem to be a confusing plethora

21 *I Corinthians 15:28.*

22 Because the question of 'God' is open to interpretation, I always apostrophise the word.

of Gods. We also have witnessed the rise of widespread scientific materialism and the assertions of thinkers from these schools. Due to the uncertainty of choosing between such widely differing conceptions, a large number of people react in a negative way when the subject of 'God' is mentioned.

Many have refused to even begin to rationally tackle the problem, saying categorically that it is impossible. This question of 'God' however is not an incommunicable enigma; it can be answered by the enlightened Mind. All enlightened beings will testify to this. By means of the Initiation process[23] this knowledge will eventually become within the common heritage of humanity.

Buddhist negation of the concept of 'God' arises partially from an erroneous assumption that the Buddha stated that a 'God' did not exist. In actuality, He simply refused to discuss the subject at all. Later, Buddhist metaphysical rhetoric focussed upon the concept of the (non) existence of an Ego or Soul *ātman* (or Spirit-Self), as the expression of divinity within our system. Edward Conze aptly summarised Buddhist and Hindu ideas concerning this:

> [W]e cannot be quite sure what notions of an *ātma* were envisaged by the early Buddhists when they so emphatically denied it. I personally believe that these notions were of two kinds, i.e. (1) the ideas implied in the use of 'I' and 'mine' by ordinary people, and (2) the philosophic opinion, held by the Samkhya and Vaisesika, that a continuing substratum acts as an agent which outlasts the different actions of a person, abides for one or more existences, and acts as a 'support' to the activities of the individual....What in general is suggested by Soul, Self, Ego, or to use the Sanskrit expression *ātman*, is that in man there is a permanent, everlasting and absolute entity which is the unchanging substance behind the changing phenomenal world...The Buddha never taught that the self 'is not', but only that' it cannot be apprehended'.[24]

W.Y. Evans-Wentz presents a similar viewpoint in his book *The Tibetan Book of the Great Liberation*:

---

23 The Initiations are explained in chapters five and six of my book *Meditation and the Initiation Process.*

24 Edward Conze, *Buddhist Thought in India,* (Ann Arbour Paperbacks, University of Michigan Press, 1967), 38-9.

Expositions of the Buddhist doctrine of non-self, or non-soul, frequently exhibit looseness of thinking and misleading argumentation, sometimes by Buddhists themselves. The Buddha did not teach that there is no self, or soul; He taught that there is no self, or soul, that is real, non-transitory, or possessed of unique and eternally separate existence. In Buddhism, salvation is not of a self, or soul; it is entirely dependent upon what the Buddha declared to be the deliverance of the mind from *sangsāric* bondage imposed by Ignorance (Skt. Avidyā), from the erroneous belief that appearances are real and that there are individualised immortal selves, or souls.

When there is no longer a clinging to selfhood, when all the external play of *sangsāric* energies is allowed to subside, because there is no longer attachment to any of them, then there is that state of absolute quiescence of mental activities which our text refers to as the natural state of the mind...The illusory microscopic mind dissolves; there is only the One Mind; there is Final Emancipation, Perfect Buddhahood.[25]

Regarding the term 'God', H.V. Guenther states that:

It may be used in the deistic sense, deism being the doctrine that "there is a certain part of the Universe which is not existentially dependent upon anything else, that all the rest of the Universe is existentially dependent upon this part of it". Another use is to apply the term 'God' to the whole Universe as having certain characteristics from which all others necessarily follow. This is a kind of pantheism. Lastly the word 'God' is used to denote those features of the Universe which actually belong to it and are not mere distortions or illusory appearances. On this view the Universe is in reality purely mental matter, space and motion are distorted appearances of this mind. There is nothing to show that Buddhism falls in with any of these three views. It eschews a First Cause as well as the mentalistic premise that the Universe in its totality is a mind or society of minds. And it also rejects the thesis that the Universe in all its aspects is 'God'.[26]

---

25 W.Y. Evans-Wentz, *The Tibetan Book of the Great Liberation,* (Oxford University Press, London, 1968), 76-7.

26 H.V. Guenther, *Treasures on the Tibetan Middle Way,* (Shambhala Publications Inc., California, 1969), 24-5.

These quotations have been presented to lay a foundation to understand what is meant when the terms 'God' or Deity are found in this work. The first and foremost thing to realise is that the question of 'God' must be related to an understanding of the nature of energy, of relativity, and of meditation. Everything is in a state of flux, which can be seen as quanta of energy in dynamic motion and interrelation. In this, nothing is permanent or remains unchanged in time and space. Such a conception is exemplified in Buddhism by the doctrine that no matter how the idea of 'God' is presented it suggests permanency, thus something that is static or lifeless. Therefore, in his consideration of the Buddhist 'pantheon', H.V. Guenther states:

> Another objection that is likely to be raised is that all these gods are doing temporal acts. If it is really true, as theologians claim, that the Divine is non-temporal, how can we ascribe temporal processes and qualities to that which is non-temporal without becoming involved in endless contradictions? This difficulty does not exist for a Buddhist, as he does not think in terms of 'things' and their 'qualities', but in terms of dynamic processes which, by virtue of their dynamics and variability, are vivid and therefore " The gods are functions and their formulations in concrete forms are symbols for the inner experiences that attend man's spiritual growth...[27]

The concept of looking at Being in terms of 'dynamic processes' is a valid viewpoint as we focus our attention upon the substance behind the form. These are energy fields that cause the appearance and fleeting existence of all manifest things in the phenomenal universe. Such a perspective dispenses with the notion of 'God' in that such an idea is itself superfluous – a 'thing' which, in terms of its essential nature and interrelatedness, is non-existent. Nevertheless, such 'things' do still exist even if only illusively and temporarily so, for they are what is presented to our cognitive faculties in the world around us. 'Things' also exist as ideas limited to the numinous level. We thus have a concept of Deity as an ineffable 'Personality' with virtually omnipresent, transcendent, and 'ever-lasting' qualities relative to the phenomenal world. At the same time, this Deity is also illusory, because of the 'dynamic variability' on Its own level of expression.

---

27 Ibid., 32.

When our vision is limited to humanity's tiny scale, we see that the human Soul (or Ego[28]) has a real permanence compared to the human lives that it causes to incarnate into *saṃsāra*. In its simplest connotation the Soul can be defined as the mediator between the undefinable, the archetypal or unmanifest aspect, and the phenomenal form. It is a self-contained sphere of the activity of Mind ensconced upon the higher mental plane. The Soul is effectively the *sambhogakāya* aspect of each human unit, whose full potential is still in the process of unfolding. The human personality that the Soul embodies is its thought-form (the phenomenal appearance) made manifest for a set purpose. The personality is the blurred mirror of the Real, unfolding its qualities (and thus evolving) by means of successive reincarnations, embodiments of the thought-stream of the Soul. Nevertheless, as with all forms, the Soul must also at some time reach the bounds of its possible attainment, and thus will 'die' (at the attainment of the fourth Initiation).

Buddhism	**Equivalent Concepts**	**Theistic Concept**
Dharmakāya The Real	The Divine/Monad Spirit	The Abstracted Deity (The Father)
	Expression = Will or Power	
Sambhogakāya Subtle body of a great One	Consciousness Soul	The Meditating Deity The Christ (The Son)
	Expression = Love-Wisdom	
Nirmāṇakāya The appearance	Phenomenal Appearance Personality	The Divine Mother The world of forms
	Expression = Activity	

Table 1: The triune principles[29]

28 A term for the Soul sometimes used by D.K. in the writings penned by Alice Bailey, as in *A Treatise on Cosmic Fire* (New York: Lucis Trust, 1951), 36.

29 This table is taken from page 111 of my book *Esoteric Cosmology and Modern Physics.*

The *Spirit* (the fundamental Buddha nature, or 'God', within) can be considered Real (unchanging, unformed, unbounded, eternal in duration), relative to the Soul. This is because Spirit's existence is gauged on a cosmic time scale,[30] in contradistinction to that associated with the lives on our planet. However, Spirit can also be considered a 'Thing' that must evolve, for it certainly exists and thus has a purpose for that Existence. When expressed in terms of words it becomes virtually meaningless except as abstract clichés (as are the attributes of Spirit). The direct experience of its energies would produce the annihilation of the mind nature that would try to contain it. (As it is the antithesis of form and manifest being. Even upon the domain of the abstract Mind wherein the Soul resides, its form cannot bear more than a portion of this energy.) This is illustrated in Table 1.

It is possible to postulate, therefore, that the essential Form of 'God' or Deity and what incorporates the totality of Being are also in a state of dynamic unfoldment. However, this is upon a scale or a state of perception that is far beyond anything that can be cognised by the intelligent person. Basically, 'God' or Deity can be defined as a great liberated Enlightened Being. That Being has Creatively built a Body of Activity that incorporates the collective consciousness existing in all kingdoms of Nature (including the human and angelic kingdoms). This provides a purpose for existence, and coherent unity.[31]

'God' is thus the originating Cause, the embodying Thought, That which is indicative of the future of all Being. This 'God' is however, a Cause that is Causeless in the sense that there is no true beginning and no ending. There is only a continuously spiralling upward progression of the All to vast empyrean states of Being far beyond human comprehension. Deity can be considered a liberated Buddha that long ago surpassed the need for corporeal evolution. Yet this Being sustains a world-sphere or universe, and the related evolving entities, for a specific Divine Purpose. This Purpose originates in That Entity's Compassionate Understanding (or Meditative Awareness of Need), on cosmic, inter-Solar, or inter-planetary scales.

30 Part of the expression of aeonic universal cyclic Durations.

31 These are kingdoms that must yet evolve to the God state. For this purpose, they have been appropriated into (or as) the Body of Expression of Deity.

It should be understood, therefore, that the terms 'Deity' and 'God' in this text refer specifically to That One who governs humanity and all other kingdoms of Nature, and their evolution in this world sphere (unless otherwise stated). All are part of 'His' Body of Manifestation. The term generally employed therefore is a planetary Logos, the embodiment of the Word, or mantric Sound, via which all things emanated.[32]

A world-sphere manifests by the projection of Divine Will. It is sustained by the expression of Love in terms of Wisdom and incorporates what is fundamentally Activity, in all its dynamic interrelatedness. These are the three aspects of Deity, anthropomorphised as the *Father, Son and Mother,* the Trinity as One, symbolised thus: .

The corporeal, the personality nature of each of us, is a sum of all the qualities and evolutionary purposes of the lesser kingdoms of Nature (such as the atomic lives) which compose our forms. In turn, the God, or Logos (the Word made corporeal), of our planetary sphere embodies the sum of the qualities of both human and angelic evolutions. This Word is explained in the opening passage of St. John's Gospel: 'In the beginning was the Word, and the Word was with God, and the Word was God'. The kingdoms of Nature represent Bodily functions or aspects to such an Entity. They demonstrate the summation of His manifest Personality. The Corporeality of this great Personality then is all that can be known by humanity, by use of analogy and the reasoning concurred by means of the mind. Later when Mind is developed then the true nature of the Logos can be directly experienced.

There is an attribute of Deity that corresponds to the archetypal Mind – the unmanifest, the Soul of a person. This cannot be known or understood by those involved as personalities, as parts of the constitution of the Divine Personality. Therefore, ancient Hindu philosophers gave the names SAT, TAT, THAT – the Immutable, the Unknown, and yet also refused to explain 'THAT' because of the impossibility of the finite mind to comprehend.

The Buddhist philosophy effectively engages in analysis of the qualities relating to, or which will be productive of, THAT. Thus, they

32 The World-Sphere of a Buddha, as described symbolically in such texts as *The Saddharma-Puṇḍarīka*, 'The Lotus of the True Law', presents a similar concept phrased in Buddhistic terminology.

emphasise the essential non-Reality of Deity. Theistic religions, on the other hand, do not concern themselves with the qualities of *THAT per se*, but rather to what Deity incorporates as a means of expression (which has been termed 'God', or the Powers of the Gods). When thinking of the abstracted concept of THAT as 'God' they simply put this 'God' as beyond everything conceivable, beyond 'all Creation'. Otherwise, they often personalise the concept in anthropomorphic terms. A theme within all of my writings is to rightly interpret and analyse the teachings from the Bible and elsewhere, wherein the idea of a 'personal God' appears to be emphasised. For the attributes of 'God' can be known and explicated, once the terminology based upon the right concepts are formulated.

In considering human beings we must view them in terms of a fusion of three aspects (Spirit-Soul-personality), which together can be considered a 'cell' in the Body of Deity. Furthermore, the fusion of a number of 'cells' (Souls) expressing a commonly embodied quality constitutes an organ in the Body of Deity. Many diverse organs (Soul groupings) constitute the summation of the internal equipment and emanatory characteristics of the Divine Personality, as far as the consciousness of 'His' corporeal Body is concerned. Just as the individual human's personality is a composite of the dense physical body, emotional body and mental body (the intellect),[33] so too does the Personality Nature of Deity have a similar composition. From the Soul all manifest Life proceeds.

What is corporeal to us is effectively below the threshold of Logoic Awareness, the constitution of the cosmic dense physical domain[34] upon which such a One literally 'Stands'. However, the domain wherein exists the essential Divinity (the 'Spirit') within us would be cognised by Deity as His proper Body of expression. Yet to humanity, the characteristics of 'the Spirit' are unknowable and unimaginable until people begin to consciously evolve transcendental perceptions that are characteristics of Deity Itself.

Following is a table depicting the aspects of humanity in relation to the *triune aspects of Deity:*

---

33 All of these are emanations of the Soul or Mind.

34 Our mental, astral and physical planes.

	Aspect of Humanity	Aspect of Deity
1	*The Spirit/Monad* The Transcendent	An aspect of the Brain structure or Mind of Deity
↑ *This is above the threshold of human consciousness*		
2	*The Soul* The abstract Mind[35]	Cellular structure of Deity Sense-perception
↓ *This is below the threshold of awareness of Deity*		
3	*The Personality*[36] The empirical mind	Dense physical substance[37]

Table 2: The triune aspects of Deity[38]

We see here that Mind becomes the common denominator that allows interrelation between Deity and humanity. All energies and factors of the Body Nature of Deity are in a constant state of mutable activity. This is an effect of the expression of His Mind, in a similar sense that the qualities of the human personality are governed by the nature of one's thought processes.

When we speak in terms of manifest Life, our concern is with That which is the result or expression of the Mind of 'God', to which the kingdom of Souls automatically responds. This kingdom then projects (as Divine Law) the results into the corporeal realms. These are the energies that condition all manifest Being.

The nature of Mind

In a passage previously quoted by H.V. Guenther, he stated that Buddhism 'eschews... the mentalistic premise that the universe in its totality is a mind or a society of minds'. This view is not consistent

35 Can also be described as archetypal Mind or the Causal form.

36 Our corporeal form, which is constituted of a mental, an emotional and a dense physical body.

37 An aspect of the substance upon which He walks. The corporeal universe is an effect of Divine Causality.

38 Adapted from my book, *Esoteric Cosmology and Modern Physics,* 115.

with the basic tenets of most Mahāyāna Buddhist schools, except as far as it relates to the idea of a 'God'. For instance, we saw earlier that W.Y. Evans-Wentz equated 'perfect Buddhahood' with the 'One Mind' that is the expression of the dissolving of the 'microcosmic mind'. The concept that 'Mind is all there is' is exemplified by the Yogācāra, a major school of Buddhist philosophy. The Yogācārins also stress the importance of meditation as means to liberation. Mind is considered in terms of transcendent Thought and empirical thought. Regarding the concept of 'transcendent Thought', most schools of Buddhism would likely agree with the following statement by Alexandra David-Neel:

> [T]he original Void *(ji ka dag)* is the inconceivable form of the Mind existing before an autogenous energy *(tsal len dup)* caused the *saṁskāras*[39] (mental composition) to arise in it, creators of the images which constitute our world. It is in this void of the mind, comparable to the special void, that are born, act and disappear all the phenomena perceived by the senses, phenomena which we wrongly imagine to be scenes unfolding outside of us, whereas they only exist in us.[40]

Mind, in its universal aspect is the *ālayavijñāna* (the universal storehouse of consciousness), which is said to be the cause of all things. Alexandra David-Neel further states that:

> "The mind is comparable with space; like space it has neither interior nor exterior; in its depths one finds nothing but the Void.
>
> "Ideas of continuity or discontinuity cannot be applied to the mind; it escapes them, just as in the case of space one cannot conceive it either as limited or as infinite.
>
> "It is impossible to discover a place where the mind is born, a place where it dwells afterwards, a place where it ceases to exist. Like space, the mind is void in the three times: past, present and future.[41]

---

39 *Saṃskāras* are predispositions, innate tendencies, impressions from actions (of emotions, etc.) done in former incarnations and which are carried through to this one, thereby becoming the basis for one's present *karma*. The action *(kṛ)* that will improve, refine or make an impression in consciousness. Once base *saṃskāras* have been transformed, enlightened principles replace them.

40 Alexandra David-Neel and Lama Yongden, *The Secret Oral Teachings in Tibetan Buddhist Sects,* (City Lights Book, California, 1972), 127.

41 Ibid.

Note the remarkable similarity of the prior words to those words of the Christian mystic Jacob Boehme (1575- 1674), who states:

> 'Within the groundlessness (that by which some writers is called the 'Non-Being' – a term without any meaning) there is nothing but eternal tranquility, an eternal rest without beginning and without end. It is true that even there God has a will, but this can be no object for our investigation, as to attempt to investigate it would merely produce a confusion in our mind. We conceive of this will as constituting the foundation of the Godhead. It has no origin, but conceives itself within itself.' (Menschwerdung, xxi, 1.) (p. 60)

> 'Divine Intelligence is a free will. It never originated from or by the power of anything. It is in itself, and resides only and solely within itself, unaffected by anything, because there is nothing outside or previous to it.' (Mysterium, xxi. I.)[42]

Whether one wishes to equate Mind with 'Perfect Buddhahood', 'God', or abstracted in terms of 'Space' is a matter of personal predilection. These are only symbols of the inexplicable, for Mind is all these things. The conception of 'God' used here thus also refers to the statement 'God is Mind', for it has validity in relation to the knowable Universe. Mind is the only facet of Deity that can be comprehended by our Minds, as we are reflections of That MIND moulded according to the patterning of the Divine Mentation.

The planetary Logos

As a person becomes 'liberated' to inevitably become a Buddha, such a One will have the faculty to identify with That which is the expression of the Buddha-Mind. The Logoic Buddha-Mind gained release aeons ago from identification with even the most subtle types of substance constituting the dimensions of perception associated with human evolution. Such a Logoic Mind incorporates this substance in a similar way to the Soul incorporating the personality for each succeeding incarnation, and yet is not bound by it in any way.

---

42 Franz Hartmann MD., *Jacob Boehme: Life and Doctrines,* (Steinerbooks, Bleuvelt N.Y., 1977), 60.

The 'God' spoken of in this book and my other writings is therefore a planetary Logos (unless otherwise stated), Who was a liberated Buddha from another planetary Scheme aeons ago, and Who has gained further education in cosmos before coming to planet earth. Such a Logos incorporates the Lives of a planetary Scheme and the related kingdoms as His Body of Manifestation. He is inclusive of these kingdoms, for He has completely evolved through and transcended the stages of evolution that must yet unfold for the various entities constituting those kingdoms. An entire world sphere is thus 'His' *Nirmāṇakāya.* My book *Esoteric Cosmology and Modern Physics* explains the method of the formation of a form such as a planetary or solar sphere.

In a similar sense that humanity comprises an integral aspect of a planetary Logos, the planetary Logos is also an integral aspect of the constitution of a solar Logos. Furthermore, by the utilisation of analogy, a solar Logos constitutes a 'Cell' in the Body of an ineffable cosmic Deity. This Entity, about 'Whom Naught can be Said',[43] has a Constitution of Mind or Purpose of such a lofty nature that even the most exalted enlightened Minds on earth could not adequately explain it in human terms. All within the local cosmos, the Logoi constituting the stellar spheres and constellations in our galaxy that broadly speaking can be seen in the night sky by the unaided eye, are part of the Mind-structure of such a grand Incorporating Logos. For lack of any better term I also call this Entity THAT Logos.

A planetary Logos has projected and embodies the Word (further explained in chapter nine) for a planetary System. His Compassionate Identification is so complete that He has befitted Himself with the

---

43 This Logos is depicted in Alice Bailey's *A Treatise on Cosmic Fire* (Lucis Publishing Co., New York,1967) as the 'One about Whom Naught may be Said'. The emphasis here is upon the term Naught, which does not mean 'nothing', though in the minds of the great majority this is indeed what exists in relation to comprehension of such a One. Rather, it means what is veiled by *śūnyatā*, manifesting as a sphere, a 'nought', the cypher zero (○), the circumscribed sphere of attainment via which a Logos builds His/Her Body of Manifestation. Such a One is a member of a cosmic Humanity consisting of similar Ones whose Bodies are constituted of *Chakras* that are stars and constellations of stars. As we all live within the Body of such a One, the true characteristics of what lies beyond such a Body can only be surmised rather than directly known, even by the highest Dhyān Chohan (liberated being) on our planet. From this perspective naught can be directly said about this Domain.

qualities needed for planetary Salvation. He is thus 'God' to that system, utilising the substance and Lives of the constituent kingdoms as the sheaths that He incarnates into.

It is possible, therefore, for an enlightened being, who possesses a similar degree of attainment to the Christ, to attain specific communication, or a 'covenant', with a planetary Logos – in a seemingly personal manner. In earlier times, there are many recorded statements of those who could hold a direct covenant with Deity. As the modern era unfolded, however, such seers became scarce. Many conflicting theological arguments have consequently developed as to the nature of Deity.

During the Buddha's time, it was virtually impossible to explain the true nature of deity, which would require understanding the characteristics of the expression of energy. His contemporaries knew very little of this, and there was little sound scientific or physiological knowledge to relate it to. Many conflicting arguments concerning the nature of deity were extant in the Buddha's time. The premise given here is that, as an expression of his wisdom, the Buddha kept silent on this subject. His philosophy was presented as the 'middle way' between all opposing views, which avoided the rhetoric of religious speculation. The Buddha concentrated on the issue of most immediate practical concern. This meant the attainment of the enlightenment that enables a person to Know. The Buddha knew that a time would come when humanity would evolve the necessary experiences and terminology to understand and describe the nature of deity; only then should specific teachings be given.

Authors of Buddhist texts, in accordance with the religious presentation of the Buddha, focussed their teaching framework in a most pragmatic manner. They focused on teaching what was directly related to a person's liberation from the form and their consequent enlightenment. The focus was hence a thorough investigation as to the nature of the manifestation of consciousness (mind) and (as previously stated) upon the THAT aspect, denoted as being–non-being, or *śūnyatā*, (Emptiness) which predisposed the entire framework of their doctrines.

Theistic religions, on the other hand, were not so concerned with the Buddhist idea of liberation. Rather, they sought a conscious mergence into (or union with) That which they saw as the Cause of all Being.

This thereby produced a holistic ontology whose efficacy concerned a transcendent and imminent relationship to the Divine Personality of God (or Gods), which thus became embodied and real.

Both of these methods of realisation eventually produce similar experiences. As the goal of either approach is reached, the method that was not previously fully expressed becomes their Path. (For there is no end to evolutionary attainment.) The Buddhist type, through internal meditative capabilities and abstract reasoning, merges into the Spaciousness that is the Heart of the Divine. Correspondingly, the theistic type is absorbed into the Personified vicissitudes of the Space that is Mind, by means of an outward going contemplation and mystical Reasoning.

The seven keys of interpretation for understanding a sacred text

There are no hard clear-cut rules or solutions regarding how to interpret sacred texts. Many different methods are utilised such as direct inspiration, philology, structural analysis, historical reference, through underlying analogy with revealed scriptures, and so forth. All methods are valid and obviously have their uses, and therefore should not be discounted.

I wish, in this exegesis, to present the philosophy and methods of interpretation that will be found to be exceedingly illuminating. A text that is truly sacred[44] will contain a condensation of the wisdom of the ages, which then may be utilised as a means towards enlightenment or salvation.

1. The literal key

This is based on a belief that the context of the scripture is true. It then relates information obtained by the methods mentioned above to conditions associated with the everyday world. By this method, an interpretation is regulated or influenced by prejudices, whims, wishes, and the subconscious desires of the interpreter. It is filtered by the sum-total of knowledge and mental-emotional equipment the person is

---

44 The word sacred means 'consecrated, made holy'.

equipped with. Results of the interpretation are therefore often dubious, sectarian, and open to much debate.

The principal value of this method lies in obtaining information concerning historical facts and geographic details; social, political, religious customs, cultural affairs, morphology, semantics and the like. Books intended to teach the Divine Mysteries to humanity were written differently in ancient times than they are now. Modern writers strive to edify readers while explicating the entire knowledge of a subject in book format. In ancient times, however, a sage gave out only succinct passages and statements. These contained the essence of the information to be imparted. The underlying reason was to provide greater value for acolytes than simply to be given answers. It was intended that readers or acolytes would utilise all their resources to decipher the meaning. The objective was to make acolytes teach themselves. By working hard for solutions, they could thereby progressively attain their own enlightenment.

Sages often codified information, imparted by use of analogy, for those who interpreted rightly to gain enlightened inspiration. From one set of instructions, therefore, disciples could obtain realisations according to the degree of their capacity. An earnest seeker would find information concerning the practical development of multidimensional states of consciousness. Conversely, those desirous of psychic power for egotistical or selfish motives (such as an ambition to dominate those around them) would find it difficult. In most cases, the intellect alone would not suffice to gain the necessary information. From the angle of the writer, codification of esoteric truths was virtually a necessity. Even nowadays people find it difficult to use words and sentences to accurately express the true nature of their thoughts and subjective emotional states. How much more difficult would it be for the sage or seer to precisely communicate regarding Revelations, Visions and glimpses of the future, memories of the far distant past, or the wisdom associated with the kingdom of 'God' and realms of enlightened Being?

In the interpretation of relations between 'God' and man, or those pertaining to the Divine, the literal interpretation method or 'key' proves far from adequate. How could it be possible for an interpreter who is aware of only physical plane phenomena to understand the meaning of inspired writings? Therefore, right interpretation necessitates the use of other methods.

The remaining six keys are concerned with deciphering the codification process. By using them, the meaning of all sacred texts can be made known. This is possible because although the outward form of the sacred teachings differs, the realisations of all enlightened beings must be similar in context (though not necessarily in scope).

Differences arise because of language, sociocultural framework, era, and religious structures that the seer or sage was born into and had to use to inspire the various groups that were being taught. All seers, however, give basically simple teachings on morals and a code of ethics, which the average being can follow. These include the necessity for compassion towards all beings, loving-kindness, and service to humanity or to 'God'. Also interwoven within these teachings was a symbology (universal in its application) that 'the elect',[45] or aspirants to the 'mysteries of the kingdom of God'[46] could use to further their spiritual progress. These veiled meanings would provide the elect with further insight into the nature of 'God' or of the enlightenment-consciousness. This was a notable aspect of the Wisdom Religions as taught by ancient schools of the Mysteries (such as at Eleusis in Greece). True esoteric teachings were also veiled due to the inherent danger of prematurely giving them to average emotionally unthinking persons, to prevent their abuse by those desirous of psychic power.

In these teachings, there are basically five levels of interpretation of which the interpreter must be conscious. The five levels of interpretation for sacred scriptures must be understood for any of these keys to be rightly applied towards hidden revelations:

a. That relating to the exoteric, or dense physical life.
b. That relating to the psychic world and to all the phenomena associated with it: to a person's subtle (psychic) constitution, the astral world of glamour, the heaven and hell realms of the various religions.
c. That relating to the kingdom of Souls, esoterically the 'kingdom of Heaven'.

---

45 See *Mark 13:22, Matt. 24:31, Rom. 8:33, Col. 3:12,* etc.

46 *Luke 8:10* – 'And he said, Unto you it is given to know the mysteries of the kingdom of God: but to others in parables; that seeing they might not see, and hearing they might not understand.'

d. That relating to the realm of enlightenment. This level relates specifically to the Hierarchy of Enlightened Being. This Hierarchy was equated with the 'kingdom of Heaven'[47] at the time of the Christ, because their domain was upon the level of the Soul at that time. It is composed of the Initiates that are completely liberated from the type of sentience or consciousness associated with the realms of form, and who are united as One by the embrace of the Christ-principle. Though they possess different methods of application they are 'messengers of the Lord of Hosts',[48] for they convey the energies and impressions from the 'kingdom of God' to the corporeal world. The explication of this level of interpretation to the reader is a major objective of this series of writings.

e. That related to the 'kingdom of God', of which an increasing amount of information shall now be revealed.

2. The numerical and geometric keys

All the letters in Hebrew, Greek, and Sanskrit alphabets have numerical correspondences, and most other sacred books were also written to a numerical code. Picture symbols, letters and numerals all convey different aspects of the forces that emanate and sustain the universe. These forces also constitute the Divine in humanity by describing the ordering of their subtle constitution. The entire story of Creation and of evolution can be read in the ten numerals, from the number 1: the Will of Deity (the first act of Creation, that is, the 'thinking of the Divine Thought'), to the number 10, the number of 'God' (crowning perfection). Even to the orthodox theologian, such numbers as 1, 3, 7 and 10 have a spiritual meaning.

The Pythagorean School in ancient Greece was well known for their concept that all manifestation is governed by numbers. In fact, they based their entire system of metaphysics on this concept. Pythagoras is said to have framed his understanding of the universe by such phrases as 'the harmony of the spheres,' and 'God geometrises'. Pythagoras also presented a cosmological theory based on numbers. This was

47 *Matt. 13:11.*

48 *Malachi 2:7.*

exemplified in his idea of the sacred Tetraktys (meaning 'fourness'). This is a form of the number ten arranged as a perfect triangle, therefore:

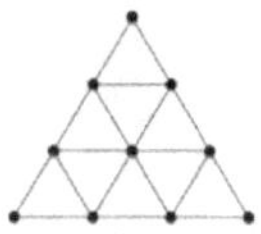

As with all truly esoteric schools, the Pythagoreans demanded that members follow strict loyalty to the edicts of the Master and maintain secrecy as to the true implications of the philosophy. The theory of rebirth, attainment of moral purity, silence, receptivity to the harmonics of music as a means for illumination, and the development of mind (which found its application in mathematics, science, and astrology) all played their part.

The use of sacred geometry by the ancients as a basis for temples has been revealed to us through the work of many authors, especially in relation to Stonehenge, Glastonbury, Druidic and Pagan temples, the Mayan and Aztec monuments, and above all, the Great Pyramid of Giza. Modern Masonic philosophy also echoes the esotericism within the ancient and sacred science of sacred geometry.

3. The astrological key

In addition to numerical correspondences, each of the ancient letter names had an astrological reference. For instance, to each of the 22 Hebrew letters could be assigned one of the ten astrological planets or one of the twelve signs of the zodiac, as elaborated in the Jewish text *The Sepher Yetzirah,*[49] and various books written on the Tarot and the Kabbalah. Also, many words and sentences have a direct astrological reference or inference. For example, the symbolism associated with each of the twelve tribes of Israel,[50] or for each of the twelve apostles, can be assigned different astrological signs. The Bible abounds in astrological data.

49 In Hebrew, the Book of Formation or Book of Creation.

50 *Genesis,* chapter 49.

4. The allegorical key

Esoterically considered, much can be related to the ancient history of humanity – to the method of evolution by all the kingdoms of Nature and of their interrelationships – if one were trained to be aware of that history. This implies the ability to vision the subjective happenings of the world and to intuit the Real. Much of the world's mythology is specifically a codification of this history.

5. The symbolical key

Each symbol such as the hand, blood, bird and fire, has hidden meaning. This is because the physical world and all the types of life thereon reflect (and thus symbolise) the qualities or the effects of the interplay of subjective energies associated with the various dimensions of perception. They are the effects of what emanates from the 'kingdom of God' and the Beings associated with it. These energies (which the symbols veil) can also be viewed as the expression of the subtle bodies of a person or 'God'. Of these, for instance, the alchemical Elements (Earth, Water, Fire, Air and Aether) are the effective representatives.

6. The physiological key

'Man', as previously stated, is built in the 'image of God', and therefore embodies the reflected aspects of God. The words of the Delphic Oracle in ancient Greece, 'as above, so below', and also the words, 'man, know thyself', have similar implications.

The doctrine of analogy has, in one form or another, been the workhorse of most metaphysical and Hermetic schools of thought. Examples are the Pythagoreans, Neo-Platonists, Gnostics, Rosicrucians, Freemasons, Kabbalists, Alchemists, and modem occult schools. Manly Palmer Hall, for instance, is of the opinion that:

> It was from the Hermetic premise set forth by the immortal Trismegistus upon the Smaragdine Tablet—'the inferior agrees with the superior and the superior with the inferior'—that the initiates of the old Mysteries established the science of correspondences.[51]

---

51 Manly P. Hall, *Man: The Grand Symbol of the Mysteries* (Los Angeles: Philosopher Press, 1937), 42.

'The notion of analogy', as Evelyn Underhill states, 'ultimately determines the religious concepts of every race, and resembles the verities of faith in the breadth of its application'.[52] This key is even echoed by St. Paul, who states in *Corinthians:* 'as we have borne the image of the earthy, we shall also bear the image of the heavenly'.[53] This key can now be fully utilised due to the marvellous physiological and anatomical knowledge that medical science has bequeathed to us. Our subtle or psychic constitution must also be well known here and related to the dense physical form into which we have incarnated.

7. The spiritual key

Interpretation as seen by one who is enlightened (that is, one is living in the 'fullness of God'[54]) is to live consciously within the embrace of the awakened Mind, which is inclusive of the consciousness states of all beings. Obviously, a type of vision incomprehensible to the average person must influence such a one. Many people have reached the stage where the Christ is newly born in the 'cave of the heart', with a touch of overwhelming Love that fills their lives, thus giving them a new purpose, warmth and devotion (to a noble cause). This is the first definite fruit of the mystical approach. However, only a few as of yet have every cell in their bodies filled with living light so that the Light of 'God', as it permeates all things, is contacted and consciously identified with.

This implies the fully developed 'Hermetic sense', thus an ability to think in the realm of meaning and of causes, and not in the world of effects. It is to be at-oned with the collective Mind of the entire Hierarchy of Enlightened Being. This necessitates a meditative awakening, leading one into an increasing awareness of that developed by all who are striving towards or have attained a similar goal. This awakening thus implies the ability to consciously contact the source or Fount of all Knowledge, Love and Light. It also implies the ability to channel this Fount so that the hearts and minds of all beings can become receptive to and be nourished by it.

---

52 Evelyn Underhill, *MYSTICISM: A study in the nature and development of Man's spiritual consciousness,* (Meridian Books Inc., 1960), 59.

53 *I Corinthians, 15:49.*

54 *Eph. 3:19.*

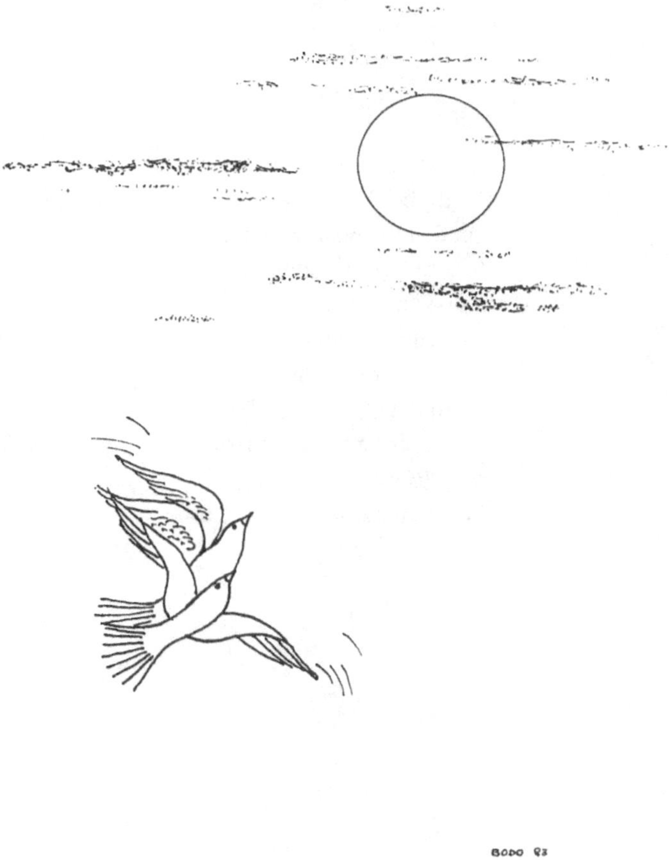
BODO 83

Oṁ

Let peace come to you
with the flight of the Dove.
Oh feel the beat of its wings!
Hear its sound
traverse the far reaches of Mind.
The clarion call of the Heart
resounds
in the clear cold Light
of prescient Awareness,
forever presenting
the adamantine jewel of Love
to you.

Oṁ

2

The Function of Energy and the Evolution of Consciousness

The entire question of enlightenment and the nature of Being is a matter of energetic reception, assimilation and transmission. The scientifically demonstrated fact that matter and energy are interchangeable – and therefore synonymous – is one of the most profound concepts ever formulated by humanity. This paradigm may also be used to define 'God' as a state or degree of organised intensified energy that causes, sustains, and then transmutes (back into fundamental energy or Being) the substance of the material universe. One can also think of the term 'God' to represent the primeval source of all Being, the Plenitude that when differentiated in time and space produced the cycles of evolution. 'God' can be conceived of as 'That which is beyond being, the summation of all that is, is not, was and will be'.

There are three basic types of energy postulated by esotericists:

a. That type of energy symbolised by *electricity,* as depicted by a lightning flash. It is the central storehouse of Power dynamically expressed in the heart of every atom (be it a physical, human, or solar atom). It is dynamic, impelling and potently destructive, or rather, transmutative: for it liberates the Life from within the confines of the form once the evolutionary goal is reached. This corresponds to the *Father* or Will aspect of Deity – the Spirit, which coordinates and impels the Life of any entity onwards in time and space.

b. That energy symbolised by *Light,* the expression of solar Fire, produced by the interaction of the other two types of energy. This is healing, illuminating, gentle, radiant and magnetically attractive. It corresponds to the Love-Wisdom or *Son* aspect of Deity, the inherent Soul that coherently embodies the evolved qualities of the Life of the form.

c. That energy symbolised by *Heat* (frictional or mechanical energy). This is the result of the activity of the form nature. It can be considered to be abrasive, coarse, cyclically generative, sensation-engendering and warming. It corresponds to the *Activity* or *Mother* aspect of Deity, the substance or matter composing the phenomenal appearance of things. The correspondence is also to our personality aspects in their most objective sense.

Using the concept of analogy, it is feasible that the 'Body of God' has its own nerve impulses and channels of supply and demand (blood vessels). These 'channels' would be composed of matter or energy existing at ultra-high frequencies, far transcending those of our neuro-physiological mechanisms. Such subjective substance presupposes a subtle 'ethereal' type of matter (or type of energy) that is interpenetrating, and thus incorporating, the dense physical form. Matter can be said to be the densest state of 'spiritual' substance.

This postulate is beginning to find testimony in recent scientific findings, as described by the biologist Dr. Lyall Watson, who states:

> [I]t now seems unreasonable to doubt that the living body produces, or at least is associated with energy that can be made visible by high-frequency electrical discharge.
>
> Exactly what kind of energy is involved is still open to question.... William Tiller, of Stanford University, believes that the evidence we already have is enough to prove that the somatic system is supplemented by at least one other. He calls the combination the 'human ensemble' and suggests that the most reasonable approach yet made to an interpretation of this complex is the yogi philosophy of the seven principles....

The first level of substance is that of the familiar somatic system which operates on the Einsteinian space-time frame – about which we already know a great deal. If we are going to assign the new discoveries to their relevant places, then Burr's life field with all its electrical effects fits in here. The second is the etheric level, which is said to be inhabited by the 'etheric double' that is unable to leave the body and is primarily concerned with health and the absorption and distribution of *prana*. The chakra[s] are apparently located at this level and so, if this is where acupuncture operates, then this is where the new bioplasmic or energy body belongs. This level forms a bridge between the first or physical and the third or astral level.[1]

The etheric body, *prāṇa* and the *nāḍī* system

This energy or etheric body, in its densest expression, is visible as a transparent (sometimes bluish-grey or purple) band about 1/4 of an inch around the body. By focussing via an imaginary eye at the centre of the eyebrows, this can be seen with practice, by looking at, yet slightly away from, a hand resting on a blank piece of paper. The etheric body appears as a tenuous type of liquid plastic interpenetrating all dense matter. It is the mould upon which the physical body is constructed. Etheric energy is the medium often shaped by the visual patterns in the brain, causing the hallucinogenic images often seen by those under the influence of psychotropic drugs.

As an intermediary between the subjective world and the dense physical body, the etheric body acts as a conveyor of energy, vitality and consciousness from one dimension of perception to the next. It embodies the channels that convey electro-chemical impulses from the nerves to the brain. It is the true medium or substance that enables the transmission of all types of energy from one form to another – even in a vacuum.

There exist a myriad of etheric channels in the human body, called *nāḍīs*[2] in the Sanskrit terminology. They roughly underlie blood vessels

---

1 Lyall Watson, *The Romeo Error,* (Dell Publishing, 1976), 164-5.

2 *Nāḍīs* are finely reticulated channels for the conveyance of *prāṇa* in the etheric vehicle. These channels stem from the three principal *nāḍīs* in the central spinal column *(iḍā, piṅgalā* and *suṣumṇā nāḍīs).* There are said to be 72,000 main *nāḍīs* in

and nerve cords. Where several *nāḍīs* intersect and interrelate, plexuses (or vortices) of energy are formed, which are termed *chakras* (further explained in chapter eight).

The energy conveyed by the *nāḍīs* is termed *prāṇa* in Sanskrit, lung in Tibetan, nephesh in Hebrew, and chi in the Taoist terminology. *Prāṇa* is directly absorbed into our systems via certain *chakras* by the process of breathing, or indirectly via food.

The word *prāṇa* is derived from the roots *'prā'*, meaning 'forth', and *'ṇa'*, meaning 'to breathe, move, live'. It is the 'breath of life' – energy drawn to the physical world from the etheric aspect of all phenomenal life. It comprises the sum-total of vital energy composing a body: be it human, planetary, or solar. There are five main types of *prāṇa*. The process of liberation from bondage to the dense form is directly concerned with transmutation and right projection of the base forms of *prāṇa* in the body.

Prāṇa is essentially the energy of the 'Son' emanating from the Sun, from the heart of That which continually radiates to the earth the vitality needed for the well-being of all entities. On a microscopic scale, it is vital, active, radiatory heat – the cumulative total of myriads of little *prāṇic* lives. Every entity absorbs what it needs and retransmits this energy after it passes through their systems. They thus colour it with their specific characteristics, which may provide either malefic or beneficent effects upon those that reabsorb it.

Prāṇa is an attribute of the aura of the planetary and solar Christ. It is the symbolic 'blood' that we were asked to drink by the historical Christ at the last supper. It can cleanse the 'robes' or sheaths of our corporeality to make them 'white'.[3] *Prāṇa* is effectively the lower correspondence of *buddhi,* the enlightenment-consciousness or energy that sustains a liberated being.

Sheila Ostrander and Lynn Schroeder present a tabulation of other terms for this energy as given to it by 'only the most famous discoverers':

---

the etheric vehicle, though this number is symbolic. Each *nāḍī* allows the passage of the five different types of *prāṇas*. Where *nāḍīs* containing twenty-one or more *prāṇas* intersect then you will find a *bīja* (seed) for the appearance of an important *chakra.*

3 *Rev. 7:14.*

Discoverer	Name of X-Force
Ancient Chinese	Vital energy
Ancient Hindu	Prana
Polynesian Huna	Mana
Renaissance	
Paracelsus	Munis
Van Helmont	Magnale
Eighteenth to Twentieth Centuries	
Mesmer	Animal Magnetism
Reichenbach	Odic Force
Keely	Motor Force
Blondlot	N-Rays
Radiesthesists	Etheric Force
L.E. Eeman	"X Force"
Current Medicine	Psychosomatic (?)
Contemporary Communist World	
Soviet scientists	Bioplasmic energy
Czech scientists	Psychotronic energy[4]

Table 3: Discoverers and names of energy

The etheric body (into which *prāṇa* is absorbed, and is practically indistinguishable from) is found in four grades. These four, and the three (dense, liquid, and gaseous) constituents of the physical body, create an interpenetrating septenary, as shown in figure 2:

4 Sheila Ostrander & Lynn Schroeder, *Psychic Discoveries Behind the Iron Curtain*, (Bantam Books, 1973), 378. The text presented in this book has here been converted into a table.

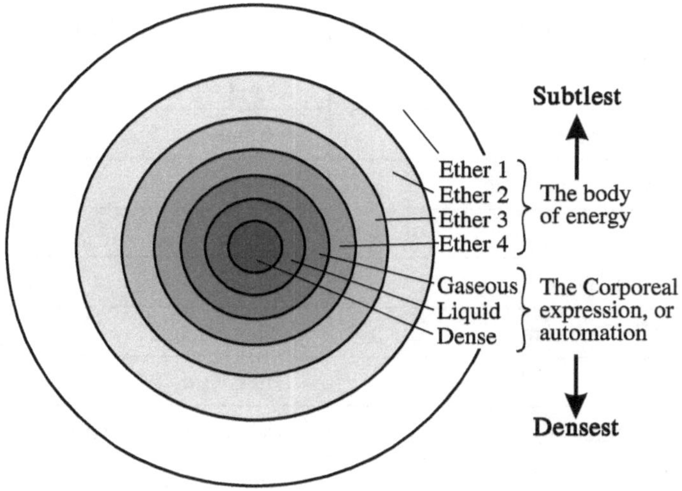

Figure 2: The physical septenary

The number seven is the most important number found in religious scriptures (occurring nearly 600 times in the Bible alone). It governs the entire ordering of Nature, epitomised by the 'seven days of Creation', the seven Rays of light (both the esoteric Rays and those found in Nature), the seven notes of the musical scale, the seven *chakras,* and the 'seven spirits of God'.[5] Physiologically there is a reflection in the seven layers of skin of the hands and feet, if the subcutaneous tissue is also included.

The etheric-physical septenary is considered by esotericists to constitute our 'physical' robe or sheath. The etheric double is our true outer form or encasement. The physical shell is but the tangible effect, an automaton, which automatically responds to the energies and impulses manifesting through the etheric double.

The etheric body radiates streams of magnetic vitality from the *nāḍī* system. This is known as the health aura, which is clearly seen in Kirlian photography.[6] One of the aura's functions is to help repel negative influences that may prove harmful to the being. The etheric double is

---

5 *Rev. 4:5.*

6 They are described in such books as: *Kirlian Photography* (East West Publications, London, 1980), by L. Genno, F. Guzzon and P. Marsigli; and *Handbook of Psychic Discoveries* by Sheila Ostrander and Lynn Schroeder, (Berkeley Publishing, N.Y., 1975).

the real seat of the brain, enabling the brain to function as amazingly as it does. This allows the transcendence of purely electrochemical functioning and computer-like patterns.

The etheric double also allows retention of memory (even after many neurons have been destroyed in the brain), the recall of past life experiences, the manifestation of psychic phenomena, and deep hypnotic trances when consciousness is withdrawn from the body. It is the medium that allows the propagation of all subjective energies (such as 'alpha waves'[7] in space).

The colour of the etheric realm is predominantly violet, gradually becoming the rose of the highest ether. The attributes of the fourth ether are currently being investigated by scientists. Many dichotomous enigmas associated with the properties of subatomic particles (e.g., the behaviour of electrons or photons as both particles of matter and waves of energy) are directly related to this ether. (Such investigation may even turn a number of physicists into mystics, though many would likely object to that term.[8])

Consciousness can survive after the death of the body because it continues to be in the subtle or energy body for an indefinite time, and then enters into higher dimensions of perception. This fact yet needs to be accepted by those governing our educational institutions. Adequately educating all responsible people in the discovery of the subtle bodies would assist endeavour to offset humanity's materialistic bias.

The Soul and the purpose of evolution

The higher Self, the Soul, of the human unit can be considered a 'Cell' in the Body of 'God'. That human unit also incorporates within itself diversified elements and qualities that seemingly occur in a separate, self-existent manner, but are unified within one body of expression. Such synthesis provides the ability to define identity by means of a person's five senses and intellect. The personalised self becomes circumscribed

---

7 See Jodi Lawrence's book *Alpha Brain Waves,* (Avon Books, N.Y., 1972).

8 As explained in such books as: *The Tao of Physics* by F. Capra (Shambhala, Boulder, 1975), *Mysticism and the New Physics* by Michael Talbot (Bantam Books, N.Y. 1980), and Gary Zukav's *The Dancing Wu Li Masters: An Overview of the New Physics*, (Bantam Books, N.Y., 1980).

in terms of this and that by saying 'I am'. In this way, on a tiny scale, the person expresses activity similar to what the Creative Deity assumes on a macrocosmic scale when manifesting as a planetary or solar Logos.

The cellular unit is therefore an aspect of the collective whole, nurtured by channels of supply and demand, of cause and effect. It is a symbiotic, homeostatic, vibrant organism. It is also a unit of diversified energy, bathing in a sea of interrelated energy impulses and currents. (For the etheric body of the human unit is an integral part of the various kingdoms of Nature, and thus of the earth, which in turn is part of the etheric expression of a solar Logos.)

Such Cells that are conscious of their place as part of an organ in the Body of 'God' represent units of consciousness within that Body. They are therefore group-conscious and are here termed Souls. As integral components of an organ in such a Body they are qualified intermediaries between the Divine and the corporeal. The vital Body of Deity directly bathes them, so they can channel particular qualities, Ray energies, or functions they are responsive to as a group. (As conditioned by the Mind or Desire Nature of Deity.) They thereby can contribute to the well being of that Body as a unit.

A Soul can therefore be defined (in its simplest connotation) as an entity that includes not only the consciousness of the personality (the human unit) in its sphere of consciousness, but also the collective consciousness of the subjective group of which it is a part. It therefore responds to the needs of that group. An enlightened being is a person whose Mind embraces such a state of perception, thus is fully Soul-conscious.

Regarding the process of evolution, the Soul is the result of a point of balance in which Spirit (ineffable Life) and matter (dense substance) meet and interact. This interaction produces consciousness. The evolution of consciousness occurs within confined and ever-changing forms. As the Soul inhabits progressively more evolved forms, the substance composing the forms becomes more refined, and the indwelling Light of the Spirit becomes increasingly brighter. The Soul thus evolves, for it contains within its sphere of consciousness all the seeds gathered by the personality, plus those radiated into it by the overshadowing Spirit aspect, to meet the needs of the gradually awakening person (and of the little cellular lives that compose its form).

The purpose of evolution is to lift gross substance from the lower to the higher planes of existence, thereby transmuting it by imbuing it with the seeds of intelligent life. This necessitates the use of the Element Fire,[9] as well as the gathering together of substance into a form to contain this Element. This is accomplished by means of that form's sentient and then conscious evolution through many rounds of birth and death, to increasingly heightened stages of perception: mineral, plant, animal, and humanity.

The Fiery Element finds complete expression in humanity. We combine the best qualities of the lesser forms of evolution and have also gained the seed of immortality – the 'spark of Mind' (the Soul). We will therefore cross the 'rainbow bridge' to the realm of enlightened consciousness. This spark is fanned, the flame is fed, until it becomes all-consuming and lights up the whole as a radiant (Christ-like) Sun.

This process is one of long continuous change and interaction with all that is. It concerns perpetual experience, then the sublimation and transmutation of the results of that experience in the realm of Light. This happens by means of the expression of Fiery energy through ever-expanding spiral unities. The fundamental sustaining Power of all Being is eventually contacted and actively becomes expressed. Thus humanity evolves.

When animal-man evolved a rudimentary intellect this was a point in the infinitude of time that marked a consummation in the long aeonic evolution of matter. It allowed the Spirit to find a medium through which it could work to influence the evolving form. Herein lies the hint as to the process producing the creation of the Soul. Only a brief outline however will be given here.

The three Outpourings and Individualisation

Three streams of Creative Energy emanating from the abstract Deity in time and space (known as Outpourings[10]) have helped to make our earth (and the solar system) what it is.

---

9 The Element governing the domain of mind/Mind, as will be elaborated in chapter four.

10 See figure 3 and pages 277-84 of my book *Meditation and the Initiation Process* for a more detailed explanation of these Outpourings.

The first Outpouring

The first stream can be likened to a downpour of an ever-congealing crystallization of virgin matter or primordial undifferentiated substance.[11] This matter is inherently sentient and is slowly preparing the bed in which the 'seed of consciousness' may germinate. It is the archetype of the Universal Mother, as symbolised by the Virgin Mary in the Gospel story. She represents the nurturing energies (the embodied Waters, or sea of substance) in which the Christ-child (the Logos or Word of 'God', the second aspect of Deity) could begin His appointed cycle. In Genesis, the first Outpouring is indicated by the phrase: 'the Spirit of God moved upon the face of the waters'.[12]

The second Outpouring

After the Womb of Life was prepared by the Universal Mother the second stream (the consciousness, or Son aspect) could descend to utilise this 'sea' as a sphere of evolution. This is also represented as the 'Holy Ghost'[13] – the streams of developed Lives (the four higher of the seven incarnated Creative Hierarchies) that have evolved formerly over past aeons or world periods. They accomplished this by mutual reaction and interblending, by progressive interplay and co-stimulation, through utilising the primal substance as the common denominator of their external forms.

At first, Life existed only on subtle levels of perception. It progressively coarsened, becoming definitely objective and physical. (Leaving behind therefore the fossils that scientists have discovered.) By incarnating into that matter, not only did the incarnating Lives evolve, but also did the highly diversified and specialised mineral elements and compounds that

---

11 The 'face of the deep', in Biblical terminology.

12 *Genesis, 1:2.*

13 Wherever the term Holy Ghost appears in the Bible, it can at first be translated as enlightenment-consciousness, in its varying degrees and capacities. (For an entity can be considered 'enlightened' relative to another lower down on the ladder of evolution than it.) It is an attribute of the universal storehouse of consciousness *(ālayavijñāna)*. When particularised as part of the enlightened or illumined Mind (or as that which enlightens), it becomes the Spirit of Truth, and for the planet it is the Hierarchy of Enlightened Being. Truth here has much the same meaning as the Gnostic term Sophia (the embodiment of wisdom) and the Sanskrit term *jñāna*. When expressed by a Seer Truth becomes the *dharma* or Divine Law.

form the substance of this world. Many experiments were undertaken by the 'Watchers', the Angels or Deities protecting and nurturing all Life. Much trial and error happened, which produced the flowering into superabundance, and eventual discontinuation, of many species of entities. Eventually, over aeons, animal forms evolved that would be capable of utilising and receiving within them the 'spark of mind'.[14]

The third Outpouring and Individualisation

This Outpouring at first produced the Individualisation process. At a later stage of the evolutionary process this Outpouring concerns the descent of the Fiery energies from the domain of the Father (Shambhala) that allow the attainment of the third and higher Initiations. Only by first introducing the 'spark of mind' could a human kingdom arise out of the animal form. At that time the highest evolved of the animal kingdom, through a collective upsurging of aspiration or of an embryonic thought process, attracted a downpouring of Fiery light to them. This allowed the higher (Spirit) and lower (matter) aspects of Deity to interact, producing a container of Mind upon the higher mental planes. The mass incarnation of humanity via the consequent appearance of their Soul-forms occurred many millions of years ago. Two types of light were blended in the mental plane: the gross and the transcendental.[15] This was obviously a significant spiritual event, producing many far-reaching consequences.

The combination of the light of the mind and that of the Spirit therefore produced a Soul-form in the higher realms of the mind (the 'heavenly realm'). This form became thereby a Cell or unit of Fire in the Mind of 'God', from which increasingly evolved the quality of the Light of the Soul. This new kingdom of Souls then appropriated animal bodies as a medium for the gathering of experience in the realms of form. This overshadowing process by the Divine allowed the appearance of two expressions of the human kingdom.

---

14 This term is derived from Blavatsky's *The Secret Doctrine*, for the implanting of the seed of the intellect in animal-man during the process of the Individualisation of humanity on earth. See Alice Bailey's *A Treatise on Cosmic Fire*, (Lucis Publishing Co., N.Y.), 719 for further explanation.

15 By 'gross', here is inferred the highest vibration or quality that the form can produce, that though bright to human eyes, is still dull compared to the spiritual Light at the centre of the Soul form (the Causal body).

a. The appearance of those that were already members of the human kingdom from a former evolutionary cycle, who could now incarnate through new forms adapted for the new conditionings. The first account of the creation of humanity in Genesis[16] is concerned with this: the formation of our animal form (the physical body) and consequently the dominion over all the kingdoms of Nature. This happened on the sixth and final day of Creation ('God' rested on the seventh day) after everything else was formed:

> So God created man in his own image....male and female created he them....and said unto them, be fruitful and multiply, and replenish the earth, and subdue it; and have dominion over the fish of the sea, and over the fowl of the air, and over every living thing that moveth upon the earth.[17]

Hinted here is that this particular 'creation' was in fact from an earlier cycle than the second more detailed account, given below of the familiar story of Adam and Eve.

b. Manifestation via those members of the animal kingdom that were ready to make the 'leap in consciousness' and enter the human kingdom. This is dealt with in the second account of Creation in Genesis, chapter two. The reference here is to the 'dust of the ground' that the 'Lord God formed man of', whereby man became 'a living soul,' after the Lord God 'breathed into his nostrils the breath of life'.[18] The 'dust of the earth' is not dust as we would recognise it (which did not then exist) for 'there went up a mist from the earth' that 'watered the whole face of the ground'[19] before humanity was formed, which would have prevented such dust from forming. Rather, the 'dust of the earth' refers to primal atomic substance as the 'material' of the supersensory realms, the archetype of our present mental plane. It was fashioned in the 'image of God' and infused with the Airy Element, the 'breath of life' *(buddhi)* that allows a 'living soul' to be formed. This mist, which 'watered the face of

16 *Genesis 1:27-28.*

17 *Genesis 1:27.*

18 *Genesis 2:7.*

19 *Genesis 2:6.*

the ground' was created before the rest of evolution, not after. This is thus contrary to the order cited in the first method. This 'mist' refers to the beginning of the formation of the astral plane.

It is stated in Genesis that 'the Lord God planted a garden eastward in Eden; and there he had put the man whom he had formed'.[20] Afterwards 'God' made to grow from the ground 'every living tree that is pleasant to the sight, and good for food'.[21] Later, there was formed 'out of the ground...every beast of the field, and every fowl of the air',[22] which were then brought to Adam so that he could name them. (Adamic man therefore resided upon the mental plane at that time, for it is only with the substance of the mind that one can 'name' all things.)

The consumption of the fruit of 'knowing good and evil'[23] caused humanity to be ousted from the subjective planes to the earth. They thereby incarnated into 'coats of skins' (meaning many sheaths, subjective and objective) that the 'Lord God' made for humanity.[24] People had to learn to utilise these 'coats' within which they could die.

The Lives of the mineral, plant and animal kingdoms were not self-conscious. They could not classify and name as Adam had done, for Spirit and matter were not interrelated in their constitution. They were not 'living Souls', as the 'breath of life' was not breathed into them. They were formed only 'out of the ground' (the material domain). The 'breath' enters their evolution as part of an entire class or group of animals. It governs, for example: all herds of cows, schools of one type of fish, one species of tree, or all oxygen atoms. For all life is Divine, they all share a collective awareness, therefore there is a common 'Group-Soul' for each species, in which the experiences of one are shared by all.

There exists no mechanism within these lesser kingdoms for the interplay of Spirit and matter wherein conscious registration of experiences can occur for the entity concerned. Animals therefore do not have individual Souls. Their experiences are collectively controlled

20 *Genesis 2:8.*

21 *Genesis 2:9.*

22 *Genesis 2:19.*

23 *Genesis 3:5.*

24 *Genesis 3:21.*

by angelic beings that are responsible for them. Compared to plants or minerals, an animal's collective awareness and experiences is more concentrated and developed. The Group-Soul of an animal will therefore comprise a smaller (more focused) number of entities than in any of the lesser kingdoms.

A Soul is essentially a completed 'Cell' in the Thought-Body of the planetary Logos. Together the kingdom of Souls represent one aspect of the prima matrix upon which the energies from that Thought directly impinge. Humanity therefore has the ability to consciously embrace both the kingdom of the Spirit and that of matter. Within the nucleus of our being, therefore, lies the doorway to 'Life eternal' that we can open and enter. Our external forms are moulded on the patterning or image of the Divine, forming the basis for the law of correspondence. The other aspect in this Thought-Body are the Soul's correspondences in the angelic kingdom (the *devas).* The entities of the lesser kingdoms collectively constitute the substance of the organelles of the 'cellular' constitution of the *devas.*

Despite this dual ability, humanity has for many ages primarily identified completely with its baser, material self (its animal component) and not with the radiant Sun of the 'Solar Angel'[25] within. People continue to identify with the impermanent, transient, non-real material world, and not the world of values. Thus the *karma* of our misapprehensions, wanderings and sufferings become perpetuated.

This need no longer be the case, for people are becoming increasingly enlightened. They are questioning the soundness of past methods of doing things. Increasingly, humanity are orientating themselves into the realm of Light, guided by those who know and can teach by example. If one wishes to fully understand the trend of the history of humanity, then one must recognise it in terms of the evolution of consciousness, not in terms of territorial acquisition and national aggression as is now the case.

---

25 Our Souls (or Sambhogakāya Flowers) are also sometimes described as Solar Angels, because of their sun-like radiance upon the higher mental plane, and because these forms, like everything else, is constituted of *deva* substance, hence are 'angelic'. What is considered 'human' are the evolving consciousness-attributes contained within that form, plus the Monadic Spark, the 'jewel in the Heart of the lotus'.

Genesis chapter three states that people are to become 'as gods, knowing good and evil', that 'your eyes shall be opened'.[26] The purpose of eating from the 'tree of knowledge' and of 'knowing good and evil' is for the opening of the 'mind's Eye' to all that conditions both material and spiritual Being. This purpose is the objective of our evolution. This is the reason why humanity was ousted from the garden of Eden into the earth, to wear 'coats of skins' in order to bear untold experiences of all types and qualities. Every incidence in our history and evolutionary journey contributed to the development of wisdom: the ability to 'see' the how and why of all things, and to walk the right direction in the immense duration of space. The phrase, 'your eyes shall be opened', does not just refer to the awakening of the physical eyes, but also of the inner ones, the *chakras,* that will allow the development of supersensory perception, the *siddhis*[27] of enlightenment, hence we are to become 'as gods'. The third Eye (the Ājñā centre) is specifically implied here.

Territorial acquisition by any nation or tribe, or the amassing of material possessions by any of us, is subject to the ravages of time, and is fundamentally an illusory activity, generating *saṃskāras*[28] and *karma.* The acquisition of wisdom, on the other hand, is eternal and continuously progresses. As the ages pass the truth of our divine ancestry has been altogether forgotten, or has disappeared within the deep recesses of human myth-making tendencies – veiled by later interpretations of the empirical mind. To counter this trend people need to directly awaken the inner Eyes by which to See what was and the true nature of the sum of Being.

The ability to reason

The evolution of humanity's ability to reason and think (the development of wisdom) is lasting. Those qualities are inevitably built into our

26 *Genesis 3:5.*

27 Psychic powers.

28 *Saṃskāras,* the unwanted attributes of consciousness, must be transformed or gradually transmuted through a succession of incarnations dedicated to their cleansing. Inevitably a complete emptying of their characteristics, or their sublimation into higher consciousness states (into subtler versions of the *saṃskāras),* is the path towards enlightenment.

constitution and thus become inherent in our consciousness. Such evolution predisposes the humanity of a certain era[29] to a certain level of activity regarding the expression of gross desires, mind, or the intuition (or any combination of these). We observe these qualities as racial, religious, or national characteristics, which can also be understood as a group-Mind. The means concerning the development of such qualities can be, and are, remembered by those who can tap the collective awareness of the group-Mind (a function of the intuition). Such ability is frequently acknowledged by the testimony of our greatest sages, saints and enlightened beings. It is the basis for their amazingly acute perceptions and revelations of the mysteries of the past, as well as prescient indications for the future.

Intuitive perception is an attribute of all Seers that have incarnated to help humanity. It concerns the development of an enlightened Reasoning that allows one to access the 'mysteries of the kingdom of God'. This is an expression of the 'hidden wisdom' of those that have been perfected, as explained by Paul:

> Howbeit we speak of wisdom among them that are perfect: yet not the wisdom of this world, nor of the princes of this world, that come to nought: But we speak the wisdom of God in a mystery, *even* the hidden *wisdom,* which God ordained before the world unto our glory: Which none of the princes of this world knew: for had they known *it,* they would not have crucified the Lord of glory.[30]

'The princes of this world' are those who shape policy relating to the temporal life of humanity. These individuals set outward objectives of personal, national, racial and territorial acquisition, or dominance of various forms. They are also the intelligentsia who rule our present society. In the phrase, 'for had they known it, they would not have crucified the Lord of glory', the 'Lord of glory' refers not just to Jesus Christ, but also to that quality ('glory') that is the next stage or aspect of consciousness being developed by humanity, which was then embodied by Jesus. Later Sons of 'God' in various religious traditions continued with the process of presenting such revelations of 'glory' to humanity.

---

29 Such as the Babylonians, Egyptians, Israelites, Romans, etc.

30 *I Cor. 2:6-8.*

(Glory here can also be considered as the radiance or luminescence radiating out as the aura of an enlightened being.)

The 'Lord of glory' must first be crucified on the cross of materiality, of human experience and suffering, before fully awakening to the transcendence and full knowledge of the 'hidden wisdom' that comes from 'God'.[31] The accumulated work of those that have manifested such glory down the ages has produced the world's religious dispensations, and other beneficial teachings (including the scientific stream) that have become an integral part of the consciousness of humanity.

The attainment of the higher levels of consciousness incorporates an awareness of the types of sentience developed by the mineral, vegetable, animal and angelic kingdoms. The sentience associated with the vegetable kingdom has been rediscovered in part by modern researchers as Peter Tompkins and Christopher Bird. In their book, *The Secret Life of Plants,* they describe the story of Clive Backster, who discovered that whenever a plant was witnessing the death of some living tissue it produced a recognisable pattern in a polygraph machine (a lie detector):

> Backster's medical consultant, the New Jersey cytologist Dr Howard Miller, concluded that some sort of "cellular consciousness" must be common to all life...Such observations seem to imply that some sort of total memory must go down to the single cell, and by inference that the brain may be just a switching mechanism, not necessarily a memory storage organ.
>
> "Sentience," says Backster, "does not seem to stop at the cellular level. It may go down to the molecular, the atomic and even subatomic. All sorts of things which have been conveniently considered to be inanimate may have to be re-evaluated.[32]

The energies emanating from the various kingdoms of Nature affect humanity, however this is generally not registered consciously (as of yet). During humanity's earlier development they were definitely

31 The proper significance of this statement will bear fruit when the significance of the fourth Initiation is explained in my book *Meditation and the Initiation Process*.

32 Peter Tompkins and Christopher Bird, *The Secret Life of Plants,* (Harper & Row, N.Y., 1973), 11-12. See also John Whitman, *The Psychic Power of Plants* (A Star Book, London, 1975) for similar information.

clairvoyant,[33] for their subtle bodies were but loosely tied to the physical sheath. They thus freely intermingled with the general astral or etheric environment. The resultant psychic impressions determined the course of all their actions. Despite being acutely psychically receptive they could not control the effects of that receptivity. They were therefore easily swayed by massed impulses, emotions and the desires of those around them.[34] (Mediumistic tendencies in certain individuals are a reversion to those times.[35])

The development of the capacity to think by humanity provided some control over the emotions, although their subtle sheaths also coarsened. Consciousness therefore became focussed downwards to the material world and radiated out from their individual selves, as centres of their own little universes. Former group awareness therefore became individualised, as humans became thinking entities with separative activities.

When this happened amongst the then most progressed of humanity, it produced extreme selfishness, darkness and evil, for they directed psychic forces towards achieving their base desires. The majority that were still the victims of a mass desire-mind were therefore manipulated by the relatively few who could think. The result was that black magic[36] became rampant. Like a dark plague-ridden cloud, it was everywhere evident. Evil and blasphemy (mantric sound against the forces of Life) ravaged the world and darkened the skies, until it necessitated the planetary Logos ('God') to cleanse the world by means of the 'great

---

33 A similar type of clairvoyance can be viewed as an animal's non-intellectual sense of knowingness, coupled with the instinct that drives them to act.

34 Various clairvoyant attributes are developed by most animal species, explaining many of the mysteries of massed animal behaviour, of how for instance, many animals move in unison, such as schools of fish and flocks of birds. In the more advanced animals, such as dogs, we can observe how sympathetically or telepathically attuned they become to the wishes of their masters.

35 Those with psychic and mediumistic tendencies have awakened minor *chakras* facilitating perception of the subtle realm.

36 Black magic is the line of least resistance for incarnate humanity. Such magic concerns the development of extreme selfishness, the ruthless psychic projection of the self-serving nature of the desire-mind in the quest for sexual and sensual gratification, money, material possessions and power. They work towards psychic and physical manipulation over everyone else.

flood'. This action was needed to prevent humanity from destroying themselves and all around them, both physically and psychically. Some people survived in many places throughout the world, and the symbolism of Noah and those on his ark is but one such testimony. Those on this arc were the righteous who did not abuse their acquired powers and were thus selected to foster a new cycle of human civilisation. This is symbolised by the appearance of the fifth, Aryan Root Race,[37] many of whom were responsible for most of the history recorded in the Old Testament. Such testimony is also in other world myths and unearthed by archaeologists. Eventually the civilisation we now live in appeared.

Humanity has slowly evolved from an unconscious or instinctual stage (in which Adam and Eve knew not their 'nakedness'[38]). From there they developed a purely emotional stage (a form of psychic receptivity). Mass emotionality is still prevalent on the earth, as evidenced by various forms of spontaneous group and mass emotion, seen in sports matches and political gatherings.[39]

Eventually the mind developed as a conscious expression within humanity, and over many millennia the mind began to properly control the emotions and desire in the foremost members of humanity. They evolved into the members of the Hierarchy of Enlightened Being.[40] They could think abstractly to reason things out for themselves, and so developed wisdom. As stated in the Bible: 'wisdom is the principal thing; *therefore* get wisdom: and with all thy getting get understanding'.[41]

---

37 See Appendix Two of my book *Esoteric Cosmology and Modern Physics* for further detail of the Root Races.

38 *Genesis 2:25.*

39 As Alice Bailey similarly states in *Glamour: A World Problem*, (New York: Lucis Publishing Company, 1998), 16, 'The bulk of the people are purely emotional with occasional flashes of real mental understanding'. She further states on page 102: 'The power of unified emotion (often expressing itself in what is called mob psychology) is everywhere recognised and feared as well as exploited'.

40 The term 'Enlightened Being' here refers to the enlightenment common to all members of this Hierarchy. Sometimes other descriptive terms may be used for them, such as 'the Hierarchy of Light and Love', often however, the phrase shall be simplified to 'the Hierarchy', or simply 'Hierarchy'.

41 *Proverbs 4:7.*

The attainment of wisdom was the onus of human development up to the time of the Christ, as emphasised by all the great religions of the time. The first step in this direction occurred when 'the sons of God' made wives of the 'daughters of men'.[42] This is a way of stating that the Divine (human Souls, which are 'sons of God') and the respective corporeal forms ('daughters of men') came to be fully interblended as a functioning unity. Through this unity, wisdom (the result of the union between the two) could begin to be expressed. Another earlier mentioned interpretation is that certain members of the then Shambhala interrelated and incarnated amongst humanity so that the Lemurians (the 'giants' of those days) could be taught the elements of understanding needed to develop the rudiments of civilisation, from which people of wisdom could evolve.

The evolution of wisdom continued unabated, as was evidenced by the later incarnation of the Buddha and also by the rise of the philosophers of ancient Greece (such as Socrates, Plato, Archimedes and Aristotle). They led people through the process of reason and induction, and away from reliance upon the powers of the various Gods (who influenced beings as if they were pawns in a seeming erratic game of chess). The fact that people in those times could do nothing without being embodied by (or having recourse to) the Gods testified to the natural clairvoyance of the earliest Greeks (as well as all of the then humanity).

The ability to 'converse with the Gods' was no longer prevalent by the time of Socrates (470 – 399 B.C.). Indeed, humanity had by then become very materialistic. The Roman Empire (a bureaucratic empire, governed by autocrats) was an experiment into a type of materialistic civilisation with religious overtones that nowadays manifests throughout the world. Materialistic attributes led to a complete disregard and even contempt for the sacredness of all life. Such thinking could be witnessed, for example, in the sadism of gladiator matches and other happenings in the sports arenas.

Jesus Christ was born during this period, in which a transition to deeper materialism was taking place. At this time, despite the above, many people had not forgotten the inner meaning of some of their myths,

42 *Genesis 6:2-5.*

especially in Egypt and the Middle East. The seekers for spiritual truth could still learn the symbolism of the ancient Mysteries, as taught in their sacred temples. Jesus was also born in that era, partly to set in motion the spiritual impetus to hopefully prevent further engendering of the spiritual ignorance that people were then sowing. He gave out new teachings based on wisdom, but also exemplifying the nature and purpose of Divine Love which everyone could develop within themselves.[43] The course of His entire life also revolved around the symbolic demonstration of the ancient Mysteries, as will be explained later.

In modern times, the ability to view the atomic and cosmic worlds has returned to us, but by the means of the development of external instruments, rather than by internal receptivity and attunement to the subjective domains. Many people are now intelligently active, and there is a growing momentum for them to ethically utilise their noetic abilities to comprehend supersensory information.

Scientists are rapidly developing the ability to control the forces constituting all manifest life, through such things as genetic engineering and the technological manipulation of the entire biosphere. The exploration of quantum mechanics and nuclear physics that has helped to explore the subatomic world and astrophysics has given access to comprehending the forces constituting the universe. The next breakthrough is to begin to properly explore the inner realms of consciousness, the domain of metaphysics and the bio-fields governing the manifestation of Life. Scientists are only beginning to explore the subjective world that was formerly the domain of clairvoyants and psychics. Here they are but infants, at the elementary stages of discovering a vast ineffable multidimensional universe of future revelation. This will evolve into a new non-materialistic science. It will have profound ramifications for human civilisation, especially when the nature of the levels of perception, and the existence of the *nāḍī* system are discovered.

In the past the control of the forces of Nature was produced through the use of the creative potency of Sound and knowledge of the subjective

43 There is much in the New Testament concerning his teachings of Love, such as in *John: 15:12-13:* 'This is my commandment, That ye love one another, as I have loved you. Greater love hath no man than this, that a man lay down his life for his friends'.

laws of Being.[44] The angelic kingdom[45] that embody all manifest things are directly receptive to this potency and knowledge. Mantra, manifested via ritualistic endeavour, produced a magical or creative action in the material world.

Today, through use of the developed mind, and knowledge of the laws of physics, technology has been developed that enables us to directly manipulate substance from the purely material level. In doing so, our technocrats are challenging the role of the angelic kingdom (Mother Nature), but they have omitted a consideration of the Life animating all forms. Thus, they have had to channel enormous energies in the most limited, material form, to achieve their results. Technocrats have assumed the role of a Creative Deity, without understanding the esoteric laws governing creation. They only consider the effects of these laws in the material world. Consequently, as Paul states: 'the whole creation groaneth and travaileth in pain together'.[46] However, the manifestation of such 'pain' has been massively increased since Paul's times. All kingdoms of Nature suffer the burden of the oppression of this massed materialism.

What was formerly sacred has been profaned by scientific materialism. Its major tool is the intellect, divorced from Love[47] and geared to manipulate all forms. The intellect can be a potently destructive force. It has produced a world full of clashing noises and strife, distorting the natural flow of Life, while endeavouring to arrange all things to suit humanity's gross desires and designs. With these effects, humanity will toil in the effects of the *karma* accrued from such destructive activity and rapine. Inevitably they must learn the consequences of wrong energy direction, for 'to every action there is an equal and opposite reaction'.

---

44 *1. Cor. 4:16* – 'Know ye not that ye are the temple of God, and that the Spirit of God dwelleth in you?'

45 The angelic *(deva)* kingdom are the conditioning intelligences embodying the substance of all forms. They are the nurturing, intelligently perceptive, feminine principle in Nature.

46 *Romans 8:22.*

47 Which allows the understanding of Divine Purpose.

The Hierarchy of Enlightened Being

Divinity, as the inherent Life in the various forms of Nature and in humanity, must in time assert its true expression in human civilisation. Divinity manifests the dominant Sound of the governing Law of all Being. This Sound was ordained as the 'Lamb slain from the foundation of the world'.[48] It conditions natural events, cyclic impulses, and the overall patterning of evolution.

The world is to be gradually sanctified, for that is the purpose of the incoming ones who follow in the footsteps of the Christ, who have evolved throughout the millennia. They are those that have passed the testings for Initiation, collectively known as the Hierarchy of Enlightened Being. They are a Hierarchy because they consist of many beings that are of different Initiation levels, from the first to the seventh Initiation (the degree of attainment of the Christ). They are 'Watchers',[49] the 'sons of God',[50] that observe and provide practical assistance to the progress of all lives on the earth. Part of the present endeavour of Hierarchy is to prevent mankind from reverting to destructive sadism, as in earlier times.

This very nearly occurred concomitantly with the brutal forces that Hitler unleashed in World War II. Such activity, in a differing guise, is also manifesting via the activities of successive US administrations. In stark contrast to this, Hierarchy guides humanity by fostering the seeds of Love-Wisdom. These seeds must be broadcast far and wide for the Christ to reappear and the New Aquarian era to manifest. If the wrongly directed effects of people's selfish materialism are to be rectified, it is now essential for the entire world to be involved, and not just localities (such as was localised to the Mediterranean region where Jesus and his disciples were concentrated).

The Buddha and Christ-Jesus are the most important historical examples of 'God-men'. They became milestones in the history of

---

48 *Rev. 13:8.*

49 *Daniel 4:13-18.*

50 *Romans 8:14* – 'For as many as are led by the Spirit of God, they are sons of God'. My book: *The Constitution of Shambhala,* volumes 1 and 2, as well as the writings of Alice Bailey, should be consulted for a detailed account of the nature of these 'sons of God'.

human consciousness, for they successfully stimulated or fostered humanity's advancing capabilities to far greater heights than ever before. Other such beings included the ancient sages, the innovators of every religion, and the great men and women of science, politics, medicine and the arts. The Buddha embodied the means for self-realisation by teaching the way to fully utilise the mind to express great Wisdom.

Christ-Jesus embodied the quality of awareness called intuition. Intuition is essentially Love instantly translated into a far-reaching vision. It necessitates a fully endowed, well-balanced mind (an all-embracive storehouse of consciousness) to effectively manifest. Wisdom and Love are two aspects of the One (energy), hence the term Love-Wisdom, denoting the expression of the second of the great Rays of Life. Only after humanity learns to think constructively can they be taught to Love effectively.

At the time of Jesus people no longer needed to devote themselves blindly to concepts of an extraneous Deity or Deities, nor to the precepts commanded (or given to them to follow) through the medium of their prophets and sages.[51] Instead, their eyes could be opened to the fact of the Christ within, as 'the hope of glory',[52] the embodiment of Divine Love. Jesus manifested as a concrete example that humanity could learn to actively follow and whose teachings they could express.[53]

The new commandment that Jesus gave, that 'ye love one another, as I have loved you',[54] was not an authoritarian dictum. Rather, it was a factual statement of what must be accomplished to fully attain conscious 'God'-realisation. This statement was not unique to Jesus; all sages have stated it in one form or another, but His method of expression of Love was new. Over the course of His life, Jesus exoterically demonstrated the context of veiled esoteric teachings, previously revealed only to Initiates of the various Mystery Schools.

---

51 The 'Ten Commandments' are an example of such precepts.

52 *Colossians 1:27.*

53 Such teachings were thoroughly abused and distorted by the Christianity that appeared some centuries after his death. Their consequent actions made a mockery of what He came to teach.

54 *John 15:12.*

An ability to achieve complete impersonality, serenity and a state of non-receptivity to any (self) engendered thought[55] is the prelude to enlightenment ('God'-realisation). Once denuded of all conception of self in such a manner, the all-being/non-being – the Unknowable ('God') – inevitably becomes one's total being. This necessitates an effortless and spontaneous response to humanity's needs, wherein intuitive perceptions continuously grow. 'Needs' become seeds that instantly fecundate a vision or direct realisation[56] of the means whereby humanity's needs can be ameliorated. Such vision is facilitated because one's earnest aspiration to assist humanity draws response from the Watchers, the Hierarchy of Love, of enlightened Being, as part of their combined meditation to similarly serve. The Hierarchy, within which Jesus resides, are liberated members of humanity. Buddhist philosophy calls them Bodhisattvas. They have 'vowed never to pass into final *nirvāṇa* until all sentient beings have been released from suffering.[57]

The laws governing Life are an emanation from the Mind of 'God'. Life consequently can be found manifest in every atom of substance. These laws can be therefore comprehended through the methodical, sensory and meditative observation of substance and its properties. Truth is inherent Divine Law and is the cause of every lasting modification of existence. It is universal in its application, but modified by the mind that registers it. It is not the prerogative of any one being, system of 'God' realisation, or method of experimental or analytical deduction. The path to Truth is open for all people to discover for themselves by any method they develop to do so. Treading upon such a path is the mode of the making of a member of the Hierarchy of enlightened Being.

It has taken aeons for humanity to evolve a capacity to understand the Truths relating to the nature of substance, the universe, and their place therein. Proper understanding was previously obtained by means of internal observation, through the meditative methods followed by *yogins.*

---

55 As is advocated by the tenets of Buddhism and equated with the *śūnyatā* state.

56 By which, past, present and future are seen in perspective.

57 There is a vast philosophy veiled here, and for proper understanding of the nature of the Bodhisattva path one needs to refer to the first five volumes of my *A Treatise on Mind* series.

It was thus realised only by relatively few. The intellect is however now the principal means to attain realisation.[58] Both internal observation and the intellect are methods that allow people to understand the nature of the energies at the heart of every atom and to release them in a controlled manner. When the *yogin* perceives such energies, and consequently liberates the *kuṇḍalinī* Fire, such a one is said to be enlightened.

Influencing the atoms of Nature upon a vast scale requires the collective action of many enlightened beings. In the past such 'collective action' was termed 'the Lord God', or the 'Lord out of heaven' who, for example, rained upon Sodom and Gomorrah the 'brimstone and fire' that destroyed those cities.[59] Nowadays scientists can manifest a similar function with their nuclear weaponry.

Unfortunately, humanity's present intellectual development is not accompanied by developed Wisdom and the force of Love. When Love-Wisdom is everywhere manifest amongst people, then the Christ will be seen to have appeared plainly before us. In His past incarnation (via Jesus), the Christ could symbolically utilise only one pure vehicle, twelve lesser vehicles (the apostles),[60] seventy disciples,[61] and an interested five hundred.[62] In His coming appearance, as part of the externalisation of the Hierarchy, and their massed incarnation amongst humanity, these numbers must be multiplied many times over.[63]

Beings such as the Apostles and disciples are all members of the Hierarchy and they have reincarnated many times in various guises amongst humanity. But soon all members of Hierarchy will incarnate in unity to help foster the New Age. They will then make the physical plane the main focus of their organisational activities, rather than upon the inner realms. Due to mass communication, the entire world will

58 Obtaining information by means of the external senses and the resultant analytical deduction.

59 *Genesis 19:24.*

60 *Matthew 10:2–4, Mark 3:16–19* and *Luke 6:14–16.*

61 Luke chapter ten.

62 *I Cor. 15:6.*

63 See the book *The Externalisation of the Hierarchy* by Alice Bailey (Lucis Publishing Co., N.Y., 1981) for further detail.

automatically be involved. Disciples will thus be found in every national or religious group and cultural situation. This advent will involve a mass descent of the Christ-consciousness into a multitude of people that were in past cycles, and are increasingly, being illumined and consecrated to work for humanity's betterment, and thus the unfolding of Divine Purpose. Their activity will be to free humanity from the oppressive force of massed lying propaganda through their multimedia, in conjunction with socio-political, bureaucratic and medical evil.[64] The entire course of our materialistic civilisation can thus be halted and changed, with an era of goodwill and peace finally descending upon the earth.

Jesus stated: 'other sheep I have, which are not of this fold: them also I must bring, and they shall hear my voice; and they shall be one fold, and one shepherd'.[65] The other 'sheep' that He had were not just the Jews and gentiles in Israel at that time, but those elsewhere in the world. Thus, they were followers of different religions that were also part of His dispensation. Bringing them into 'one fold, and one shepherd' refers to the fact that all beings working to serve humanity, no matter the religion, race or creed, are members of the Hierarchy of enlightened Being, whose spiritual head is known as the Christ in the New Testament.

Despite this pronouncement the churches have taught that amongst billions of incarnated humans on earth, the only ones to have attained such Revelations were the Hebrew prophets. Also, they state that the statements contained in the Bible are the only Revelations from 'God', that any other religious presentations are misguided, and that other teachings are the work of an adversary of 'God'. Unfortunately, here is seen a sad travesty of misinterpreted or misrepresented scriptural passages. Such pronouncements made possible the highly successful theological bid for ecclesiastical supremacy and temporal power (especially during the early formative years of Christianity). Specifically related are two main factors:

---

64 The reference here is to the present Covid 19 'plandemic' that has caused immense damage to many countries, whose governments amassed a vast tyrannical overreach, at the behest of the pharmaceutical companies that they serve.

65 *John 10:16.*

1. It helped the gullible to zealously accept the edicts of a theology by appealing to their desire nature. It promised them roles as central figures on a stage where a world (and even a cosmological) drama was enacted. They were declared as the 'chosen of God' – the elect – who were therefore superior to all other people. Hitler used similar tactics with his idea of a 'master race', achieving similar (though shorter lived) success.

2. It enabled the church fathers to amend into scriptural passages whatever they wished. Thus, their actions, no matter how extreme, would be condoned as the 'Word of God', by the fostered desires of the ignorant masses. It allowed such eventualities as the Inquisition, Papal infallibility, and the 'divine right of kings'. Such activities have constituted a real threat to the appearance of the Christ-energy amongst humanity.

The outward appearance of a religion matters little, or even the terminology of spiritual concepts. What truly matters is the religion must present a vehicle of approach to the Divine, as a gateway to develop illumination. The Christ Presence (Hierarchical Love and Wisdom) is manifest everywhere, always, but it must work within the constraints of the *karma* generated by humanity and their inviolable self-will.

All beings innately find that which is related to their own level of development, as governed by their mental-emotional equipment. Their development will naturally orient them towards a philosophy or system of realisation that offers a sense of accomplishment satisfying their needs, aspirations, or desires.

The indoctrination of a particular religious or philosophic system further moulds a follower's mental-emotional environment until the revelations possible through the teaching have been achieved. Thereafter, a follower may need to find another source of inspiration to bring them to reveal deeper insights and new heights of awareness into the Mysteries of Being. (This proviso rests upon the laurels of past achievements.) The conscience (or 'inner Voice') always urges one to climb to the mountaintop of all experience.

The inevitability of change

Evolution, spiritual or otherwise, is non-static. The principle of change and adaptation governs all of Life. The old, debilitated, or generally unsuitable must die or transform to meet ever-changing conditions. From the perspective of evolutionary time, we see that no entity or species can forever adhere to the outer forms or cycle of activity they are involved in. Similarly, everyone must eventually break away from the old and familiar to seek a more complete and comprehensive union with their sources of inspiration.

Change is inevitable. One eventually becomes maladjusted (emotionally, mentally, or spiritually) and dies in the face of advancing times. This process affects nations and tribal groups, as well as the individual. Often this happens without the entity concerned being aware of these processes at all. The objectives of enquiry produce pain due to the separation from long cherished and adhered-to forms. Greater comprehension always involves deep inner inquiry, analysis, and subsequent pain. Changes may take fractions of a lifetime, a whole life, or many lifetimes to accomplish.

Humanity learns and evolves through the process of trial and error. We are constantly propelled towards Deity by the Christ-Light, the 70 (or Spirit) within the human frame. Eventually, after a worldly and dissolute life, the prodigal son must return to his 'Father',[66] through his own free will.

True and lasting change can come only from within the heart, not by imposition of external force,[67] as some believe. Becoming spiritual robots is clearly not the purpose of human evolution; change must therefore occur as people increasingly realise the deeper implications behind the meaning of Love.

Each person must learn to walk in the footsteps of the Christ. We must follow Him subjectively to the crucifixion experience. Humanity is now ready to demonstrate this, which was not possible 2,000 years ago (as will be gradually explained). Thus, part of the agony of Jesus

---

66 See Luke chapter fifteen.

67 Such as fear of the 'wrath of God', the jurisdiction of Deity, or the proclamations of a religious or cult leader.

in the garden of Gethsemane was the realisation that even His own disciples were not yet ready to constructively use the message that He came to bring; even Peter was not able to stay 'awake'.[68]

The true message of Christ was, and is, available for all His disciples through the esoteric aspects of His teaching (to the degree that they are able to receive it). For instance, Jesus states 'I have yet many things to say to you, but ye cannot bear them now'.[69] To 'bear' the full weight of the esoteric teachings implies an enormous spiritual responsibility. This involves the capacity to give (as a Bodhisattva) and necessitates a highly sensitised and attuned corporeal body to receive the accompanying intensities of energisation from Divinity.

The ability to bear vibrational intensity of the highest order requires a gradual purification of the body, of all related emotional states, and the meditative training needed to master the mind. Christ's disciples were not then ready. This training allows the energies of 'Will' or 'Power', of which the 'Father' is the custodian, to manifest. (This will become clearer once the Initiation process is understood.) Jesus later states:

> When he, the Spirit of truth, is come, he will guide you into all truth: for he shall not speak of himself; but whatsoever he shall hear, *that* shall he speak: and he will shew you things to come.[70]

The 'Spirit of truth' that is to guide us to 'all truth' is synonymous with *bodhicitta,*[71] the compassionate force or energy driving one to attain enlightenment. Here *bodhicitta* is personified, or takes the guise of, a Buddha (of meditation), 'the Spirit of truth'. Such a Buddha is the embodiment of all-Wisdom, Love and Light. *Truth* is the Law of 'God' expressed via the associated Mysteries, the *dharma,* the spiritual Law of the Buddhists and Hindus,[72] which manifests as the Wisdom to impel one upon the path of righteousness.

---

68 *Matthew 26:40.*

69 *John 16:12-25.*

70 *John 16:13.*

71 The generation of *bodhicitta* lies at the heart of Mahāyāna Buddhist practice. It concerns awakening the properties of the Heart centre, and consequently the 'Eye' of insight. With the awakened Heart, that directs the energy of *bodhicitta,* all attributes of the Buddha *dharma* ('all truth') can be perceived.

72 The Gnosis (Sophia) of the Gnostic religion.

'All truth' can also be viewed as an expression of the *ālayavijñāna,*[73] the universal storehouse of consciousness of the Buddhists. A Buddha (or any enlightened being) is able to guide us to experience the *ālayavijñāna.* He does so, for He does not speak of Himself (as all those that are bound by their egos and the concept of 'self' necessarily do), 'but whatsoever he shall hear' from the 'kingdom of God' (Shambhala), in the form of the Voice of Silence.[74] A higher interpretation of 'all truth' relates it to the *dharmakāya,* which can be equated with cosmic consciousness.

The silent Voice is the sound of the *dharma* within, which the enlightened one externalises through speech to the 'hearers'. (The inner and the outer then esoterically become a unity.) This *dharma* is the Voice of the Law governing all Being, the Word that was 'in the beginning' and which 'was God'.[75] One that is an exponent of this 'Voice' can show us the 'things to come', for the *dharma* within sums up the entire milieu of Being: past, present, and future.

The esoteric truth within the parables

Jesus states:

> The time cometh, when I shall no more speak unto you in proverbs, but I shall shew you plainly of the Father. At that day ye shall ask in my name: and I shall say not unto you, that I will pray the Father for you.[76]

Once Jesus's disciples (literally the members of humanity attuned to the Hierarchy of Love) have developed the capacity to be able to

---

73 *Ālayavijñāna,* universal storehouse of consciousness, is the mind as basis of all in the Yogācāra philosophy. *Ālayavijñāna* is *ālaya* + *vijñāna,* where *ālaya* is a place of storage of mental images. *Ālaya* indiscriminately harbours what flows into it through the *vijñānas* (the faculty of discriminating). The attributes of consciousness perform actions, hence evolve, however the *ālaya* always abides in its self-nature. The *ālayavijñāna* can therefore be considered the store of all knowledge (mental images) impressed from the kingdom of 'God' or derived through human evolution. See my book *The Astrological and Numerological Keys to The Secret Doctrine,* Volume 1, 269, and elsewhere in my Buddhist books, for further information.

74 See also Helena P. Blavatsky, *The Voice of the Silence* (The Theosophical Publishing House, Adyar) for detail.

75 *John 1:1.*

76 *John 16:25-6.*

bear the 'Spirit of truth', it will allow the Christ to be able to show them 'plainly of the Father'. He will therefore no longer have to act as a mediator between humanity and 'God' ('that I will pray the Father for you'). Disciples will then have developed the ability to directly know that 'the Father himself loveth you, because ye have loved me, and have believed that I have come out from God'.[77] 'The Father' (or the personal 'God' to Jesus) here refers to the planetary Logos residing in Shambhala.

To be shown 'plainly of the Father' necessitates one to esoterically See. One will then know the process whereby the Christ, the Love-Wisdom principle, emanates ('come out from God') and is thus made manifest in the world. To answer the question of His apostles as to why He spoke in parables to the common people, Jesus stated:

> Because it is given unto you to know the mysteries of the kingdom of heaven, but unto them it is not given. For whosoever hath, to him shall be given, and he shall have more abundance: but whosoever hath not, from him shall be taken away even that he hath. Therefore I speak to them in parables: because they seeing, see not; and hearing they hear not, neither do they understand.[78]

Jesus was not the only *guru*[79] or Master that reserved such esoteric teachings for his disciples. It was, in fact, a common practice by all sages and schools of divine realisation. In the Buddhist and Hindu schools for instance, we note the concept of the 'pith' (seed) instructions that could only be transmitted orally as 'ear-whispered truths' from *guru* to disciple. Only the foremost developed 'sons' of the *guru* were entrusted with the complete teachings. They thereby became the Master's spiritual successors. In the West is seen the development of the various Mystery Schools such as those at Eleusis in Greece and Heliopolis in Egypt. Therein, beings were gradually Initiated into the Mysteries, and were pledged to never reveal these secrets to the non-Initiated. Such schools have existed throughout time. They presented a universal Wisdom-

---

77 *John 16:27.*

78 *Matthew 13:11-13.*

79 The word *guru* is derived from the Sanskrit roots *gu*, meaning 'darkness', and *ru*, 'to dispel'. Therefore, a *guru* is a bringer of light, which dispels darkness.

Religion – a substratum of esoteric teachings that were heavily veiled by the orthodox presentation to the non-Initiated. The knowledge veiled by them has however always been retained by the modem successors of those ancient sages, the members of the Hierarchy of enlightened Being. They are part of the apostolic lineage of those that have received the 'ear-whispered truths'. In this form, Christianity existed long before the advent of Jesus in Jerusalem, as St. Augustine (A.D. 354 – 430) has informed us:

> "That which is called the Christian religion existed among the ancients, and never did not exist, from the beginning of the human race until Christ came in the flesh, at which time the true religion which already existed began to be called Christianity". *(Epis. Retrac., Lib. I, xiii. 3)*[80]

It is a small wonder that the real context of our myths and religious teachings are so little understood, for only what is exoteric (the 'profane') has survived the course of time as texts. The esoteric truths can however be rediscovered by us all if we develop the qualities needed to listen to the silent Voice of the *guru,* the Christ within.

Theologians who only believe in the literal interpretation of the Gospels are thus effectively just like the common people who are spoken to in parables (despite their many eclectic theorisations and rationalisations). They are esoterically blind to the nature of the Mysteries and to the true context of the statements in the Gospels. If people are to realise the 'mysteries of the kingdom of heaven' and understand the context of sacred scriptures, they must develop 'eyes that see' and 'ears that hear' before those secrets can register upon their consciousness.

The first step in this direction is to rightly utilise the developed intellect (the light of the mind). The next step is the opening of the 'wisdom Eye' through the development of compassionate Reason (Love). This is fostered by right meditative techniques that will allow

---

80 William Kingsland, *The Gnosis or Ancient Wisdom in the Christian Scriptures,* (George Allen & Unwin, London) 163. This is an excellent companion to this present book. In reference to this note Mr. Kingsland states: 'But surely this "Christianity" to which he refers was not that which has come down to in an ecclesiastical form. No. It was this same ancient Gnosis which has always existed with the Hierarchy of Initiates'.

the Light of the Soul to illumine oneself. When this Light manifests in the collective body of human consciousness (as is now beginning to happen) it will illumine the world.

The Christ-Light (as transmitted by the Soul) is the universal storehouse of knowledge, the repository of the sum-total of human experience. This is the 'light of the world',[81] the substance of all enlightened Minds. Therefore, when the energies of Love and the fully developed intellect are united in common accord, then great strides can be made towards the advancement of human evolution. No hidden secret will be able to withstand the prying 'Eye' of mankind. For this objective, we must all earnestly strive. The reason why these teachings were hidden is indicated by the words of a similar, more poignant passage:

> Unto you it is given to know the mystery of the kingdom of God: but unto them that are without, all these things are done in parables: That seeing they may see, and not perceive; and hearing they may hear, and not understand; lest at any time they should be converted, and *their* sins should be forgiven them.[82]

This enigmatic statement has long been overlooked or misconstrued by theologians. It is not that Jesus feared those that knew not his teachings ('are without') could escape eternal damnation if they should be 'converted'. That is opposite to the mainstream of His entire dispensation, which is to broadcast His Love equally to all. Instead, like all *gurus* and Masters of the esoteric Wisdom, He was concerned with the effects of the esoteric teachings upon 'them that are without' the necessary moral purifications, right motives and adequate spiritual training. His concern was that they may wrongly utilise what they had seen and misperceived, or heard and misunderstood.

The esoteric teachings concern the path of practical 'magic'. This is the conscious use of very potent subjective energies to manifest the types of 'miracles' that Jesus often did. The great danger concerning the 'converted' here is because of their unreadiness – their unrelinquished gross desires and tendency to profane and distort the doctrines. This would tend to manifest as the 'left hand' tendencies of a black magician

81 *John 8:12.*

82 *Mark 4:11-12.*

and the related evils (which are explained in chapter eight). Their 'sins' (wrong actions on a psychic or gross level) would be forgiven if they acted sincerely on the knowledge received, but the resultant *karma* would fall upon the shoulders of the Master that had erroneously revealed the teachings; it would be his responsibility.

There is much power, for good or for evil, in psychic energy. The responsibility of the custodian of such power, as was Jesus, is therefore great. Thus, the esoteric teachings of such Teachers are necessarily veiled. They are not to cast their 'pearls before swine, lest they trample them under their feet'.[83]

The novices of most Mystery Schools had to discipline themselves and were often required to spend a number of years in silence. They had to learn to rightly utilise the potency of speech, which is sacred and has power. The potency of Sound is that which creates, sustains and destroys all forms. In Sound, colour and number are hid all the Mysteries of Being.

Clarifying ancient history

Many modern writers have attempted to seriously investigate the invaluable testimony of sacred texts. They have endeavoured to interpret the inner meaning of the parables and have developed valuable insights into the nature of the evolution of consciousness and the ancient civilisations.[84] However, the full understanding of this history has been retained only by the enlightened. These ones have been termed Adepts, Gurus, Masters of Wisdom, Arhats, Rishis, Bodhisattvas, and the like. Such understanding includes an awareness of lost continents and civilisations (such as Atlantis and Lemuria) of primal human beginnings involving unknown millennia, and the conditionings that motivated these peoples.[85]

The means to the complete attainment of such awareness is necessarily a secondary theme to the process of enlightenment. This concerns direct contact with the stream of realisations associated with

---

83 *Matthew 7:6.*

84 This is despite the fact that the deductions of some authors have been marred by spurious claim making or sensationalised speculations.

85 The writings of H.P. Blavatsky and A.A. Bailey should be perused for detail here.

the continuity of human consciousness, for things that happen in time and space are sequential, the result of past actions. They are not chance happenings but are the planned effects of the Thought process of 'God'.

When archaeologists, anthropologists and historians can finally investigate the course of evolution from the angle of consciousness, the Mysteries concerning the past will then be brought to light. Many of the enigmas associated with human suffering and conflict – the rise and fall of civilisations, the advent of catastrophes, and the Law of Cycles – will then be understood. People will be led into the realms of true values: the comprehension of the role of the Divine in history through the unfolding Love principle and not the glorification of human aggression and selfishness (as is now the case).

The *Revelation of St. John* is actually a detailed codification of this entire history. Much early history is contained in Genesis, as well as in all other sacred texts. Jesus often utilised such history within His allegories and parables, yet the message of the Gospels can be profoundly simple. The reader does not need much learning to be inspired (despite the fact that there are many levels of interpretation to them), for the truths are universal in their application. The keys to this are:

- A heart open to the idea of loving-kindness, the expression of the Christ within.
- Hands that are willing to serve.
- A mind that is predisposed to contemplation.
- A steadfastness in aspiration to seek the Divine in all things.
- A faith in the surety of the Law *(dharma)* that can 'move mountains'.

The gist of many of Jesus's teachings have however been distorted by theological arguments and interpretations. This is especially so when coupled with the emphatic following of the Old Testament's emphasis on such statements as: 'an eye for an eye, a tooth for a tooth'.[86] The reformation of the practices and theology associated with the Old Testament and the fulfilment of its prophecies were major objectives of

86 *Exodus 21:24* and *Leviticus 24:20*. See also *Matthew 5:38* for Jesus' refutation of this statement.

the Christ. For this, and the apparent blasphemy of being proclaimed the Messiah,[87] He was crucified.

Through following erroneous doctrines the orthodox and often sincere Christian has often been diverted from the expression of the real purpose of the Christ – to provide true God-realisation by means of the path of Love in service. People continue crucifying the Christ whilst base human motives, ideals and values remain unchanged. There has been a revolution in the collective quality of human thought over the past few centuries and people everywhere can think more intelligently. The doctrines of the various churches are now changing to meet the newly informed attitudes and ways of thinking of their constituents. The resultant reformation and cooperative ecumenicalism, such as the World Council of Churches, is a welcome development.

Such new liberalism is necessary if the Christ principle is to arise from out of the ecclesiastical doctrines. This will thereby provide religious followers with greater ability to meet the needs of an increasingly enlightened world. What has been crucified for so long must now be resurrected and shown to the world,[88] in such a manner that people can no longer ignore the testimony of His Light and active Love in their lives. The 'Christ principle' therefore also represents the appearance of the entire Hierarchy of enlightened Being. Mass human awakening necessitates right interpretation of sacred scriptures, in conjunction with the benefits of scientific discoveries. The development of wisdom will allow an understanding of the purpose of Love in everyday life to be spread in a meaningful manner to all.

---

87 Via such statements as: 'I am the way, the truth, and the life: no man cometh to the Father, but by me' *(John 14:6)*.

88 That manifests as a 'doubting Thomas' (see John chapter twenty).

While sitting in a
suburban
room-yard jungle,
I escaped in my mind
with a volley
of remembrances
of yesterday gone by
re-enacted today,
in seeing those around me
play games
in a cycle of returning,
and walking in feet
that must pass
many a graveyard
of tears.

3

The Nature of Karma and the Rebirth of Consciousness

The fact that life on earth is normally full of selfishness, pain, fear and violent reactions is a travesty of the true expression of our human heritage. If the motives for our actions are changed, a life of harmonious interrelationships – peace and joy – will be in store for each of us. This is approached by means of a developed meditative awareness to the subjective causes of all conditionings (adverse or otherwise) that affect us on the physical plane. This necessitates a true understanding of the concept of the rebirth of consciousness. As such understanding becomes an accepted realisation, established as fact within the mind structures of humanity, it will cause people everywhere to ardently work towards the goal of enlightenment with sighted aspiration. When enough people do so, fostering the type of civilisation that will arise in the awakening Aquarian epoch, then peace and harmony can reign on the earth.

What is termed 'life' will then become viewed as a means of opportunity for the indwelling Soul to gain certain types of experiences. Experiences become qualities that are built into the personality that the Soul can use to perform its tasks in the world.

By accepting the hypothesis that a human Soul forms a cell in the Body of 'God', we see the life of the personality is the field of expression, wherein the creative work of Deity can be accomplished to perfection. In this way dense physical substance and the lesser streams of Divine Life can become exalted. This is by being brought to the relative perfection that humanity represents, for all Life is evolving to self-consciousness, or from it.

Heaven and hell states

As humans become increasingly enlightened (that is, identified with the consciousness of the Soul), the states of awareness associated with other dimensions of perception gradually become apparent, whilst incarnate on the earth. This refers to specific 'localities' of existence, such as the heavens and hells of the various religions. The earth also comes to be viewed as one of these 'localities'.

What is known as hell is then seen to be only relatively so. It is not an eternal condition, nor is it as portrayed by the major religions. Rather, hell will be seen as an effectively self-imposed state of consciousness that can be the result of 'coldness', self-enclosing selfishness, or extreme passions (heat engendering) whilst incarnate.

One's 'outer raiment' is cast aside at death. This leaves one 'naked', clothed only in the subjective mental-emotional conditionings of the former life, or lives. Thus, much of the *karma* of one's emotional and thought life which is not dissipated during physical existence will be experienced in the life after death. Once the physical body is expired, then one will be robed directly in one's emotional body and later in the thought body. The true causes or intentions behind one's actions (such as subjective hatred, spite, jealousy, selfishness, etc.) now become what one is clothed in, which must be lived out in consciousness. They become one's *karma,* which may form a hell state.

Such astral plane conditionings will disappear gradually as people realise (or are helped to realise) the causes of their self-engendered suffering and begin to rectify their past actions. (This necessitates the use of the energy of Love.) Such realisations must inevitably come as part of the inherent evolutionary urge of Life on all realms of perception.

All aspects of Life are embodied by Deity. The Soul within the form therefore always prompts one towards greater receptivity to Light. The shells that enclose a person in the hell realms will therefore eventually dissipate by the action of attrition. The Light and warmth of ever-present Divine Life must increasingly manifest, though this is assisted by the actions of inner plane helpers who work to help the denizens of the lower zones. In being so helped a being will inevitably ascend to the 'heavenly realms'.

The idea of hellfire is somewhat a misconception. Coldness and murky desolation would be nearer to the truth for most, unless referring to the 'fire' of intense emotional zealotry and bigotry, or the karmic expression of hatred. Interestingly, concerning the concept of hell, *The Interpreter's Dictionary of the Bible* states the following (where OT refers to the Old Testament and NT refers to the New Testament):

> In the NT the abode of the dead is invariably called 'Hades'....and nothing is added to the OT description of it...Nowhere in the OT is the abode of the dead regarded as a place of punishment or torment. The concept of an infernal "hell" developed in Israel only during the Hellenistic period, probably under the influence of Iran ideas.[1]

Under the heading of Gehenna, the book states:

> The general idea of a punitive conflagration appears, to be sure, in the earlier portions of the OT (e.g., Deut. 32:22; Isa. 33:14), but it is only in the Greco-Roman period of Jewish history that the quite distinct concept of a blazing hell – a lake, or abyss, of fire – begins to emerge...The concept was doubtless influenced by the infiltration of Iranian ideas, for the articulation of it is clearly patterned on the Avestan doctrine of the ultimate judgement of the wicked in a stream of molten metal *(aya khsusta;* cf. Yasna 31.3; 51.9; etc.)...Gehenna is clearly conceived by the NT writers as identical with the "lake of fire" into which Hades (i.e., Shoel, the general abode of the dead) will itself ultimately be cast (Rev. 20:14). The conception seems, however, to have been somewhat fluid, for the sundry rabbinic statements dating from the first and second centuries A.D. declare that Jews, by and large, will be delivered from it, and that none of them will remain there permanently except certain historic reprobates, the adulterer, and he who shames or vilifies his fellow man.[2]

---

1 *The Interpreter's Dictionary of the Bible,* Vol. 1 (Abingdon Press, Nashville Tennessee, 1962), 788.

2 Ibid., Vol. 2, 361-2.

From the perspective that Hell is a state of being caused by the collective mental-emotional actions of humanity, it must eventually disappear from the experiences of humanity, once their mental-emotions are refined. This is one of the outcomes that the rapidly approaching New Age will produce through people's heightened awareness. Heaven also may be viewed from a similar angle, as a state of being created by the collective consciousness of people. In this state, a person lives out the most beautiful, exalted, or compassionate attributes that have been engendered in consciousness.

Individual and group *karma*

Everything is conditioned by the law that determines the process of rebirth, called *karma* in the East. It involves the most detailed and exact rendering of the words that Paul used to explain this law – 'Whatsoever a man soweth, that he shall also reap'.[3]

One reaps the consequences of not only physical actions, but also of the emotional and mental life, and of non-action or non-involvement when one had the ability to help. This concerns the means by which consciousness evolves and is gauged by both the observable and subjective motives underlying actions, as well as the consequences of such actions. It is the law of perpetual fulfilment. Through the consequences of past actions and the resultant suffering or happiness, a person (or later reincarnations) is eventually impelled to transmute grosser states into the refined and subtle. Desires then become aspirations; petty and selfish ambitions become a selfless expression of the *dharma;* ignorance becomes wisdom; darkness becomes (a resplendent vehicle of) Love and Light. The early stages of a person's evolution proceed very slowly – one makes many mistakes and produces much *karma.* Ever the Light of the spirit within guides one forward, even though one is not aware.

One eventually awakens to the Light of the Christ within. Then, evolution is comparatively rapid. Although mistakes may still be made, they are mostly of a subtler nature – concerned with aspirations and social activities rather than the sensual and desire nature. One is then

3 *Gal. 6:7,* see also *II Cor. 9:6.*

effectively no longer making *karma,* rather, the concern is with 'working off' the *karma.* One becomes desireless in motive and simply allows 'the law' to condition all actions. The 'inner Voice' then directs one's entire being. Despite this, the outer form is buffeted every which way by the tides and waves that are the effects of past actions, and the social conditionings within which one is born. However, these actions no longer agitate the karmic sea of retributive activity. Instead, they build up a compact environment within it, obviating the necessity for its agitation. Eventually all dies down and becomes still (and thus becomes known in its entirety). The production of such a state is termed *dhyāna* (meditative calm, a state of absorbed insightful contemplation). One then finds that this 'sea' is but a drop in an ever-expanding ocean.

Karma is primarily a group law that affects civilisations, nations, races, and all kingdoms of Nature. People come into and out of incarnation according to the *karma* of their subjective group. This is what prompts masses of people towards experiencing certain events collectively. (Such as wars, sports gatherings, and the effects of government edicts.) People live in a sea of conditionings that constitutes their *karma,* urging them towards fulfilment.

In conjunction with cyclic law, *karma* is the prime agent that regulates the manifestation of all natural disasters, wars and everything else that conditions human evolution. *Karma* thus also causes the beneficial effects of, for example, rain and sunshine, because all aspects of manifest life are expressed in accordance with *karmic* law. The very soil we live on and the air we breathe is effectively the residual *karma* of a planetary or solar Logos. They are the result of an ineffable cosmic *karma* that caused Deity to create all that is manifest, for even a Logos must work with the massed *karma* generated in a former cycle.

Karma, therefore, conditions the cause and effect of the purpose for the existence of any evolving entity. Its real nature is thus inexplicable to the thinking minds of people, who can be considered as the atoms constituting a 'grain of sand' that is the earth sphere, and all are karmically propelled in the immense duration of cosmic Being. The prime objective of *karma,* in its seemingly destructive aspect, is the disintegration of old forms (e.g., a geographical, national, or religious form). This is followed by the birth of a new form to wield higher types of energy more adequately and effectively. Thus, via *karma* a truer more expansive aspect of Deity is expressed, freed from the constraints of the old, rigid, or limited expression. The new forms of evolutionary expression are conditioned by the past effects and actions of humans, or of 'God'.

Karma exists on all levels of a manifest universe. One can thus think of the causative *karma* producing the planetary form by the Creative act of a Logos. There is also the *karma* engendered by a humanity, which exists whilst people are engendering it. The evolutionary process *(manvantara)* enters into dissolution *(pralaya)* when all of humanity begin to wisely cleanse their karmic activity from former cycles. The humans produce their own liberation from *saṁsāra* through their enlightened activity, thus everything else is transformed, transmuted. Then the purpose for the manifestation of a planet has been accomplished.

The objective of *karma* is thus to produce future beneficent results. When viewed in the light of the aeonic evolution of time, an entire solar system, galaxy, or even universe benefits. This can be seen when looking at the history of the earth – all the various changes and cataclysms of the past (geological, biological, and historical) have resulted in humanity's present awareness.

Karma is controlled by great angelic Beings *(devas),* for they embody the substance of all that is. Out of the *devas* the subjective or objective sheaths of the various kingdoms of Nature are wrought and manifest on a mass scale. All substance is in fact angelic, being part of the body of manifestation of their kingdom. This esoteric fact will become clearer once etheric vision is obtained by humanity, when people will be able to see and contact the *devas.*[4] The angelic kingdom are therefore the active agents of *karma.* They wield karmic energy in such a way to produce the required results, thereby rectifying imbalances wrought in the substance they embody. They are continuously impacted or modified by the Sounds of the Word (of 'God') that act to modify manifest space. The *devas* evolve by responding to Sound, and its expression forms the concretion of the substance that manifests the material world.

---

4 The nature of the angelic kingdom will be further elucidated in chapter five. Control of *deva* substance forms the basis of all magical endeavour.

People are generally not aware of these subtle sounds. They manifest mental, emotional or physical actions, which are but modifications of (noisy) sounds that impact the *devas* concerned. In time the *devas* work to harmonise (rectify) the modulations of sound affecting the substance of their forms (which incorporates the human three-fold persona) and so karmic effects are produced. This is obviously a very simplified statement, as there are many levels of these agents of *karma*. The *devas* are units of active Intelligence, for all is Mind conditioned. Mind and its response to Sound is the order of things. The Sound reverberates the patterns of the colours that we see. Such subtleties of the subjective domains are difficult for the empirical mind to conceive, but understanding can come when one perceives that all is but an expression of energies conditioned by Mind.

When a human Soul incarnates it appropriates *deva* substance to do so, which we erroneously think of as the bodies that we 'possess'. There is however far more affecting these forms than what people normally think. The personalities of most humans, for instance, are swayed by the mass agitation of the common emotional mood, and thus by the sea of *karma* within which the person is immersed. For a long evolutionary period, the angelic kingdom have worked with the Soul to control the *karma* of the people concerned. (For people are still in the womb of the Great Mother. The Mother being but the sum total of all *deva* Lives.) When people learn to think constructively and start to transmute their personality nature, they begin to control the lesser angelic units ('Elementals') that embody their form natures. They then start to master their own destiny. Many of the strict moral precepts[5] stressed in meditation techniques are very potent devices to control such elemental forces. As one wields *karma* one is thus liberated from its stranglehold. Upon the path of Initiation the human Soul begins to properly take control of the person (constituted of *deva* units) it has incarnated into, for the person's mind becomes one with the Mind of the Soul. This is part of what constitutes the making of an enlightened being.[6] Only an enlightened being can truly be called a 'Lord of *karma*'.

5 Such as control of speech, breathing, the mantras and *yantras*.

6 Such a being consciously resides in the archetypal Mind (the domain of the Soul),

If one thinks only of oneself, and thus is separative (taking from others to satisfy the desires of the self), then inevitably the *karma* of self-centred action rebounds upon that person to take from them what they formerly cherished. Such action may happen in a later life to produce a perceived real loss in some way, entailing the consequent pain of frustrated personality ambition. (The manifestation of people's painful or joyous states can thus be viewed as self-engendered.) Effectively, the 'bloodstream' (the subjective energies in the Body of Deity uniting oneself with others) is constrained or severed by separative self-serving actions. When the flow is restricted then what the 'bloodstream' is meant to nourish becomes accordingly malnourished and diseased. When a person thinks of others as oneself and gives to them compassionately (thereby using the energies from the Heart centre), this connects to the source of all Light and Love. The consequence produces joy. Such an idea can be broadly expanded to encompass groups, even at the national or international scale. The process of compassionate action, to eventually become consciously absorbed into the expression of the Heart centre, produces enlightenment.

A liberated (enlightened) being technically has no more *karma* left associated with the material world (the three planes of perception where humanity has its being). People must learn to perfectly control and express the qualities of these three planes. They are the dense physical, the emotional (or astral), and the mental planes.[7] A liberated person continues to be involved with the material world for compassionate reasons and they can also be conduits for planetary or Logoic *karma*. Herein is also veiled the esoteric concept of the *dharma,* or law of 'God' that conditions such a one's activities. The term 'technically' above was used, for all who are considered 'liberated' (except the highest Initiates) still have remnant *karma* that they are working off or processing in such a way to best benefit the humanity that they have incarnated to serve. Such *karma* allows them to incarnate amongst us.

---

or a higher realm (e.g., *buddhi* or *ātma),* and can thus control the manifestation of the law of *karma*.

7 The mental plane is dual, consisting of the concrete (empirical) mind and archetypal, abstract Mind. The empirical mind is conditioned by or is bonded to form, and the archetypal Mind is liberated from form.

Karma and the conditions of rebirth

The type of body that one incarnates into depends entirely upon one's past *karma* (and upon the evolutionary goal of the Soul-group). In addition to the type of body one inhabits, *karma* also dictates the emotional, mental, social and national environments that one is born into.

To the Soul, emphasis is not upon the amount of money, personality influence, or the ambitions one may have. Instead, the Soul is focused upon the ability to convey the force of Love and further the Plan of Deity. The Soul also works towards its own liberation from the constraints of the form it resides in. All such activity is further defined by the Soul's Ray colourings.

Karma always manifests so as to bring about the Soul's intent. This has naught to do with the personality, except so far as the personality is an expression of the Soul (and Soul-groups). The type of body, personality and environment one incarnates into are therefore the external means through which such forces must manifest.

Two basic postulates of physics are:

a. Energy can be neither created nor destroyed, but is only transformed from one state to the next.

b. Newton's third law states: 'mutual reactions between two bodies produce equal and opposite reactions; or, to every action there is always an equal and opposite reaction'.

These laws are subjectively of great importance. When all human interactions are viewed in terms of energetic interrelationships (which is always the esoteric viewpoint), then it will be obvious that all physical laws are related to such interrelationships. They are but the outer effects of inner conditionings. The terminology of the scientific and esoteric communities differ because of the differing sources of their views; one being empirical in nature, and the other derives vision from the abstract Mind. However, these Laws are universally applicable and emanate from the subjective universe.

The 'equal and opposite reaction' is the *karma* that we incur ourselves by our actions. It is 'opposite' in that the consequences are relayed back to us in a similar fashion to a mirror image. Nothing is created or destroyed; only the forms are changed or modified to suit the needs of various evolving external conditionings and environments.

The laws that govern motion or energy are reflections of the subjective laws of cause and effect, of thought and thought transference, and of 'Creation' by the Mind of 'God'. In them, the true nature of Deity or humanity can be intuited and realised, as well as the causes of the *karma* that impel us to action.

Jesus stated, 'it is easier for heaven and earth to pass than for one tittle of the law to fail'.[8] Thus, it is for the law of *karma*. Indeed, 'heaven and earth' will pass one day. However, this 'law' (of 'God') will be eternally with us as long as Life exists. No entity can escape the consequences of it, whether through action or non-action.

All of one's actions are instantaneously recorded in such a way that they can be directly utilised by one's own Soul. As far as the life of the personality is concerned, the Soul is the 'God' within, because it is a direct expression of (and always works in accordance with) Divine Law. The intentions and consequences of the prior actions of an entity thereby unfailingly manifest. This occurs in such a way that the entity will grow in experience, to produce eventual spiritual maturation. By the mechanism of *karma* one is made to realise the extent of such consequences by living them fully in consciousness.

No one can evade karmic consequences. No compassionate being can therefore relieve another person from experiencing the weight of the repercussions, until such a time that the cause of these sufferings are realised and the first step towards Light are taken. Then, and only then, can they be helped – for only that which a person has experienced themselves can be known, thereby becoming an integral part of the person's constitution.

Once having experienced every type of suffering and experience possible, then one can comprehend the causes of suffering and learn the means whereby they can be remedied. Only then does one truly begin to tread the compassionate path. By having identified completely with the sufferings, trials, hopes and desires of another, one knows where these paths will lead. This produces the next steps towards the conclusion of the long and eventful evolutionary path.

8 *Luke 16:17.*

Happiness is just as common an aspect of the human condition as pain, as are all aspects of Life. An uplifting spirit of the transition of happiness to joy increasingly manifests as the compassionate part of the cleansing of *karma* is fulfilled, for then only spiritual *karma* remains. Such *karma* lifts one to great heights of revelatory awareness that governs Life in the realm of enlightened Being.

The evolution of a Christ

Only through many lifetimes of experience and aeonic evolution along the path of Love-Wisdom can a Christ – an all-compassionate being – eventually be born as a world Server and Saviour. He knows exactly what to give at the perfectly timed moment, so as to bring true and lasting benefit upon those that form the object of His Vision. This requires virtually absolute patience, steadfastness in motive, and the incalculable wisdom to know precisely what and when to give. The development of such patience is one of the most difficult of accomplishments for all to achieve, but this is a major requirement of all that desire to become a Master of Wisdom or a Lord of Compassion.

One as fully realised as the Christ is able to touch the source of primeval *karma* (the timeless cause of all suffering) and bear it in His Heart. This can then be expressed as a metaphorical ocean of quietude, beating out the Rhythms of Being:

The Christ can be considered to have the total world picture in His consciousness. This picture is but a drop in the ocean of Being.

The Christ, the eldest of all our brothers, the head of the Hierarchy of Enlightened Being, must have experienced every possible human attribute, having long ago fully developed and then transmuted them.

The Christ has thus also contacted the fount of the omniscient One Life, becoming a pure vehicle of That Life.

Accordingly, the Christ possesses an immense compassion for human frailty (as it is buffeted by the mass agitation of the elements, the 'Waters' constituting our environment).

All those who are to measure up to His Stature must similarly demonstrate the potency of the Christ's compassion possible at their level of expression.

The way of developing the attributes of the Christ concerns progressing along the Initiation path to pass all of the associated testings, from the first to the highest of the Initiations possible to attain upon our planet.

Eventually the way is found to travel upon any of the cosmic Paths after the purpose of the service work of the Initiate has been completed upon the earth. This happens after the attainment of the sixth Initiation. The Christ is one whose cosmic Path incorporates earth service, to fulfil a Need (or divine office) within the kingdom of 'God' (Shambhala) for a set duration associated with the development of the principle of Love-Wisdom by humanity.

Life after death

Evidence is now accumulating concerning the survival of life after death, as well as of its nature and qualities. In this way the world's religious testimony is validated. Such evidence includes:

- Results of regressions under hypnosis.
- Investigations at the death bed (by qualified specialists) of those that had suffered 'clinical death' and yet lived to tell about it, remembrances.
- Clairvoyant investigations.

Dr. Raymond A. Moody, Jr., presents the following as his 'model', or 'composite of the common elements found in very many stories'. This refers to people either resuscitated after having been pronounced clinically dead, coming very close to physical death, or descriptions of the death experiences by those who were dying:

> A man is dying and, as he reaches the point of greatest physical distress, he hears himself pronounced dead by his doctor. He begins to hear an uncomfortable noise, a loud ringing or buzzing, and at the same time feels himself moving very rapidly through a long dark tunnel. After this, he suddenly feels himself outside of his own physical body, but still in the immediate physical environment, and sees his own body from a distance, as though he is a spectator. He watches the resuscitation attempt from his unusual vantage point and is in a state of emotional upheaval.

> After a while, he collects himself and becomes more accustomed to his odd condition. He notices that he still has a "body," but one of a very different nature and with very different powers from the physical body he has left behind. Soon other things begin to happen. Others come to meet and to help him. He glimpses the spirits of relatives and friends who have already died, and a loving, warm spirit of a kind he has never encountered before – a being of light – appears before him. This being asks him a question, nonverbally, to make him evaluate his life and helps him along by showing him a panoramic, instantaneous playback of the major events of his life. At some point he finds himself approaching some sort of barrier or border, apparently representing the limit between earthly life and the next life. Yet he finds that he must go back to the earth, that the time for his death has not yet come. At this point he resists, for by now he is taken up with his experiences in the afterlife and does not want to return. He is overwhelmed by the intense feelings of joy, love, and peace. Despite his attitude, though, he somehow reunites with his physical body and lives.[9]

Doctors Karlis Osis and Erlendur Haraldsson have similar information to present to us:

> When patients had visions which were predominantly environmental (Heaven, beautiful gardens, and so on), the positive emotional response was even more dominant: mainly serenity, peace, elation, or religious feelings. This leaves only a small portion of patients with negative emotions. They were, to a great extent, those who hallucinated mundane, this-life scenery. Although otherworldly images were fashioned after this world scenery, they were greatly heightened and refined. Brightness and intensity of colours were mentioned...of those reports which supplied enough information for interpretation, visions seemed to portray death as a transition to a gratifying existence in five out of six cases.[10]

This compares well with the esoteric viewpoint. Generally, the expression of Love and a sense of the Divine will confront the average emotionally polarised and genuinely good-willed person after death.

---

9 Dr. Raymond A. Moody, Jr., *Life after Life,* (Stackpole Books, Harrisberg, PA), 21-2.

10 Karlis Osis and Erlendur Haraldsson, *At the Hour of Death*, (Avon Books, 1977), 186.

Since the physical body has expired, one of the veils (or 'robes') that separate us from the true inner being is now discarded. There will be no sense of separateness (as conditions most of our actions on the earth). Often, one's old friends, occupations, and pursuits are continued but in a more perceptive manner, conditioned by new values.

As there is no longer a physical body nor the conditionings associated with it, so there will be no sense of time, sleeping, or waking day and night experiences. None of these cycles will be present which are so common to mundane life, upon which our concept of time is based. Timelessness therefore prevails. Also, there will be no diseases or sickness, for there is nothing that is corruptible. The laws concerning rebirth become understood and may be worked with, for those in the heavenly realm are aware of beings that are entering into and out of incarnation.

The means of propulsion and travel, building of forms such as houses, and creation of works of art may all be achieved by means of thought energy alone. They result from the direct expression of varying degrees and hues of the energy of light (which is synonymous with the energy of thought). All that is beautiful, aesthetic, joyous on the earth (such as flowers, trees and water) have subtler correspondences there, which also includes much that cannot be found here.

'As he thinketh in his heart, so is he',[11] and so one will be. One always reaps the consequences of one's actions. If the motives to one's actions are right – that is, in accordance with the laws of Love and good will – then entry into the heavenly realms becomes a certainty. Such laws should lie at the heart of, or form the basis of, any scripture worthy to be called sacred. It matters not what faith one follows, or even if one is an atheist.

The essence of what truly matters is the degree of freedom one has from selfishness or self-centredness. Spite, hatred, and all similar attitudes of mind will enclose and deform a person from within, and these energies thereby imprison that person after death. Regarding 'How the dead are raised up', [12] Paul states:

---

11 *Proverbs 23:7,* see also *Luke 12:34.*

12 *I Cor. 15:35.*

> One star differeth from another star in glory. So is also the resurrection of the dead. It is sown in corruption, it is raised in incorruption.[13]

To be 'sown in corruption' means to have been born into the ever-dying, transient, material world. This is into the sense-perceptive and information gathering apparatus that is our dense physical form. This form is corruptible and also corrupts the impressions associated with the Divine. In the physical realm, change is recognised as a progressive manifestation of the ideal for that person, which is generally directed by the will, and gauged by the intensity of Light that can be withstood. The realm or state of being one finds oneself in after death depends upon the Light (or 'star') that shines from within. This determines the strength or intensity of external spiritual Light that can be withstood in the subjective realms. Meditative development can be viewed similarly, for here a person gradually dies to the personality nature, which enables the withstanding of greater intensities of Light (illumination).

By the time one has become fully enlightened, the personality (the bearer of the 'I'-concept) no longer exists – it has died. The enlightened one can thus 'sit together' with similar beings of Light 'in heavenly places in Christ Jesus'.[14] Paul states that:

> In a moment, in the twinkling of an eye, at the last trump: for the trumpet shall sound, and the dead shall be raised incorruptible, and we shall all be changed. For this corruptible must put on incorruption, and this mortal *must* put on immortality'.[15]

The phrase 'the trumpet shall sound' refers to the note or sound that signifies the Presence or emanating quality of the Soul as it withdraws

---

13 *I Cor. 15:41-42.*

14 See Ephesians chapter two, where Paul begins with the words: 'And you *hath he quickened,* who were dead in trespass and sins', the nature of which he explains, and then states 'But God, who is rich in mercy, for his great love wherewith he loved us, Even when we were dead in sins, hath quickened us together with Christ, (by grace ye are saved;) And hath raised *us* up together, and hath made *us* sit together in heavenly places in Christ Jesus'. (Eph. 2:4-6.) That which is 'quickened together with the Christ' is the entire Hierarchy of Enlightened Being.

15 *I Cor. 15:52-53.*

its energy from the 'corruptible form'. It thereby calls forth the Life of the personality as ones dies to the dense physical body.

The concept that the 'mortal *must* put on immortality' implicates the Christian idea of living forevermore in a heaven or hell state, but this concept is the result of not comprehending the nature of life after death. The human Soul is literally immortal, for it incorporates the sum total of the incarnations of the personalities it sends into incarnation. The astral body is not so, as its form must eventually die to that plane when the inherent consciousness (the immortal aspect) moves to the higher domains. It will then be absorbed into the construct of the Soul before the next incarnation.

Note Dr. Moody's previously quoted description of the moment of death: 'He begins to hear an uncomfortable noise, a loud ringing or buzzing, and at the same time feels himself moving rapidly through a long dark tunnel'. This bears favourable resemblance to Paul's statement, because 'a trumpet' can easily be described as a 'long dark tunnel' that emits an 'uncomfortable noise'.

Esoterically, the trumpet or 'tunnel' is exactly how each *chakra* appears to the eye of a seer. They are whirling vortices of energy emanating from points in the spinal column to the surface of the body (where they assume a disc-like shape).[16] The specific centre implicated here is the *brahmarandhra vidhāra*. This is the subjective opening at the top of the head through which, according to all systems of yoga-meditation philosophy, the person is said to exit and enter at death, birth and deep meditation. It is an expression of the *sahasrāra padma*[17] (the 1,000 petalled lotus), the *chakra* situated on top of the head.

---

16 They are, for instance, described on page 204 of *The Romeo Error* by Lyall Watson as 'spiral cones of light'.

17 The Head centre (*sahasrāra padma*) of each human unit reflects attributes of the *Sambhogakāya* Flower into active manifestation. The yogin that properly accesses the *sahasrāra* can then be liberated from illusional activity. Wisdom and eventual Buddhahood is the gain. The *sahasrāra padma* can also link to the spiritual triad *(ātma, buddhi, manas)*, the higher, enlightened sheaths of a person, because the structure of its petals facilitates sympathetic receptivity. More information regarding the *chakras* is provided in chapter six, as well as in my *A Treatise on Mind* series, such as Volume 6: *Meditation and the Initiation Process*.

Biblical references to rebirth

Regarding the concept of rebirth, there are at least two places in the New Testament where this is hinted at. For example, Jesus told His disciples that John the Baptist was a (re)incarnation of Elias (Elijah in the Old Testament):

> For all the prophets and the law prophesied until John. And if ye will receive *it,* this is Elias, which was for to come. He that hath ears to hear, let him hear.[18]

Elsewhere, even clearer support for rebirth is provided by this statement:

> But I say unto you, that Elias is come already, and they knew him not....and then his disciples understood that he spake unto them of John the Baptist.[19]

The idea of rebirth was known in those times. This is indicated in a question the priests and Levites directly asked John the Baptist:

> 'Art thou Elias?' And he saith, I am not. Art thou that prophet? And he answered, No.[20]

This query is specifically asking if he was the actual reappearance of the prophet Elias, as prophesied.[21] In answering 'No' to the question 'Art though Elias? Art thou that prophet?' a seeming contradiction exists between the statements of Jesus and those of John. Their statements are in fact complementary, for it was specifically queried if John was the *actual physical reappearance* of Elias, which he was not. Those that understand the law of *karma* know that the (re)incarnation process is not at all concerned with the reappearance of the physical form, or

---

18 *Matt. 11:13-15.*

19 *Matt. 17:10-13.*

20 *John 1:21.*

21 *Malachi 4:5,* at the end of the Old Testament, which concludes with: 'Behold, I will send you Elijah the prophet before the coming of the great and dreadful day of the Lord: And he shall turn the heart of the fathers to the children, and the heart of the children to their fathers, lest I come and smite the earth with a curse'.

a specific previous personality, as the priests and Levites evidently enquired of John.

What Jesus is implying, on the other hand, is that the Soul or 'Spirit' of Elias is incarnate in John. This is suggested by the phrase 'and they knew him not'. This true knowledge of the aspects of the Elias cannot be known by those not Initiated into the Mysteries of Being.

The orthodox background behind this discourse is provided in *The International Standard Bible Dictionary*:

> Jewish eschatology in the intertestamental period picked up the reference to Elijah in the prophecy of Malachi and – in part, no doubt, due to the dramatic translation of Elijah – included the return of Elijah as a distinct element in its expectations for the end time. From the NT also it is evident that the expectation of Elijah was widespread in Palestine in the 1st cent. A.D.[22]

The text continues:

> When John the Baptist described Jesus as the one who would "baptize with the Holy Spirit and with fire" (Mt. 3:11 par.), he may have hinted at an analogy between Jesus' ministry and Elijah's. James and John clearly made the association when they asked Jesus if He wished them to "bid fire come down from heaven and consume" the Samaritans (Lk. 9:54). The nature of Jesus' ministry itself suggested to many that He was the Elijah to come (Mk. 6:15 par.: cf. 8:28 par.). Jesus Himself alluded to Elijah's journey to Zarephath and suggested a parallel between His own ministry and Elijah's (Lk. 5:25f.). He may also have alluded to Elijah's ministry when He said of Himself, "I come to cast fire upon the earth" (Lk. 12:49).[23]

One can obviously speculate as to exactly how the various ancient Jewish sects conceived of the return of Elijah, but for those that have 'eyes to see' and 'ears that hear' the meaning of Jesus's statement above clearly refers to the rebirthing process. To 'hear' here does not simply refer to listening to Jesus' words, but also to what the Buddhists call

---

22 G.W. Bromiley, general editor: *The International Standard Bible Dictionary, Vol. 2.*, (William B. Eerdmans Pub. Co., Michigan, 1982), 67.

23 Ibid.

'the ear-whispered truths'. These are the innermost instructions from their gurus heard in the silent recesses of their Hearts. To listen is thus symbolised by the long ear lobes of Buddhas and Bodhisattvas. This is also why Milarepa for instance is often depicted sitting with one hand cocked behind his ear. These truths are those of the esoteric doctrines *(dharma)* revealed in my writings, and the main sources that I refer to.

The quote of Jesus that 'I come to cast fire upon the earth' is of interest, especially when the passages following it are also analysed:

> I am come to send fire on earth; and what will I, if it be already kindled? But I have a baptism to be baptized with; and how I am straitened till it be accomplished! Suppose ye that I come to bring peace on earth? I tell you, Nay; but rather division.[24]

Fire is the Element that governs the mental plane, hence what Jesus is referring to is that He has come to awaken people's minds with right logic, that of the spiritual truth. The question 'what will I, if it be already kindled?' denotes that Jesus was but following in the footsteps of his predecessors, and continues with the next step of the message that they originated. The 'baptism to be baptized with' refers to the attainment of the second Initiation, which will be elaborated in chapter seven. Jesus also passed His version of this Initiation. He was consequently Baptised by John and the 'Spirit of God'.[25]

'Division' comes when those following the Initiation path are contrasted to the activities of the average person. The average person has no cognisance of 'the ear-whispered truths'. They are also selfishly oriented, whilst the Initiates are compassionately focussed. The clash between the path of compassion and that of selfishness produces the division. This observation is also veiled in the statement:

> 'Verily I say unto you, No prophet is accepted in his own country.'[26]

---

24 *Luke 49-51.*

25 *Matt. 3:16.* The type of baptism that Jesus provides is given by John the Baptist in *Matt. 3:11* – 'he shall baptise you with the Holy Ghost, and with fire'. As previously explained 'the Holy Ghost' is the Hierarchy of Enlightened Being.

26 *Luke 4:24.*

Jesus and the blind man

In the Gospel of St. John it is stated that Jesus passes by a man who was blind from birth. The disciples queried: 'Master, who did sin, this man, or his parents, that he was born blind?'[27]

The only way for one who was 'born blind' to have previously sinned would be to have previously lived, and in that prior life to have committed the acts that karmically resulted in blindness in the next life. If however it was the blind man's parents that had 'sinned' (acted in such a way during the pregnancy so as to have caused deformity in the foetus), then this could have resulted in the physical defect of the newborn child.

The disciples' question also presupposes that some of the Jews were familiar with the law of cause and effect and the doctrine of rebirth in one form or another. Certainly, the way was opened for contact with, and the assimilation of, Buddhist and Hindu doctrines after Alexander the Great's conquest of northern India. Also, testimony in Plato's Republic, the works of Pythagoras, Herodotus, Heraclitus, and others, tells us that the doctrine of rebirth existed in the Middle East long before Alexander's time.[28]

Jesus' answer here is interesting – 'Neither hath this man sinned, nor his parents: but that the works of God should be made manifest in him.'[29] This indicates that the man was predestined to accomplish certain things – for instance, to meet the Christ. This phrase also indicates that this man's *karma* (as that of all other beings) is directed by the guiding Light of the Spirit within ('God').

By the means of 'blindness' the man could therefore be made to know 'God', or certainly the nature of the manifestation of 'the works

---

27 *John 9:2.*

28 Joseph Head and Silvia Cranston's book *Reincarnation: The Phoenix Fire Mystery* (Point Loma Publications, San Diego, 1991) is an excellent anthology of quotations from some of the world's greatest minds concerning the subject of reincarnation. Note also that the important Gnostic text, *The Apocryphon of John* (circa the earliest portion of the Christian era), certainly teaches of reincarnation – as do the works of the most eminent of Church Fathers, Origen.

29 *John 9:3.*

of God' within him. These 'works' relate to the development of an awakened awareness, which the man would eventually accomplish. This is illustrated by the rest of the chapter (in his answers to the Pharisees and to Jesus).

We see, therefore, that logically the man's Soul chose that life for him to be born blind. This is what most who are spiritually evolved do (figuratively) when they take a new body – they become 'blind' to their former state of perception. In this way, through mastering their new conditionings, they can best identify with the problems of the humanity around them, and so work out how to appropriately help those with whom they are incarnate. Such a person's entire life (as a Bodhisattva[30]) becomes a ritual of enlightenment, through which others may gain inspiration. Average humanity may thus gain insight by listening to and following the example of such an enlightened one, living in normal conditions. Enlightened beings have mastered the exact obstacles and conditionings that the rest of humanity also must master, yet they choose to live amongst the rest of humanity out of compassion. In this way, the 'works of God' will be made to manifest by the enlightened.

In the context of the Gospel story, the blind man was born physiologically blind in that life as a symbolic illustration, or embodiment, of the above point. He still had some ways to go to enlightenment, but through seeing the Light – hearing and believing in Christ – this path was set straight for him.

All of us are 'blind' spiritually speaking; we are ignorant of the Light that is the Christ within us. Our eyes must eventually be opened to see That Light. This explains the meaning of the verse:

> And Jesus said, For judgement I am come into this world, that they which see not might see; and they which see might be made blind.[31]

Those that 'see not' are average people. Although they may be born with normal eyes, they 'see not' the beauty of the subjective realms – the nature of the Mysteries of Being, of the Christ Light. Such ones are esoterically blind and must be taught how to 'see'.[32]

---

30 They can be considered members of the Hierarchy of Enlightened Being.

31 *John 9:39.*

32 As I state in Volume 1 of my series *A Treatise on Mind,* page 5. 'An enlightened

Correspondingly, those who 'see' are Initiated into the Mysteries of Being. They are thus 'made blind' to the temptations and the enticing lasciviousness of material *(saṃsāric)* life. By the means of this blindness, they would 'have no sin',[33] as nothing could cause them to be limited or tied to the *karma* of the material world.

While the average person is also born 'blind', it is for different reasons. Humanity's present selfish and self-centred attitudes tend to prevent the proper objectives of the law of *karma* (and thus of evolution) from being met at the appointed times. Self-centredness, coupled with psychic vision, would be disastrous for the person concerned (and those with whom he/she has relationships). Such is the way that leads to the path of black magic.

People must evolve by gaining the qualities that enable them to 'see'. These developed qualities are the major objectives of the evolutionary impetus, while the ability to 'see' is simply an effect of that evolution. Jesus' answer[34] also shows it is immaterial whether the blind man or his parents have sinned, for the only thing that matters are the results – the works of God. The law of *karma* is primarily concerned with the effects, that is, the manifesting Plan of 'God', and not the causes. The effects of those causes are arranged in such a way so as to eventually produce freedom from 'sin' (liberation) upon the enlightenment path.

Even Herod seems to think that Jesus was John the Baptist risen from the dead (i.e., reincarnated).[35] Other statements in the New Testament, when deeply pondered on, also provide convincing evidence for the likelihood of evolution through a multiplicity of births and deaths. As an example, let us look at Paul's statement in Philippians:

> Work out your own salvation with fear and trembling. For it is God which worketh in you both to will and do of *his* good pleasure. Do all things without murmuring and disputings: That ye may be blameless and harmless, the sons of God, without rebuke, in the midst of a crooked and perverse nation, among whom ye shine as lights in the world.[36]

---

one is needed to help properly awaken the inner tools and organs of perception that allow multidimensional visioning'.

33 *John 9:41.*

34 *John 9:3.*

35 *Mark 6:16.*

36 *Phil. 2:12-16.*

Achieving the perfection of the Christ

Note that in the above statement Paul asked the Philippians to become 'sons of God'.[37] The appellation 'son of God' is therefore not exclusively that of the Christ (as orthodox theologians would have us believe). Rather, it indicates a very high degree of spiritual attainment whereby one has become 'blameless' (that is, *karma* producing actions are no longer caused). Such a person also becomes 'harmless' to the extent that the complete knowledge of the Mysteries of the Kingdom of 'God' has become manifest within. This is because all beings that become vehicles for the 'work of God' must partake of 'His' Divinity and be included consciously as part of That Mind. They will thereby become 'lights in the world', as was Jesus. A Lord of Compassion is the gain. From this perspective it states in Ephesians:

> That the God of our Lord Jesus Christ, the Father of glory, may give unto you the spirit of wisdom and revelation in the knowledge of him.[38]

One must express the 'works' of this Kingdom in the world, 'without murmurings and disputings', in a completely desireless and spontaneous fashion. (This will be made clearer in the chapters on Initiation.) The Christ is a perfected example of such a Being. This is definitely within Paul's mind, as indicated earlier:

> Let this mind be in you, which was also in Christ Jesus: Who, being in the form of God, thought it not robbery to be equal with God.[39]

Elsewhere, Paul asks us all to:

> Come in the unity of the faith, and of the knowledge of the Son of God, unto a perfect man, unto the measure of the stature of the fulness of Christ.[40]

We also find a statement of the Christ at the end of chapter five in Matthew, which effectively summarises the context of that chapter: 'Be ye therefore perfect, even as your Father which is in heaven is perfect'.[41]

---

37 See also *Romans 8:14, Galatians 3:26, John 1:12,* and *John 3:1.*

38 *Ephes. 1:17.*

39 *Phil. 2:5-6.*

40 *Ephes. 4:13.*

41 *Matt. 5:48.*

What does it mean to become as perfect as the Christ, or as His 'Father in Heaven'? How is it possible in merely one lifetime to become 'equal with God', especially if one has to 'work out' one's own salvation? 'Salvation' thereby implies utter perfection. This is precisely why Adam and Eve ate the forbidden fruit that caused them to be ousted from Eden, as explained previously. Surely, these statements mean exactly what they indicate and not the orthodox misinterpretations (or rather their avoidance).

Theologians tell us that the reward given to all people who faithfully believe and follow their doctrines is the right to be with the Christ in heaven. The idea that followers can also become 'equal with God' is seen as a heresy. The dogma is that Christ is consubstantiated with the Father, but the rest of us (other than Mary) are considered as lesser beings, that if we are not sinners we will remain in heaven presided over by 'God' and His Son 'for ever and ever'. Such a concept does obviously not fulfill either Paul's or Jesus' expectations for us, from the above quotations.

The 'faith' that is so much brandished by Christians is important for all spiritual activity. It should be faith in the certainty of the Law of Love and the providence of 'God' that enables us to figuratively 'move mountains', as Jesus stated was possible.[42] Faith in prescribed theological assertions will only lead to bondage and blindness.

To come to be 'equal with God' surely requires a large expanse of time, and myriads of progressively fulfilled enlightening experiences. These experiences allow forms that no longer serve their purposes to be eliminated, transmuted, or transformed, as a consequence of working off *karma* from past lives, and so also treading the Initiation path. There are cosmic paths to eventually travel upon as a liberated Buddha, to learn the mode of becoming a planetary Logos upon various star systems. Vast are the schools of learning in cosmos.

One's needs thus become served as they come within a field of increasingly expansive perception. In so doing, one progressively becomes perfected, then 'perfect'. Divinity (or 'grace' as Paul puts it) increasingly manifests until it obliterates all opposition in the form.

---

42 *Matt. 17:20-1.*

Inevitably there is naught but the Divine That is 'God' inhabiting the Mind of the liberated One. This is what the rebirthing process eventually confers upon a person.

One who is thus 'perfected' has become steadfast in spiritual Being. Having overcome the vicissitudes of incarnate existence, then there is no need to further incarnate. This partially explains the meaning of the statement in the Revelation of St. John: 'Him that overcometh will I make a pillar in the temple of my God, and he shall go no more out' [43] (into incarnate life). To further illustrate, note the statement of Jesus: 'He that believeth on me, the works that I do shall he do also; and greater works than these shall he do'.[44]

How is it possible for all those that 'believeth' in the Christ to perform 'all the works' and also 'greater works' than what He performed, if they unquestioningly accept naïve theological arguments concerning human spirituality? The factor of rebirth guarantees that each person shall eventually perform such works, as one evolves to embrace the consciousness that Jesus possessed, and then to transcend it. Following the Initiation path guarantees this.

Evolution is non-static; there is no feasible end to it. Every person must strenuously work out his/her own salvation, till eventually the 'grace' of God within is made manifest. The orthodox Christian belief of only one life, followed by a perpetual life after death in heaven was gleaned from certain statements in the Bible such as one by Paul, 'And as it is appointed unto men once to die, but after this the judgement'.[45]

This statement and other similar beliefs, are perfectly true in reference to the physical body of a person and the personality nature. The person dies, along with their former personality. One is judged (by *karma*[46]) according to the actions and the state of consciousness wherein one is polarised. One can thus stay in the subjective realms for an eternity (for time does not exist in that state). When one does reincarnate, it is into a new body with a new set of conditionings and

43 *Rev. 3:12.*

44 *John 14:12.*

45 *Heb. 9:27.*

46 The agents of *karma* are the angelic *(deva)* kingdom. This is a subject touched upon in chapter five and elaborated in more detail in my other writings.

personality qualifications, based on the results of old actions and the appropriate karmic judgements.

One may have been a male in one life and a female in the next, or a millionaire in Europe in one life and a beggar in India in the next. Racial, family, or religious ties as they exist in the world offer significant scope for many types of activity and experiences for incoming Souls, and that is all. The Souls are not in any way bound by previous exoteric ties when they are to reincarnate.

It is important to realise that only the Spirit within and its instrument, the Soul, are everlasting, and then only relatively so (in comparison to the personality life). Everything else is corruptible, dies, and once dead cannot return, except in the form of *karma,* and memories.

The censorship of reincarnation

We have seen therefore, that the rebirth theory was unquestionably prevalent during and after the time of the Christ. However, by the sixth century A.D. the then emerging Roman Catholic church excluded the tenets of reincarnation from its agenda. This was the purpose of the edict of the second Council of Constantinople in A.D. 553. Specifically, the church threatened excommunication (anathema) and therefore hellfire, upon anyone believing in, or propagating, the 'mythical doctrine of the pre-existence of the soul and the consequent wonderful opinion of its return'.[47]

The history of the early ecclesiastical councils is very interesting. There were many ecumenical councils between the fourth and the

---

47 This is quoted from W.Y. Evans-Wentz, *The Tibetan Book of the Dead,* (Oxford University Press, London, 1957), 234. This edict was specifically directed against the teachings of Origen, who W.Y. Evans-Wentz states was 'the pupil of St. Clement of Alexandria, and the best-informed and most learned of the Church Fathers, who held the doctrine of rebirth and *karma* to be Christian, and against whom, two hundred and ninety-nine years after he was dead, excommunication was decreed by the exoteric Church, on account of his beliefs, has said: 'But that there should be certain doctrines not made known to the multitude, which are [revealed] after the exoteric ones have been taught, is not a peculiarity of Christianity alone, but also of philosophic systems, in which certain truths are exoteric and others esoteric' *(Origen Contra Celsum,* Book 1, c. vii)''.

eleventh centuries which endeavoured to settle theological and liturgical differences concerning the Divinity of Christ. For example, Christ's relation to God – whether He was God-man or man-God, the nature of the Divinity of Mary, the question of consubstantiation, etc.

Disagreements led to a final schism between the Eastern (the Greek Orthodox) and the Western (the Roman Catholic) forms of Christianity in 1054 A.D. Later, the opinions of many other differing sects evolved out of the Reformation. What texts to include in the Bible of the many that were then extant (such as the Gnostic codices[48] and the texts that found their way into the Apocrypha), was finally settled in A.D. 381 in the Council of Rome. This basic ruling has been followed ever since by the Catholic and Protestant faiths. It may be of value to the reader to further investigate the origins of present theological arguments, regarding the context of the Bible and the nature of Deity.

Transmigration of Souls and lesser rebirths

The idea of the transmigration of Souls (metempsychosis) concerns incarnation of a Soul into a human body or a lesser evolved species, such as an animal. Once the progressive nature of evolution, the law of *karma,* and the nature of the Soul are better understood then metempsychosis into lesser species will be seen as infeasible. Certainly, human consciousness did inhabit and evolve through the medium of animal forms, over many millions of years. However, after the formation of the human Soul (the Sambhogakāya Flower) only human forms were incarnated into.[49]

The idea of metempsychosis might be partially justified if one only takes into account the physical body of a person, which is an animal form. The sentience of the component organs can also be considered to reincarnate from an animal reservoir of substance. Although an 'animal' form is appropriated by the human consciousness for each incarnation, the form in and of itself is not in reality the human being. Rather, it is the human consciousness that inhabits the form. The animal kingdom

48 Fifty-two tractates of which (producing 49 newly recovered texts) were discovered at Nag Hammadi in 1945. See James M. Robinson (general editor), *The Nag Hammadi Library,* (HarperSanFrancisco, 1990).

49 Note that the evolutionary process from the esoteric perspective differs from that of modern scientists because we also take the subjective planes of perception into account.

is evolving to embrace the human kingdom and the human is evolving to embrace the Divine. Therefore, 'man' the thinker (the indwelling consciousness that utilises the dense form in its totality) does not, and cannot transmigrate into any other form other than what has evolved to contain that consciousness.

No aspect or attribute of Deity or category of experiences is uselessly repeated or wasted. Therefore, once a set of experiences becomes part of a being's equipment of response, they progress onwards. Hence, a human's highly developed consciousness (that even the basest person has, when compared to the lesser kingdoms) will have no need to retard further development by incarnating into highly confining forms, such as the animal kingdom provides. Such forms provide zero capabilities for a human consciousness to express itself, for the intelligence bearing factors are not there.

The greater sphere of consciousness always includes the experiences of the lesser in its radius. It thus would gain nothing by reincarnating within the bodies of lesser kingdoms of Nature. Furthermore, even if transmigration were possible, *karma* would not be fulfilled or served by that means.[50] While it is possible for the Divine to overshadow the animal (and thereby 'enlighten' it), it is not possible for the human to incarnate into it. (Except from the perspective that the physical bodies we inhabit are primarily animal forms, which include within themselves the sum-total of what is most necessary from all the other kingdoms in Nature to enable our continued evolution.) There are also significant differences between the psychic constitution of humans and animals (for example, we are direct extensions of our Souls) that further clarify the impossibility of lesser rebirths. Thus, in considering the evolution of consciousness, experiencing repeated births into the animal kingdom would be a useless exercise.

Note that in some human incarnations, certain animal-like qualities may seem to predominate. This idea, when extended, allowed many

---

50 There is a type of exception to the rule, in those cases of complete identification with the animal nature (as in some forms of black magical practices). Then a degeneration into animal-like states, a breakdown of the human personality (not the Soul) is possible, after many such self-willed incarnations. My book *Karma and the Rebirth of Consciousness* (Munshriram Manoharlal, New Delhi, 2006) delves into the subject of *karma* and rebirth in detail.

religions and philosophers to teach an exoteric doctrine based on a concept of transmigration. The symbolic context of such teachings, therefore, should not be overlooked. For example, a birth as an ass may imply one who is basically stupid and obstreperous in temperament, whereas birth as a lion carries the meaning of one who is courageous or ferocious in his temperament.

Such tenets were advocated many millennia ago in order to induce the people concerned to live rightly through fear of such rebirths. At that time, people apparently needed the element of fear to prompt them to right values. Nowadays, this should no longer be the case. Newer and more accurate teachings have arisen which are more suitable for humanity's increasingly intellectual and enlightened attitudes.

Dr. Evans-Wentz complements these statements concerning rebirth in his explanation of *The Tibetan Book of the Dead (Bardo Thödol).* He speaks regarding the Buddhist and Hindu doctrines and their relation to Plato's description in *The Republic,* all of which proclaim metempsychosis. Evans-Wentz emphasises the great difference between exoteric and esoteric views on this subject:

> The exoteric interpretation, namely that the human stream of consciousness, that is to say, the human life-flux, not only can, but very often does take re-embodiment in sub-human creatures immediately after having been in human form, is accepted universally by Buddhists, both in the Northern and Southern Schools – as by Hindus – who, referring to Scriptures, invariably regard it as being incontrovertible... Over against the exoteric interpretation, which without any doubt, the *Bardo Thödol,* if read literally, conveys, the esoteric interpretation may be stated – on the authority of the various philosophers, both Hindu and Buddhist, from whom the editor has received instruction – as follows:
>
> The human form (but not the divine nature in man) is a direct inheritance from the sub-human kingdoms; from the lowest forms of life it has evolved, guided by an ever-growing and ever-changing life-flux, potentially consciousness, which figuratively may be called the seed of the life-force, connected with or overshadowing each sentient creature, being in its essence psychical. As such, it is the evolving principle, the principle of continuity, the principle capable of acquiring knowledge and understanding of its own nature, the principle whose normal goal is Enlightenment. And, just as the physical seed

> of a vegetable or animal organism – even man's seed – is seen by the eyes to be capable of producing after its own kind only, so with that which figuratively may be called the psychical seed of the life-flux which the eyes cannot see – if of a human being it cannot incarnate in, or overshadow, or be intimately bound up with a body foreign to its evolved characteristics, either in this world, in *Bardo,* or in any other realm or world of *sangsāric* existence. This is held to be a natural law governing the manifestation of life, as inviolable as the law of *karma,* which sets it into operation.
>
> For a human life-flux to flow into the physical form of a dog, or fowl, or insect, or worm, is, therefore, held to be as impossible as would be – let us say – transferring of the waters of Lake Michigan into the depression occupied by the waters of Lake Killarney.[51]

Evans-Wentz later states:

> Human life is far richer in possibilities for the workings out of evil *karma* – no matter how animal-like the *karma* may be – than any sub-human species could possibly be.[52]

Concerning the doctrine of rebirth one can also presume that Buddhist conceptions of birth into one of the six realms associated with the wheel of birth and death is also an exoteric account. All such doctrines must therefore be reinterpreted esoterically, to gain proper insight into their meaning.[53] Needed for such interpretation is the recognition that all things originate in the mind; the six realms are accordingly also 'mind-created'.

The context of these realms pertains to the 'real' that is experienced by the desire-minds that created and continually perpetuate them. Similarly, they have a non-reality to other minds with differing

---

51 W.Y. Evans-Wentz, *The Tibetan Book of the Dead,* (Oxford University Press, London, 1957), 42-3.

52 Ibid., 58.

53 These realms are the heavenly realms, the human world, the realm of tantalised ghosts, the various hells, the animal world, and that of titans *(asura).* My book *An Esoteric Interpretation of the Bardo Thödol,* Parts A and B should be consulted for an in-depth explanation of the subject of the six realms and everything else concerning Tibetan concept of the life after death in relation to the meditation process.

philosophic backgrounds that have created other heaven or hell states. Symbolic and philosophic interpolations of the after death states have been moulded into the context of what is actually experienced, in order to suit the religious dispensation of any era.

The laws governing all life processes are immutable, but human imagination moulds and adapts what may be perceived to a desired outcome, or to suit a specific narrative. All states after death and any related Deities formulated by the imaginative minds of humanity are thereby easily accommodated. What is consequently created becomes *karma* that must be lived through and worked out before a truer state of perception manifests, as assuredly it must. The salvation of all kingdoms of Nature and the Deification of the human kingdom rests on this concept, which later chapters will further clarify.

Ephesians 3:8-11

Unto me, who am less
than the least of all saints,
is this grace given, that I should preach
among the Gentiles the unsearchable
riches of Christ;

And to make all men see what is
the fellowship of the mystery,
which from the beginning of the world
hath been hid in God,
who created all things by Jesus Christ:

To the intent that now unto the principalities
and powers in heavenly places
might be known by the church
the manifold wisdom of God,

According to the eternal purpose
which he purposed in Christ Jesus
our Lord.

4

The Development of an Enlightened Attitude

There are states of consciousness (dimensions of perception) that exist far beyond the comprehension of the average person, just as the intellectual abilities of humanity are beyond the instinctual (and sometimes emotional) abilities of animals. That there are many possible dimensions of perceptions can be understood by all but the most adamant skeptics. Accumulated evidence is found in the fields of parapsychology, clairvoyant realisations, mediumistic utterances, near death experiences, and the testimony of mystics and sages from all religions throughout human history. Readers that are seriously interested in these subjects can research this for themselves, for libraries now contain many relevant books.

Even one who has not researched these topics may have had experiences of the 'inner voice', dream states, telepathic communication with others, extra-sensory abilities, and awareness of psychic, phenomenal, or logically perplexing happenings. These examples should suffice to denote there is more to life than simply what the five senses and the intellect can explain.

Nowadays, few educated people remain entirely ignorant of these fields, for there has been an enormous awakening of interest in the esoteric sciences. Despite some negative aspects, much good has arisen from this development. The negativities are exemplified by many societies (both secretive and open), as well as by cults that are deluded by the grosser psychic powers (the 'raising of *kuṇḍalinī'*). Prematurely trying to awaken this energy is a dangerous practice.[1] One can also observe the misuse of hypnosis, the appearance of Satanism, forms of witchcraft, fortune telling, and pseudo-miracle making. Various occult groups will be found promoting speculative and erroneous ideas.

These developments have occurred concurrently with the opening of people's minds to both the feasibility of an afterlife and the existence of invisible intelligences. Such entities include angels, fairies, nature spirits, disincarnate beings, Masters of Wisdom, and the like, that influence people in various ways. The entire mass movement towards enquiry into paranormal phenomena, alternative religions and the psychic domains represents a necessary and important stage in the evolution of consciousness. This stage must precede the externalisation process of the Hierarchy of Light, which is synonymous with the concept of the reappearance of the Christ.

This awakening of humanity is part of a continuing series of revelations that have been rapidly freeing human minds over the centuries, which has sped up in the past few decades. These revelations (or events) are preparing and conditioning the common mind of humanity. This ensures that when the Christ (the head of the Hierarchy) does appear, humanity can be receptive to the teachings that He and the Lords of Light will bring. The New Age will consequently be birthed.

These teachings will, in effect, be a profoundly modified reinstatement of the arcane philosophy associated with the ancient wisdom religions. They will incorporate the esoteric doctrines that support the mysteries of Initiation. The manifestation of the consequent revelations will necessitate that people understand the basis of the meditative approach to life. This must include embracing the livingness of Love and the One Life that pervades all Lives. The word meditative infers a system of realisation by which the hidden laws that condition all we see around us can come to be known. The meditative way of life is attuned to these laws.

---

1 These dangers are explained in my Buddhist books under the topic of *kuṇḍalinī*.

Societal progression from the 1950s onwards

The explanation below will be brief. It will provide only a basic idea as to the progress of human thinking during the past decades. There has been a notable trend, consisting of distinct stages that reflect a quickened evolution towards mass human enlightenment. This progress however, has intensified efforts by the forces of evil to counter the progress of humanity and the activities of Hierarchy to rightly educate them.

The 1950s represented a period where many restrictive, narrow-minded and Victorian era type of attitudes (such as relating to sexual and social norms) began to crumble. People began to put the privations from the war years behind them and so to seek new freedoms. The movie industry led the way by providing mass education about interesting concepts. In many ways, the cultural flowering amongst the then youth found an outlet in a 'beatnik' type of philosophy. This was based principally on Zen Buddhism, western existentialist philosophy, and the oriental religions in general. It was epitomised in the writings of such authors as Allen Ginsberg, Jack Kerouac, Alan Watts, as well as through the abstract tendencies of the visual arts.

The next decade, the 1960s, saw the popularisation of using hallucinogenic drugs among a large minority segment of radical youth. It also saw the rejection of many existing norms in living standards and social ethics by many of the youth. They espoused long hair and the 'hippy' style antiauthoritarianism. Popular music was used as a means of carrying this message to a wide audience. The 1960s also witnessed the beginnings of humanity's real exploration of space (both physically and in terms of consciousness).

To pursue a more mystically oriented, less restricted, style of life, ideals such as 'make love not war' emerged. During this era many in society were encountering a rapid awakening to things occult. The worst aspects of this were found in the popularity of such movies as *The Exorcist* and *The Omen.* This period also saw a popularisation of fortune-telling, divination methods such as astrology, the I Ching, and intense interest in psychic phenomenon. Eastern religious and meditative methods (especially religious leaders from India, as well as Tibetan Buddhism) had much success in the West. This counteracted some of the negative impacts from the rising interest in psychism. There was also an increase in the activity of some charismatic, fundamentalist and splinter Christian groups.

Social movements also became a real force, and radically transformed society. The 1960s witnessed social outcry and demonstrations against the Vietnam war, nuclear armaments, pollution, and enforced impoverishment.[2] Politically, many world leaders began to seriously strive towards détente, mostly to address basic common economic needs. The intense rivalry between Communist and Western nations reached its zenith with the Cuban missile crisis (1962) and began a slow road to decline. The value of cooperative action began to be realised; this was evidenced by events such as the signing of a nuclear non-proliferation pact (N.P.T.).

During the 1970s, scientific research into subjects that were formerly the domain of mystics and esotericists began to bear fruit. An energy crisis became a matter of mounting interest, which provoked governments throughout the world to seek alternatives to fossil fuels. This spurred the development of solar energy. Other technological developments led to increased multinational communications. A greater understanding of the earth sciences enabled humanity to offset worldwide hunger to a large extent. Influential ideas circulated, such as farming the world's oceans and direct utilisation of mass-produced vegetable proteins (such as soybeans) to feed the world's population, instead of the indirect consumption of plant resources (by first feeding farm animals).

The end of the 1970s produced a period of comparative quiet as new ideas were digested. The field of space research rapidly progressed. The Viking landers landed on Mars (1976), and probes were sent to the outer planets Jupiter and Saturn. Instrumentation from a host of satellites also provided an information explosion about the cosmos.

Initially, there was hope that the 1980s would produce solutions to worldwide systemic issues, such as the right distribution of world resources, proper control of diseases, pollution and the constant threat of famine for many on earth. Such activities were derailed by the entrenched narrow-minded and self-serving interests of many nations. They blocked opportunities to alleviate such easily solved problems.

---

2 This impoverishment increased over the decades in many communities, to produce, for instance, the urban slums of the USA.

Thus, these goals would have been achieved if the United Nations functioned properly in accordance with the text of its charter of rights. There was a superficial easing of the arms race, such as the reduction of short-ranged nuclear weaponry in Europe, but elsewhere internecine strife continued. Because international forms of aggression continued, a large proportion of world resources were funnelled into the military establishments of various nations.

Various grass roots movements increased their activities with vociferous vigour, protesting forest denudation, acid rain, the greenhouse effect and the precarious condition of the ozone layer. This prompted many of the world's scientists to contribute well-timed documentation and research. It became increasingly evident to many that a materialistic civilisation, largely based on greed and fostered fear was no longer viable, and was doomed to a slow, self-emasculation. A continued orgy of over-consumption propping up the edifices of economic viability was destroying the environment and produced many social evils. Such activity is, however, the mainstay of the consumer society that is the basis of modern capitalism. There was thus little incentive by governments to change this course of action. The elimination of forest reserves, coupled with the effects of widespread industrialisation and pollution, gradually threatened human survival on earth. Such concerns increasingly became the objective of governmental legislation.

Some people possessing communal idealism went back to the land to seek saner lifestyles in the sixties and seventies. Many of them achieved basic self-sufficiency and adequate life-support systems in their immediate environments by the end of the 1980s. Their hope was to cushion themselves from any possible disasters that might overcome civilisation as it then existed. Others endeavoured to effect radical changes within the structure of civilisation by bringing enlightened ideas into arenas of life they had 'dropped out' of in the past. Everywhere, there were people inspired by a sense of urgency to effect the right changes in all facets of society before it became too late to rectify the imbalances. Hope was widespread that humanity could build bridges leading to a new world of heightened co-operative harmony.

Legislators and thinkers began to alter many materialistic motives and actions, as they strove to improve humanity, as a whole. The biosphere of the earth began to be viewed as an interconnected whole (the Gaia theory[3]), rather than in terms of what this or that group or Nation possessed. Many realised that without such changes in attitude, international aggression and self-serving interests would eventually bring disaster for all.

Some viewed the events of the 1980's as having already progressed so deeply into the moneyed concerns of the stock market's ups and downs that widespread chaos and destruction were inevitable. Others perceived the future as being in the hands of a comparative few, so they prepared to implement the needed changes that would foster a New Age civilisation through the applications of Love and goodwill within their immediate environment. The objective was to allow humanity to prosper as one global community in the twenty first Century, rather than as many warring and competitive nations that create frequent disasters. Visionary idealism saw that one humanity, one earth, and the force of Love must triumph over the evils of separateness and selfishness to ensure our collective survival.

The Internet was developed, allowing people everywhere to communicate and to share new ideas rapidly. This united the entire world in a web of information explosion. As a result, much of the world's knowledge became easily accessible, and every facet of governmental and social interaction rapidly became dependent upon this new technology.

After the fall of the Soviet bloc in 1998, the remaining superpower (the USA) became the world's hegemon, using its vast military power to enforce its political dominance over the rest of the world. The resources of many nations were plundered through the absolute control of the USA over financial institutions such as the World Bank, the IMF, the means of monetary transaction (SWIFT), and making the US dollar to become the world's reserve currency. These were privileges the USA egregiously abused. Its form of capitalism became a corporatocracy that ruthlessly used its power to enrich the very few at the expense of the vast majority of the people on the planet.

As we entered the early decades of the 2,000s, Western governments became increasingly tyrannical. They suppressed, with the complete

3 Popularised by James Lovelock & Lynn Margulis, *Atmospheric Homeostasis by and for the Biosphere: The Gaia Hypothesis.* (Tellus, 1974).

powers of a police state, any real dissent to totalitarian authoritarianism. Both left and right political parties of most Western governments effectively became a uni-party, by having only one voice on the issues that matter. Citizens saw these governments as being won over by the power of big corporations and the billionaires owning them. Corporatocracy (a disguised Fascism) thus became the norm. The power of money to corrupt governments and all state institutions was amply demonstrated. Leftist politics that favoured labour and the working class were nearly completely eliminated in a race to impose the ruthless wishes of a kleptocratic banking class.

The mass media also became beholden to the dictates of the powerful few who controlled all mainstream media outlets. Those independent voices who promoted truthful and informed opinions on the internet were suppressed and censored by government controllers. The onset of the Covid 19 'plandemic' was based upon overblown dangers of the Covid 19 virus, widely promoted by the mass media. As events unfolded, this allowed the utter ruthlessness and tyranny of governments to become increasingly clear. Civilisation now awaits the ending of these despotic institutions, so that the New Age can emerge. It will arise out of the testing grounds for the mass first Initiation, through the efforts of stalwart fighters for basic human freedoms. The frenzy of a media disinformation campaign reached its peak with the onset of the war between Ukraine and Russia. The foundation to the eventuation to a future world war is thereby established.

The above history shows what has allowed the forces of evil (the dark brotherhood) to gain control over all governmental institutions in our so-called democracies. Nevertheless, there is a Hierarchical Plan to bring about a forthcoming New Age. The objective will be to free humanity from the powerful grip of the forces of evil that is now so clearly upon us. This process is described in this book. The books of Alice Bailey can also be referred to,[4] as well as the two volumes of my book *The Constitution of Shambhala*.

---

4 See Alice Bailey, *The Externalisation of the Hierarchy,* and *The Reappearance of the Christ,* published by Lucis Publishing Co., N.Y. The phrase 'the Reappearance of the Christ' relates to the process of the implementation of the Hierarchical Plan.

Transforming conflict

An indefinite continuation of the present materialistic attitudes of humanity is adverse to evolutionary law. (Although evolving through materialism was certainly part of the Plan for humanity.) Such law is an expression of the Meditative Mind of the planetary Logos. Many are the enlightened agents[5] that exist to help propel evolution along according to the pattern of the Plan established since 'before the foundation of the world'.[6] The continued progression of egregious materialism will inevitably stimulate an onslaught of natural catastrophes as an effect of Divine Law. Such activity also occurred during Atlantean times, causing the sinking of that island. Much of the *karma* from that epoch is manifesting today in this (parallel) cycle. Today this *karma* is redefined with a more material emphasis, rather than the psychic bias of the past.

The destruction of our particular Root Race and materialistic civilisation has been prophesied by ancient seers to be by the Element Fire.[7] The mass use of modern armaments is certainly one way such a prophecy could be fulfilled. By a similar token, the Atlantean civilisation was destroyed by the Element Water. This was a consequence of the extreme cupidity, selfishness and self-assertive psychic (Watery) predation of humanity. These Watery qualities were aggressively fostered by the members of the dark brotherhood that arose during the Atlantean epoch. The evolution of each Root Race concerns a gradual development of needed characteristics out of the parent stock. Although there is an overlapping between each cycle, the termination of each racial cycle is heralded by widespread catastrophes. This is similar to the sickness and disease that is frequently experienced by people in old age before they die.

Whatever the exact incidents that produce the new epoch may be, their general trend will manifest so as to eliminate much of the materialistic bias of humanity. Much will happen that encourages good will, builds a sense of comradeship, and reveals the purpose for

---

5 *Devas*, Hierarchy and the members of Shambhala.

6 *John 17:24, Eph. 1:4.*

7 See Appendix 2 of my book: *Esoteric Cosmology and Modern Physics*, (Sydney: Universal Dharma Publishing, 2020), for further detail concerning the nature of these Root Races.

existence. Disasters and natural catastrophes are major forces that often bring people together to assist each other. They generally encourage serious consideration of the transitory nature of life and contemplation of the purpose of death.

Despite many adverse conditions, and the proclivities of the amassed evil that govern our lives, there are hidden forces working to rectify the situation for the better. For example, the advent of the mass media is also a mechanism for educating the disciples of the world. The opportunity for world-wide beneficence is thus great. Humanity has long been bound in chains that limited various forms of spirituality from being expressed. The rapid development of intelligent reasoning however facilitates critical thinking in arenas of metaphysical thought. These chains are therefore being broken as advanced types of religious and socio-political thoughts are actively pursued. Innovative thinkers are transforming all fields of knowledge, and technology keeps apace with novel advancements. Nevertheless, the resultant conflicts between opposing viewpoints also create a bewildering plethora of differing arguments that are seemingly only understood by specialists.

The consequent uncertainty has produced much dismay, confusion, turmoil and discontent in the world. These challenges represent a testing ground for those of humanity that are probationers and aspirants to the Mysteries of Being. The advent of rapid communication and exchange of ideas and views via the Internet represents the birth pains of a mass awakening of higher consciousness for a great deal of humanity. Lying propaganda on a mass scale is however also everywhere evident.

People are now demanding answers to many of life's riddles. The best possible solutions, or middle way between opposing issues in all fields, must be, and are, gradually being produced. The required labour is being accomplished by the intelligentsia in every department of life. Thus, the Child of the New Age is being procreated.

This Child will bring new freedoms of Revelation – to love and be loved, and to know and be known by the beloved. The gained vision will produce international peace, cooperation and harmony, as people recognise their common humanity and thus work together for similar goals. Humanitarians of the world must all work together to achieve the birth of the New Age Child.

Miracles can be achieved if willed via our Heart's compassionate activity. They must be achieved for the errors of the past to not be repeated. All-inclusive qualities must be developed by humanity on the long road to (Divine) Realisation. The common heritage of a united humanity can propel an astounding journey into the immensity of the universe.

Continued war, famine, international catastrophes, world-wide depression and inflation, may however be aspects of the 'signs of the times'[8] and of prophecies concerning the reappearance of the Christ.[9] It seems unlikely that the fundamental differences between totalitarian and the forces of freedom will be resolved without warfare. Even now, there are frequent proxy wars being fought all over the world, fed by these differences. Nowadays, what people believe to be Democracies have been surreptitiously co-opted by totalitarian forces. These governments have mostly been taken over by a cabal of super-rich individuals that manipulate the minds of our elected officials. It is also doubtful that votes are being honestly counted by using the electronic methods that are becoming increasingly prevalent. Various methods of wide-scale electoral fraud are employed to disinherit voters from their rights. People need to become aware that their governments may be selected for them, rather than actually being elected.

Ultimately, most wars of the past few decades are a continuation of the type of ideological conflicts associated with the past world war. Dictatorships and totalitarianism (whether fascist, kleptocratic, or communist) are anathema to everything related to progressive evolution of the human spirit and its basic freedoms. Most people on earth however live under such systems. The resultant conflicts with those of the 'free world', may be seen as part of the 'abomination of desolation, spoken of by Daniel'.[10] The phrase 'free world' here no longer refers to a grouping of democratic countries. Rather, it refers to those arenas of civilisation where the basic freedom of expression for people to think and act responsibly has not been curtailed by kleptocrats abusing the powers of the mass media and the political pawns they control.

---

8 *Matt. 16:3.*

9 *Matt. 24:42, Mark 13:1-37,* and *Luke 21:5-38.*

10 *Matt. 24:15.*

We are told in the same verse to 'stand in the holy place' when we see such abomination happening. This means to stand (in consciousness) within our innermost spiritual centre, the Heart of all Life, Love and Light. This refers to the central points in the Head and in the Heart that relate Spirit to matter. Enlightenment proceeds from there. This is the stance that all responsible beings in this era must endeavour to attain. Such attainment is now possible for many (via the Initiation process). From that place great heights of spiritual vision can be reached by us and as groups.

Through such a stance in the innermost spiritual centre the proper course of action needed to rectify the imbalances in our world will be revealed. Such vision is increasingly needed for disciples and aspirants, because the greater the effects of disease in a body (here of the planetary Logos) the more drastic the remedy generally needed to combat it. The healing activity is facilitated by the development of enlightened attitudes and the virtually instantaneous modern communications that nowadays connect humanity. The agents of Love and Light utilise this facility in a mutually co-stimulating and beneficial manner in order to counteract the malicious propaganda of the agents of darkness.

Other such beneficial progressions may also be seen through the advancement of science and the development of socio-technological achievements. Fruitful progress continues to occur, despite the negative attitudes fostered by ideological differences and partisan competitiveness between nations. Partisanship and self-serving mentalities are also being progressively abnegated by karmic impetus, working subjectively to rectify the imbalances in the world. This promises that peace will inevitably truly manifest on the earth, concurrently allowing the Christ (the Hierarchy) to reappear (externalise).

Preparing for the return of the Christ

For Christ's return, humanity must not only be prepared in consciousness, but must also strongly desire the type of energies that the Hierarchy of Light embodies. All concerned servers of humanity are presently working towards this educational goal (whether they are fully aware of the esoteric objective or not). The children of those that survive the present-day 'abominations' should see this appearance before the ending of the present century. Peace, and the enlightening of humanity by all educational means possible (within the auspices of karmic law) will consequently manifest. Right spiritual education is the main import of the statement: 'Therefore be ye also ready: for in such an hour as ye think not the Son of man cometh'.[11]

Humanity must 'be ready', thus must be prepared for this advent. The evocative appeal of united human desire must be sufficiently demanding to see the end of the present machinations of the forces of evil. Humanity must unitedly call forth this eventuality. The phrase 'in such an hour as ye think not' does not just mean that the Christ will come when a person least expects it; more specifically, it refers to when a person 'thinks not' – when the empirical thought processes have been superseded by 'no-thought'. Within that space is found the seeds of the intuition. This is part of the enlightenment process, the awakening of the Christ-consciousness.

Intuition (a display of the Christ-consciousness) will not come when one is thinking empirically upon self-serving activity that stimulates the ego. Intuition normally comes when one is lost in service and is so inspired with the confronting task that there is no longer recognition of a separate self or of any cognitive processes whatsoever. This creates the space for the Christ (or Guru) to come, whilst there is no expectation of such experience. One is emptied or Void of ego-forming qualities (to use Buddhist imagery). This thereby allows the mind into a meditative state (*dhyāna*) wherein the most profound realisations are attainable.

'Thinking not' also alludes to information already presented concerning the manifestation of Light (producing enlightened realisation). The manifestation of such Light nearly always occurs when a person least expects it (as in the form of a 'lightning flash'[12]). Such is the 'light from heaven' that suddenly shined round Paul (Saul) on the road to Damascus.[13] It contained a vision of the Christ that radically altered his life. The three days without sight that followed,

---

11 *Matt. 24:44.*

12 *Matt. 24:27:* 'For as the lightning cometh out of the east, and shineth even unto the west; so shall also the coming of the Son of man be'.

13 *Acts 9:3-10.*

in which he neither ate nor drank, are similar to the time one spends in the crypt or tomb of Initiation. (As explained in my book *Meditation and the Initiation Process.*)

Jacob Boehme, for instance, was said to have gained instantaeous enlightenment after seeing reflected sunlight on a pewter dish. Socrates, as related by Plato, sometimes stood immovable in one spot for a long time in a type of ecstatic trance-like state. The sudden 'lightning flash', when least expected, is also the means to enlightenment, as is exemplified by the concept of *satori* in the Zen Buddhist doctrine.

Jesus was therefore voicing an esoteric truth in the statement in *Matt. 24:44*. Most mystics and sages have also testified to such truth. The gaining of sudden illumination *(satori)* is an indicator that one is upon the path to enlightenment. It betokens the fact that such a person will have gained enlightenment in a previous life, and so is experiencing some of the karmic consequences. The developing force of the experience of further intuitive flashes *(pratyakṣa)* should lead that person to gain a similar awakening in the present life. An aspirant comes to be fully receptive and prepared for incoming greater intensities of Light by means of the attainment of right esoteric knowledge and the related meditative practices. The process will lead such a one to find the Teacher that can instruct the candidate in the ways of passing Initiation testings.

No being, not even the Christ, can give wisdom to another if that being is not ready, or does not desire it. This also holds true for experiences of peace, love, or joy. People must therefore ardently desire peace, ardently desire the 'kingdom of God', and steadfastly work towards that end before the means to their attainment may be provided. We must be able to take the 'kingdom of God by storm'.[14]

Humanity's desires centre around material comforts and social security, for people have been strongly conditioned towards them. They must be reconditioned in a wholesome way, so that gross desires may be transmuted into a higher desire for enlightenment and its implications. This is a necessity before the Christ will reappear.

Each past era has seen an expansion of human thinking, laying the foundations for greater freedom of movement, perception and living styles. This has produced the so-called permissive society of today. It

---

14 *Matt. 11:12.*

provides freedom of expression, which allows one to discern whatever may be truth – even in the face of a host of contradicting opinions that are presented as facts. In this society, one may live life without having to conform to rigid and unyielding rules of behaviour and modes of thought such as dictated by state, social, or religious laws and customs.

Self-directed freedom of expression in body, speech and mind in our societies, to pursue whatever course in life that is chosen, was possible within reasonable bounds, until the event of the Covid 19 tyrannical overreach by governments. Nevertheless, humanity still generally possesses the freedom to think as they choose and to experience all possible types of experiences. Having been shown practical alternate modes of living by the advanced thinkers amongst us, our understanding of real values must accordingly become greatly expanded and more inclusive. This is a fertile bed within which our spirituality can grow. When the mind finally becomes freed of all material conditionings, then half the battle to the enlightened attitude has been won. This will allow a person to recognise the new teachings that the reappearing Hierarchy of enlightened Being will bring.

The development of leisure time for people assists meditative development. Due to the importance of humanity possessing enough leisure to pursue higher spiritual advancement, the forces of evil have worked hard to prevent this. They try to enforce a monetary regime where most people are denied leisure through pecuniary deprivation, forcing them to work much longer hours to meet basic survival needs. The rule of corporatocracy (or kleptocracy) has ensured that vast amounts of humanity's resources have been siphoned to the super wealthy ruling 'elite'. Humanity must fight for the return of their rights, to overcome this creeping form of neo-feudalism that is being imposed upon them.

In this modern era, the luxury of leisure for most people has been brought about primarily by humanity's technological achievements (such as mechanical and electrical appliances) that free us from many formerly time-consuming tasks. Rightly used, leisure time provides the opportunity to read, study, and pursue any course of research and thought. Once a society has been adequately educated in the appropriate directions then 'this gospel of the kingdom' can be 'preached in all the world for a witness unto all nations; and then shall the end come'.[15] The 'Gospel', as thought of by the modern Christian commentator, is not what is indicated here. Note that the Gospels were not in existence during Jesus' time. Rather, the 'gospel of the kingdom' implicates the high attributes associated with the 'kingdom of God' known to those Initiated into the higher Mysteries. This has not been understood by orthodox Biblical commentators, which explains why it has not yet been 'preached in all the world' (though the mechanism exists to do so).

From Pisces to Aquarius

During Greco-Roman times at the beginning of the Piscean age humanity began to fully develop the intellect, via the rise of the empirical philosophers of Greece. Similarly, the current materialistic era provides opportunity for large-scale development of the intuition. Such development will be increasingly expressed by small groups of people as the Aquarian age develops. It will tend to propel them to incorporate their particular brand of philosophic, religious, social, scientific, artistic, or political thought into a homeostatic inclusion with all similar spheres of activity in the world. The keywords of the future will be co-operation, brother/sisterhood, amalgamation, peace, equanimity, good will, synergy and syncretism.

Astrologically, we are in a transitional period between the past age or era, governed by the sign Pisces, and the New Age governed by Aquarius. There is no sudden jump from one era to another. Rather, a gradual transition ensues, in which the qualities associated with a new sign supersede those of the old. It is not necessary to enter into an analysis of the qualities of the various signs here.[16] What must be understood, however, is that all possible systems of Divine realisation and enlightenment have their place in our particular era. This is either to eliminate ancient *karma,* or as a training school for the type of consciousness that is to be the foundation of the forthcoming world civilisation.

---

15 *Matt. 24:14.*

16 Many of my future writings will examine the esoteric interpretations of astrology.

There are very few beings that are truly Aquarian in their motives, lifestyles, ideals and innovations. Most of them will presently be found in communal situations that allow meditative development. Such a communal system will be the basis of the type of civilisation to come, which will be slowly developed over the next 100 – 1,000 years. Modern socialist doctrine (as promulgated by Marx and Lenin) was an adaptation of this idea, although true communal living is far-removed from the totalitarianism that existed in the USSR. (There we saw abuses of power and constraints to the freedom of expression for individual thoughts, political beliefs, religion and social life.)

Any manifested life is governed by characteristic cycles. Breathing, circadian, and diurnal rhythms are associated with day and night (and thus sleeping and waking). Other examples are cardiacal, reproductive, seasonal, and planetary cycles as well as the wave motion that is characteristic of the propagation of energy through space. Similarly one can postulate that the process of birth and death is also cyclic. These cycles are spirallic, propelling the evolving entities forward, and inevitably upwards through the dimensions of perception, for that is the path of evolution. We are constantly dying and being reborn in our consciousness in a progressively enlightening way. This is what Paul meant when he stated 'I die daily'.[17] Every time we experience something new our old experiences become memories, laying foundations for the new. Thus we grow. In effect, these experiences go through the process of birth and death. The sum-total of these experiences, as retained by the mind, must continue in cycles after the death of the form, which was momentarily the container of the mind. This is the philosophic basis for the continuation of consciousness in an after-death state.

The mind perpetually changes through well-recognised cycles of birth, adolescence, maturity and old age. The theme of the continuance of consciousness after the death of the form has already been introduced and will be further developed later. Of importance here is to realise that the principle of cyclical change is a constant factor associated with incarnate life.

---

17 *I Cor. 15:31.*

The Four Noble Truths and the Eightfold Path

Change is invariably accompanied by the factor of pain; we learn by means of pain and suffering. Pain arises due to attachments to things that are transient. All material things grow old, change and decay – like our physical bodies. However, the lessons (experiences) learnt and assimilated are of real value, laying the foundation for the development of wisdom and compassion.

In the modern world there are many obvious self-engendered causes of suffering. People often live in a continuous state of daydreaming, yet they suffer when dreams do not eventuate. They build up utopias in their minds based on imaginative longings and how they expect the future to be. They consequently do not live in present reality.

Many people suffer from emotional insecurity and become dependent on other emotionally unstable beings for security. Some look to various forms of drugs, which become prime causes of suffering. It is common for many to attempt to satiate their desires by collecting a superabundance of material goods, endeavouring to offset their fear of insecurity and of impermanence. They thereby hope to somehow ward off the process of dying. People may even be enslaved to the concept of time, to regurgitating of the past, which thereby limits their future freedom of expression and they suffer for it.

Examples of the causes of suffering are legion. This teaches us that the satiation of sensual desires, amassing of material empires, or assumed positions of temporal power cannot produce lasting emotional or mental happiness.

No amount of attachment to anything that can change (or decay, become lost, stolen, or destroyed) can bring true happiness. All material possessions are left behind at death. What, then, produces true happiness? The Buddha answered this question 2,500 years ago in His formulation called the Four Noble Truths.

These Truths concern the means whereby suffering can be relieved by cultivating non-attachment to material or transient things, and consequently the generation of wisdom. Wisdom is effectively the end product of the process of experience. Learning in the material world delivers the accomplishments of the incarnation process. Inevitably, a transmutation of the effects of that experience is produced, rather than mere negation.

- The *first Noble Truth* states that all life is (or inevitably results in) suffering.
- The *second Noble Truth* describes the cause for suffering, which is desire – the never-ending craving of the senses. In effect, it is an aspect of the selfish grasping of the separative, lower self, for things it wants from all around to sustain 'itself'. This concerns the illusion of a 'self' that is separate from all other 'selves'. It produces indifference to, or avoidance towards the real needs of others (except when self-serving).

  The attitude of separateness causes the thirst for sentient existence, whilst the innate desire for union with the complementary self at first produces vehicles (by means of the sexual experience) through which a person can manifest the illusion of self. Later, this desire is transmuted into the necessary quality to tread the path to liberation – a deliverance into, or fusion with, That which can be considered to be the All-Self (or Non-Self).

  The battle between the concept of self and the innate promptings for consummatory union with the 'All' produces the major sufferings of the mystic and the aspirant on the path. At first, separateness is instinctive, as a result of being caught up in the urgings and promptings of the great mass of beings, sponsored by ignorance. Later, as understanding comes from continued experiences, separateness is wilfully manifested. The potential for suffering is then increased exponentially unless steps are taken to abnegate these effects. As the person begins to tread the path to self-realisation the process causes a consequent diminishing of suffering. This is the result of the realisation of the third Noble Truth.

- The *third Noble Truth* states that through eliminating desire and craving, by fostering an enlightened attitude and through compassionate understanding, the causes of all man-made suffering are no longer sustained.

- The *fourth Noble Truth* is constituted of the various steps that facilitate the cultivation and development of an enlightened attitude and compassionate understanding. These steps consist of following the Eightfold Path.

The *Eightfold Path* is thus:

1. Right understanding.

This implies obtaining an intellectual grasp of the essence of all religious philosophies, the causes and results of the evolutionary process, of wrong actions and attitudes, of the mysteries of our Being, and of the basic laws and precepts discovered by scientific investigation.

2. Right aspiration or attitude of mind.

This implies aspiration towards the development of Love-Wisdom, of compassionate understanding. It follows naturally from the obtaining of right understanding. This concerns setting one's feet upon the path that leads to Initiation into the Mysteries of Being, thus to the portals of the zone of residence of the Hierarchy of Love on our planet.[18]

3. Right speech.

Once the right attitude of mind has been developed then the person curbs all idle chatter out of necessity and cultivates silence. Speech is then only for what will benefit others or is productive of the right (magical) results. Speech is sacred, as an act of Creation. The effect of erroneous or zealously misdirected speech (or writings, as an extension of speech) often produces the most long-lasting and serious damage to the development of the aspirant who is endeavouring to cultivate harmlessness. The power of the written word for good or for bad is obvious to all. Truly, 'Not that which goeth into the mouth defileth a man; but that which cometh out of the mouth'.[19] The cultivation of silence is necessary if an aspirant is to meditate and utilise the Word (Oṁ, or other mantras) with effectiveness.

---

18 This Hierarchy can also be depicted as the Council of Bodhisattvas.

19 *Matt. 15:11.*

4. Right action.

Once an aspirant is actively able to rightly cultivate speech, which necessitates the development of an effective meditative rhythm (or Mind), this automatically finds expression in all aspects of life. All sentient beings will be served thereby. This is the keynote of the Eightfold Path. For action, rather than mere belief, is central to the Buddhist religion. Only direct (experimental) action will produce the concrete expression of the other aspects of the path. Action involves what we do or refrain from doing, it thus concerns the deepest self-analysis and scrutiny of the true motives behind everything one does. This involves the ability to cultivate an attitude of deep receptivity to the 'Voice of Silence' within, to obey the laws of Life, the dictates of *karma,* of 'God', thus the inner and external *dharma.*

5. Right livelihood.

Right action carries naturally through into right livelihood. This means taking naught from others that is not given, nor manifesting actions that harm the development of any other being. It therefore implies a path of complete harmlessness and service to others. Such service is the result of life-long contemplation upon other's needs, or of humanity in general. One must work to develop the right characteristics and possessions that enable one to rightly give.

Such contemplations cause people to be robed in qualifications (according to Ray type) that befit them to be a scientist, teacher, artist, etc. They glean the best of past life experiences, plus those developed in this life, as conditioned by the various environments they are in. In essence, they must be able to vision the direction that the course of events in a chosen field may take. The thought is to develop the qualities that may be of greatest future benefit to those, or the society, they are endeavouring to serve.

Right livelihood also means sincere heartfelt, and even ritualistic devotion, to Mother Nature and the Lord of all Being. Through such livelihood, all manifest Life is sustained from the realms of divinity. One is provided with the resources that are the mainstay of one's livelihood through being part of the beneficence of the planet that one is a part. Right livelihood concerns therefore the application of

Love-Wisdom in all fields of endeavour. The inner Divinity is contacted and seen to be but a reflection of what exists outside, and that Divinity is what is served.

6. Right effort.

One must learn to strive for enlightenment with all one's heart and mind, and yet also be able at any time to seemingly 'abandon' that quest in order to help the other. I have apostrophised the word 'abandon' because this is an illusion, seen from the context of time and from the point of view of a 'self' that is striving. In fact, the quest for enlightenment necessitates the death of a self-concept, whilst the generation of far-sighted compassion is an automatic expression of this quest. Thus, in fact nothing is abandoned, except the façade of attachment to an illusion. Only thus is enlightenment acquired. It is an effort that is steadfast, persevering, and one-pointed in its motive. One can, with persistent certainty, overcome all the obstacles to obtaining the goal, while developing qualities and goods needed to meet all needs. This effort underlies the five previous precepts, and manifests in each of them with differing degrees of intensity at various stages of the path. It is something that the aspirant works upon, or with, in a conscious manner.

7. Right concentration, or mindfulness.

In the final two precepts, an aspirant must be so imbued with the course of the path that effort is automatic and spontaneous. For all intents and purposes the path becomes effortless, below the threshold of consciousness. When related to meditative development the idea of striving or trying to concentrate becomes meaningless. Complete relaxation of all cognitive processes is what is needed here. The act of mental effort, though useful at the beginning, prevents concentration in its final stages. Perhaps the phrase 'effortless effort' best describes the mode of action involved.

If all other precepts are followed, then everything preventing the aspirant from obtaining lasting release from suffering (and thus from the wheel of birth and death) falls away. He/she is left with concentrated energies, physical, emotional and mental, that are assimilated and projected towards the goal. This produces perfect mindfulness of all things. The concentration is such that the only elements that remain allow meditative development and the demonstration of the *dharma*. After the types of *karma* that tie one to material existence have been eliminated, it is a concentration of the aspects that relate to the Divine. This results in a specific effortless 'tension', or a state of being in which naught that distracts from the application of the meditation-Mind exists. It is a point of focussed receptivity where the mind is held steady, unwavering, in Light.

To do this necessitates the application of the Will – the positive, dynamic fruition of the aspirant's long drive to liberation. (It is also the impetus sustaining that drive.) When focussed (upon a form or idea), the Will becomes the seed or germ. When increasingly generated it can explode into That which empowers the complete unfoldment of any stream of realisation. It can also direct one to realms beyond all thought. Such Will is then effortless because it is the outcome of long periods of meditative unfoldment that have become a spontaneous state of transcendence. This state manifests through the aspirant,[20] there is naught then to resist the realisation of the most potent energies or Revelations.

8. Perfect Bliss or Absorption.

This is an absorption into That which is Void of all discernible characteristics, which is absolute and unconditioned. It has also been termed the enlightened Mind, the *dharmakāya*. This can also be seen as an absorption into the Heart of the Hierarchy of Enlightened Being, to which an aspirant is now a fully Initiated member.

The significance of death

Experiences that lead to illumination and the development of Love are the only things possible for the indwelling Soul to be receptive to, by virtue of its exalted position. (See figure 1.) That, plus the type of mental-emotional consciousness that we have built, are the only things taken with us in our astral forms after death. People who resist the lessons that life strives to teach them will retain their selfishness, desires,

---

20 Who at this stage would be an Initiate.

glamour and other self-focussed attitudes after death. Consequently, they often find themselves after death in a type of self-imposed hell, or in a clouded, confused, dream-like state. All such conditionings do not, however, last forever.

There is no break in the process of evolution. We are always propelled closer to the Divine. For this reason, the force of yet unrealised experiences and the subjective purpose of the Soul-nature eventually causes human rebirth. (Similarly for all forms of Life.) We are born again into a new world of experience, propelled by the accumulated weight of tendencies left over from past lives.

Death is a type of deep 'sleep' – an intensely active and vividly purposeful 'sleep' between births, just as sleep is a state of awareness between periods of being awake. It is possible to leave the body consciously in either an astral or thought body during sleep. This is widely recognised by those interested in clairvoyant and psychic research. Such a body is also occupied by the inhabiting consciousness after death (as will be elaborated in chapter five).

All Life can be viewed as units of consciousness inhabiting or embodying forms composed of lesser units of awareness or sentience. The cycles of evolution of consciousness encompass ever widening and more comprehensive realms of perception, which become increasingly inclusive of every state or attribute of being possible. The various attributes of Deity are gradually unfolded, until eventually the Ineffable Mind of Deity is realised.

Where, then, is hell – unless it (as it so often does) exists in the consciousness of the person concerned. Therefore, is hell self-engendered? If so, can it also possibly be self-dissipated? If the beauty of the death process and the fundamental divinity in all aspects of life are better understood, then people will no longer so adamantly wish to hold on to their physical forms when it is time for them to depart (causing unnecessary suffering for them). Nor will they fear the unknown, which will hold no secrets for them.

Death can only signify a birth into a freer realm of experience, just as how when a baby is born it dies to the enclosing walls of the womb and enters into the life of the immense world outside. People's ignorant and unpleasant reactions at the deathbed will disappear when they realise that death[21] simply frees them from a very limited and restricted form. Death should be a time of rejoicing, not weeping. It should be a process of inward reflection of what the death process means, and an outward acceptance that 'God' calls for His children when He wills. Each of us must eventually die. For this event, or liberating experience, we should prepare ourselves whilst we live.

For those awakening to the path of Love-Wisdom such understanding entails following the precepts associated with the Eightfold Path. Each of them deals succinctly with overcoming the process of dying and the transmutation of its effects. The gains in perception are consciously realised. At the last stage, death as humanity understands it, becomes meaningless. The person becomes immersed in That to which such terms as Eternal or Absolute Life are guarantors.

As one experiences the processes of death throughout life,[22] so too is physical death a continuation of that process. The assimilation of experience thus does not terminate at death. It is the ending of one large cycle of experience and the beginning of a new one that continues until we are ready to be born again into a new physical body. When we do so, it is in full accord with the evolutionary plans of the subjective Soul-group of which we form a part. There is no sense of separateness in the higher dimensions of perception. Many of the members of our Soul-group incarnate with us. According to the nature of the group and our subjective training, so the qualities we bring with us predispose us to certain activities within the context of the social settings manifested by the group as a unit. These qualities are the result of the store of experiences that we have reaped in our former lives.

This viewpoint is being validated by such investigators as Dr. Helen Wambach. In her book, *Life before Life,* she describes the results of her investigation of 750 subjects by hypnosis and regressing them to their existence before their birth. She states:

> My subjects were nearly unanimous in rejecting any purposes involving increase in wealth, status and power. Their responses indicate that at a subconscious level, the Golden Rule is the basic law of the universe.

21 Of which the butterfly emerging from its chrysalis is the symbol.

22 As Paul said: 'I die daily' *(1 Cor. 15:31).*

> But apparently this rule – that we should treat others as we would like to be treated – is "enforced" by reincarnation. We *will* be treated as we have treated others; we come back to experience being on the giving as well as receiving end. As soon as we finally learn the lesson that we are creating the realities around us – based on our expectations in this life and circumstances chosen by us to redress the wrongs we did in the past lives – then there is one more lesson to learn. All of us are part of one giant soul organism, all linked together at the higher levels. Jesus said, "What ye do for the least of them, you also do for me." And we are linked with Christ as we are linked with a prisoner in death row at San Quentin. We are one. This is the Higher Consciousness.[23]

She further states:

> In summary then, 87 percent of all my subjects reported being aware of how they had known important people in their current life from past lives. These relationships were quite varied. Most interesting was the fact that the relationships are not just from past lives, but from the state between lives. This was surprising to my subjects, as indeed it was surprising to me.
>
> My subjects all tell the same story. We come back with the same souls, but in different relationships. We live again not only with those we love, but with those we hate and fear. Only when we feel only compassion and affection are we freed from the need to live over and over with the same spirits, who are forced to live with us![24]

Dr. Wambach's statements can be compared to the information dictated by the Tibetan (D.K.) many years earlier, as compiled by A.A. Bailey (these writings are of the most esoteric nature extant in the West today). I will quote in part some statements from the book *Esoteric Healing*. D.K. states that 'immediately after death', the person 'is as much aware and alert to his environment as he was upon the physical plane', and that the 'first reactions and activities' of the average person are:

---

23 Helen Wambach, Ph.D., *Life before Life* (Bantam Books, 1981), 90-1.

24 Ibid., 97.

1. He becomes consciously aware of himself. This involves a clarity of perception unknown to the average man whilst in physical incarnation.
2. Time (being the succession of events as registered by the physical brain) is now nonexistent as we understand the term, and—as the man turns his attention to his more clearly defined emotional self— there ensues *invariably* a moment of direct soul contact. This is due to the fact that even in the case of the most ignorant and undeveloped man, the moment of complete restitution does not pass unnoticed by the soul. It has a definite soul effect, something like a long and strong pull at a bell rope, if I might use so simple a simile. For a brief second the soul responds, and the nature of the response is such that the man, standing in his astral body, or rather in his kama-manasic[25] vehicle, sees the experience of the past incarnation spread before him like a map. He records a sense of timelessness.
3. As a result of the recognition of these experiences, the man isolates those three which were the three major conditioning factors in the life which has gone and which also hold the keys to his future incarnation which he will next initiate. All else is forgotten, and all the lesser experiences fade out of his memory, leaving nothing in his consciousness but what are esoterically called "the three seeds or germs of the future". These three seeds are in a peculiar manner related to the permanent physical and astral atoms, and thus produce the fivefold force which will create the forms later to appear. It might be said that:

a. *Seed One* determines later the nature of the physical environment in which the returning man will find his place. It is related to the quality of that future environment and thus conditions the needed field or area of contact.

b. *Seed Two* determines the quality of the etheric body as a vehicle through which the ray forces can make contact with the dense physical body. It delimits the etheric structure or vital web along which the incoming energies will circulate and is related in particular to the special one of the seven centres which will be the most active and alive during the coming incarnation.

---

25 The desire-mind *(kāma-manas).*

c. *Seed Three* gives the key to the astral vehicle in which the man will be polarised in the next incarnation. Forget not, I am dealing here with the average man and not with the advanced human being, disciple or initiate. It is this seed which—through the forces it attracts—brings the man again into relation with those he previously loved or with whom he had close contact. It can be accepted as a fact that the group idea governs subjectively all incarnations, and that reincarnated man is brought into incarnation not only through his own desire for physical plane experience, but also under group impulse and in line with the group karma as well as with his own. This is a point which should receive emphasis. Once this is truly grasped and understood, a great deal of the fear engendered by the thought of death would disappear. The familiar and the loved will still remain the familiar and the loved, because the relation has been closely established over many incarnations...It will be apparent, therefore, how necessary it is to train children to recognise and profit by experience, for this, once learnt, will greatly facilitate this third activity upon the astral plane after death.

4. Having completed this "isolating of experience," the man will then seek and automatically find those whom the third seed influence indicates as possessing a constant part in the group experience of which he is an element, consciously or unconsciously. The relation once again established (if those sought have not yet eliminated the physical body), the man acts as he would on earth in the company of his intimates and according to his temperament and point in evolution. If those who are closest to him and whom he deeply loves or hates are still in physical incarnation, he will also seek them out and—just again as he did on earth—he will remain in their neighbourhood, aware of their activities, though (unless highly evolved) they will not be aware of his. I can give no detail as to reciprocal give and take or to the modes and methods of contact. Each person differs; each temperament is largely unique. I only seek to make clear certain basic lines of behaviour pursued by man prior to the act or acts of elimination.

These four activities cover varying periods of time—from the angle of "those who live below," though there is no time recognised on the part of the man on the astral plane. Gradually the lure and glamour (of a low or high order) wears off, and the man enters into the stage where he *knows*—because the mind is now more incisive and dominating—that he is ready for the second death and for the entire elimination of the kamic body or of the kama-manasic vehicle.

One of the things to remember here is that once restitution of the physical in its two aspects has taken place, the inner man is, as I have earlier said, fully conscious. The physical brain and the swirl of etheric forces (mostly somewhat disorganised in the case of the majority of men) are no longer present. These are the two factors which have led students to believe that the experiences of the man on the inner planes of the three worlds are those of a vague drifting, of a semi-conscious experience, or indicate a repetitive life, except in the case of very advanced people or disciples and initiates. But this is not the case. A man on the inner planes is not only as conscious of himself as an individual—with his own plans, life and affairs—as he was on the physical plane, but he is also conscious in the same manner of the surrounding states of consciousness. He may be glamoured by astral existence or subject to the telepathic impression of the varying thought currents emanating from the mental plane, but he is also conscious of himself and of his mind for of the measure of manasic life developed) in a far more potent manner than when he had to work through the medium of the physical brain, when the focus of his consciousness was that of the aspirant, but anchored in the brain. His experience is far richer and fuller than he ever knew when in incarnation. If you will think this out for a little, you will realise that this necessarily would be so.

It may therefore be assumed that the Art of Elimination is practised more definitely and more effectively than was the restitution of the physical vehicle. Another point must also be considered. On the inner side, men *know* that the Law of Rebirth governs the experience-process of physical plane living, and they realise then that, prior to the elimination of the kamic, kama-manasic or manasic bodies, they are only passing through an interlude between incarnations and that they consequently face two great experiences:

1. A moment (long or short, according to the attained point in evolution) wherein contact will be made with the soul or with the solar angel.

2. After that a contact, a relatively violent reorientation to earth life takes place, leading to what is called "the process of descent and calling," wherein the man[26]:

   a. Prepares for physical incarnation again.
   b. Sounds his own true note into the substance of the three worlds.
   c. Revitalises the permanent atoms, which form a triangle of force within the causal body.
   d. Gathers together the needed substance to form his future bodies of manifestation.
   e. Colours them with the qualities and characteristics he has already achieved through life-experience.
   f. On the etheric plane arranges the substance of his vital body so that the seven centres take shape and can become the recipients of the inner forces.
   g. Makes a deliberate choice of those who will provide him with the needed dense physical covering, and then awaits the moment of incarnation. Esoteric students would do well to remember that parents only donate the dense physical body. They contribute naught else save a body of a particular quality and nature which will provide the needed vehicle of contact with the environment demanded by the incarnating soul. They may also provide a measure of group relationship, where the soul experience is long and a true group relation has been established.[27]

The wealth of talents developed in former incarnations allows great artists, people of science and geniuses to be born. They often focalise or embody within themselves a keynote or the manifested quality of a Soul-group (which other members often learn to emulate). In any era, the combined activities of such Soul-groups shape civilisation, by characterising particular qualities and prevailing attributes. All of humanity progresses thereby. All qualities developed will evolve and then eventually die (or rather, be absorbed into the animating Life) once

---

26 By this time the consciousness will have merged with the Soul, which makes the needed decisions.

27 See Alice Bailey, *Esoteric Healing,* (Lucis Publishing Co., N.Y., 1971), 490-6.

utilised and the entities evolving them have achieved their purpose. This process continues from life to life, thus eventually the path of aspiration to Initiation into the mysteries of Being will be found and trod.

The power to vision

One can speculate that the interaction between all the Soul-groups within the planetary Logoi (Heavenly Men) throughout the aeonic history of our solar system have produced the quality of Life that embodies the Personality Nature of the 'God' that is our solar Logos. Since the consciousness aspect (the evolved quality of the form) reincarnates again and again by means of progressive incarnations, so it is possible to eventually expand consciousness sufficiently to embrace the Mind of 'God'.

An entity such as the Christ, Buddha, or any highly enlightened Being can know beforehand the probable destiny of the collective action of any group of people or civilisation in general. This may be understood by realising that before coming into incarnation each being composes a plan of what will be achieved while incarnate. The being responsible for the course of evolution (or the Soul) meditates and builds a thought-form (a picture in mental substance), a paradigm or *maṇḍala,* that will delineate the course of action of the incarnate personality. People are thus preconditioned to accomplish certain works. A being whose consciousness has embraced the entire group-Mind of the Soul-group must be able to see, or know, the combined picture forms of that group in its totality. Such a One can therefore predict with reasonable accuracy what the future is to be.

Karmic effects are built into the Thought-construct, which will condition the actions of the incarnation. Such constructs are however not inviolate, and personalities often create new karmic meanderings that will have to be rectified later. The Builder of the Plan will however have taken such possibilities into account. The formulation of a Logoic Thought-Form, which is embodied by an act of Will, causes the manifestation of phenomena, the appearance of the material universe, or a world-sphere. The planned evolutionary events of such forms can also go awry once human units that possess self-will come into existence and express their rights of self-determination.

The Christ embodies, or holds within His consciousness, the entire collective consciousness of all groups concerned with the (seven) departments of Life. He thus has clearly before Him the collective picture image of their course of action when they are to incarnate. Therefore, He also senses the most probable course of the civilisation which is to develop. He is thereby able to see with great accuracy far into the probable future. In effect, Christ can be considered the Group-Soul (or 'over-Soul') that embodies the collective-consciousness of the human kingdom, and of the angelic kingdom associated with them. His immediate disciples (the Masters of Wisdom) each embody a particular Soul-Group, and so forth.

It is possible for those that have evolved the necessary sensitivity, to be in tune with such group formulations, to a varying extent, depending upon their attained Initiation level. This realisation may then expand, until eventually the full 'Plan of God' is known. Seers, prophets, clairvoyants and Intuitives generally only cognise small fractions of the entire world-Plan of the future. Often their fragmentary visions are distorted and great care must therefore be taken in accepting any of them at face value.[28]

True visions nearly always concern the advancement of human consciousness in some way. They can thus be intuited accurately only by one dedicated to the welfare or proper education of humanity. Such visions are not the property of the personality, but of the Soul (or of That which the Soul veils). They may also come from members of the Hierarchy, or from the *devas* (the angelic kingdom). The Soul utilises the highly trained mental resources of a quiescent personality to impart the vision that is to affect others and inspire them in some way towards spiritual fulfilment.

---

28 The 'akashic records' that most seers, mediums, and clairvoyants contact is the astral plane reflection of the impression discernable from the higher mental plane. This is accordingly distorted by the state of agitation and colouring of the Waters (emotions, desires), both of the person's own astral body, and via the sub-plane of the astral from where such impressions are derived. They generally 'See' fleeting images through a veil of glamour, and their desire bodies often add the missing portions. We thus have the many erroneous pronouncements and cryptic impressions from such sources often published as 'revealed truths' from an enlightened one.

Far-reaching visions therefore always emanate from domains beyond the realm of the mind. This is needed if the vision is to be inclusive of an entire world picture, or to present accurate prescient prophesies. The necessary prerequisite is to be absorbed in a meditative state for the duration needed for the vision to manifest. It requires a tranquil 'moment', in which the essence of the entire sequence of events that caused a person's life purpose, or future events, can be seen in revelatory imagery.

A vision can slowly grow over time as the Seer becomes increasingly meditative. It does not require any particular yogic postures or austerities to be accomplished. The meditative Mind is slowly built by a life lived in an exemplary fashion and cannot in any way be forced. The vision (and enlightenment) is something that happens from above down, or from within-without. A person must therefore become completely passive, yet intensely aware, to allow the divinity that is to be expressed in a dynamically active fashion to become embodied in consciousness.

Visions often manifest (at first) as any number of infrequent or frequent (concurrent) flashes of intuition. They generally take the lifespan of the person concerned to develop. Many are incarnate that have visions to impart to humanity, and the entire sequence of their lives might revolve around the imparting of those visions. This can manifest as the inspired works of our greatest sages, saints, artists, scientists, legislators and reformers. Such people are often termed 'visionaries'. The more esoteric understanding possessed, the greater the faculty to truly vision. Visions can therefore only effectively manifest in one that has adequately built and stabilised the mental body and controlled the emotional nature. Also, it is facilitated for one who has attained conscious *buddhic* perception in a former life.

In the case of a 'trance medium' and some 'visionaries', the entire emotional and mental nature is held in abeyance in the hope that a highly evolved being can speak through that vehicle (such happenings are rarer than is normally supposed). Normally a dark brotherhood impersonator of a Master of Wisdom is contacted instead.[29]

A higher correspondence to the trance medium is the spiritual mediator, such as was Jesus. He mediated between the Christ and

---

29 See my book *The Constitution of Shambhala,* Part A, 330, 423-32 for further clarification on this subject.

humanity. Jesus, it is said, gave his threefold personality nature in its entirety for the use of the Christ for the three or so years of his ministry in Jerusalem, while consciously controlling and being aware of the entire process. This is not the case of the trance medium, who is normally unconscious during the process of mediumship. Note that there is a great difference between what is here termed a vision, a recollection, mediumship, or clairvoyant states.

The enormous range, context and depth of meaning of the types of vision accorded to such beings as the Christ (who was the mediator between His 'Father in Heaven' and the lesser kingdoms in Nature) is indicated to us in such works as the *Revelation of St. John*. (Which has never yet been adequately explained.)

Trite information concerning people's petty emotional affairs are of little concern for any enlightened source. It is easy to fool the gullible that are desirous for such information. Unless people are seriously working upon themselves for human betterment, or that they are highly evolved ones (Initiates) yet to awaken, there is little gain in feeding the ignorantly gullible with impressions they cannot understand. Nevertheless all people have the capacity to receive impressions, flashes of realisation that may help them out in some way.

Visionaries are intrinsically disciples of the Christ[30] and are able to help Him in His work. A portion of the Christ's Mind that is associated with their place in the scheme of things (as units pertaining to a unity) can then be made known to them.

The Buddhist concept of the 'three times' in one – the past, the present and the future that are instantaneously at one point of time in the eternal Now – comes as a consequence of this ability to vision the future. The actions, activities and happenings of the past producing the present moment lead on into the future, and yet the future is simply the present moment becoming the past. Reality, in many ways, is the past experiences (stored as memory and imagination) that are continually being utilised to experience the future. It is all happening in that eternal expanse of timelessness that is the Now. Seen here is that there is really no such thing as time, except in the minds of people, where it is reckoned as a distance or interval between two cycles of events.

---

30 As are all Initiates.

A person who is enlightened is fully aware of that eternal now. This includes causes and effects, of how the past has karmically manifested through the present to make the future – physically, subjectively, psychically and spiritually. Due to this, one is able to live fully in the present moment, thereby perfectly fulfilling their function for that cycle without being distracted in any way. Their mind is tranquil and serene, like a mirror. It perfectly reflects the Ineffable Mind (the future) into the corporeal world (the past) and adjusts the expression of the vision in such a way that it can benefit the members of that world (in the present).

The idea of the three times is indicated in *Ecclesiastes 3:15:* 'That which hath been' (the *karma* of the past) 'is now' (the cause of the present). 'That which is to be' (the future) 'hath already been' (as the Thought Form of 'God'), 'and God requireth that which is past'. The Creator, the Magician (be he 'God' or man), must mould past causes (the primeval substance) to manifest the present, and thus further the course of evolution.

The Seven Rays

All Soul-groups, and everything else in Nature, embody one or other of the seven Ray aspects of Deity. These are the subdivisions of the one fundamental Light that emanates from Shambhala. The Rays also relate to the seven planes of experience (dimensions of perception), the seven major psychic centres in the body, the seven principal planetary Regents, the 'seven Spirits' before the Throne of 'God',[31] and a host of other septenaries that abound in mythology and religious teachings.

Each of these seven major Ray groupings have seven associated sub-Rays, making 49 such groupings altogether. All of the Ray lines have obvious esoteric definitions, the explanations of which would cause us to digress too far here.[32] In my writings I enumerate the qualities of the seven major Rays thus:[33]

---

31 *Rev. 4:5.*

32 More knowledge can be gained by studying the writings of A.A. Bailey, specifically the books *Esoteric Psychology,* Volumes 1 and 2, and *The Rays and the Initiations.* Also my book *The Constitution of Shambhala,* 97-102 (and elsewhere) presents significant detail of these Rays, especially in relation to the Ray Ashrams.

33 D.K. generally denotes them as: Will or Power, Love-Wisdom, Activity, Harmony

Ray 1 of Will or Power.
Ray 2 of Love-Wisdom.
Ray 3 of Mathematically Exact Activity.
Ray 4 of Beautifying Harmony Overcoming Conflict.
Ray 5 of Scientific Reasoning.
Ray 6 of Devotion, Idealism.
Ray 7 of Ceremonial Cyclic Activity, Actualising Power.

Comprehending the science of the manifestation of the Rays lies at the heart of the esoteric doctrine. Their associated properties condition all things, manifest and subjective, hence the Rays must be a major theme of study for all who wish to become enlightened. It is no longer possible for those who wish to walk upon the enlightenment path to be ignorant of them. For this reason a thorough explanation of the Rays is incorporated in the seven volumes of my *A Treatise on Mind,* wherein I delve deeply upon the corpus of Buddhist ontological and eschatological doctrines.

Through Conflict, Concrete Science, Devotion, and Ritual or Ceremonial Magic. It is a little difficult to properly define the fifth Ray. Properly speaking it is the mode of application of the forces of the mind to segregate, classify and to build. D.K.'s depiction of the third Ray as 'Activity' relates to the activity of the empirical mind, whereas my rendering relates more to the Activity of the awakened Mind.

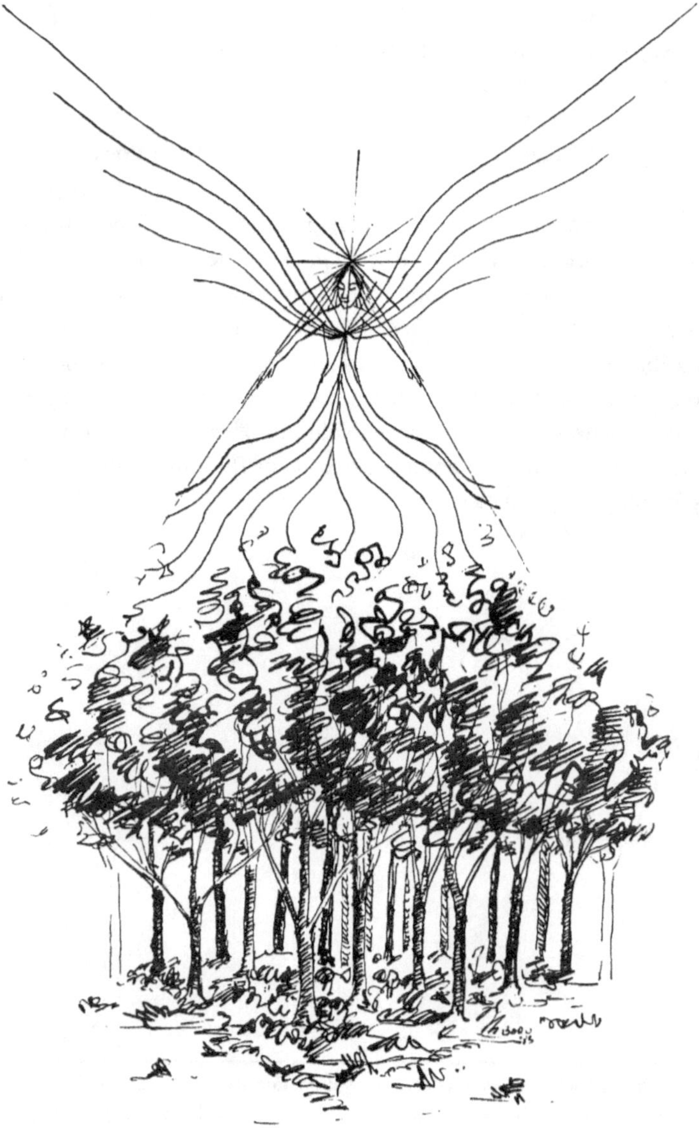

Wherever there is Life
there is Love,
and whoever Loves
need no longer hide
in his tears and fears,
for all such evaporates,
is washed away,
and is absorbed,
like the rain on the soft earth.
And whoever Loves
need no longer seek,
for the song of the chirping bird,
or for the forest brook,
or the ocean's waves,
for s/he shares forever
a moment of tranquil peace
that contains all sounds
and songs, far and near.
For Love's embrace
is Nature's ocean
that contains all things,
yet expands with
each passing day.

5

The Function of Life and the use of the Physiological Key

It has been postulated that as each entity cyclically incarnates into the physical realm, evolution continues through a process of assimilation, utilisation, and transmutation of experience. Moreover, the substance that composes the bodily sheaths is stimulated and made to evolve by this means. The entity is ultimately able to function as a conscious Deity, unhindered by any material limitation. It can also be postulated that though consciousness and matter seem distinctly different, they are directly interrelated in a synonymous evolutionary process. One is the vehicle for the evolution of the other. As such, because physical matter is also embodied Life, so it is Divine.

In totality, the evolutionary experience of the atoms of matter symbolically expresses the desire of the Mother for the birth of a Son. This is catalysed by the 'Will of the Father'. From the Womb of matter, the self-conscious human entity is born. Life is the potent germ of activity infused into matter (as a continuum of conscious expression) by the Will of Deity during 'His Hour of Creation'. It is sustained by the action of the Son through the assimilation of experience. All manifest life is in a constant state of activity. Activity causes change, and change causes further cycles of experience.

The Life principle manifests as an inherent (unconscious) Will, which scientists have termed instinct. Plants and animals utilise instinct to ensure their survival. Nature uses this tool in Her endeavours to perpetually transmute the various denizens of Her kingdoms into freer and more comprehensive beings that are more adaptable and better able to withstand ecological and environmental changes. The role of Nature is to maintain an ecological balance and harmonious cooperation between units, forming an omnipresent and autonomous whole, whilst allowing for evolutionary developments and other changes.

Having developed the intellect, humanity has transcended the instinctual stage (which is now innate within us). This explains our ability to radically alter or destroy the environmental harmony of the earth. These destructive actions are generally a by-product of human determination to seize the transitory. These are attempts to make objects, concepts, or phenomena permanent – by building concrete boxes and mental-emotional shells around them. The 'shells' that people build are based on fostered fears. Their fears are primarily enabled by the union of imagination with emotional reasoning faculties, motivated by social conditioning.

The fear of loss intensifies the human instinct of self-preservation. This provokes the formation of protective barriers of animosity against all that threaten self-made delusions. Based on these selfish mental attitudes, competitive or hostile behaviours often result. By so doing, people reap the karmic rewards of such actions and experience suffering. Nevertheless, even humanity's destructiveness is part of Nature's plan. Note that people are given the freedom to choose their own path to perfection (or to destruction) through the assimilative progression of experience.

In ignorantly forestalling or delaying evolutionary progress by massively raping Nature's resources (normally for selfish corporate gain) significant *karma* is produced by humanity. Such *karma* is seen as a destructive friction in the workings of the munificence of the great Mother. Metaphorically, friction produces heat, which manifests as pain between individuals, groups, nations, or the various kingdoms of Nature. Nature reacts with Her Laws; She reasserts Herself to replace the parts of Her body of manifestation that have become desecrated. These parts are oft closely interrelated with humanity. During the rectification of energetic imbalances in the earth, we thus experience many environmental catastrophes. By reacting rightly to these catastrophes, we can eventually learn to prevent them by tearing down the separative walls and barriers built of selfish and avaricious motivations and thought tendencies.

Thoughts, energy, intelligence and will

The idea that substance can be influenced by human thoughts is no longer unique to esotericists and *yogins*; it is beginning to be echoed by the findings of modern physicists. Arguments to this effect are well formulated in many books. They need not be recapitulated here. Michael Talbot, for instance states, with reference to Eugene Wigner, a physicist with the Nobel Prize to his credit:

> According to Wigner, all that quantum mechanics purports to provide is probability connections between subsequent apperceptions of the consciousness. He asserts that it is impossible to give a description of quantum mechanical processes without "explicit reference to consciousness." (86) In the dilemma of Shrödinger's cat it is the consciousness of the observer that intervenes and triggers which of the possible outcomes is observed. Wigner also suggests that search be made for other effects that consciousness may have upon matter.[1]

What must be emphasised is that since consciousness has an effect upon matter, then the sum of all human thoughts obviously must have ramifications. Thought is an expression of energy. Massed thoughts and emotions will therefore have vast effects upon the sea of energy and substance interrelationships forming the biosphere we live in. These thought-forms may be seen as energy fields of different colourings and potencies that have potent subjective effects upon Nature. The most obvious effects from the direction of such energies can be perceived in

---

1 Michael Talbot, *Mysticism and the New Physics,* (Routledge & Kegan Paul, London, 1981), 34. My book *Esoteric Cosmology and Modern Physics* explores the relation of consciousness (mind/Mind) to the appearance of phenomena of all types in great detail, including the process that is productive of world-formation, or even that of a cosmos.

all physical aspects of our civilisation. These effects are well studied by scientific investigators, yet the majority of the subjective effects remain a mystery to them. Research in this area will represent a fertile bed of hitherto undreamed-of possibilities for new discovery.

Research on the karmic implications of all sorts of action-reactions between humans will include many advances. For instance, breakthroughs in the understanding of the nature of collective expressions of thought, the associated emotional energies that produce all types of sicknesses and diseases in our societies, and the origins for other catastrophes in Nature. Such investigations will lead to a greater understanding of the true nature and function of Life. They will also inevitably produce revelations concerning the nature of the etheric body and the *chakras,* as well as the functions of the *deva* kingdom.

It should be apparent that all lesser species of Life are evolving aspects of consciousness, precursors to the intelligence that humanity is endowed with. This is especially notable when observing the qualities of our domesticated animals. Intelligence must therefore be inherent in all manifest life, its functions being a primary impetus underlying the evolutionary urge. Intelligence begets intelligence, as it acts upon substance that is mindless yet malleable and impregnable. This works through ordered self-replenishing cycles of ever-increasing momentum. Eventually, the needed qualities become so thoroughly imbued into the substance that it becomes a bearer of intelligent capacity as 'a free will', which is both self-contained and self-motivated.

The intelligence that acts upon substance is a reflection of the Logoic Mind, which causes and underlies all manifest things. This Mind is embodied subjectively within Forms that manifest as agents of active Intelligent Will: the Will-to-Be, the Will-to-Create, the Will-to-Sustain and the Will-to-Destroy. The agents that can be considered units of Logoic Intelligence are the *devas* (the angelic kingdom). They embody the sum total of Nature, from the greatest to the smallest atomic form. From them, therefore, come the physical laws known to science, of gravity, of attraction and repulsion that all forms are subject to. Lesser Elementary evolved streams of Life react to the Will of the greater Lives by responding to the emanations of Sound, according to their varying capacities. These Elementals are esoterically called 'the army of the

Voice', because they listen to and then retransmit or resonate the Sound frequencies in diminishing levels of energy expression according to their capacity to do so.

The attributes of the triune Logos (Father-Son-Mother) are abstracted upon the three highest realms of perception. From there Divine Will manifests on all other realms via the mediating Creative Hierarchies that disseminate Logoic Intelligence and Love. The Hierarchy of Love and Light on earth is one such agency. These Creative Hierarchies qualify Divine Will, to the degree that the laws and attributes of the planes of perception whereon they are polarised limit their expression. On the lowest plane (the dense physical realm), Divine Will generates the force of the instinct that governs the kingdoms of Nature. The sum of various instincts (of which there are five[2]) becomes translated into the intellect derived from the five sense-consciousness possessed by a human kingdom.

The intellect (often coupled with desire) is the personal will of a human unit that directs the five senses. When the intellect is directed downwards to analyse the material world then empirical science is the result. When the intellect is used as an organ of the will to master the sense-consciousnesses then supersensory perception can be developed. When that will is used to intensify selfish or separative self-focussed motives and ambitions to dominate, then a black magician is the result. If the will is used as an aid to master *saṃsāra* by developing higher awareness through compassionate undertakings, then enlightenment is the gain. Focus must also be upon what lies behind and sustains the form – the cause of all being. Once the intellect becomes sublimated, transformed into the abstract Mind, one becomes intuitive and resides in the world of enlightened Being. The empowerment of Divine Will then becomes the onus of attention.

Those that have evolved intelligence normally act as *unconscious* mediators between Divine Will and the lesser streams of Life. Those that have transcended the intelligent stage do so *consciously*. The conditionings inherent within an intelligent being's thought sphere allow modifications of the originating Creative Impulse of Deity. In contrast,

---

2 They are the instinct of self-preservation, the sexual instinct, the instinct towards knowledge, group or herd instinct, and the instinct of self-assertion.

lesser Life forms respond to such qualifications without modifying them in any way. They are automatically conditioned thereby.

The self-conscious stage is thus effectively the most important in the entire milieu of Being. Evolution is either proceeding to, or evolving from self-consciousness. This is the stage that allows one to stand within one's own innate resources, to determine one's own course of actions, and to walk either the 'left hand' (black magic) or the 'right hand' (the way of Love-Wisdom) path.

The Will-to-Be of Deity expresses itself as:

- *Intuition* – in the supra-human kingdoms.
- *Intelligence* – expressed by the human kingdom.
- *Instinct* – the sub-human kingdoms.

Life manifests by means of a corporeal body. There is, however, a difference in the quality of life between a person and a lump of clay, although even clay is 'alive' at its own level of perception. Life is the cause of physical manifestation and its laws, and thus is not subject to them, except when incarnate. Whilst the quality termed 'Life' is there, the physical body and related (human) mental-emotional states function instinctively. For Life is what coherently integrates its various sub-components, using the aggregate for a purpose greater than what is possible through separate parts.[3]

When something happens to impair or prevent the body's functioning – such as the destruction of a vital organ – then the will to live disappears (subconsciously, if not consciously). Disharmony between all organs of the body results, spelling the eventual death of all the organs and cells in the body. First, Life abstracts itself from the body as a unit (the being dies). This then occurs for all the cells in turn, and so they die. Finally, all the little Elemental Lives scatter and diffuse into the ether. After it has discarded the physical form that no longer serves a functional purpose, the abstracted Life finds itself occupying the etheric construct upon which the dense physical is based. (To which it also must inevitably die.)

---

3 The physical form may be considered as something tangible, like a human body; loosely structured, as in the case of a hive of bees; or intangible, such as the forms of the angelic kingdom.

All forms could not exist unless controlled by some type of intelligence, for 'coherent integration' is a function of intelligence. Inanimate matter is organised according to laws that are but expressions of the natural functioning of a meditative Mind. Such a Mind imbues its life force into each atomic unit that it galvanises into its corporeal form. That Mind then attracts to the form the necessary flavourings and colourings of energy that allow its manifest purpose to be expressed. The manifestation of such energy, as directed by Mind, then governs the activities of the manifest form. On the grossest sphere, these colourings then become crystallised units of embodied force (called atoms) that are comprehensively governed by the Will of That Mind. Such a Mind can be that of a human Soul, or of a Logos.

Atoms are the base 'lives' moulded into the corporeal forms of all sentient beings, yet they qualify that sentience according to their own inherent characteristics (e.g., as chemicals in the effect of drugs). In the form of large groups of units they are able to influence or modify the evolving sentience of an incarnate life. However, the characteristics of those groups of atoms are in their turn modified by intelligent Life, by mind/Mind in one form or other. Intelligence conveys the Fiery energies that condition or create the appearance of things in accordance with the Will projecting a thought onwards into space-time. If directed downwards into the domains of form, the Will gathers to it congealing Watery substance that precipitates what must be into the domains of material space. This thought-construct has a planned existence for a duration of time, thereby allowing the atomic units that have been built into the construct to gain evolutionary traits. They are embodied by the 'Life' of the directing Will, after which a point of deconstruction occurs – once the purpose of the thought-construct has been achieved.

The angelic *(deva)* kingdom

All is imbued with the Life of 'God', and all Lives and forms are an expression of this Life. Although each atomic life must possess its own inherent 'will' (a directive rhythm, motion or purpose for existence) each atomic will would be conditioned by, or be subordinate to, a collective Will (or Law). Such a Will is viewed as a collective group-Soul (or group-Mind) that is an embodied Life responsible for the collective action of a large group of atoms, and the relations between that group and other similar groups. Group-Souls become mediators between the Intelligent directive Source (ultimately the Mind of a Logos) and the individual atom.[4] They convert intensified energies into what can be utilised by the atoms. As they evolve closer to the originating Logoic Mind they bear greater comprehension of the nature of the building of Thought Constructs. Because the attributes of Mind are inherent throughout manifestation, so sentient atomic lives thereby eventually evolve intelligence.

Such group-Souls (Intelligences), as agents in the Mind of 'God', are commonly called angels *(devas* in the Sanskrit terminology). Substance, such as that which composes the mineral kingdom (e.g., the human body), etheric, astral or mental substance, is therefore but angelic, *deva* lives.[5] Working as aspects of the form of Mother Nature the *devas* evolve the Lives (involving various planes of perception) that eventually become the animals wherein the Fires of the substance of mind *(citta)* can coalesce to form a rudimentary intelligence. Such is technically the beginning of their work, for they also evolve – to eventually become a world Mother, producing (embodying) every form of a world-sphere such as the earth, and so on to eventually form a galactic sphere, etc.

The sex interplay between positive and negative forms or ions (valency) is an expression of atomic 'will'. Similarly, male and female energies, as well as the expression of instinct, are possible through individual atomic responses to the collective-consciousness of a group-Soul. For instance, an oxygen atom subordinated to a 'group-Soul' means that the experiences of that particular atom would be collectively incorporated with all oxygen atoms. Thus, all experiences from each atom add weight to the total experiences of its group-Soul and are conditioned by the subjective laws governing that Soul.

---

4 As stated above, the atoms are but embodied Elemental Lives.

5 *Deva,* meaning 'shining one', is the general term for the celestial beings of the heavenly worlds in Hindu and Buddhist philosophy. The derivation is from the Sanskrit roots *dā,* 'making gifts' (as a god does), *dip,* being radiant, and *dyut,* the sphere of heaven. The members of the angelic kingdom, such as fairies, nature spirits, Seraphim, undines, *ghandaravas*, *apsaras*, and *ḍākinīs*, are the feminine counterpart to the human kingdom.

If the inner life of an atom were removed (such as by a nuclear reaction) then it would no longer function as part of the group-Soul, thus the atom would cease to exist. As the ladder of evolution is ascended, a group-Soul becomes more condensed and complex. It involves an increasingly smaller number of members (correspondingly, each individual member is more complex and more responsive to the environment). Eventually, a group-Soul individualises into a single self-conscious entity[6] with many lesser entities subordinate to it.

As an example, there might be a particular group-Soul *(deva)* controlling the growth and experience of a particular species of tree. Subordinate to it might be a lesser hierarchy of *devas* controlling a single tree (called Dryads in the Greek mythology). They would thus be included within the consciousness of the greater angelic entity. Similarly, nature spirits (fairies, etc.,) may embody each individual flower, or lesser species of the plant kingdom. On a tiny scale, there are even Elementary Lives that control the actions of cells and atoms. Each individual entity works harmoniously for the well being of the tree. Each tree abides by the same principles, under the auspicious care of a higher *deva* who ascribes to a landscape *deva* containing vast energies and scope of visioning, and so forth. Herein lies the basis for the conception of such mythological figures as Pan, the Lord of Nature, presiding over all the *devas* and nature spirits within the mineral, plant, and animal kingdoms.

The collective consciousness of domesticated animals that directly interrelate with humanity, such as cats, will be limited to very few entities. This is because their proximity to humans concentrates their rate of assimilation and utilisation of experiences. This process is much faster, and of a wider scale, than for example, a gazelle. Note that entities belonging to a group-Soul may be physically incarnate (such as cats), while the entities of another group-Soul (such as the fairies) are not. All, however, will live out their lives and undergo experiences that are conducive to their particular evolutionary impetus.

Angels *(devas)* are intelligences clothed in robes of matter of a greatly refined and subtle quality. They resonate at a far higher frequency than gross three-dimensional matter. They are thus imperceptible to

6 Such can be considered an Individualised human Soul, but here the teaching directly relates to the nature of the evolution of the angelic kingdom.

our senses. All Life is permeated with the Mind of 'God', which, as substance, is angelic.

As a collective unit, the angelic kingdom is the great Mother. They are the nurturing entities that are actively intelligent and whose purpose is to produce the forms through which consciousness can evolve. They are concerned with the appearance of the 'Son' in time and space through the forms that they build with the substance of their bodies. The 'Son' is essentially a human kingdom, which is the parallel stream of evolution to the angelic. We occupy the same time and space as them, but manifest different qualities.

All of the planes of perception are thus spheres of sensation embodied by great angelic Beings.[7] All entities find homes and build their environment within the spheres of influence of these Beings (by utilising the substance of their forms). This environment creates the outer boundaries of the world in which the entities live and move and have their being. For humanity, this 'outer boundary' is the dense material world that people live in, plus the boundaries of our inspirational, thought and emotional lives.

The vehicles that people inhabit when coming into incarnation are thus appropriated from the angelic kingdom and are therefore an integral part of their forms. This is how *karma* manifests with the exactitude that it does. There are myriads of interrelated angelic units that channel karmic impulses, or energies, from Causative Sources to the lesser entities (the 'army of the voice') that they embody, and who constitute the sum of manifest space. This makes a vast ocean of interlocking energies, allowing the most intricate weaving of intelligently directed karmic impulses. All entities that have energetic interrelations with other entities are largely impelled by eddies in this ocean.

---

7 This concept is elaborated in detail in my book *The Constitution of Shambhala, 7B,* where I state on page 3, for instance: 'The substance of each of the planes of perception is presided over by a great Deva Lord. Here we must view them as agents of *karma,* for the substance of the planes is the effect of the weaving together of karmic streams of force. Such *karma* emanates from and resolves into the *ātmic* plane. It is the plane of the Third Logos, the great Mother, the feminine aspect of Deity, as are the *devas.* This plane is ruled directly by that Great Deva Lord we term the Mother of the World. She is the Great presiding Mother of all, for from Her 'Womb' all that we know of and have come to view as 'real' has come to be'.

Those beings that are self-willed can produce actions contrary to the general flow. Such ego-based activities produce instantaneous chains of interactions in the ocean, which eventually reach angelic karmic adjudicators. They note the effects of the newly formed eddies, and their relation to the overall Plan, then instantly manifest action that will rectify the imbalances. This adjusts the expression of energy in such a way that karmic law and the Plan of 'God' are fulfilled. (There is a truism in the Christian belief that each of us has a *deva* complement, the 'guardian angel'. They evolve with their respective human unit.) Lesser *devas* adjust the *karma* that is affected by conscious units on the terrestrial sphere and by the subhuman kingdoms in Nature. The greater angelic Entities (Archangels, Cherubim, Seraphim etc.) have travelled further along the evolutionary path than humanity at present. Therefore, these Entities are responsible for the direction of karmic streams that emanate from the joint actions of large groups of beings. This will often involve immense durations of time.

The interlocking, interdependent hierarchical chain of intelligent and supra-intelligent angelic Lives progresses upwards to increasingly subtle realms of perception. It progressively encompasses greater expanses of Being (Space) till the total multidimensional cosmos is included as part of a Causative Law – far beyond the speculative ken of anyone incarnate on the earth. (Which is a relative dust speck in the universe.) The Thought-Form of what constitutes Life and the nature of the Lives contained within the solar system alone is in fact well nigh staggering to any mind that would try to comprehend it.

The great angelic Beings that clothe the causative Thought-Forms that emanate from the Mind of 'God' to embody manifest space (the various realms of perception) are thus denoted as *Lords of karma*.[8] On a lesser scale, elementary Fires clothe the thought-forms that emanate from the human mind. Thus, as stated, the angelic kingdom embody and empower the objective Activity and functioning of Logoic Thoughts. All the autonomic, integrated qualities and workings of the organism

8 The Lords of *karma* are titled Lipika Lords. They adjudicate the sum of the *karma* of humanity, for every Life is integrated as part of cosmic Law, for all are but one interlocking system. The lords of evil also have their place and will be relegated to their right zone of destination, or to the eighth sphere.

in that Body thereby manifest appropriately. This ensures that the Logoic Body of Manifestation is sustained and adequately nourished. The angelic kingdom therefore allow the indwelling Thinker to pursue His Meditative activities, freed from concern for the maintenance of the functioning of various parts of the Thought Construct.

Esoteric physiology

The angelic kingdom embodies the functions of the *involuntary nervous system* within the Body of 'God', which regulates such analogous functions as the rhythmic beating of the heart and the workings of the digestive system. The internal regulatory maintenance of the body is seen effectively as karmic adjustment (just as, on a small scale, there is internal monitoring of our human bodies to ensure well-being and to rectify the imbalances). When one is in tune with this regulatory maintenance then good health (expressed as joy, harmony and radiance) is the natural karmic reward of right action. Action produces reaction both in our system and in Nature.

The human kingdom, i.e., the Hierarchy of Light and Love, embodies the coordinated activity of the entire Body of 'God' – *the voluntary nervous system,* governing the manifest Purpose of that Incarnation (or to pursue those qualities which are being evolved). They embody the functions of consciousness – experience directed by the brain and the cerebrospinal system. The mental-emotional qualities of humanity also produce the secretions of the endocrine glands, hence the hormones that are carried by the circulatory system. We express the quality of the conscious response of Deity, while the angelic kingdom are the field through which such responses must manifest. The *devas* thus govern the factors which carry the quality of conscious response, allowing it to function as it does.

We see here another reason why the angelic kingdom represents the Great Mother, as they are fully responsible for the early evolutionary journeying until self-consciousness evolves. After this the kingdom of 'God' (Shambhala) establishes itself on earth, to help regulate the process of the evolution of humanity. Nevertheless, the consciousness-principle (human Souls) incarnate into substance appropriated from the *devas*. The *devas* therefore embody the substance of the three-fold personality that a human unit 'borrows' from them for each incarnation in order to gain the experiences that consciousness needs so as to evolve.

The involuntary nervous system manifests in three divisions: the sympathetic, parasympathetic and the enteric (gastrointestinal) nervous systems. Similarly there are three classes of *devas* that embody the substance of the three worlds of human evolution (mental, emotional and physical). The *devas* that govern the Fiery mental domain are the Agnishvattas, those that govern the Watery (emotional) domain are the Agnisuryans, and those that govern the Earthy physical domain are the Agnichaitans.[9]

The sympathetic nervous system prepares the body for the thinking process and physical plane activity, as well as regulating the heartbeat so that the principle of Life can manifest, assisted by the action of the lungs in breathing. This system also governs the response mechanism of an animal, such as whether to fight or run, with respect to a perceived danger. These functions are an analogue to the effect of the activity in Nature of the Agnishvattas. They work from the mental plane, from which they embody the evolution of the attributes of mind in Nature. Consequently, they are the hidden architects for the development of the five instincts (explained in the next chapter) that form the basis for the human sense-consciousnesses.

The parasympathetic nervous system is responsible for bodily functions when we are at rest. It stimulates digestion, activates various metabolic processes and helps us to relax, especially after eating. Sexual arousal, tears, urination, digestion and elimination of bodily wastes are also controlled by this system. All of these functions are the analogues to the effect of the activity in Nature of the Agnisuryans that embody its Watery disposition.

Finally, the enteric (gastrointestinal) nervous system largely regulates the movement of the bowels as a consequence of digestion, allowing the elimination of waste products. Such 'products' esoterically represent the physical domain whereon we manifest our conscious activities. This entire activity in Nature governing the appearance and functions of physical plane phenomena is ruled by the Agnichaitans.

---

9 I shall not delve into the detail of these categories of *devas* here. Those who wish to pursue the subject in depth need to consult Alice Bailey's *A Treatise on Cosmic Fire* (Lucis Publishing Co., N.Y.), or my book *The Constitution of Shambhala*, volume 7B.

The objective of the functioning of the Body of 'God' is to facilitate the manifestation and evolution of a human kingdom. Via the development of mind/Mind humanity can control all aspects of the three-fold form. The analogue is that the autonomous nervous system will eventually take control of all 'bodily functions' in Nature, apart from those that are rhythmically self-regulating.

Humanity (the Son, the repository of future glory) will properly begin its dominance of the planet, subjectively as well as objectively, through overcoming the attributes of desire, selfishness and the personal will. Taking their place will be loving-kindness, wisdom and the manifestation of the Divine Will. The bridge thereto will at first be the development of impeccable rational thinking.

There are points in the evolutionary journey where human and angelic evolutionary streams touch. They then merge and fuse their qualities, becoming as One, thus signifying the nature of the Divine Marriage in the Heavens.[10] This represents the consummation of one cycle of evolutionary attainment before a new higher cycle is begun. The human kingdom is masculine, dominant in quality (or will evolve thus), whilst the angelic kingdom is feminine and receptive.

The human kingdom evolves by expansion of consciousness, from a point (the 'ego') to embrace the totality of space. Conversely, the angelic kingdom evolves by lessening the sphere of contact – a consolidation of resources, by focussing energies from the pervasive (sphere) to a point of intensified energy. While humanity learn to command substance (by the use of the Will), the *devas* learn to acquiesce to the Word. Humanity sees colour and hears sound, while *devas* see sound and hear colour.

While Love is innate in humanity (viewed as the kingdom of Souls), Intelligence is innate in the angelic kingdom. Clearly, both humanity and *deva* complement each other's evolution. In a mutual evolutionary embrace (yin-yang), both learn to interrelate with the other's qualities. From this, Love-Wisdom is the gain. Love-Wisdom produces the orderly merging and blending of all qualities that facilitate one's Initiation into

---

10 The points of interrelation of this marriage and eventual consummation concern the path of Initiation, from the second to the fourth Initiation. At the sixth Initiation there is a complete fusion of *deva* and human elements into a non-dual bliss, and thus a Chohan (a sixth degree Initiate), veritably a Buddha, evolves from out of both kingdoms. The mysteries of Monadic evolution are veiled here.

the Mysteries of Being. When taking the devas into account one can see that the abundance of Life is far greater than has ever been imagined by the wildest speculations of the average philosopher or science fiction writer. Life's mysteries can however be wrought by all who are willing to undertake the necessary journeying into consciousness.

The physiological key[11]

For insight into the nature of Life and the relation between 'God' and humanity (or the other kingdoms of Nature) *the physiological key* is virtually indispensable. This is a major postulate by which the complete understanding of all relationships can be derived.

A cell is a unified, coherent, functioning entity composed of many diverse parts. So too, an organ constitutes a large number of cells with specialised qualities and diverse functions that are found together in the body of a person. The totality of many organs providing a multiplicity of functions, and working rhythmically and harmoniously, is what constitutes the physical form of a person. If the analogy is extended, we can describe a person (personality-Soul-Spirit) as a cell (or atom) in the Body of a sensed but unseen greater Entity, such as is described as 'God' in various religions. Rephrasing the concept: 'God' has within His constitution a large number of self-conscious units ('cells') all interrelated in some way to form a coherent unity.

From this postulate of interrelationships it can be observed that there are unseen messengers (hormones), channels of supply and elimination (blood vessels), and cellular communications (nerves) between the various organs in the body of a person. Similarly, there are also correspondences within the body of 'God', as channels and mediators of energy flow and utilisation. These can be divided into three categories:

1. The Earthly dense material world – the Flesh and Bones of That Body.
2. The Watery world – the Circulatory and Digestive Systems.
3. The Airy and Fiery worlds – the Breathing and Thinking mechanism.

---

11 The information presented here was also published in a more condensed version in my book *Esoteric Cosmology and Modern Physics,* 84-94, in the chapter entitled 'The Question of 'God' and the Physiological Key'.

The above tabulation shall be explained below.

1. In the Earthy world

The 'Flesh and Bones' of the Logoic Body can be seen and touched, forming the body of action – the corporeal form of both a person and 'God'. When considering 'God' one must think in terms of transmuted correspondences, where, to a planetary Logos, the corporeal form represents the realms of *saṃsāra* (our mental, astral and physical planes). The physical body provides our consciousness the ability to gain experiences via contact with the external environment, and to make and manipulate things.

There are *seven main analogies,* or parallelisms, between the observable dense physical universe (the solar system) and human physiology that can be noted.

1. The physical sun is the dense heart of the solar system, to which there is an approximate twenty-two year cycle of sunspot activity (areas with intense magnetic fields). Sunspots increase in frequency over a roughly eleven-year cycle, and then diminish. Often accompanying them are solar prominences, which discharge an immense amount of energy to the solar system. They can seriously disrupt humanity's communication systems. This activity is analogous to the cyclic coursing of blood (or rather, *prāṇa* coursing through the *nāḍīs)* through our veins, which conveys nutrients to all parts of our bodies.
2. The solar system travels on an interstellar path and is influenced by the motions of other stars and constellations. It thus responds to external stimuli (just as humans travel on their paths in life and are influenced by their friends). Such stimuli have a profound effect upon the Logos incarnate as the solar system. This is similar (though in vastly transmuted levels of correspondence) to the way that emotions, moods and mental impulses of our friends influence us. The entire science of astrology, esoterically considered, was founded by ancient humanity to analyse the effects of such influences, and those from the planetary Regents. Astrology endeavours to prognosticate future events by understanding the nature of energy qualifications from celestial sources. Sidereal astrology is specifically concerned with how these influences condition our civilisation and the related environments.

3. The solar system also breathes. It expands and contracts, depending upon whether the planets are in aphelion (the point furthest from the sun in the orbit of a planet) or perihelion (the closest point to the sun). In a similar manner, the chest cavity of a person expands and contracts as one breathes in and out. Our entire life can also be viewed in terms of expansions and contractions as we undertake a course of actions that provide a set of experiences (an expansion). The contractions of those actions then manifest as the experiences serve their purposes, and so forth.
4. The solar system was born, it undertakes many evolutionary stages, and shall eventually die (as also does a person). By a similar means both entities gather the experiences or qualities they need to further their evolutionary progress. (The sun does this during its interstellar journey by absorbing stellar energies from those cosmic Entities with which it has relationships. The solar Logos also works out His quota of cosmic *karma* through the evolutionary unfoldment of the Lives manifesting within His form.)
5. One can look to the fact that when all aspects of phenomena are observed, a nucleus or centre of life can be seen that coheres or holds around it a number of lesser entities that act as 'electrons' to it. That nucleus may also be considered an 'electron' orbiting the nucleus of the greater Life of which it is a part. It is seen, for instance, that:
   - Every atom has a nucleus (the positive centre) and surrounding electrons (the negative particles) that are not inseparably bound to the centre.
   - Every cell has a nucleus and surrounding protoplasm.
   - The solar system has a nucleus (the sun) and surrounding planets ('electrons').
   - Every personality gravitates around a central nucleus, such as their home circle, social group, professional or business group, ideological or religious faction. The group holds their focus of attention as their central sun (the source of their emotional, idealistic and/or mental life). There is a life span for the purpose of that group centre, and when that purpose no longer exists another group centre may be found. This corresponds to the rebirthing

process, which changes a Soul's focal point from life to life. A person also manifests in a similar fashion:

- For a mentally polarised person, the head (thinking process) is the positive nucleus and the body constitutes the 'negative particles'.
- For a purely sensual person, the desire body and organs of reproduction form the positive nucleus. Everything else is subsidiary, the 'negative particles'.
- For an emotionally polarised person the Solar Plexus centre region is positive and the thinking process is subsidiary.
- For a spiritual being the Heart centre is positive in orientation and everything else is subsidiary.
- For an Initiate, the higher Self or Soul is the positive centre and the sum of the three-fold personality represents the 'negative particles'.

6. Each atom, or unit of life, is basically spherical, or else evolves towards a spherical or ovoid shape. However, the human body can also be likened to a pentagram.

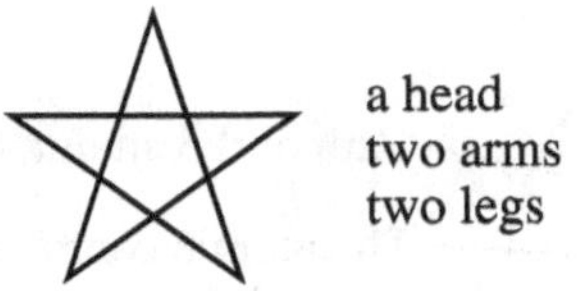

Figure 3: The pentagram

Nevertheless we have, as the seat of that principle which distinguishes us from animals, a head that is spherical in shape. The start of all life is a cell, and the ultimate form is spheroid in shape – the Soul of a person.[12]

Most ancient religions had a symbol for the sun to signify the supreme Deity: ⊙. This symbol can also be interpreted in terms of the figure below.

12 The qualities of the Soul (Causal Body, the Sambhogakāya Flower) are explained in volume three of my *A Treatise on Mind* series, as well as in my book *Esoteric Cosmology and Modern Physics*. See also Alice Bailey's *A Treatise on Cosmic Fire*.

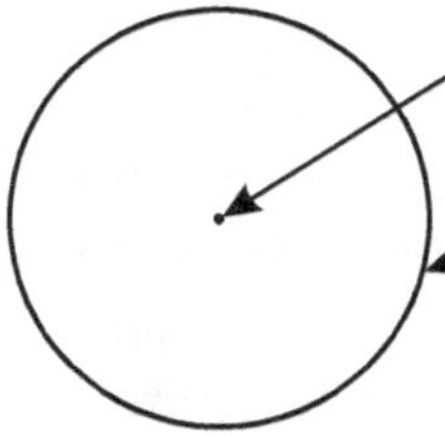

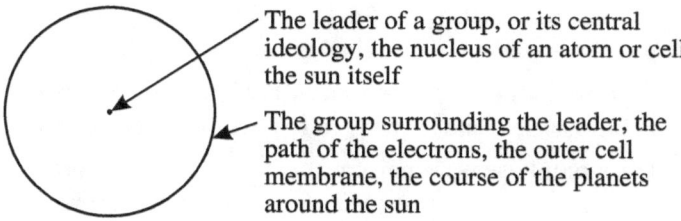

Figure 4: A group centre

7. Ultimately, form is transcended. Formlessness, the energy at the heart of every atom or sun is released – freed from bondage. The atom becomes radioactive and disintegrates. A sun often becomes a nova, and this is also the eventual destiny of the Soul.

At present, people largely limit or confine themselves to certain forms that relate to the experience of living in their thought processes: the use of words, circumscribed ideas, ideals, and picture symbols ('bits of information'). This can be symbolised as in figure five:

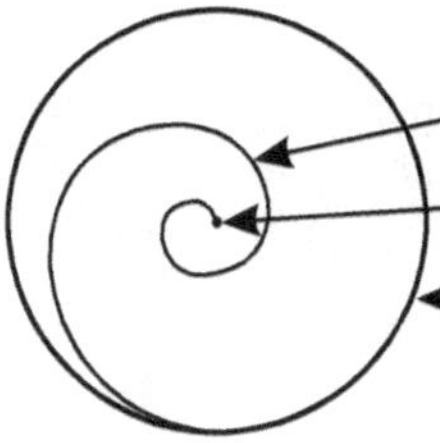

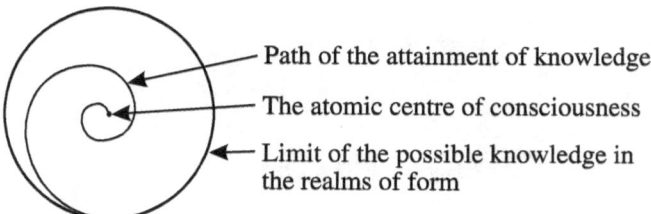

Figure 5: Self-conscious (self-centred) individual

Those upon the path to enlightenment work to transcend the need for thought processes to think with. The universality associated with *dharmakāya* (the Mind of 'God') is their goal, and gaining abstract 'thoughtless thought' *(śūnyatā,* which is void of thoughts of 'self', or any other empirical mental activity) is the means to its attainment.

Enlightenment can be likened to an atomic explosion in the realms of consciousness, although it is perfectly controlled and slowly brought to the critical stage. The mind is then no longer self-centred. It is focussed upon the greater whole – the infinite multi-dimensional universe, the symbol of which is a boundless and therefore formless 'sphere'. This somewhat paradoxical symbol imparts a notion of the nature of the enlightened Mind.

Humanity has evolved the capacity to reason and think. They must now progress to the stage of evolution where such ability becomes instinctive, or 'below the threshold of consciousness'. The entire Life process should be viewed in terms of relationships, seen from the angle of the viewer and the relation to the object of perception. However, far vaster perspectives can also be contemplated. Just as the consciousness of a person is ineffable and 'boundless' as related to that of an animal, so the Consciousness of 'God' (or the higher forms of Life) is seemingly ineffable, boundless, or formless, when related to that of a person. The enlightened Mind relates the one to the other.

The greater Mind is always inclusive of a lesser mind, which can therefore be viewed as part of its constitution. Although states of consciousness may be ineffable to the sentience below it, all are bound by form. Such manifests both as a sphere of contact and a means of expansion (that is limited by natural or self-made laws), for all spheres have an objective purpose.

The entire universe that our minds can cognise has been said to be the result, and the unfolding of, the Thought process of the One in Whom we 'live, and move, and have our being'.[13] This concept can be extended to the ONE in which That Great Entity lives and moves and has Its Being. The nature of the embrace of the Mind of 'God' cannot however really be understood. We can only think of 'limited infinities', or a series of successive greater embodiments of lesser units of consciousness.

Deity can therefore also be defined as that Life or Mind that embodies and abstracts the collective consciousness of all lesser unities, by including them in Its sphere of activity as Its subtle, psychic, and gross constitution. These parallelisms in life are generalised and not necessarily true in detail, nevertheless, the same general principles and laws govern the evolution of all forms of Life. This can be understood by acknowledging that every atom or form has latent sentience and is evolving towards consciousness, which then evolves beyond the human stage.

---

13 *Acts 17:28.*

2. In the Watery world

The Watery world is generally only seen objectively (outside of the system) in the form of excretion. (The precipitation that has caused the formation of our rivers, lakes and oceans.) Psychologically, its effects are principally experienced as emotions, feelings, pain and sentimental warmth. The circulatory and digestive processes are what provides Life and sustains our being. In many ways this is an expression of the 'Desire of God'. This Desire caused the manifestation of physical plane phenomena, and will also cause its cessation. Manifestation incorporates the cycles of experiences and assimilation (digestion) of those experiences, eventually leading to spiritual fulfilment.

It is interesting to note that Genesis opens with the following words that indicate the importance of the Watery world in the process of Creation:

> In the beginning God created the heaven and earth. And the earth was without form, and void; and darkness was upon the face of the deep. And the Spirit of God moved upon the face of the waters'.[14]

The Watery world of Creation:[15]

- *The Void* – The unknown, the unknowable, the totality of the space in which the cycle of emanatory Being is enacted.
- *The Deep* – The psychic, the fathomless, the immaterial, and the bowels of the Entity wherein the digestive process occurs. Here it represents the Womb, in which the new world-system must be formed. The Deep therefore represents the triune aspects of the Great Mother, the feminine principle in Nature.
- *The Waters* – With this, a being digests or procreates, or else (as blood) it sustains Life. Here it symbolises the actual substance to be used in the Creative process. The Deep is an aspect of the Void and manifests the Waters.

The statement 'the earth was without form, and void' relates to the time before 'God' circumscribed this matter with His Thought.

---

14 *Genesis 1:1-3.*

15 Note that the various mythologies concerning the symbolism of water are well presented in Mircea Eliade's book: *Patterns in Comparative Religion*, (New American Library, N.Y., 1974).

'Darkness' relates to a state of abstraction: the realms of perception beyond human ken that precede the light of day and the light of knowledge. The 'face of the deep' relates to Uranus in the Greek myths, and the great Father-Mother (when wedded to Gaia, the earth), of all the forms and primeval forces (Titans) that sustained the universe.

The 'Spirit of God' that 'moved upon the face of the waters' refers to the Ineffable Mind of 'God', whilst 'the waters' refers to primordial substance – the fluid, psychic, receptive, feminine counterpart of 'God'. The implication here is to the act of procreation, wherein semen is implanted into, and then 'digested' by the Waters of the Womb. This process refers to mass consciousness, or rather, mass (un)consciousness ('the face of the waters') and its gradual stimulation and evolution by means of the 'movement' caused by the 'Spirit of God'.

The concept of 'face' implies the seven facial orifices: mouth, two nostrils, two ears and two eyes. They relate to the attributes of the seven planes of perception, when the functions of these organs are analysed.[16]

In terms of energy, the relation or union between the Spirit and the Waters produced light. At first a type of light appeared that softly diffused all forms. Seen clairvoyantly, this is known as the astral light. Later appeared that type of light that can be described as solar,[17] of the sun or Son (Soul) aspect of Deity. This was 'the greater light to rule the day'.[18]

The 'lesser light', which is to 'rule the night' (as the moon), is what shines in the darkness (by reflecting sunlight), and thus symbolises the evolving light of the form nature.[19] This eventually becomes the

---

16 The interpretations of the facial orifices can differ. H.P. Blavatsky in Diagram 1, facing page 426 of *The Secret Doctrine,* vol. 5, (The Adyar Edition, Theosophical Publishing House, 1971), lists them as: right eye = *buddhi,* left eye = *manas,* right ear = lower *manas,* left ear = *kāma-rūpa,* right nostril = life principle, left nostril = life vehicle, and the mouth = 'the Organ of the Creative Logos'. *Buddhi* is the principle of enlightenment. *Manas* relates to mind, whose subdivision is the higher abstract Mind and the lower empirical mind. *Kāma-rūpa* is the body of desire (also the astral form). The life principle is *prāṇa.* The life vehicle is the etheric body wherein reside the *chakras.* The physical body is not esoterically considered a principle, hence the mouth embodies the function of precipitating material forms (by means of *mantra).*

17 *Genesis 1:15-19.*

18 *Genesis 1:16.*

19 *Genesis 1:16.*

personality light, which is co-ordinated by the intellect.[20] The appearance of both solar and lunar lights happened on the fourth day of Creation.

On the fifth day of Creation (or month of the gestation period), the Waters were to 'bring forth abundantly the moving creature that hath life'.[21] The implication is to the vivification (with living Light) of the Blood Stream of 'God' (the Waters), so that all creatures that have Life could be sustained by it. The foetal Christ-consciousness in the Womb of Nature was then born. This allowed the 'creation' of humanity on the sixth day. They became the vehicle of that living Light in the Waters of Being.

Note that there are only seven days of Creation. This relates to the foetal life, in the fact that all the organs of the foetus are fully developed by the seventh month, and technically, the child can be born. In the remaining two months, it grows in size and viability.

Esoterically, the Sun and the Heart are virtually synonymous terms, for both are active dispensers of Life and vitality. On the earth, Light and Life are absorbed by the watery principle that is contained by the plant kingdom as sap. Sap is rich in the energy (sugars) made by photosynthesis that is used to build the plant's tissues. This energy then finds its way into the blood streams of members of the animal kingdom, after their digestive processes release the vitality captured by the plant.

The sun is the physical Heart of the solar Logos, and transmits the circulatory fluids of the Body of Deity. Life is sustained by the ability of the Watery principle to absorb Light energy, as regulated and directed by a transmitting Heart. Such action is termed 'the Love of God', of which the Christ, the head of the Hierarchy, is the active representative on the earth. In this guise, the Christ is the 'light of the world'.[22] He is also 'the way, the truth, and the life'[23] for both angels and men. He is the spiritual Sun, the repository and transmitter of the

---

20 Exoterically, the 'greater light' is viewed as the light from the sun and the lesser light being the reflected light from the moon. Esoterically however, the 'greater light' shines from the domain of the Soul, and the 'lesser light' is what illumines the life of the personality.

21 *Genesis 1:20.*

22 *John 8:12.*

23 *John 14:6.*

subjective energies from the Heart of 'God', which bathes our Souls with illumined splendour.

Just as the blood, the conveyor of nourishment to the human system, is pumped cyclically to the heart, so all entities will partake in the cyclic activities of the Heart of all Life if they 'drink' freely of the symbolic 'Blood' of the Christ (as He asked us to do).[24] We then become enlightened extensions of the Christ, outposts of His consciousness, so becoming the various messengers (hormones) and agents of protection and nourishment (e.g., red and white blood cells), within that Blood stream.

The Watery Element is fluid and easily moulded into the shape of whatever contains it. Thus, it is conditioned by the moods, feelings, glamour and emotional states of an individual. Psychics and mediumistic people generally perceive via this Element. The realm of perception pertaining to such Watery functioning has been termed the astral plane in various books on occult or hermetic philosophy.

The astral plane and the silver cord

The alchemical term Water is used to describe the substance that is affected by our moods, feelings, glamour and massed emotional states, because its intrinsic nature is fluid. This fourth-dimensional substance[25] is normally equated with the astral plane. Astral substance thus constitutes our body of emotions, desires and feelings. The associated *prāṇas* and *saṃskāras* are regulated by the Solar Plexus centre and the minor *chakras* in the body. The word astral means starry or luminescent. The term is however somewhat of a misnomer, for that quality really depicts the *etheric body* (the intermediary between the astral and the dense

---

24 *Matt. 26:27-8*, 'And he took the cup, and gave thanks, and gave *it* to them, saying, Drink ye of it: For this is my blood of the new testament, which is shed for many for the remission of sins'.

25 A confusion in terminology is possible here because earlier the emotions were said to act in a 2-D way, whereas here the substance of the astral plane, which consists of the sum of people's emotions, desires and glamours, is depicted as 4-D. Also *manasic* perception was labelled 3-D. Effectively, the way of perceiving with the mind, *via* external objects is 3-D, but the nature of the expression of the substance of the mind is 5-D. Hence we can imaginatively control *manasic* input, build empires of mind, and project pathways to the future without having recourse to the forms of the 3-D world.

physical realm, housing the energy field of the corporeal form). The astral substance is often confused with the etheric body by clairvoyants. These two forms of substance are practically extensions of each other. The etheric body is auto-luminous, as is the astral. Those with psychic and mediumistic tendencies have awakened minor *chakras* facilitating perception of this subtle realm, which includes therefore the subjective states described above.[26]

The first-dimensional perception can be viewed as the type of sentience developed by the mineral kingdom. (This concerns direct interrelation between individual molecules, atoms, or subatomic particles, from a linear perspective.) The second-dimensional perception can be seen as that developed by the vegetable kingdom. They grow principally upwards and downwards, but can also spread out sideways, such as the action of vines and creepers. They are composed of layers of generally highly geometric interrelated superimposed cells. Such layers of receptivity (two-dimensional planes, as for instance observed in the form of leaves) are fully developed in this kingdom. Thus we can deduce that plants view things as if they are on a plane surface. They are also a basis for the life in the animal kingdom. Third-dimensional perception is represented by the type of sentience developed by animals, whilst fourth (or rather, fifth-dimensional perception) is the birth right of humans. Esoterically, our view concerns the way of the mind (the fifth-dimension), as everything is mind-conditioned. The astral realm is really an illusional zone of residence created by the human desire body and mental-emotions. We see therefore that the terms fourth and fifth-dimension depend upon the way that the mind expresses itself. Animals can also share in the fourth-dimensional experience.

It is commonly known that during deep sleep many of us leave our bodies in our astral forms and experience many and wonderful things that may be remembered as vivid and euphoric dreams.[27] Such dreams

---

26 The perceptions of psychics are generally fragmentary and distorted. There normally is much glamour involved, and rarely do they properly scrutinise or validate their impressions. Many are the traps and lures that such individuals can fall prey to, and rare are genuine knowledgeable instructors to guide them safely through the lower astral miasma of their psychism.

27 The term used in the relevant texts for this function is 'astral projection'. Probably the best book on this subject is by Peter Richelieu, *A Soul's Journey*, (Thorsons, London, 1996).

are usually in colour and often manifest as precognitions, educational scenes, pleasant floating sensations, and lyrical wanderings. These usually appear when the dreamer had previously strongly desired (even subconsciously) to see something or someone that is loved, or when there is a strong desire to know about something. An example can be seen in a mother's concern for her separated son in the case of a war, and she has a true prophetic dream of him being killed in action. In general, astral experiences are often not remembered because most have not manifested a cognisable alignment between the two realms of perception (by having stimulated the psychic centre concerned). Some very physically biased people have also not sufficiently developed their astral form.

The ordinary concepts of time or motion with respect to distance are transcended in the higher dimensions. Because the astral body is really the Watery sheath of the mind so motion is instantaneous with thought. Time is only related to 3-D cycles or events, whilst distance is perceived astrally by changes in vibrational rates, by the earth's astral boundary, or else in relation to 3-D perception.

There is a link called the *silver cord* uniting the astral and physical bodies. It has similar functions to the umbilical cord, the dense physical manifestation that conveys nutrition from the greater life (the mother) to the foetus. In Ecclesiastes, it is stated that:

> Or ever the silver cord is loosed, or the golden bowl be broken...Then shall the dust return to the earth as it was: *and* the spirit shall return unto God who gave it.[28]

The 'golden bowl' is the sum of the *prāṇa* that vivifies every cell in a being. *Prāṇa* is the energy conveyed by the 'silver cord' and which sustains the life of the person. Once this cord or link between the subjective and corporeal person is severed, then the body dies and the subjective person, the 'spirit', is freed. It is composed of the subtlest type of astral matter and is able to instantaneously absorb the energy, or matter, from the astral sea that the person needs in order to travel in that realm of perception.

---

28 *Eccles. 12:6-7.*

Most people do this during their sleep life, but only a few have developed the ability to consciously travel thus. The silver cord is able to stretch indefinitely to wherever the person wishes to go within the astral environment. At all times it is anchored in the physical body, which, during the process, is in a sleep or trance state. It can be linked to the physical body in one of three places:

- Average humanity: the emotionally centred and sensually oriented individual – in the region of the spleen.
- The mystic: the type of person that loves much, and/or is involved with groups of people – in the heart.
- The intelligentsia or esotericist: the definitely mental polarised individual – at the top of the head.

When the indwelling Life (the Soul) has no more use for the physical vehicle, then the life force and consciousness are withdrawn through one of the three apertures of release (Splenic, Heart, or Head centres). The silver cord is then severed from the body. The astral body consequently becomes the densest sheath of the person (after a brief sojourn in the body of vitality, the etheric form).

Those that have continually reinforced desire, emotional and sensual thoughts, or glamour and illusions, must live astrally through the effects of these after they die. This is because thoughts and desires are concrete things on the subjective realms. They clothe the person as an aura, becoming the objective form when death ensues. 'Gods' or 'devils' of various forms, religious or non-religious, socio-political, and all types of unpleasant, as well as aesthetic forms, can then become visually real. For instance, the devotional type of person that has strong preconceived ideas on the nature of a personal beneficent Deity would live the emotional aspect of that ideal, having imagined what it would be like whilst incarnate. Inconsistencies with the 'ideal' will inevitably present themselves in an unavoidable manner, for the astral substance that was bound to that form will gradually dissipate.

There are no hard and fast rules governing astral experiences. For everything depends upon the personality's inbuilt desire qualities and karmic relationships. Those residing on the astral realm must be far more group conscious than those on the earth, for this realm is largely created by the united efforts of people's collective desires, emotions and aspirations throughout the ages. Their common glamour and massed thought forms are thus what one experiences. This is the reward for involvement in social, national, racial or religious groups (from which many of our addictions and cravings arise).

A person lives and 'works out' emotional thought forms on the astral plane to the degree that they were affected (and not annulled) during the incarnate life. They are the resultant *karma* for wrong or right attachment and desires and become an incentive for future right action. Part of the objective of all meditation techniques is to eliminate these desires and thought forms whilst still incarnate, obviating the need to experience that realm after death. This ensures abstraction into the highest heaven, the Kingdom of Souls, or of Enlightened Being.

Descriptions of torture in Hades, of the Greek and Roman mythology, Hell in Christian theology, Amenti of Egyptian theology, or the *preta lokas* in Hindu and Buddhist theologies, are all actual references to astral experiences. This fate befalls beings who were highly cruel and insensitive to other's sufferings, and/or definitely selfish and separative in motivation whilst incarnate. These people have much to eliminate karmically by this means, for their former state of awareness encaged them in a self-made hell that they must live through. Even so, many pictures of hell with flames and furnaces are purposely exaggerated, invented, or made horrendous. This was to induce the members of the diocese or religious community to do 'right', or to conform to the dictates of a religion through fear of torture in the afterlife, if their religious doctrines were not obediently satisfied.

It is necessary for people to eliminate all concepts of fear of the afterlife if a righteous life has been lived. It should be emphasised that emotion, pain, (etc.) are greatly modified on that realm. There is no pain as we understand it, for there are no physical nerves. Nor are a person's values and identifications involved. Thus, there are no means for sensuous addiction or experiences.

People must learn to control the forces and properties within every new sphere of sensation, contact, or realm of perception. This is achieved by being born into such environments until they eventually learn to completely master those qualities. Eventually the properties, glamour and illusions of *saṃsāra,* the three worlds of experience (aspects of the physical, astral, and mental realms with which we have karmic obligations), are completely mastered. We can then rise out of the corporeal world and reside in the realm of enlightened Being. Grosser contacts and expressed sensations are gradually eliminated as karmic lessons are learned. Useful elements are absorbed, refined, and eventually abstracted when a new higher cycle of experience is entered. The intimate and frequent contact with the enlightened members of one's group, in conjunction with the energies from our Souls (which always play upon us), will stimulate and draw us higher – closer to our true Being.

The higher levels of the astral realm are conditioned by the musical interplay of sound and colour, the 'music of the spheres'. From here is derived much of the inspiration to musicians and artists. Often those found on these astral levels are devotionally engrossed in the development of the creative faculties of their imaginations, building astral utopias.

There are various categories of service work in the astral realm, plus the ability to research in all scientific fields. What will be the focus of their next incarnation will gradually influence all their actions.

The nature of multidimensional perception

To understand the nature of the astral plane and other realms of perception we must accustom ourselves to the notion of dimensions of conscious awareness and existence. Each dimension is a boundary that signifies a level of attainment for our ability to perceive all things in the subjective or objective universes. The boundaries thus depict different levels of perception and can extend to domains far beyond what we recognise as consciousness. The dimensions can be accessed according to the developed capacity gained through awakening the various subjective organs of perception for the inner realms, and the sense-perceptors for the dense physical domain.

When one thinks one discriminates between this and that. Such thought process is needed to survive in the three-dimensional world of experiences that we reside in. Each thought-stream represents a line of knowledgeable representation, each line is a discriminatory process, and each point of that line can expand into a sphere of higher dimensional perception, which can produce visionary domains beyond thought.

If one is to construct a *maṇḍala*[29] as a thought construct, the concept of dimensionality is important. Dimensionality can be thought of in two ways:

a. Mathematically, where size, numbers of objects, length, depth and breadth of inclusiveness, new elemental expressions, linearity or non-linearity, and overall geometric structure is taken into account.[30]

b. Levels of abstraction or density of dimensions of perception implied by various aspects of the construct.

Most thoughts are depicted upon printed pages and in painted images in a two-dimensional fashion. Utilising our logic we can extrapolate much information from them because we are capable of thinking in multidimensional terms. The moving spiral of consciousness unfolding is depicted two-dimensionally.

In reality the spiralling manifests within a sphere of consciousness, which also can expand exponentially in all directions in multidimensional space. This figure depicts esoterically the nature of the appearance of the *saṃskāras* that underlie the manifestation of the attributes of mind/ Mind. The associated philosophy is explained in detail in chapter six ('The Spiral of Consciousness, the Energy View') of my book *Esoteric Cosmology and Modern Physics*.

29 Literally a circle, or circumference, a diagram filled with religious symbolism drawn by one wishing to contemplate things divine, or to evoke potencies and forces associated with Nature and the subjective realms. A perfected, completed, state of being and perception encompassing all phenomena when presented symbolically in a specific form or blueprint of what is to be. Used as a visualising tool in meditation.

30 The actual geometry of dimensional perception is described in my book *Maṇḍalas: Their Nature and Development*. 124-37. This passage should be read to obtain the background to this present section on the nature of multidimensional perception.

The appearing *saṃskāras* arrive via a (one-dimensional) line of conveyance (a *nāḍī*) and then quickly demonstrate a three-dimensional mode of interrelatedness of their qualities once the *saṃskāras* become expressed in terms of consciousness volition. The neuro-chemical impulses obtained from sense contact with external phenomena travelling along the nerves to the brain can also be considered in one-dimensional terms, until the impressions are correlated by the brain to produce the images we think with. This one-dimensional attribute is equated with the expression of the Element Earth. (One-dimensional lines of relationship also betoken how chemical compounds interrelate and combine.)

When divorced from *manasic* control the emotions manifest in this two-dimensional manner. They can engulf and surround the object of desire, of that wished for, but the image of what is contacted can never produce the full three-dimensional (3-D) reasoning that consciousness produces. The emotions can produce awareness of only a slice or surface area of what is contacted, thus they immediately distort the true image. They also curtail reasoning in terms of the 'I' and the object of desire, where the image of that object is coloured according to what is desired. True penetrative reasoning is not obtained, rather, a quick truncated two-dimensional impression is obtained. Later in quieter moments, the mind can derive further realisations from the initial emotional contact, when logic is activated.

The associated *saṃskāras* are clothed in the Watery Element, which manifest torrent-like to grasp an object without penetrating the three-dimensional relationship between various objects, or of the complete perspective of that which the emotions contact. The rounded out inclusivity of the view of the *manasic* perspective is needed. The combination of desire-emotions coupled with the mind is called *kāma-manas,* and signifies the way that most people 'think'. Therein lies the generation of most of their *karma.*

Humanity views the universe in terms of 3-D rules and limitations. In this way, for instance, we perceive the illusive three-dimensionality of a painting or photograph, despite the fact that it is really a 2-D object. Similarly, the fact that there are higher, subtler dimensions, escapes the attention of most. If we over-rule our 3-D conditioning from giving things a 3-D flavour, then we will be able to view things from a more comprehensive angle.

The Fires of the mind come to the fore in 3-D thinking, producing the ability to gauge depth, and to reason in terms of all points of view, the length, breadth, and depth of a mental image. The information gleaned from all sense-perceptors are correlated in this manner by the intellect. All commonplace *saṃsāric* events can thus be visualised throughout the sequence of time. (In this analysis time is *not viewed* as a separate 'dimension', but rather as an expression of, or an addendum to, the third dimension.) The visioning of the time-sequence is conceptualised in terms of 3-D events as perceived by consciousness.

It can be claimed that the content of what is to us solid three-dimensional physical matter is really empty space with specks of matter (atoms) separated by relatively great distances and linked by definite laws. The atoms also obey the laws of conservation of energy and are in constant vibratory motion, whilst their 'matter' is almost wholly concentrated within the nucleus of every atom. There is also a relatively vast distance between it and the cloud of electrons spinning around it. The electron's mass is about 1/1840th of either that of a proton or neutron, which together constitute the atom's nucleus, there being an increasing number of neutrons and protons to each atom as we ascend up the periodic table of elements.

As the first-dimension is represented as a line, so the second-dimension could be viewed as a square, and the third-dimension as a cube. Each dimension is viewed at right angles to the preceding dimension, and speaking metaphorically, its principles or faculties (of perception) progressively transcend its correspondences in the previous dimensions. Thus the fourth-dimension must have all the possibilities of the above-mentioned dimensions of perception and yet transcend them. Therefore one in the fourth-dimension could clothe oneself in any of the shapes that are represented as form in the third-dimension and yet that form would not limit the person. This would present the added characteristic of being able to interpenetrate all aspects of the third-dimension. One would be able to see and move freely within and about the solid (3-D) matter (similar to the action of x-rays) without the loss of one's own form.

This is feasible if the comparatively enormous distances between atoms of 3-D matter is considered. The much smaller subtler 4-D atomic unities existing at much higher frequencies and permeating the spaces between ordinary physical atoms can then be taken into account. To a being with 3-D perception or instruments (such as those possessed by the average person and the scientist) such matter would to all accounts be undetectable.[31]

This can be further illustrated by the idea of a stick that is moving to and fro. As the stick is vibrated faster and faster, the object of perception (the stick) becomes a blur. The analogy is completed if we imagine a whole forest of such sticks rapidly vibrating in an engulfing forest of slowly swaying trees (representing the world of atoms). In comparison, the perceiver would have the dimensions of a huge mountain but be able to see only the trees, even with the help of instruments.

In order to detect matter composed of such minute entities, one's faculty for visual perception would have to resonate at that ultra-high frequency, and that faculty must be trained or focussed to observe the matter before one.

Such ability is termed *clairvoyance,* and will manifest if one's physical, emotional and mental bodies are refined, and then adopts a rigor of concentration or meditation upon the subject at hand (utilising the appropriate psychic sensory organs). Some types of drugs will also induce psychic visions, and certain people, such as mediums, are born with these abilities. This does not mean, however, that these people are more 'spiritually' advanced than others, but rather indicates that there are flaws in their psychic constitution. Psychics normally manifest the lower psyche, involving mediumship, aberrant clairvoyant and clairaudient perceptions that are often clouded by emotions and misleading ignorance.

The alchemists attributed the property of Water to this form of (astral) matter, for by analogy with the physical plane, 4-D matter is fluid like water. It permeates the dense form and is easily moulded by external forces. In this case thought energy is the mechanism of

---

31 The argument that many of the subatomic particles detected by physicists, such as quarks, are but the 'atomic' constituency of this fourth-dimensional world is detailed in my book *Esoteric Cosmology and Modern Physics.*

application. This is because its molecules (or rather, the arrangement of its form) are not as rigidly bound as those of 3-D matter. The molecules of 4-D matter freely discharge themselves from the 4-D atmosphere, and vice versa. The Watery Element is thus fluid and easily moulded, therefore, a 4-D being can assume whatever shape desired through using the will directed by the mind's image-making faculty.

Just as a person with 3-D eyes can read all of a 2-D world (such as a newspaper) at a glance, so a person with 4-D eyes could be able to simultaneously read the facial markings on each of the plane surfaces of a 3-D object from an external point in space, as well as perceiving its inner nature. One would thus not need to open a book to read it. This is because the organs of perception of a 4-D person are diffused to all parts of his/her body. This is possible because 4-D matter is highly tenuous when compared to the physical 3-D body, which has its organs of perception localised to certain areas of the body, such as the eyes in the head. Localised perception is therefore transcended. The whole body, literally every atom, now functions as an organ of perception. (Similar to the sense of touch.) As the 4-D matter interpenetrates the 3-D matter, so the internal as well as external features of an object would be able to be simultaneously discerned.

It could also be said that because 2-D perception is at right angles to the first dimension, and 3-D perception is at right angles to the 2-D, so 4-D perception must be at right angles to the 3-D. This means that a person with 4-D vision will be looking perpendicularly, that is, on all the (six) sides of a 3-D world, from one point in space.

The particles of 4-D substance represent particles of sentient response. They clothe the impulses of the mind. The intensity of the energy of the desire-mind provides the vibrancy, or propelling force. This substance is instantaneously galvanised into activity by the impulse of desire, and is quickly coloured by the force of human emotions. These emotions consist of minute Watery *devas*, which introduce the factor of *karma*, because this energisation affects the *deva* lives that inevitably must return the energy to the original source. Thereby equilibrium is restored in the field of Life. All substance is in fact constituted by *devas,* who can be considered minute units of sentience.

Achieving the equilibrium of the pristine condition thus becomes the *modus operandi* of karmic purpose. What manifests therefore is ordered purpose. This therefore opposes the effects associated with the second law of thermodynamics.[32] Entropy can be considered the state of chaos existing at the primeval beginning. Entropy manifests when atoms are no longer directly controlled by a encompassing mind, or field of desire (which produce order out of chaos). This represents the state of elementary substance during *pralaya,* the dissolution of things (a world-sphere) at the end of time. A *maṇḍala* of incarnate expression then no longer serves its purpose. Elementary substance may enter into entropy, but what is bound by mind/Mind is held in ordered harmony and enters into higher dimensions of perception. The macroscopic body is calm, but the minute particulate matter that has been discarded is chaotic. (Except when it is again directed or galvanised by some energy field or Life force. This happens at the new dawning of a world or universal sphere of activity.)

In the field of life each atom of matter carries with it a unit of gain, a quantum increase or added colourisation of the type of energy that swayed it as part of an organised force. The gains are qualitative and each unity grows in experiential quality over time. Because of this, chaos imperceptibly slowly moves towards greater order when *manasic* embodiment becomes the goal of the elementary Lives concerned. The activity of mind is thus what organises chaos. The entire universe marches this way in a cyclically reincarnating expansion, not towards some far distant 'heat death', as some scientists imagine. The progress of all things is thus away from chaos into a congenial state of order. Myriads of cycles come and go before an elementary Life evolves to organise itself into the comprehensive system that is a Buddha Mind.

Karma and the life after death

Elementary substance that is incorporated as part of human emotional expression differs from its primal condition. Over the course of human evolution such substance has accumulated upon the earth and has enriched the biosphere of the human experience. It has created the heaven and hell states, described in an exaggerated fashion by our

---

32 In a closed system entropy (disorder or the randomness of elementary particles) always increases with time.

religions. This substance has become a special, compliantly malleable experiential zone for human consciousness, experienced after the death of our physical bodies. The 4-D Watery (astral) substance of these zones has been moulded according to the way it is conditioned by massed human imagination. Images of all types created by human desire-minds hold sway. Entire landscapes of desirable places and homes are thereby created, the most pleasurable of which are depicted as heavenly or 'godly' realms.

The entire astral zone of human habitation is inextricably governed by the law of *karma*. The quality of the energies of emotional thought determines the type of substance one is clothed in after the physical form has died. *Karma* but represents the nature of the manifestation of the consequent energy forms. Previously developed selfish *saṃskāras,* for instance, then clothe the individual, producing a squalid environment.

Herein lies the basis for the *asura* and *preta* realms claimed by Buddhists, and the purgatory of Christians. Also, according to the degree of rapacity, cupidity, hatred, separateness, or spite manifested throughout that life, so an equal force implodes upon the individual after death, enforcing a hell state for those that manifested such attributes. People thus experience the true effects of the pain they have caused to others. This however is not to be confused with the pain people create for themselves due to uncontrolled emotions in reaction to something that may have happened to them. An individual is not karmically responsible for the irascible, petulant, tetchy, spiteful, fractious, etc., emotions of another. Such emotional ones are very apt to blame others for their 'hurt feelings', and must learn not to do so. *Karma* will manifest in a way to teach people not to blame.

Pain-inducing *karma* is produced by those responsible in changing the environment or living conditions that produce hell-like, squalid life-styles for others, where the direct infliction of pain is caused, or where people's resources are stolen in some way. What is termed 'good *karma*' is produced through acts of kindness and charity, whereby the 'good intent' engendered is experienced after death, and in the physical effects of the charity provided when later they are incarnate.

Everything equilibrates in the end. *Karma* is an exact law, and most people have to think out more logically as to the karmic repercussions of every action manifested with their thoughts, emotions and physicality.

The resources one possesses for instance is karmically measured in terms of how a person obtained it and what it means emotionally to them. Monetary value has a conceptual meaning in terms of the value people assign to things, however true value is represented by the sacrifice or effort a thing took to acquire, or the hardship caused when it is gone. A poor widow's 'two mites' for instance may be worth more than a rich person's treasure.[33]

Digressing a little, it should be mentioned that there are many people that use the 'letter of the law' to unjustly steal another person's wealth (viewed in terms of physical and emotional effort to obtain) through the money they are awarded by a judge for some perceived (often emotional) abuse. The plaintiff does not understand the karmic debt that will be owed to the one thus stolen from. It must be paid back in a later life. Receiving money in a lawsuit does not atone the *karma* of being assaulted, for instance. One has simply accrued a karmic debt through this legalised theft. Society must obviously provide checks to individuals that perpetuate violent (etc.) actions against others, but stealing from them does not rectify their wrong. If one meditates upon the subject of such crimes, we see that the 'victim' (in this case the one assaulted) is generally paying karmically for crimes perpetuated (i.e., having assaulted someone) in a past life. The karmic slate may have been wiped clean in the unfortunate incident, but by thieving, the 'victim' is now bonded in a new karmic debt. People must beware their avarice and feelings of revenge. Karmically, the effects of such emotions produce heavy burdens.

The above information concerning the nature of the after-death state is generalised and thus suffers from errors natural to all generalisations. The notable factor is, however, though it is seemingly wonderful, the astral realm is really an illusion. It is the realm of the psychic, and the source of much of the inspiration of the mystic, being the home of many of the visions colouring the effects of devotion. It is also the world of glamour, of imagination, emotions and feelings. Here exist picture forms of all kinds that humanity's combined hopes and dreams have built throughout the ages. Therefore, it has no substantiality of its own, as D.K. states:

---

33 *Luke 21:1-4.*

> The energies taking form upon the astral plane are not pure emotion and feeling, clothed in pure astral matter, for there is no such thing. They are the instinctual desires, evoked by the evolving substance of the physical plane and this, in its entirety through the activity of the human family, is being redeemed and drawn upwards until some day we shall see the transfiguration of that substance and the "Glorification of the Virgin Mary" – the Mother aspect in relation to divinity. They are also the descending thoughtforms which the developing human being is always creating and drawing downwards into manifestation, clothing them with the substance of desire. When the descending forms of thought (a reflection in the three worlds of that vast "cloud of knowable things" in process of perception, as Patanjali calls it, and which hovers upon the buddhic plane, awaiting precipitation) and the ascending mass of instinctual demands from the lower aspect of the human unit and from humanity as a whole, meet at a point of tension then you have the appearance of what is known as the astral plane – a man-created sphere of activity. The subhuman kingdoms of nature know no astral plane; the superhuman kingdoms have surmounted it and discovered the secret of its delusion and no longer recognise it except as a temporary field of experience wherein man lives. In that sphere he learns the fact that reality is "none of these but only the One and the Other in relation with each other".[34]

In its grosser aspects the astral plane can be visualised as a dark, murky cloud hovering over our planet, which is almost impenetrable to Light. This is the 'darkness' that is equitable with hell, as often mentioned in the Bible. For example, this is the 'outer darkness', where 'there shall be weeping and gnashing of teeth',[35] 'mist of darkness',[36] and 'the darkness shall cover the earth'.[37]

A purpose of the Christ is to dispel the world's 'darkness' – all the fogs, mists and glamour that keep us bound to the prison of the earth. He is the Light that 'shineth in darkness; and the darkness comprehended it not'.[38] Each of us must become bearers of the Light to disperse the

---

34 A.A. Bailey, *Glamour: A World Problem,* (Lucis Publishing Co., N.Y., 1982), 220-21.

35 *Matt. 8:12, 22:13* and *25:30.*

36 *II Peter 2:17.*

37 *Isaiah 60:2.*

38 *John 1:5.*

darkness of ignorance and the fogs and miasmas associated with the Watery realm. As stated in Matthew, you must let your light 'so shine before men that they may see your good works'.[39]

Whenever the astral realm or psychic phenomena are discussed, we are therefore dealing with the *saṃskāras* of glamour, darkness and illusion, of substance wherein people are trapped and from which they must in time free themselves. Liberation from such phenomena is to be found on the higher mental realm (wherein resides the Soul), or the realms of perception where exists the Light of the intuition.

3. In the Airy and Fiery worlds

If a person previously had an intellectual life, then the *karma* of his/her thought world will eventually draw that person from the astral realm[40] into the mental realm. At the borders of this realm, one undergoes a second death and dies to the astral body before entering the mental sub-planes, called *devachan* in the Sanskrit terminology.

Here the doors of higher spiritual knowledge open. Complete understanding of the laws of Nature concerning humanity on the lower planes is available, for thinkers are now regents in their own estate. The domain now resided in is Fiery, the substance that constitutes the thought forms. Fire here is but rarefied energy. The registration of thought thus becomes instantaneous and in the form of an unbroken and expansive vista of any subject the person is engrossed in. For the thinker, the result will be one of sublime ecstasy of a directly involved realisation.

On the *lower mental sub-planes*, the abstract and archetypal ideas and ideals from the realm of enlightened Being are fragmented into set patterns and forms that can be directly experienced by the thinker. Here also a person experiences thought forms that were formerly built, bringing all the latent ideas and mental tendencies or problems that were engrossing whilst incarnate to their fullest expression. For example, a scientist will now be able to fully explore the most intricate and deepest thought patterning that may have frustrated them before. In the mental plane, there is no way for the mind to be clouded and marred by the astral emotionalism and glamour, or to be limited by the sensations and

39 *Matt. 5:16,* See also *II Cor. 4:16.*

40 Hell, purgatory or heaven of the Christians.

lower instincts of the physical body. For this reason, consciousness, as people normally understand it, does not exist on this realm. Also, there is no imagination on the mental plane there is only direct cognitive perception in a vast stream of realisation, which becomes the entire body of experience.

The physical plane is the realm of reasoning and experimentation. The astral is the realm of imagination, and the mental is the realm of direct illumination. For instance, if the history of the world is the object of the person's attention, then one can become that history to the extent that one is absorbed in the collective group-Mind of all beings. One lives out the *karma* of one's thought life, until that life has been transcended when one is absorbed into the Clear Light of the Soul.[41]

The mental plane is associated with the Mind of 'God'. It is related to the central nervous system and the electrical impulses that direct the entire organism. It is the field of Fiery electrical energy that constitutes mind/Mind, from which all Lives emanate, and which governs their evolutionary Purpose.

Air is not seen, nor can it be touched; yet it impels, as do, for instance, nerves. People and animals build shelters to protect themselves from the ravages of storms and the effects of the seasons. They are – figuratively speaking – carried in the air. Rain, hail, snow and heat all impel people and animals to live in certain ways. Air can take the guise of the destroyer aspect of Deity (such as in the form of a storm), or resurrect (as does fresh air and the sun that shines through) and it preserves all life (even that of fishes). Similarly, nerve impulses preserve the life of our bodies by regulating our conscious reactions to external stimuli.

Blood, the watery principle, is really the carrier of the air through the bloodstream. Air is invisible to us and thus is principally known by its effects, just as we know of 'God' by the results of His effects. It is universally effective and all-pervasive, for the air that we breathe and which sustains us is the same air that is breathed by all animals and utilised by their cellular constitution. Air is thus directly related

---

41 In Buddhist philosophy, the abstract Mind possesses the attribute of Clear Light of Mind, pristine cognition. When a thought enters that Mind it instantaneously and completely sees the true nature of that thought. This is the enlightened Mind, and the next step beyond that is *śūnyatā,* called Emptiness, which reflects cosmic Mind (the *dharmakāya),* or what some might call the Mind of 'God'.

to our nervous system and thinking process (we think as we breathe). Likewise, the food that we eat is related to our emotional process (we eat as we desire).

Air is the fuel that keeps a fire ablaze, just as nerve impulses are the 'fuel' keeping our mental processes active. The nervous system gives humanity the ability to consciously evolve, thus to conquer the vast open spaces embodied by the airy domain – to conquer space (which is an extension of the airy world). 'Air' keeps the Mind of 'God' bound to the outer form.

Fire, which is produced by the substance of the earth (our worldly experiences), is enflamed and sustained by the Air (here synonymous with the intuition, the enlightened Mind). This relates to the mental principles of both humanity and 'God'. Indeed, 'God is a consuming fire'.[42]

Fire relates to the intellect (the empirical mind) and to its abstract permutation (the higher, or pristine clear Light of Mind). Fire is transmuted into the synthesis that is the Mind of 'God'.

Air, in the form of the intuition, the archetypal Mind, relates the mind of humanity to the Logoic Mind. Air represents the energy field that sustains all Being, within which consciousness evolves.

The present result of the entire evolutionary process is Fire – the Fires of the mind. This is the substance that burns, liberates, consumes and destroys. Yet Fire is also the furnace from which all things are made. It warms, sustains and protects a person from the storms and cold produced by the violence of Nature (for example, from the Watery emotional nature). Fire can also be used to fan that violence. All depends upon how the mind is used. When Fire is united with desire and emotionality (Water), it produces clouds of steam and fog. However, when united with Air, Fire allows the Light of the sun to illumine the person. Fire is Nature's transmutative agent.

Jesus stated: 'I am come to send fire on the earth; and what will I, if it be already kindled?'[43] Therefore, He came to give humanity the ability to think with real perceptiveness (though his predecessors had already started the process). Luke describes the development of the mental principle, symbolised by the work of 'the servant who knew

---

42 *Hebrews 12:29.*

43 *Luke 12:49.*

his lord's will' and of whom 'much is required', for 'much is given'.[44] In the passages from *Luke 12:42-49,* Jesus states:

> Who then is that faithful and wise steward, whom his Lord shall make ruler over his household, to give them their portion of meat in due season? Blessed *is* that servant, whom his lord when he cometh shall find so doing. But if that servant say in his heart, My lord delayeth his coming; and shall begin to beat the menservants and maidservants, and to eat and drink and be drunken; The lord of that servant will come in a day when he looketh not for him, and will cut him in sunder, and will appoint him his portion with the unbelievers, And that servant, which knew his lord's will, and prepared not *himself,* neither did according to his will, shall be beaten with many *stripes.* But he that knew not, and did commit things worthy of stripes, shall be beaten with few stripes. For unto whomsoever much is given, of him shall be much required: and to whom men have committed much, of them they shall ask the more. I am come to send fire on the earth; and what will I, if it be already kindled?

Here 'the steward' relates to the mind, 'the Lord' to the Soul, and being 'beaten with many stripes' signifies the effects of the law of *karma.* The entire passage is an explanation of the nature of the workings of *karma,* thus should also be analysed as such. 'Menservants and maidservants' are attributes of the mind, whilst to 'drink and be drunken' relates to manifesting emotional attributes that are detrimental to the developed consciousness. The ability to reason and think provides the ability to know the powers inherent in the universe. Much can therefore be expected of one that knows, and further esoteric knowledge can be given as experiences grow. With knowledge comes responsibility, spiritual as well as temporal, as is evident with the knowledge that people now possess. The seemingly endless conflicting ideals and philosophies that are the result of humanity's use of the mind[45] create 'division' on the earth.[46]

44 *Luke 12:48.*

45 Numerically, the mind is symbolised by the number five and the pentagram (for it is the fifth plane of perception) – the 'five' that are 'in the one house divided' in *Luke 12:52.*

46 *Luke 12:51, which states:* 'Suppose ye that I am come to send peace on earth? I tell you, Nay, but rather division'.

The early philosophers stated that the Elements: Earth, Water, Fire and Air together constituted the totality of Being.[47] In their search for the philosopher's stone, alchemists sought to fuse them together, under the following names:

- Salt – *Air,* the intuitional realm of perception.
- Sulphur – *Fire,* the mental plane.
- Mercury – *Water,* the astral or emotional realm.
- Earth – Earth, the dense physical realm.

This stone is the wish-fulfilling gem that would grant the possessor immortality and the ability to transcend all known laws of Nature, as well as to make gold – symbolic of spiritual superabundance.

Of all external forces needed to keep the body alive, air is the most critically important. A person can only last minutes without air (the Life principle) as compared to days without water (the Love principle), and weeks without food (the matter aspect of Deity).

Water functions as the universal solvent. It absorbs the Life principle (Air) so that the entity can utilise it. It also dissolves physical matter so that it can nourish. Water (Love) thus relates Spirit to matter. It is of prime importance in the foetal development of a child, whilst Air, which completely surrounds the newborn child, is also of key importance in the growth to maturity. Thus, Water nurtures the primeval stages of evolution and develops the animal form to the extent that a human unit can evolve and eventually be born into the Air, into the 'Spirit'.

Humanity has been nurtured in the Womb of the Earth (Water) and is now ready to be 'born anew' into the all-pervasive life of the 'fullness of the Christ' (Air). The human conquest of the airy sphere by means of the aeroplane is the symbol of this. At the place where Water and Air meet and interact, there is produced electric-fire ('lightning'), the intuition that illumines those on the earth. This somewhat explains the meaning of that obscure passage in the book of Matthew: 'For as the lightning cometh out of the east, and shineth even unto the west; so shall also the coming of the Son of man be'.[48] The type of consciousness

---

47 The fifth Element Aether, is generally not mentioned, as it is so refined that most people have no cognisance of its qualities. It expresses the attributes of the *ātmic* plane.

48 *Matt. 24:27.*

that originated in the East, from where the sun (the Heart of Life) first rises, must be brought to illumine people's minds in the West (where the sun sets). There is an esoteric reference to the type of philosophy developed in the eastern hemisphere (India, Tibet) that must also be brought to the West. Eastern philosophy is based on the understanding of the nature of meditation and of its accomplishment, such as what the Buddha advocated. (He also endeavoured to reform the Hindu religion.) When coupled with Western metaphysical development and empirical attainment, it will produce an enlightened world.

The Eastern and Western types of ontologies and philosophies must thus become integrated with the coming of 'the Son of man'. Such understanding is now rapidly affecting an increasingly large number of people. Consequently, as the Sun shines from the East to the West, so also must shine the illumination that the Christ (the Hierarchy of Light) is to bring. The outer manifestation of Nature is ever the symbol of inner Law and happenings. The intuitive Mind must be developed by thinking people, in such a way that it illumines and completely irradiates all of the 'dark places' of the earth.

BODO 83.

Life is not known
for what it is,
nor seen for what it was.
Neither can it be what we wish,
for our dreams
become sea mist
with passing time, and our life:
a leaf floating in the breeze.

6

Instinct, Glamour and Thought-Forms

Instinct, desire (or the Will) and thought-form construction are factors necessarily taken into account by any causative agent during the concrete manifestation of empirical or divine Impulse. Causation is effectively the vitalisation of the *Great Symbol* that delineates time and space as the Womb of Being. From there all the lesser evolutionary symbols emanate, embodied as manifest (and even imaginary) forms. This Symbol is the sphere ○, abstract and undefined. The Great Symbol is the cause and result of evolutionary being, the path of enlightened perception.[1] It is the Mystery, from which the other symbols embodying the lesser mysteries of the kingdom of 'God' emanate. They are depicted in such forms as:

The analysis, therefore, of the Mysteries of this and all related symbols will lead to an understanding of the fundamental nature of Being.

---

1 The attributes of this Symbol are analysed in greater depth in my book *Esoteric Cosmology and Modern Physics*, 5-12.

When rightly pursued, it develops into fully enlightened perception and liberation from the realm of cause and effect. This provides the ability to wield causative energy in the guise of a creative Deity.

The Symbol is embodied in our temporal forms, and manifests as all related qualities. The quickest way to understand its intrinsic nature, therefore, is to understand the nature of ourselves. This includes all of the qualities and energies, latent or empowered, that cause us to exist and to manifest the full potential of our evolutionary journeying. For, as all sacred books say, we are built in the image of the prime Causative Agent embodying our planetary sphere, that sustains all related manifestation.

A developed intelligence is needed to understand the nature of Being. It is the key tool whereby we must interpret and deduce. The factors that influence intelligence should therefore be carefully analysed and understood. Depending upon how the mind is controlled and directed, so our ability to think (and the related opinions) is accordingly swayed. The intellect is thus the first major tool to be developed to analyse and deduce the nature of the symbols, and therefore the process of releasing the energy and qualities that they embody. Consequently, the intellect is an instrument to be developed upon the process of self-mastery.

The factors influencing intelligence are:

A. Those that relate to the physical plane, and thus the factor of instinct.

B. Those related to the emotional and desire realms – the factor of desire *(kāma),* auras and desire forms.

C. Those related to the mental body *(manas)* – the intellect and the creation of thought-forms. This necessitates comprehending the method of causation.

D. Those factors arising from beyond the mental, the planes of Divine Causation – *(buddhi, ātma, anupādaka* and *āḍi).*

E. The interblending of the various Ray and astrological energies constituting the sum of human life.

I shall limit the present analysis to only the first three, for they are what directly concern the average intelligent person. The higher factors concern the realms of enlightenment, which are explained in my other books.

A. The question of instinct[2]

Instinct represents the *intelligence of matter* itself. It is the expression of the various little unconscious Lives that evolve to become self-conscious entities. They are cellular or atomic unities animating the bodies of all corporeal beings. Together they voice an urge, a pull of matter, which always modifies the outward expression (the personality) of the indwelling consciousness. They are often antagonistic to the spiritual Will of the entity concerned, especially during the path of aspiration and probation to Initiation.

The true nature of instinct is not easy to comprehend, as it involves the type of consciousness developed by the mineral kingdom. It can therefore at first only be fully understood by an Initiate of the third degree (whose consciousness necessarily embraces and controls that kingdom) and is one of the imparted secrets of that Initiation.

The rationalising ability of the intellect often reinforces the basic instincts. When coupled with imagination, ignorance, and prompted by desire, this is the cause of most of our miseries and misunderstandings. The actions of most people are thus largely dominated by unconscious reactions to these instincts.

Instinct is the expression of the evolutionary Will, and is found in all kingdoms in Nature. However, it finds its most evolved or specialised forms in humanity. There are five distinct types, categorised as:

1 The instinct of self-preservation

This is basic to the *mineral kingdom*. It is the result of the various laws of the conservation of energy, and of the laws that bind the factors of the nucleus of an atom, whereby their attributes are derived. The strength of this instinct is indicated by the fact that only under extreme conditions can most atomic nuclei be destroyed or changed.

This instinct also allows the concretion of substance into a dense planetary or solar sphere and its consequent aeonic evolution.

In the plant and animal kingdoms it is seen as what allows the

---

2 This section on instinct is adapted from the information originally provided by D.K. in Alice Bailey's book: *A Treatise on White Magic,* (Lucis Publishing Co., 1991), 626 –29.

'survival of the fittest', and prompts the natural selection of the most adaptable entity to any environment.

In humanity it produces an innate fear of death, the death of all aspects of the nucleus that constitutes the personality, or at the fourth Initiation, the Soul-form.

2 *The sexual Instinct*

In the mineral kingdom this instinct is expressed as the various laws of valency – the union of positive and negative ions that produce the many molecules and compounds that constitute our dense sphere.

This instinct is, however, most specifically developed and brought to perfection in the vegetable kingdom. It is seen in their abundant use of colour, perfume, and the myriad different hues, tonalities, floral shapes and specialisation of petals that greet all of us in the cities and fields. Its principal objective is to attract the insect world by offering them nectar and pollen as a reward for the act of cross-pollination that fertilises them, ensuring genetic diversity. Its other objective is the production of a pleasing and healing environment for all kingdoms in Nature.

The fact that the vegetable kingdom constitutes the foundation of the food chain or Life energy that sustains the other kingdoms should also be emphasised here, for the sexual instinct essentially allows the life of the form nature to be adequately sustained and brought to an integral perfection. The wellbeing of our material selves is aptly likened to a blossoming or flowering of vitality, joy and beauty. Such wellbeing is often obtained by eating the sexual parts, or that which encloses the sexual parts of our fruits,[3] vegetables, grains and nuts. By desiring such foodstuffs we manifest actions that help propagate the plant species in a progressive manner.

In the animal kingdom the sexual instinct is expressed in the many courtship rituals and mating displays. These are geared towards the propagation of the most adroit and viable members of the genetic pool of any species.

In humanity this instinct is closely allied with that of self-preservation, and stems from an innate fear of isolation. At present, it

3 The apple's core, for instance, is an ovary, that is enclosed by the edible portion.

is one of the strongest forces motivating most people, especially when reinforced by imagination.

3 The group or herd instinct

In the mineral kingdom this is seen as the union of the various classes of atoms into molecules. In turn, the amalgamation of these molecules creates the myriad groupings of solid and liquid shapes (crystals, rocks etc.) that form the dense world of our environment.

This instinct is brought to perfection in the animal kingdom, and is seen in their banding together in flocks, schools and herds composed entirely of one type of animal.

In the vegetable kingdom, on the other hand, the tendency is for the flower to disperse its seeds (progeny) as far away from the parent or group as possible. They need sufficient space between them so that they do not over-compete, thus choke each other for scarce resources. This tendency then (via this instinct) produces, for instance, a field of flowers of predominantly the same type, appropriately spaced from each other. This instinct therefore is not dominant in this kingdom, where this instinct is essentially integrated with the sexual instinct. The seed dispersal method of the species may thus be inefficient, for the ideal in that kingdom is to produce significant diversity of different species in any locality. This assists its interrelation with the members of the animal kingdom for their mutual benefit.

In humanity, the herd instinct fosters our fear of loneliness, causing us to seek friendship or comfort in the form of social, political, aesthetic, national, religious, or racial groups.

4 The instinct of the self-assertion of the personality

This instinct is seen in the mineral kingdom as the tendency of atoms and molecules to attain those reactions and forms that produce the greatest stability.

In the vegetable kingdom it is seen in the poisonous and spiky plants, and in those with defence mechanisms against hostile entities.

This instinct is specifically developed (exemplified) in the human kingdom, with obvious effects, seen in the many examples of 'man's inhumanity to man'. It also produces the various personality traits and characteristics, the self-willed, self-determined attributes that are so important in the latter stages of our evolution, which precede the Initiation process.

This instinct produces the fear that we may fail to be recognised by our group, and thus be left out of the group activity, or that we may lose what seems (to us) to be necessary for our survival as individual entities.

5 *The instinct towards knowledge*

In the mineral kingdom this is seen as radioactivity and the disintegration of matter into the rays that pierce or travel through space and solid matter.

In the plant world this instinct is seen in their aspiration towards light and their empathy with the animal kingdom (e.g., the insect world).

It is seen in the animal kingdom as their increased mobility (the use of feet and wings) and in devotion/aspiration to the human kingdom (by our domesticated animals).

In the human world we see this instinct prompting our fear of the unknown and thus our present determination to learn about it. From this instinct arises scientific investigation.

This instinct is, however, most developed by the kingdom of Souls, and is the major property of their expression. This kingdom is urged towards the gathering of knowledge, first on the corporeal planes of perception (by the process of repeated incarnation into it), then in its own realms, and finally in the realm of enlightened Being *(buddhi).*

These instincts together are the foundation for the evolution of consciousness in all kingdoms of Nature. They produce an interrelated unity within the human framework wherein they become fully expressed. They are developed into their transmuted aspects by means of the conscious mind as an embodiment of Divine Activity, Love-Wisdom, and Will.

The lower mind (intelligence) can either modify, be influenced by, or dominate these instincts, producing most of our personality traits when allied with desire. The development of Love-Wisdom implicates their replacement with aspects of the intuitive Mind. The focussed expression of the Will completes the process by translating the instincts into higher spiritual types of perception as possessed by members of the Hierarchy of Enlightened Being. When instinct is fully controlled by intelligence rightly applied (as a vehicle of the higher Mind), then the fears enumerated above will be negated and the corresponding perfections brought about.

The right application of the knowledge obtained from understanding the *instinct of self-preservation* (from which all other instincts stem) will produce immortality through the negation of the fear of death. The vital processes of the physical form will then be consciously held in place by the Initiate's Will, and there can be no death unless willed so. This instinct will then find its expression as that type of awareness known as 'isolated unity', which is basic to all that have attained the higher Initiations.

The *sexual instinct* eventually results in the perfect blending of positive and negative energies within and without the Initiate's body. It will allow an interrelation with all human and *deva* groups associated with any desired sphere of activity. The 'life more abundantly'[4] Jesus promised us will thereby be known for what it is, leaving no place for any sense of isolation. The Initiate will be completely engrossed in the higher creative impulse, producing the children of an inspired meditative awareness, in conjunction with others who are so working. The entire Hierarchy of Enlightened Being are the Initiate's co-workers. The sexual instinct will find its expression in the progress towards the 'divine marriage' between the *deva* compliment and the human unit at the fourth Initiation.

The *herd instinct* must eventually evolve into group consciousness, and then interrelation according to Ray type and Monadic purpose. It thus implies eventual absorption into a Master's Ray Ashram and the complete development of the higher enlightened perceptions. Loneliness thereby loses its meaning.

The *instinct of self-assertion* develops into a Will-to-Good, an expression of the Will of 'the Father', qualified by the person's Soul Ray working in accord with the entire Hierarchy. The fear of being unrecognised by one's group is thereby fully negated. One then walks in the 'fellowship' of the Christ's sufferings.[5]

This instinct finds transmuted correspondence in the Will-to-Be of a Creative Deity, Who manifests a ring-pass-not – a sphere of self-

---

4 *John 10:10.*

5 *Phil. 3:10.*

contained activity, the boundaries of which He will not step out of for the duration of that incarnate existence. When seen from the higher perspective, all circumscribed atomic unities can be considered ring-pass-nots.[6] Such, for instance, can be considered the boundaries of a planetary or solar Logoi, the skin of a physical form, or the spheres of influence of the Ray Ashrams of the Masters of Wisdom.

Finally, the *instinct towards knowledge* eventually produces the enlightened standing and wisdom that will dispel all fear of the unknown, making the person a Master of Wisdom. This instinct will eventually translate into the ability to choose and then travel on any of the cosmic Paths that lead away from the earth Scheme altogether.

What is termed instinct in the dense realm is really the evolved reflected attribute of the Thought process of the Mind of Deity when the universe (or Thought-Form) was emanated. It could be said that the Logos used the higher correspondence of the *instinct towards knowledge* to form a world-sphere of self-contained activity. (This is a consequence of the cosmic Path chosen by Him, to become a planetary Logos, upon a much earlier cycle.) This Path eventuates in the embodiment of a dense sphere through which countless Lives can evolve their evolutionary Purpose. It is one field of activity out of many for the *nirvāṇees* of an evolutionary sphere, such as is the earth. A Logos can then assert Himself as an incarnated Personality, thus becoming objectively distinct from the other world or solar spheres in the universe.

The manifestation of the substance of a world sphere happens from the highest plane wherein such differentiation is possible, the *ātmic plane*. When later reflected on the lowest plane of perception (the dense physical) the emanatory force becomes the *instinct of self-assertion*. It can be viewed as the originating karmic impulse.

In the greater sphere (Thought-Form) of the solar Logos, the Brothers of our Planetary Logos also formed similar spheres of sensation. The planets and planes of perception, the organs or *chakras* in the Body of the solar Logos, thus came into being. The interrelatedness of these

6 A ring-pass-not does not mean that an entity can't escape its bounds, it just means that an incarnating Being limits itself to its constraints for the duration of that incarnation in order to obtain the gain for that cycle of expression. There are a succession of levels for such constraints (physical, astral, mental, etc.).

Brothers (connoting the sum of the solar *chakra* and *nāḍī* system) caused the *herd or group instinct* to manifest as a natural reaction to their combined energies in the concrete realms. This activity emanated from (and caused the properties of) the buddhic plane.

On the mental plane the various dual forces – the lesser *(deva)* builders (the Agnishvattas) – came into play by reacting to higher energy impulses. They qualified those impulses with characteristics inherent in their constitution. Being of mind-substance, they caused the multitudinous differentiations between the various categories of forms, their reactions and interactions. All of the basic qualities (the yin-yang interrelations) inherent throughout manifest space (the expression of the manifestation of all sentient creatures) were thereby caused. This was the innate expression of evolutionary resolve by the means of union between all entities and their complementary selves. It allows the great play of action-reaction, the cause-effect universe that we live in, to come into being.

The principle of duality and the effect of the resolution of that duality to produce a fusion or unity (the Son) is inherent in all manifest space. It essentially emanates from the Mind of the Creator. The product is an effective duality between the originating cause, the seed point of the *maṇḍala* of expression, and what becomes the entire body of manifestation. When reflected into the dense physical realm, this energy expression manifests as the *sexual instinct*.

For humanity, the *instinct towards knowledge* emanated via the second plane of perception, *anupādaka,* as an expression of our Monadic form (the Spirit within) therein. This instinct is therefore an effect of their Reason for incarnate expression. This expression manifested in the kingdom of Souls on the higher mental realm. This kingdom became the various cellular units in the Body of the planetary Logos. Their interrelated evolutionary impetus then became the reflected source of the *instinct towards knowledge* in the dense physical realm. Human Souls can be considered the evolving quality that was inherent in the application of the Logoic Thought-Form, whilst Human Monads represent the energies of the Ideation of the Logos. The *deva* kingdom represents the substance utilised to build the incarnate Form.

The *instinct of self-preservation* is fundamental, a product of the Will of the Thinker that sustains His Creation. It thus underlies all the realms of existence, relating the highest to the lowest. Naught could exist without it, yet all Life evolves away from it, from death to Life and from Life to death: expansion after expansion, above and beyond the concept of 'self'. Everything will inevitably be merged into the All-Self, the Oneness that is ALL. This instinct is the expression of the various laws of conservation of energy that cause the bondage of atomic nuclei into integral forms, be they solar, planetary, or human atoms. This instinct thus emanates from the highest of the seven planes of perception *(ādi)* and underlies all the realms of existence.

The consolidation of these instincts into the various kingdoms of Nature took an enormous period of evolutionary time. The qualities impinged upon, then manifested through, substance. They eventually became innate properties of that substance, projecting also through plant and animal forms, and governing their mode of behaviour.

The three Outpourings

Before continuing, the three Outpourings of the Creative Essence from the triune Logos need to be considered. The information here shall be relatively brief, as it is a summary of what was given in my book *Meditation and the Initiation Process.*[7]

The *first Outpouring* concerns the pouring forth of the primal substance that caused the formation of the planes of perception, as well as the globes or spheres of activity whereon Life must find scope for evolution. This substance is *Fiery* in nature and concerns the evolution of the way of mind by means of concretion and consolidation into the forms of the various streams of the evolving Lives. It is an aspect of the work of the *third Logos,* the *great Mother,* and has as its basis the unfoldment of the five instincts and senses. The third Logos externalises Herself upon the *ātmic* plane (the fifth from below upwards), from whence emanates the primordial *karma* that conditions all aspects of the evolution of mind (the fifth principle). The form of motion concerned is rotary in nature.

The *second Outpouring* concerns the outpouring of the myriad Lives constituting the various kingdoms of Nature, thus the emanation

7 Pages 276-84 and figure 3 in that book.

of the twelve *Creative Hierarchies*.[8] This concerns those that en-Soul all forms, the activation of the petals of the *chakras* in the Body Logoic that are controlled, or dominated at first, by that of the Solar Plexus. Later, we see the twelve petals of the Logoic Heart rule, of which the Hierarchies are emanations. This concerns the awakening of consciousness. The work of the *Son,* or *second Logos*, externalises upon the plane *anupādaka*. The Lighted Lives come into being, and the form of motion is considered spiral-cyclic.

The third Outpouring emanates from the first aspect of the Logoic Body – *the Father* or Will aspect (the Initiatory Will), externalising upon the first plane, *ādi*. This concerns the Individualisation process of the animal kingdom, thus the formation of the human Soul upon the higher mental plane. This produces the consequent evolution of the fourth kingdom in Nature along the way of Initiation. In this manner they eventually become embodied Deity. The Fiery Life manifests via the associated process of Initiation, where this Outpouring comes as a consequence of the application of the rod of Power of Sanat Kumāra[9] for the higher Initiations. It concerns the Abstracting Impulse of the *Father*. The type of motion is forward-progressive.

All these Outpourings of the Creative factor of Deity are spread out cyclically through evolutionary time. The third Outpouring waits for the second to reach the appointed expression, and the second for the first to sow the fertile ground, but there is much overlapping of cycles. The greater cycle encompasses the activity of all lesser cycles, like the mechanism of a clock, with its wheels of cogs.

Notes to figure six

Figure six shows the evolution of instinct and is summarised below.

1. The seventh sub-plane of the *cosmic astral plane*. (The sixth of seven cosmic planes.)

---

8 The Creative Hierarchies are explained in *Esoteric Astrology* by A.A. Bailey and in more detail in the two volumes of my books *The Astrological and Numerological Keys to The Secret Doctrine*.

9 Sanat Kumāra, 'the Eternal Youth', is the planetary Logos, the great King of Shambhala (the planetary Head centre).

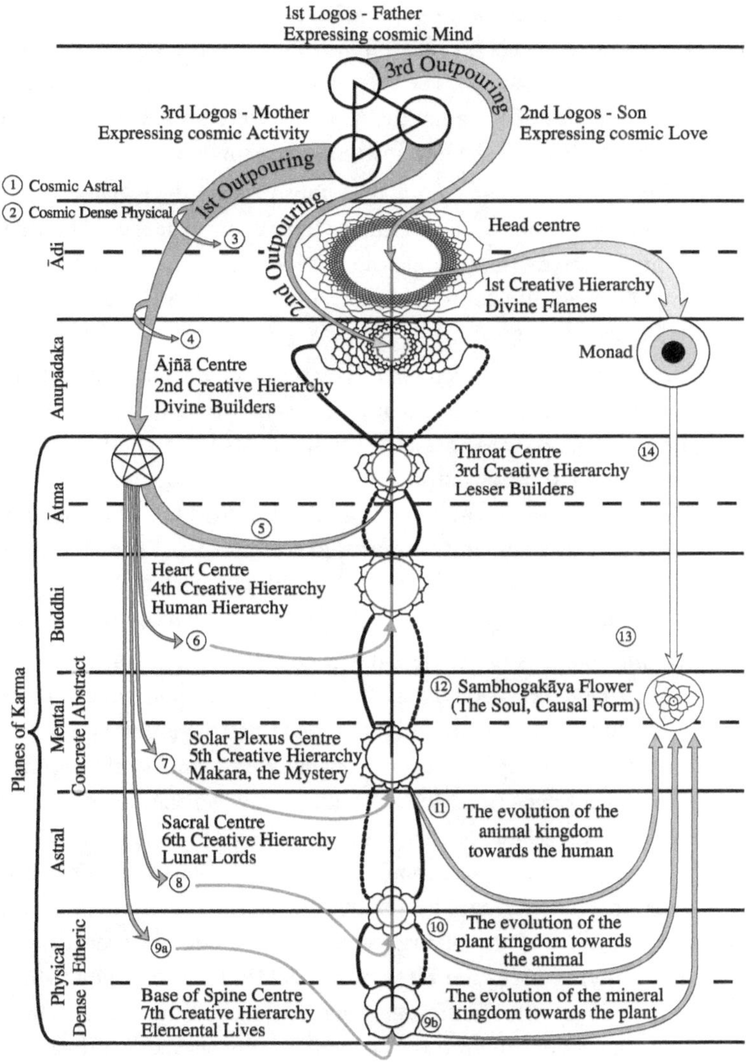

Figure 6: The evolution of instinct via the three Outpourings

2. The *seven systemic planes* whereon humanity finds scope for evolution in this solar system. These planes are the sub-planes of the cosmic dense physical plane. They are divided into four cosmic

etheric sub-planes *(ādi, anupādaka, ātma* and *buddhi)* and three concrete sub-planes (the mental, astral, and dense physical). Each manifests as a septenary. The five planes from *ātma* down are termed the five planes of Brahmā (the Mother). Here, Mind is developed and the qualities of the five instincts are expressed.

3. The *first* systemic plane is *ādi,* that of the plane of the Father (Divine Will) aspect, from which the third Outpouring proceeds. The first of the Creative Hierarchies, the Divine Flames, are established here. They administer to the main function of the Head centre of the Planetary Logos.
4. The *second* plane is *anupādaka.* Here resides the Monad, denoted in the Bible as the Spirit. It is a unit of cosmic Mind, and for humans (the fourth Creative Hierarchy[10]) it manifests the archetype of the instinct towards knowledge. This instinct is consequently the main propelling force for humanity. After the third Outpouring this instinct propels humanity onwards to cosmic space. The second of the Creative Hierarchies, the Greater Builders, also manifest here. They manifest the functions of the planetary Ājñā centre.
5. The *third* plane is *ātma.* Here the Logoic Thought-Form first takes proper shape (is objectivised). It utilises past *karma,* which, when ensconced in the human kingdom, becomes the archetype of the *instinct of self-assertion* of the personality. Here manifests the energies of the third Logos (the Mother), which empower the five planes of Brahmā. This pentad of energies is symbolised by the pentagram in the diagram. It is the focal point for the distribution of the substance of the first Outpouring. This Outpouring pours forth the *deva* Lives, who are guided by the mantric power from the Logoic Throat centre. This centre governs the Fires of mind/Mind. Here Logoic Mind (Mahat) directs the manifestation and evolution of the instincts, thus their conversion into the five sense-consciousnesses[11] utilised by

10 This Hierarchy are the human Souls. Though externalised upon the higher mental plane, their true home is *buddhi,* the plane of at-onement and of liberation for humanity. Also, though the human Monads are found upon the plane *anupādaka* they are not the second Creative Hierarchy. That Hierarchy is far more spiritually advanced than our humanity.

11 They are the types of awareness developed by the five sense-perceptors (the skin, eyes, ears, nose and the mouth).

humanity. On this plane manifests the work of the third Creative Hierarchy, the Lesser Builders, who build the forms into which the streams of Lives incarnate.

6. The *fourth* plane is *buddhi.* This plane, where the *nāḍī* system of the Logos is externalised, is the higher correspondence of the fourth ether. The overall distribution of these energies are governed by the Logoic Heart centre. The integration of these energies becomes the archetype of the *group or herd instinct.* This is the place of residence of the fourth Creative Hierarchy as liberated Souls (the Hierarchy of enlightened Being). They embody the attributes of the planetary Heart centre.
7. The *fifth* plane (upon the descending arc) is the *lower mental.* Here the various 'cells' (units of consciousness) in the Logoic Body come into activity. This represents the activity of the fifth Creative Hierarchy (Makara, the mystery), the *devas* who are ultimately responsible for the appearance of the dense physical form. The interaction of these *devas* with the appearing streams of Lives that will inhabit the manifesting forms produces the archetype of the *sexual instinct.*
8. The *sixth* plane is the *astral,* which is non-existent at this stage of evolution. It is a Watery field of crystallising energies that is practically indistinguishable from the etheric domain. This dynamic energy dispensation underlies the appearance of physical phenomena, and is controlled by the activity of the Logoic Sacral centre. The sixth Creative Hierarchy, the Lunar Lords, here embody the substance of humanity's emotions and desires. These 'lunar' forces can run amok and control those who misuse the lower psychic powers.

9a. The *seventh* plane is the *physical.* This concerns the appearance (concretisation) of the mineral kingdom that expresses the reflected attributes of the archetypes of the abovementioned instincts. At first, however, only that of self-preservation is prevalent. Many aeons pass in a nebulous ('Fiery Whirlwind'[12]), or plasma state, before forms appear. Mineral forms evolve and eventually radioactivity ensues.

---

12 See Stanza 5:1 of H.P. Blavatsky's *The Secret Doctrine,* and explained in detail in my book *The Astrological and Numerological Keys to the Secret Doctrine,* Vol. 2, 164-5, 167-8 and 172-3.

When the *sexual instinct* dominates, in terms of the manifestation of many organic chemical compounds, this allows the emergence of the second Outpouring. The plant kingdom thus appears.

9b. The four *etheric sub-planes* of the physical. These sub-planes are the true home of the plant kingdom. The objective of plant evolution is the perfect expression of the sexual instinct, which, as was seen, is innate to the mental plane. (On the inner realms this plane is the source of light, the light of the Soul, to which the plant kingdom technically aspires.) When this is achieved, then it is possible for plants to eventually be born into the animal kingdom by interaction with it (such as by the act of pollination), and by embracing their qualities. (For example, the development of a rudimentary nervous system, and sensitivity to touch, as some plants, such as the Mimosa family, already possess.) The seventh Creative Hierarchy, the Elemental Lives, en-Soul the evolution of the mineral kingdom.

10. The *astral plane*. The animal kingdom is naturally energised from this plane by its Watery attributes, which stimulate the principle of desire. The main astral energies however work to develop the group or herd instinct amongst them. This activity is directed by *devas* upon buddhic realms. The animal's way of evolution concerns the awakening of mind, which is a function of the work of the fifth Creative Hierarchy (Makara) whose energies permeate the entire sequence of animal evolution. All five instincts are therefore seeded in this kingdom. The integration between these two main forces produces the distinction between carnivorous and grazing animals. The herd instinct develops by diversification of animal qualities, and then their separation into smaller group unities[13] that have a greater aptitude for hastened, enriched learning experience. They develop cunning, devotion to a group leader, and complex social behaviour. The domestication of animals by those in possession of mind (humanity) has hastened this process, for humanity conditions these animals with many human characteristics.

11. When a sufficient number of animal units develop a rudimentary mind and true devotion, then such activity (aspiration) prompts the release

13 From large herds, to packs of animals, such as wolves, then, for instance, litters of kittens.

of the energies and processes to produce the *third Outpouring*. This, in turn, produces the appearance of the kingdom of human Souls.

12. The *higher mental plane*. Here Monadic Thought-Forms are incorporated into *deva* forms. They are differentiated into the various interrelated organs, *chakras,* or groupings of the human Hierarchy in the Body of Deity. The human kingdom (the human Soul, the Sambhogakāya Flower) is then formed on the abstract realms of the mind. From here the entire evolutionary journeying of humanity in the formed realms is eventuated by means of the '777 Incarnations' of each Soul.[14]

13. *Buddhi.* The true home of the human kingdom (the fourth Creative Hierarchy) is the buddhic (or fourth) plane, wherein the transmuted correspondence of the *group instinct* rules. This is the Love that sustains the Hierarchy of Enlightened Being that embody the petals of the Heart centre of the Logos. (The Dynamic driving Impetus behind all group participation.) Compassion, the shedding of the Heart's blood for the welfare of others, rules all enlightened beings. This Hierarchy embody the all-embracive consanguinity of Mind, yet they also work to perfect the transmuted aspects of the *instinct of self-assertion* of the Personality. In its higher connotation this instinct implies the development of the first Ray of Will or Power, and to direct *antaḥkaraṇas* (explained later) into the higher domains towards Shambhala (the Logoic Head centre) and into cosmos. The concept of 'Personality' here is that of the 'isolated unity' of the group-conscious Initiate.

14. *Ātma.* A Master of Wisdom (a fifth degree Initiate) is inevitably brought into being through bringing into manifestation attributes of Logoic Mind upon *ātmic* realms. This signifies the perfection of the objective of human evolution. Liberated humanity eventually move out of our earth Scheme via the second plane of perception, *anupādaka*.

An Initiate of the *third degree* has transmuted the *sexual instinct*, for the fusion between the basic dualities within one's constitution (the

---

14 See Alice Bailey's *A Treatise on Cosmic Fire,* 825-7, and elaborated in detail in my book *Maṇḍalas: Their Nature and Development,* 221-37.

iḍā and *piṅgalā nāḍīs)* has been achieved. This has allowed *kuṇḍalinī* to rise up the spinal column, producing the ascension up the Mountain of the Lord to produce complete integration with the Soul. This is the first true Initiation, productive of enlightenment. The first and second Initiations are called Initiations on the threshold.

The *fourth degree* Initiate has gained the transmuted correspondence of *the group* or *herd instinct.* The plane accessed *(buddhi)* is that of at-onement and universality. The 'I am' consciousness becomes merged into the whole, the That, which is expressed via the cosmic *nāḍīs* found on this plane. Thereon is experienced the collective Awareness of vast streams of evolutionary Lives, of planetary and solar spheres. The *anima-mundi* (world-Soul) can be experienced, as well as the collective Awareness of the Hierarchy of Enlightened Being. *Buddhi* is the main plane of their activities, from whence decisions are made concerning planetary evolution.

The *fifth degree* Initiate is responsive to the Logoic Mind *(dharmakāya).* The intellect (as the base to compassionate understanding) then resides below the threshold of consciousness, thus is effectively an instinct. Its function is automatic, basic, the ground level of Awareness. The Initiate's developed Will becomes the higher transmuted correspondence of *the instinct of self-assertion.* Utilising the Divine Will,[15] the Master of Wisdom can control the sum of *saṃsāra.*

Those that have attained the *sixth Initiation* (Chohans) have transmuted the *instinct towards knowledge,* for these Initiates are so completely identified with the Monad (Spirit) that there is nothing that they can further learn by contact with what is material. They have completely transcended the stage of being 'human', having fused the traits of both human (masculine) and *deva* (feminine) evolutions. The Chohans normally pass out of the earth evolution and the solar system altogether, to travel on one or other of the cosmic Paths.[16]

Those of the *seventh Initiation* (such as the Christ) can empower the laws governing the manifestation of corporeal Being, as far as the cosmic dense realm is concerned. All (mantric) Power associated

15 See chapter 7 of my book *Maṇḍalas: their Nature and Development,* for an explanation of this and the other permutations of the will.

16 Explained in *A Treatise on Cosmic Fire* by A.A. Bailey.

with the planes of perception are given to them, in accordance with the purpose of one or other of the three major Rays. They thus wield with effectiveness the transmuted correspondence of the *instinct of self-preservation*, to help maintain the conditionings associated with what the Spirit-Souls utilise in their evolutionary journeying.

The above information can be tabulated as shown below:

<table>
<tr><th>Instinct</th><th>Related Fear</th><th>Kingdom[17]</th><th>Plane</th></tr>
<tr><td>Self-preservation</td><td>Of death</td><td>Mineral</td><td>Physical</td></tr>
<tr><td colspan="4">Transmuted quality: immortality, control of the cosmic physical by a seventh degree Initiate.</td></tr>
<tr><td>Towards knowledge</td><td>Of the unknown</td><td>Soul</td><td>Higher Mental</td></tr>
<tr><td colspan="4">Transmuted quality: enlightenment, then Monadic perception by a sixth degree Initiate.</td></tr>
<tr><td>Self-assertion</td><td>Of failure</td><td>Human</td><td>Lower Mental</td></tr>
<tr><td colspan="4">Transmuted quality: the Will-to-Good, ātmic perception by a fifth degree Initiate.</td></tr>
<tr><td>Herd or Group</td><td>Of loneliness</td><td>Animal</td><td>Astral</td></tr>
<tr><td colspan="4">Transmuted quality: group consciousness. Hierarchical involvement. The fourth degree Initiate.</td></tr>
<tr><td>Sexual</td><td>Of isolation</td><td>Plant</td><td>Etheric</td></tr>
<tr><td colspan="4">Transmuted quality: spiritual fusion by a third degree Initiate.</td></tr>
</table>

Table 4. The five instincts and their relationships

17 The kingdoms and planes indicated here are considered at a lower level of correspondences to those of their transmuted qualities.

B. The factor of desire *(kāma)*, auras

The next principle influencing intelligence is *the astral body,* known in Sanskrit as *kāma-rūpa*, the body of desire. Desire is so closely allied to the intellect that it generally clouds, mars, and overrules clear rational thinking, to the extent that the dividing line between intellect and desire is often difficult to find.

The genesis of *kāma* (desire) is found in the vegetable kingdom, for many plants express the germ of desire as sense-response. In the animal kingdom desire is innate, but undistorted by thought processes. Humans develop the mind, which quickly directs the desire impulse.

The desire-mind that dominates the activities of most of us strongly influences the qualities of the aura, generally strengthening the baser colourings. The effect of spiritual development and mental discipline refines, intensifies, and then transmutes auric colourings. Nothing is static in the three realms of *saṃsāra:* everything is constantly modified and changed according to the effects of energy interplay between all beings.

The auric colours are perceptibly real to those with vision, yet like all else in Nature, they are essentially illusory, as D.K. aptly explains. He defines the aura as 'the quality of a sphere of radiatory activity', and then says that:

> The aura is usually spoken of in terms of colour and of light, due to the nature of the vision of the one who sees and the apparatus of response which is in use. Two words only describe an aura from the point of view of occult knowledge and they are "quality" and "sphere of influence." What the clairvoyant really contacts is an *impression* which the mind rapidly translates into the symbology of colour, whereas there is no colour present. Seeing an aura, as it is called, is in reality a state of awareness. That the seer may in all sincerity believe that he has registered a colour, a series of colours, or light, is entirely true in many cases, but what he has really recorded is the quality of a sphere of radiatory activity; this he does when his own individual sphere of radiatory activity is of the same nature and quality as that contacted. Most seers register the astral range of vibrations of a person or group and this through the medium of their own astral body. The impact of a truth or of a mental concept and its recognition is an expression of a similar contact, carried forward this time into the realm of the mind.[18]

18 Alice Bailey, *Discipleship in the New Age,* Volume 1, 752.

The colours or areas of such 'radiatory activity' in the emotional body of a person can be analysed thus:

Yellow has one of the most intense vibratory effects of all the hues. It usually is seen only around the head, and thus connotes that the person has the ability to think abstractly, or else is intuitional *(lemon yellow).* We often see pictures of the Christ and saints with yellow or golden halos around their heads. This part of their aura was so strong as to have been seen physically, and such observation has been preserved in our religious art.

The various *grassy green* shades indicate qualities related to the many forms of teaching, those that spend much of their time disseminating practical and useful information. *Light blue-green* implies the qualities of a healer, one who has the ability to truly ameliorate other's woes by means of generally physical palliatives and remedies, the right application of energies, and comforting speech. Many have this gift naturally, without necessarily setting themselves up as 'healers' per se. A *yellow-green* indicates the same quality manifesting upon a more subjective level (such as compassionate understanding), implying the ability to heal subjective causes and not just effects. Also, they are natural philosophers.

A *deep greyish-blue* tinge indicates adaptability, the ability to meet headlong all of life's manifold changes. It is the most common of auric colours in the average person.

The various shades of *red* denote the aspects of anger, pride, jealousy and sensuality. Thus sensuality is indicated by *dull brick red,* anger an explosive *vivid red*, and pride is a *deep red.*

Dark blue indicates devotion, the deep religious sentiment based on faith without real spiritual understanding, whereas *light blue* corresponds to the higher spirituality and inspiration.

Indigo is aurically deep blue tinged with green. It indicates the ability to manifest abstract thought, united with Love and intuitional capabilities.

Violet indicates a trance or psychism, or the development of higher spiritual abilities *(siddhis).*

Grey indicates fear, serious sickness, or a dulling of the senses.

A *dull White,* here, is an absence of characteristics and indicates immaturity, what has yet to be developed, whilst *black* indicates intense malice or hate (usually impinged with *flashes of red*, showing anger).

From studying the astral colourings described above, it can be seen whence such sayings as 'red with rage', 'a green thumb', or 'scarlet woman', derive their meaning. An emotion, such as affection, is a radiatory activity of a more subtly intense quality than, for instance, sensuality or hate. Its observable colour would therefore be more refined, clear and pure. Its sphere of influence is consequently greater. Sensuality or hate however can be strongly projected with the force of the will, hence their penetrating ability will be more powerful.

Habitual and frequently recurring emotions and actions stabilise and reinforce the corresponding astral matter. Such stabilised sensations continually cry out for stimulation. A person, for instance, who is strongly sensual possesses a large amount of brick red colouring around the sensual regions. If he/she tries to curb this habit the person would find that the intensified emanatory quality of the astral body would strongly influence the mind, thus continuously inducing sensual thoughts. The resultant imagination will then stimulate the desire body, and thence physical urges. The cycle is self-propagating.[19] Through lack of stimulation the radiatory activity centred in that area takes time to die out. It can only effectively be eliminated by lack of sustenance through much vigilance. The desired highly refined attributes are thus not so easily developed.

For a similar reason, *yogins,* seers and saints, usually require long periods of solitude before they achieve the continual revelation that is their life purpose. (Solitude also removes them from the major centres of astral and physical turmoil.) We see also why such beings as St. Anthony,[20] who (as it can be inferred) had no real understanding of the nature of the astral body, were plagued with hallucinogenic visions and dreams. Trying to force divinity whilst 'the devil' (i.e., astral conditionings) is still within, courts many psychic problems.

The astral particles that constitute an aura can easily dislocate themselves and dissipate into the atmosphere, or be attracted to anyone nearby. A person, therefore, who is violently angry, shoots out astral

---

19 Addiction to drugs and hallucinogens manifest in a similar way.

20 St. Anthony the Anchorite (251-356), a father of Monasticism in Christianity, is well known for his struggles in the desert with sexuality and various demons. His temptations are well known and are often depicted in Christian art.

emanations that afflict not only the object of anger but also anyone who happens to be there, giving all those present a tendency to anger. This partially explains why such emotions as anger and laughter are so contagious, and why the mob orator (for instance) has an immediate effect upon those around him. Almost everyone in close contact with another person absorbs some of the astral emanations from that being. Note the effect upon one's constitution when entering a room after there has been intense discharge of gaiety or anger by those in the room.

Energies accompanying mass psychological conditionings, such as sport displays and political gatherings, as well as the more subtle types induced by our media and advertisement campaigns, swirl through the astral atmosphere in accolades of expression of differing degrees and colourings. They have such a powerful effect upon people's subtle vehicles that very few can escape them, especially when reinforced by their imaginations. Massed astral energies are responsible for the fogs and clouds of glamour that enshroud our planet with 'darkness'. These self-made delusions, by individuals and humanity as a whole, constitute major obstacles upon the path for the average aspirant and disciple.

Aspirants on the spiritual path are necessarily concerned with overcoming the problem of glamour and illusion, both within their constitution and within the environment of which they are a part. They must eliminate such mass conditionings (especially from the mainstream media). This constitutes the beginning of the path to enlightenment for them. They must be able to stabilise their consciousness in vision and beauty so as to cleanse their own astral conditioning. This also assists in purifying the mass astral miasma. The meditating disciple clarifies the general auric environment by being impregnated with the seeds of divinity. (Accompanied by the intensity of the energies of the Ray colourings or white Light.) These seeds assist all creative contemplatives. They are the inspired ones working in any of the seven Ray departments of Life.

The astral characteristics are *transmuted* on the higher dimensions of perception, thus also the qualities associated with the various colours. (As stated, what is seen depends upon the clarity of perception of the perceiver.) True auric colourings, reflecting the qualities of enlightened Being, are those seen upon the higher mental plane, or *buddhi,* and are exceedingly vibrant. Deep red, for instance, manifests as that of the first Ray of Will, indigo blue as the second Ray of Love-Wisdom, and so forth. The vibrant light from the auras (radiatory emanations) of enlightened beings can be blindingly brilliant to those with the developed inner eyes that can perceive. For most seers or psychics, however, enlightened beings will manifest their presence through a veil of substance, often with symbolic imagery. This necessitates the empirical mind to correctly deduce what has been perceived.

The astral plane thus represents a major field of work and service for disciples up to Initiates of the third degree, who are immersed in it. Those of the third Initiation or greater work from the realms of light above the astral domain, hence manifest vaster responsibilities, according to the level of their Initiation status.

Glamour

Most of the world's religious teachings about the objective of love and selflessness effectively concern the rules of training associated with the dissipation of glamour. They also have many devotional aspects that contain seeds of glamour. Glamour can be depicted in terms of the nature of the astral fog, the cloud of emotional thought-forms that surrounds one's aura. Glamour thus relates to the way that the emotions and desire condition the mind. It normally dramatises the needs or image of the personal-I (or self-love) in relation to something 'other' that is desirous to it, or which it wishes to shine before. Glamour can also be conceived in terms of *kāma-manas*. Glamour can be contrasted with illusion, in that illusion is far more mental in quality, where images are formed by the creative imagination that the personality believes in.

Aspirants must utilise the total weight of their mental perceptions and understandings, held steady in the light of the Soul, in order to tackle the problem of the fogs of astral substance associated with their own constitution. Only the mind, divorced from the emotions, can adequately recognise glamour and thus act towards its elimination. This subject is fully explained in the book *Glamour: A World Problem*, therefore needs no recapitulation here. Below is a quotation from the book, listing some of the types of glamour that might affect people, according to Ray qualifications.

Ray I.

The glamour of physical strength.
The glamour of personal magnetism.
The glamour of self-centredness and personal potency.
The glamour of "the one at the centre."
The glamour of selfish personal ambition.
The glamour of rulership, of dictatorship and of wide control.
The glamour of the Messiah complex in the field of politics.
The glamour of selfish destiny, of the divine right of kings personally exacted.
The glamour of destruction.
The glamour of the superimposed will—upon others and upon groups.

Ray II.

The glamour of the love of being loved.
The glamour of popularity.
The glamour of personal wisdom.
The glamour of selfish responsibility.
The glamour of too complete an understanding, which negates right action.
The glamour of self-pity, a basic glamour of this ray.
The glamour of the Messiah complex, in the world of religion and world need.
The glamour of fear, based on undue sensitivity.
The glamour of self-sacrifice.
The glamour of selfish unselfishness.
The glamour of self-satisfaction.
The glamour of selfish service.

RAY III.

The glamour of being busy.
The glamour of cooperation with the Plan in an individual and not a group way.
The glamour of active scheming.
The glamour of creative work—without true motive.
The glamour of good intentions, which are basically selfish.
The glamour of "the spider at the centre."
The glamour of "God in the machine."
The glamour of devious and continuous manipulation.
The glamour of self-importance, from the standpoint of knowing, of efficiency.

RAY IV.

The glamour of harmony, aiming at personal comfort and satisfaction.
The glamour of war.
The glamour of conflict, with the objective of imposing righteousness and peace.
The glamour of vague artistic perception.
The glamour of psychic perception instead of intuition.
The glamour of musical perception.
The glamour of the pairs of opposites, in the higher sense.

RAY V.

The glamour of materiality, or over-emphasis of form.
The glamour of the intellect.
The glamour of knowledge and of definition.
The glamour of assurance, based on a narrow point of view.
The glamour of the form which hides reality.
The glamour of organisation.
The glamour of the outer, which hides the inner.

RAY VI.

The glamour of devotion.
The glamour of adherence to forms and persons.
The glamour of idealism.
The glamour of loyalties, of creeds.
The glamour of emotional response.
The glamour of sentimentality.
The glamour of interference.
The glamour of the lower pairs of opposites.
The glamour of World Saviours and Teachers.
The glamour of the narrow vision.
The glamour of fanaticism.

RAY VII.

The glamour of magical work.
The glamour of the relation of the opposites.
The glamour of the subterranean powers.
The glamour of that which brings together.
The glamour of the physical body.
The glamour of the mysterious and the secret.
The glamour of sex magic.
The glamour of the emerging manifested forces.[21]

---

21 A.A. Bailey, *Glamour: A World Problem, 120-23.*

The glamour of psychic perception is perhaps the main glamour that will increasingly come to the fore as the New Age develops. This is because that epoch will increasingly produce a higher psychic receptivity within humanity and consequently a widespread interest in occult arts. Hallucinogenic and related drugs also produce major forms of glamour along this line.

The Atlantean epoch

It should be noted that psychic perception (as related to the powers of the *chakras* below the diaphragm), be it under the influence of drugs or otherwise, means a reversal of the normal *prāṇic* forces in the body. (These powers need to be wisely directed by an Initiate working via the centres above the diaphragm.) Such stimulation occurs in the centres made spiritually redundant since the Atlantean era, when they were needed by humanity. This reintroduces a type of atavistic clairvoyance, reversing the evolutionary trend – from psychic sensitivity (astral consciousness) to intellect, to wisdom (enlightened consciousness). Higher spiritual powers *(siddhis)* can then rightly manifest.

The widespread use of drugs today is a karmic reverberation from those ancient times. People were then pre-eminently emotional and had an uncontrolled desire for material things. They had clairvoyance associated with the involuntary nervous system. (Whereas the type of powers to be developed nowadays should be based on the cerebro-spinal system, dominated by the brain and the use of the mind.)

When humanity began to develop the intellect, then this reinforced astralism with extremely potent desires and psychism. This caused people to pursue black magical practices, witchcraft and related sorceries en masse, to try to satiate their overstimulated imaginative wishes and desires. Rapacious desire for luxury and possessions produced massed forceful selfish incantations. The consequence was the formation of enormous clouds of desire forms, and huge psychic beasts: of aggressiveness, of burden, of lasciviousness, of fright, and of material comfort. People's actions were so much dominated by the Lords of evil Intent, the hosts of darkened countenance, that it threatened to destroy the fabric of the Plan for evolution for the world. This caused the Lord(s) of Life (the 'God' of the book of Genesis) to cleanse away a large part of the glamour (muddied astral/Watery aspect) of humanity by means of the great flood that sank the Atlantean continent.

Much of the potency associated with the Atlantean sorcery was precipitated into the plant kingdom. (Such precipitation was possible because of the then humanity's strong affinity with the plant kingdom.[22]) This psychic potency has remained there to this present time, to be released at this turn of the cycle by the users of the various hallucinogenic drugs. Many of their effects (such as the consequences of addiction) can be viewed as a karmic heirloom from those times.

The astral plane still contains much that was then built into it, and revitalised during succeeding cycles of evolutionary activity, such as the mythos of the ancient Egyptians based on theriomorphic deities, and strong magical rituals focussed mainly on the belief of an afterlife (Amenti or Duat). Our present world era is but a recapitulation of that ancient Atlantean epoch, but on a higher, more materialistic cycle. What was once almost purely psychic is now objectivised and materialised. The pollution covering the face of the earth, the wanton destruction of all forms of vital life through greedy materialism, constant warfare, the building of 'concrete jungles' (and much more), are all symbols of inner plane astral conditionings. They are the reverberated effects of that ancient *karma* being intensified anew. The Lords of selfish and evil might again dominate the flowing psychic currents of our civilisation.

All true texts on meditation and spiritual or psychic development warn us to beware of the lower psychic powers, and for good reason. The dangers of abuse of such powers are great. Similarly are the effect of psychism upon those who presume they have contacted entities from the highest realms, or that their abilities are divinely inspired (thinking that they come from higher centres than they actually do), or that the revelations they receive are of the highest order, etc. Generally, naught could be further from the truth. The veil of glamour weighs heavily over their minds, obscuring their vision by colouring it with the traits of the cloud of astral substance that they have attracted to themselves. Often such people will need to spend a number of lives eliminating the *karma* they have thus engendered.

---

22 There is a close numerical affinity, in that the Atlanteans were the fourth Root Race, the astral is the sixth plane, and plants are the sixth kingdom in Nature.

It can almost certainly be ascertained that a system of spiritual teaching is governed by glamour when it justifies itself by stating the revelations have come from this or that cosmic or heavenly Entity, 'God', Christ, or any such liberated or ascended embodiment of Divinity. When the jargon of such teachings are closely examined we often see many absurd claims, with very little presented that is of true value for human betterment. It can also be an advance upon that elsewhere presented. Sensationalism is often the order of the day.

The qualities of true teachings will speak for themselves. They are not true if they serve to stimulate devotion in any of its many forms, are basically emotional in their appeal, or provide no further teaching above and beyond what has already appeared in written form. Then it can be ascertained that they come from the realm of glamour or illusion (the personality realm). Such teachings do not come from enlightened realms. Nevertheless, nearly all teachings have at least a small basis of truth or seek out the kernels of truth. Beware, however, the reticulation of distorted information that may be woven through them. The trusted discriminative mind, utilising past experience and held steady in the light, must be one's major tool here (and for all other topics).

True New Age teachings are based on the sum of tried and tested truths of the past and will allow the seven keys to be applied with effectiveness. They focus upon imparting revelations associated with the higher powers and qualities of enlightened Being. This necessitates the wise utilisation of the mind for understanding. The enlightened teachers write for wise thinkers and not for devotees who would tend to distort the teachings through their desire minds, wish-fulfilling intuitions, and feeling-perceptions. These are major causes for glamour. No enlightened person will encourage or vitalise the Atlanteanism that is no longer viable for the evolutionary development of humanity. They will not foster devotional pursuits that are doomed to failure by lacking true wisdom as their basis.

C. The intellect and thought-forms

Fundamental to the understanding of the causative process is the analysis of the qualities of the mental body. It was shown earlier that the mind is divided into a higher (or archetypal) and a lower (or empirical) aspect.

Further qualities of the lower mind, or intellect, will now be explained, specifically in relation to desire and the subjective side of things. The intellect is a classifying tool, the cognised result of sense perception that acts as a medium between objective physical experiences and the subjective domains. It does this by differentiating phenomena in terms of the observer and the observed. Therefore, it is responsible for the idea of separateness. (A function that the human kingdom must inevitably learn to transcend.)

The intellect is born in humanity as an effect of the external relatedness between all pairs of opposites, which is inherent in matter during the progress of its sentience. (Specifically, the instinct towards knowledge.) Intelligence is sustained by means of the evolved senses and associated contact with all forms of phenomena. Intelligence is used to enumerate and classify the different categories of things. The angelic kingdom embodies its substance. They wear it as a corporeal sheath, and the lesser *devas* are moulded by its inherent qualities to make the forms of all things.

Intelligence is the 'I am' principle that allows a personality to come to be, allowing contact with all that is not the personal self. For only when people can intelligently think can they truly begin to differentiate from the herd mentality of those ensconced in emotionality. A personality can thus only manifest after the intellect dominates the astral and physical environment, and thus is no longer manipulated by the incessant tides of desire and thought forms that sway and afflict people. (Such things as public opinion, social mores, and fashionable attitudes.) A personality is a free will that can intelligently pursue whatever path in life is chosen.

A personality can thus be defined as the bundle of mental aggregates that coherently dominate the instinctive and emotional qualities developed by the evolving form. (Which is cyclically collected by the incarnating Soul for a specified purpose.) As a functioning unity the personality can intelligently register impressions from the phenomenal and subjective realms. These are then collated and stored so that they can be consciously recalled to satisfy a specific purpose. The developed intellect is therefore the gain of personality development.

The intellect is however normally integrated with desire or the emotions, termed *kāma-manas* in Sanskrit. *Manas* is derived from the root *man* – to think, whilst *kāma* is desire. The intellect is conscious to the phenomenal world of action/reaction, whilst desire (or the emotions) focuses perception on any object that is wished for, or that manifests the allure of glamour.

Attachments to such objects normally produce feeling-sensations, or emotionality, in relation to them. Attachments manifest as idea-forms (thought-forms) in astral-mental substance that have a life or duration of expression, to the extent of the energy put into them. The impetus of desire (or the will) can project such idea-forms to any imaginable place on earth.

We think by utilising the elementary Lives (the *devas)* from the emotional and lower mental planes, moulding those Lives (the substance of the planes) into our thought-forms. By doing this we imbue that thought with an inherent life that emanates a particular vibrational quality, hue, or combination of hues, circumscribed as a form that expresses the quality of the thought. These thoughts are intermingled with, or else emanate out of, our auras.

The principle behind the life of an average thought can be pictured thus:

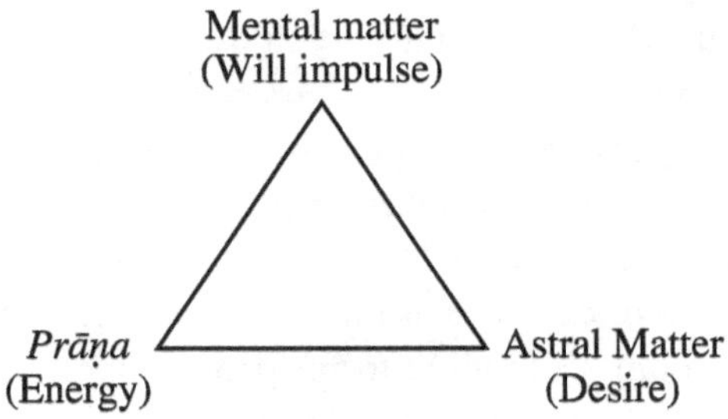

Figure 7: The energy of thought

This triad of energies can be seen, for instance, in a well-intentioned compassionate thought, represented pictorially below (as apparent to clairvoyant sight):

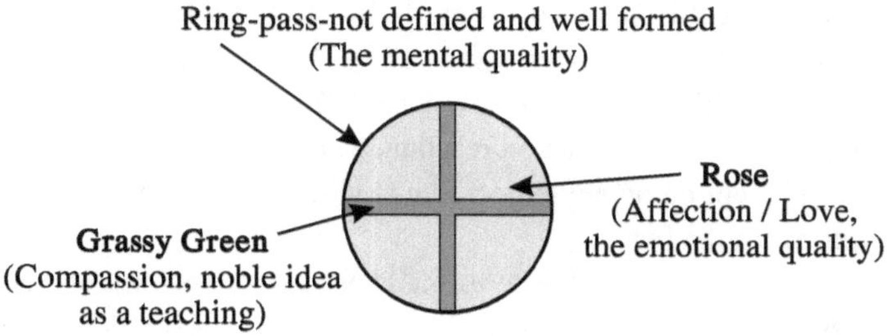

Figure 8: A compassionate thought

This thought-form is strongly vivified with energy because it has a clearly developed and well-outlined form. It therefore has a long life and can be sent unerringly to perform the task assigned to it. When absorbed it will produce a definite thought based upon the qualities inherent within (via the four directions in space). The fixed cross therein is of compassionate intent, as related by its colour (here of a grassy green). The cross also indicates a form of a teaching or instruction. As depicted, the rose colouration indicates that this thought-form is imbued with an affectionate energy.

Figure 9 indicates a sensual thought-form, seen as a reddish-brown cloud brooding over the creator. It therefore is constantly fed by the person's sensual desires and imagery. It can be sent to the object of desire, in which case the 'hooks' may try to latch on to that object.

Inspirational thought-forms take the shape of triangles, coloured rings, flashes and stars. In fact they can take any geometrical shape or form. Sensual, selfish and desire forms, or those with nebulous intent, are generally clouds of coarse astral matter enveloping the person.

The lifespan of all thought-forms depend upon the amount of *prāṇa* imbued in them, and the nature of the thought. A thought that embodies an aspect of the force of Love has a far longer life and greater penetrability than a selfish form directed to and centred around a person. There are thus oceans of swirling torrents of thick clouds of sensual and selfish desire-forms created incessantly by people. They are, however, constantly being washed and annulled by the fewer (though far more powerful thought-forms) engendered by Love and aspiration. In this idea lies the hope for the salvation of humanity.

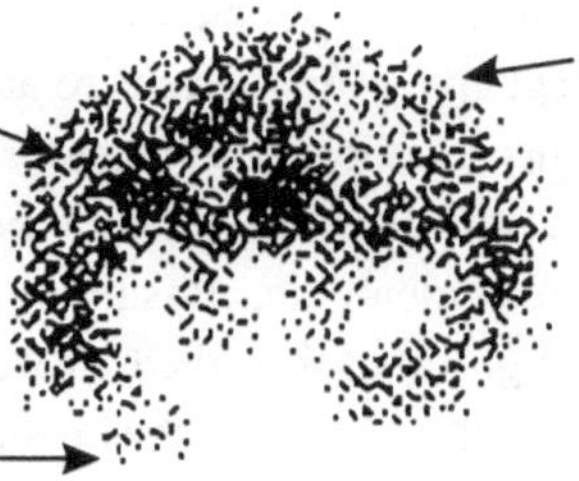

Figure 9: A sensual thought

The cumulative effect of thinkers throughout the ages has produced a sea of thought and desire forms in which most beings are constantly bathed. Those who look for inspiration must invariably, by the nature of their concentration, send out probes that will attract the appropriate type of thought-form needed. Thus ideas, mental flashes, or revelations are obtained, allowing the completion of the work they are engaged in. Thought-forms are absorbed into the consciousness, though people often modify them according to the qualities and characteristics composing their mental and astral auras.

Everyone builds thought-forms whenever they think. People automatically project them towards the object of their thoughts (if there is one), and these can also be absorbed into a recipient's aura. Thus, one often 'feels' what someone close[23] is thinking, or gets a flash, a telepathic message from another. This is virtually ascertained if there is an affectionate or loving bond between those concerned, as a link is produced between them facilitating telepathic rapport.

If the atmosphere in a room is tense, undermined with emotional currents, then a person entering feels this because his/her aura is bombarded with such thought-forms. Everyone lives in all types of thought-forms: individual, national, religious, scientific, racial, cultural and those that are divinely inspired. They are attracted to us by way of the similarity of colourings possessed in our auras, affecting us accordingly. This happens far more than a self-centred person would

23 By 'close' here is not necessarily meant physical closeness, but rather, one who is in the person's thoughts.

like to admit. Many dreams, spontaneous desires and realisations, come by this means, especially impressions related to mass conditionings.

There are immense collective thought-forms engendered by countless beings throughout the ages. They are constantly fed by the glamour, emotional, inspired, idealistic, illusional and devotional thoughts of people. There are prototypes of the Christ, the Buddha, hell, heaven, etc., — not as they actually are, but as people have imagined them to be. They act as reservoirs of the qualities with which they are imbued, and constantly influence everyone susceptible to such conditionings. This happens by means of innate desire, the quality of their mental constitution, *karma,* and present life indoctrinations.

Many psychic or telepathic people receive their visualisations, prognostications and understandings from such sources, thinking erroneously, but in all sincerity, that they have contacted highly evolved spiritual entities. Much so-called 'occult' information and 'divine revelation' can also be inspired by thought-forms coming from higher levels. Sometimes enlightened beings can also be contacted thereby. This would be the case, for instance, when a Master of Wisdom may be contacting his student.

Most psychics and spiritual people, however, rarely contact such exalted beings. They need to possess a proper sense of proportion and knowledge of the higher domains and the beings residing therein if true spiritual contact is to be made without distortion. The glamour-forming nature of the astral plane also needs to be adequately considered.

It can be intuited that cosmic Entities and Beings from the kingdom of 'God' (Shambhala) produce planetary and interplanetary effects. They project Thought-Forms and energies affecting whole categories of Life and the kingdoms of Nature during various appointed cycles. They have naught to do whatsoever with communicating any information to personalities. Only an Initiate of the third degree or greater could have any true awareness of their influence at all.

Initiates of the higher degrees in fact rarely, if ever, provide esoteric teachings to those who have not achieved personality integration, those who do not walk upon the path of Love-Wisdom. Disciples who will have taken the lesser Initiations are those directly responsible for the education of spiritual 'children'. Their training directly concerns the overcoming of glamour and illusional thought-forms. The 'children' normally innately seek mediumistically inspired and sensationalised information, thus teachings wrapped in glamour. They must consequently be taught to look towards the realms of reality, not the astral depths. For them this is often a very difficult achievement.

One cannot overestimate the effect that thought and desire forms have upon our subjective selves. We will even have to live out the intensity of our created thought forms in the afterlife.

Nowadays the grosser aspects of the thought-forms associated with outmoded systems of thought are being rectified and transmuted by the world's aspirants and the intelligentsia. This happens through the effects of scientific investigation and by thought geared towards concrete proof before acceptance of any theory of phenomena. A prime duty of every new religious, social, philosophic, or scientific movement, is to dissipate or destroy the unsatisfactory forms built by their predecessors. Humanity originally created them, so they must also destroy them.

All forms of glamour and illusions can be rectified by the light of the mind, of reason, and then by developing receptivity to the Christ Light (the intuition). Those that utilise their thoughts constructively are spiritually helping the evolutionary progress of Nature's kingdoms. They help to tear asunder and to transform the veil of darkness surrounding our earth so that Light may enter.

There are also large inspirational and educational Thought-Forms sent to humanity by Hierarchy (and also from Shambhala). Their objective is to set up the appropriate psychic atmosphere that will help condition humanity to planned spiritual events. Many major revolutionary epochs in human history have been conditioned this way. The inspirational mantras of Hierarchy manifest to assist those who incarnate to carry the new epoch into manifestation. A major Thought-Form along this line concerns the reappearance of the Christ in the New Age. Such a proceeding is a major world event and will radically change the face of human history. Since the Renaissance period in Europe humanity has been unconsciously conditioned in preparation for this.

Such teachings have also been part of the general expectation of Christians for 2,000 years, but theirs is an exoteric doctrine that has preserved the general idea of such an eventuation. Christian dogma however no longer controls the Western world. People are now better educated as a consequence of the scientific, philosophic and academic criticism of past theologically inspired propaganda (such as the world being flat). There is an ever-increasing inability of the churches and propagandists in government to control people's thoughts. Humanity's bias however has become much more materialistic, with all of the attendant evils. Humanity must consequently again learn the basics of spiritual reasoning, but now genuine and logical information must be presented that can lead people to liberation and enlightenment upon the path of Love and Wisdom.

Alice Bailey presented the more esoteric aspects concerning the Reappearance of the Christ, which was further elaborated in my volumes of *The Constitution of Shambhala*. This esoteric information has been presented because such knowledge is truly needed in the world to help foster the dawning of this New Age. This process is proceeding according to Hierarchical schedule, despite the current social, economic and political fiasco.

Some thought-forms are consciously made for a specific purpose, like those engendered by the Egyptian (black) magicians to protect the tombs of the Pharaohs. They are limited in scope but powerful, and can function even after a lapse of many thousands of years. Others, such as the (fabricated) conditionings associated with the twelve signs of the zodiac, are far more pervasive, influencing the lives of millions, conditioning their play in *saṃsāra* for aeons.

The power of thought is potent, and humanity needs to learn much about it. Before they learn the arts of conscious thought-form building (thereby becoming creative magicians) they must comprehend the meaning of Love (compassionate understanding) and of complete selflessness as a force. Otherwise the potency of such knowledge will be used to destroy and not build. Weapons of mass destruction with their ability to annihilate life are exoteric symbols of a similar ability that can destroy the civilised world using mainly psychic forces. To prevent such eventuation is a major reason why teachings concerning the raising of *kuṇḍalinī,* for instance, have always been heavily veiled. To present safe teachings concerning the way to liberation has always been the motive behind the work of all disciples of the Christ. Such teachings will be increasingly needed when the mass of people become awakened to the reality of the psychic realms as a prelude to the Reappearance of the Christ.

The societal conditionings and values of people are being changed, and this change is concomitant with the discovery of Nature's finer forces. The human mind (with its selfish materialistic values) that has so far been focused downwards into the concrete world will slowly turn upwards to focus upon the Hierarchical Light. This is necessary, if more detailed, advanced information than previously presented in esoteric and meditation texts is to be revealed.

Thought-forms are living entities that are nearly always clothed in astral matter, and thus enter and influence the person through the Solar Plexus centre (for most people are emotionally polarised). A purely mental thought enters via the Throat centre, whilst direct ideation or inspiration from planes beyond the mental enters via the Head or Heart centre. All occult, psychic or mental creation, or the transference of thought, is done with the aid of the *chakras*. The process is threefold:

1. The *initial inspiration*, the seed point *(bīja)* of the thought. This may consist of the substance of the higher or lower mental plane,[24] or for the most sensual people, astral matter (though technically not a thought-form). The nature of the seed determines the quality of the substance that is attracted to it and necessitates the focus of the intent of the will, or of desire.
2. The thought-form *is projected upon its errand*. If it is to be purely subjective, then it remains upon the mental plane to influence the minds of thinkers. If it is to be objectivised, then it is first clothed in the appropriate astral matter, then etheric substance, and consequentially is crystallised into dense form. The physical plane automatically builds in terms of whatever energies manifest through the etheric body.
3. After it has performed its task the thought-form *must be destroyed* or drawn back into the aura of the thinker, otherwise it becomes a

24 Seeds can also emanate from the higher liberated domains, if generated by a high Initiate.

karmic liability. The thinker would sooner or later be compelled to offset its (malefic or redundant) effects. All thinkers must pay the price for the effects of their thought forms. This is a subjective reason for why the Christ-Jesus must come again, because the effects of the wrong interpretation of His teachings must be rectified. It also explains one of the main things that binds the Christ with us until the 'end of the age'[25] (when coupled with His Love and Compassion), for the thought-forms engendered as a result of Jesus' former appearance are immense, far reaching in consequence. They will take a long time before they become invalidated, which necessitates their dissipation.

It is possible for an illumined being to create things directly by the use of thought power.[26] Our technological age, with its miraculous labour-saving devices, can also be considered to be a result of materialised thoughts.

Mental telepathy is the result of thought energy sent with sufficient *prāṇa* by the transmitter to impact upon and be absorbed into the mind of the receptive person. Telepathic communication from mind to mind (rather than the emotional type from Solar Plexus to Solar Plexus centre) should become increasingly frequent as the mental unfoldment of humanity progresses, and their psychic receptive facilities become more developed. Conscious mental communications between more advanced people should become a common happening during the next few centuries.

This activity is facilitated through the process of meditation. One must have an attitude of non-attachment, with no strong emotions or feelings, and then concentrate one's energies upon the required thought-form. The thought must inevitably be dissipated when its purpose is accomplished. Emotion or desire for anything (e.g., to achieve success, or fear of failure) by the receiver will create eddies, or currents of force, that will tend to rebuff the sender's thought-form. If strong enough they will be sent back.

---

25 *Matt. 28:20* – 'Lo, I am with you alway, *even* unto the end of the world'.

26 See, for example, Alexander David-Neel's *Magic and Mystery in Tibet* (Dover Publications, N.Y., 1971) for illustrations of this.

To send a mental thought to another the receptive part of the receiver's brain must be attuned to the frequency of the thought. People who are in telepathic rapport with each other have built an *antaḥkaraṇa* (consciousness-link) between each other's mind, along which a thought can travel at any time without modification.

Every person that thinks effectively re-enacts the primal act of creation, when the Logos utilised Thought energy to animate substance into form. The form persists as long as the thinker continues to vitalise it. This would be aeons for a solar Logos, and a lifetime in the case of the Soul's meditation upon the personality. Regarding what is usually a person's idle glimmerings of mental stimulation a few minutes may suffice.

Those who wish a deeper comprehension of the nature and projection of mental telepathy should refer to the book *Telepathy and the Etheric Vehicle* by A.A. Bailey.[27] Much further valuable esoteric detail is contained therein.

Mental telepathy incorporates the use of the *Fiery Element*, some of the properties of which have been explained earlier. Mental substance is the source of all light and warmth, the furnace within which all alchemical and transmutative processes are accomplished. Its higher correspondence is with what Deity fashioned or wrought whatever manifest is. Fire destroys and consumes all things, and yet this Fire also moulds and makes anew. The Element also embodies the internal heat that sustains every aspect of Life. Without this incandescent energy (and therefore light), no Life could exist, for all are aspects of the Mind of 'God' (Who is a 'consuming fire'[28]). Our ability to reason and think is but a tiny aspect (or 'spark') of that Fire.

When the mental process is conditioned by *kāma* then the Fires of the mind become focused upon a point – the object of desire. This point is the looking glass that allows our intellects to perceive the objective world. People that function through *kāma-manas* can only view one particular thing or point at a time in the immensity of space. A scenery (such as a landscape) is made by the mind instantly collating a sequence of a myriad of such 'points'. The minds classify those points according

---

27 A.A. Bailey, *Telepathy and the Etheric Vehicle,* (Lucis Publishing Co., N.Y., 1950).

28 *Heb. 12:29.*

to their own preconditioning. The mind is necessarily self-centred, for the points are only understood as such in relation to the perception of oneself as a viewer. The general patterns produced by a picture image composed of many such points can be distorted, according to one's desires, equipment of response, and other conditionings.

This point is also the focal point of the eye of the creator during the 'moment of creation'. The energy of the mind is concentrated upon that point when the will is applied. In Nature the 'point' can be seen as an atom of substance, as well as, for instance, a planetary or solar sphere in the cosmos.

To understand the process of Divine Causation will thus concern a comprehension of the nature of the manifestation of a point in time and space. (This is depicted pictorially as the central point within a sphere.) Such knowledge provides a fuller idea of the subjective nature of the atoms that compose all manifest space. (Be this space in the body of a person or of Deity.) The process normally involves the use of the intellect that discriminates, classifies, and restricts the Fires of the mind to a seed point or 'germ'. The point then evolves into a sphere of activity through which a being manifests the purpose for that evolutionary cycle. The chapter on the Question of Evil will provide further understanding of the manifestation of the energy of Fire in relation to the causation process (without which naught could exist).

BODO 83

What your Life brings

However your Heart sings
that is what your Life brings.
In your Heart you will find
the One who guides mankind.
He you must seek,
whose Light comforts the meek
and grows from week to week.

I am His shadow.
I follow in His footsteps.
I travel in the wake of the Way
He has prepared for me.
I am His servant.
I add my Heart to His Glory
for ever and ever.

Amen.

7

The Organs of Sensation and of Action

The mode of interaction of the five Rays of Mind[1] as they traverse the planes of perception wherein the Divine Mānasaputra[2] (the human Soul) finds its livingness, constitutes the corporeal Body of Brahmā. (The Creative Deity.) The sum of the realms of form (from the *ātmic* plane down) wherein mind/Mind *(manas)* evolves is His Body of Manifestation. When reflected in the human constitution this 'mode of interaction' forms the basic quintuple division of our external constitution – our bodily nature, as governed by the five senses. These senses find their localised means of expression in the five organs of sensation, producing the sense-consciousnesses, as depicted below.

---

1 The third to the seventh Rays.

2 The term *mānasaputra* relates to the body *(putra)* that is composed of the mind, as is the Soul. The term I also often use is the Sambhogakāya Flower, which depicts the form of the Soul on the higher mental plane, where in the Buddhist philosophy the attributes of this plane are described as the *sambogakāya.* (See my book *The Buddha-Womb and the Way to Liberation* for detail.) As earlier stated, sometimes the Soul is also called the Causal form.

Sense Perceptor	Sense	Ray[3]	Element
The Ear	Hearing	Ray 7	Earth
The Skin	Touch	Ray 6	Water
The Eyes	Sight	Ray 5	Fire
The Tongue	Taste	Ray 4	Air
The Nose	Smell	Ray 3	Aether

Table 5: The five organs of sensation

The totality of the stored and assimilated perceptions from these five senses, and the means whereby they are consciously utilised, constitutes the human personality. Likewise, it is the totality of the five lesser Rays and the sensations stored and received from their interaction and contacts in the Body of Deity that connote the nature of the Divine Personality. Deity is robed with the Rays, just as we are robed with our organs of sensation. To understand, therefore, the function of our senses is to get an idea of the function of the Rays in the Body of Deity. Humanity or Deity can use them either selfishly and sensually, or to gain illumination. (Though in the case of Deity one must take care not to materialise the subject.)

There are higher correspondences to the senses on the subtle planes of perception. They are expressions of the various psychic powers, such as those found on the astral plane:

Clairaudience	hearing
Psychometry	touch
Clairvoyance	sight
Creative imagination	taste
Emotional idealism	smell[4]

3 The kingdoms and planes indicated here are considered a lower level of correspondences to those of their transmuted qualities.

4 This list is adapted from detail found in Alice Bailey's, *A Treatise on Cosmic Fire*, 185-207.

Upon the higher liberated planes, these states of perception necessarily become abstractions.

Each of the five senses is pre-eminently related to a particular plane of perception, and therefore to the Ray that governs that plane. Thus *hearing* is related to the *physical plane*,[5] therefore to *Ray seven* of Ceremonial Magic, Materialising Power, because here the Logoic Word finds its densest expression. Deity created the physical universe by means of Sound and ritualistic Activity, as explained in detail in my book *Esoteric Cosmology and Modern Physics.* Such Ritual is observed for instance in the cyclic turning of the moon around the earth and the earth around the sun. Also by means of a Word of Power, the prodigy is abstracted back to its Source.

The seventh Ray is the reflection of the first Ray into the dense physical, and Sound is the medium that relates the two. Divine Will (the first Ray) directs the Primal Word and represents the Father aspect. The *devas* (whose materialising activity is governed by the seventh Ray) build the dense substance as they listen to the *Word.* They are the activity of the Mother. Sound is the product of 'the whole creation' as it 'groaneth and travaileth in pain together'[6] through its evolutionary path. Except possibly for the sense of sight, hearing was the first sense developed by primeval humanity. (Adam and Eve *listened* to the Word of 'God'[7] before they could *see* their nakedness.)

Hearing, via the medium of sound, is the most limiting or confusing of the senses, as it is easily mistaken or misunderstood. (Just as the physical plane is the most limiting of all the planes of perception.) Yet it is through the media of sound that the sacred Word, when rightly understood and aspirated, finally enables us to escape from the limitations of *saṃsāra*. This necessitates listening to the Voice of Silence that emanates from the innermost recesses of the Heart.

---

5 This statement is not quite true, for this Ray actually governs the etheric substratum, whose energies control the manifestation of what eventuates in the dense form.

6 *Romans 8:22.*

7 *Genesis 1:28.* See also *Genesis 3:7,* that after hearing the wiles of the serpent and eating the forbidden fruit: 'the eyes of both of them were opened, and they knew that they *were* naked; and they sewed fig leaves together, and made themselves aprons'.

Touch or *feeling* is related to the astral plane, and therefore to *Ray six* of *Devotion* and *Aspiration*, because touch is strongly associated with desire, and is often the result of emotional stimulation. It is through the sense of touch that a person can contact the higher planes of perception and thus obtain an understanding of his/her own constitution. Just as we must touch before the objectivity of the physical plane becomes a reality to us, so we must occultly 'touch' the matter of the other planes of perception before their nature can be ascertained.

The eyes are easily deceived by images and mirages, the cause or purpose of sound is often confusing, and very little can be tasted or smelled. They all help, but touch is the final authority ascertaining the concrete reality of an object. It is strongly related to the second Ray aspect of Deity (Love-Wisdom) and is thus the preeminent sense, for to gain Love-Wisdom is the purpose of evolution in this solar system. Our sexual expression and the continuity of the species by means of touch is an indication of the importance of this sense.

The expression of this organ of sensation is also subjectively demonstrated in the meditative process. By the means of subjective touch a union or fusion of all the dualities ('sexes') inherent in us (of our psychic and mental-emotional forces) is accomplished. Both the higher and lower forms of union (via touch) guarantee immortality. So it must also be with a planetary or solar Logos as they seek out their polar opposite. They utilise the systemic or solar correspondence to touch to eventually consummate a Heavenly Marriage. This parallels the ecstatic embrace of a *yogin* with the Source of His Being, of the lover with his beloved, and is universally applied to all in the body of the solar Logos at the end of the cycle of Logoic Activity.[8]

Sight is related to the mental body (and therefore to *Ray five* of the Scientific mode) because it produces the correlation of ideas and develops the intellect. Sight coordinates the sensations or information obtained from the other senses. Sight and the mind both direct the personality in any given direction. The eyes see the way and the body follows. The mind is the mediator, the discriminating faculty between the good and the bad, the light and the dark, the jungle and the path, etc. It is the discerner of hidden truth.

---

8 *Manvantara* and *pralaya*, where *manvantara* is evolutionary activity and *pralaya* is its cessation.

Accordingly, Thomas was not content in merely hearing about the resurrected Christ but needed to see and touch Him before he was convinced of His reality.[9] Light is the essence of being, which, when not screened by the wall of corporeality, dispels the darkness of ignorance and glamour. This enables the awakened person to visualise his higher Self. Thus Jesus said:

> The light of the body is the eye: therefore when thine eye is single, thy whole body also is full of light; but when *thine eye* is evil, thy body also *is* full of darkness. Take heed therefore that the light which is in thee be not darkness.[10]

It is interesting to note that with the advent of *Ray five* (the esoteric cause of the era of scientific materialism) many of the dark places of the earth have been lit up, especially at night. We can now see further in all directions of space and to better discern the causes of things than was ever possible previously.

Taste and *smell* are minor senses. In humanity they are the most underdeveloped and are also somewhat subordinate to the sense of touch. They relate to the two higher planes (*buddhi* and *ātma)* that humanity rarely contact. Therefore our ability to perceive via these senses are likewise underdeveloped. For instance, we do not have the olfactory abilities of a dog.

Taste is akin to *buddhi* (therefore to *Ray four* of *Beautifying Harmony overcoming Conflict),* which is the domain of the intuition, the oneness of being, and universal consciousness. The experience of this fourth plane of perception produces the *taste* of universality. Taste is the result of discrimination. First, the eyes and the analytical mind select what one desires to eat, then it is tasted to see if it is nourishing. One must learn to discriminate right from wrong, the real from the unreal, before the way out of the jungles of illusion can be found. The Heart of Being (the energy of *buddhi)* is then realised, which one esoterically 'tastes' in order to savour the subtleties of the associated revelations.

---

9 See *John 20:27.*

10 *Luke 11:34–35.* The single eye refers both to one-pointed direction or purpose, as well as to the development of the 'third Eye' (the Ājñā centre). This Eye is also known as 'the all-seeing Eye'.

The body is fed via the *mouth* and the person is sustained by physical, intellectual or spiritual food. The energy of *buddhi* is reflected into consciousness as the manna or spiritual sustenance from 'God'. It feeds the spiritual person. As has been noted, the Christ personifies the buddhic plane, thus He states that:

> I am the living bread which came down from heaven: if any man eats of this bread, he shall live for ever....He that eateth my flesh, and drinketh my blood, dwelleth in me, and I in him.[11]

The symbolism here is at once apparent. If 'any man eats' of 'the living bread' then he gains sustenance from the fount of Wisdom and energies wherein resides the Christ, which come via the buddhic plane. The doors to Ineffable Wisdom then lie open, and one becomes integrated with the Christ, Who is incorporated within.

Smell is the most ethereal and universal of the senses, for the odour that pervades a room is common to all. Therefore it is related to the ātmic plane (and the third Ray of Mathematically Exact Activity), for *ātma* affects all simultaneously, not just the individual or even groups of individuals (as does *buddhi).*

An odour is carried by the wind (or air), just as *ātma* uses *buddhi* for its vehicle. Smell and taste are very closely interrelated, and in many ways are interdependent upon each other. Smell is taste transcendent. A subtle aroma has a direct pacifying, alleviating effect upon the mind, far more than any of the other senses (which tend to stimulate one or other of the emotions, or the imagination). Yet smell is the most limited sense in humanity. It can stimulate us to a meditative attitude without the medium of thought. It directly translates the sensual into the Divine.

Though the five senses are the *raison d'etre* of the personality and its delusions, they are thus also the instruments of enlightenment when rightly controlled and directed. They are coordinated or synthesised by the intellect (which is considered the sixth sense in Buddhism). All are abstracted into the Causal consciousness of the Soul.

The intellect translates sensual experiences into codes (sequences of images) and stores them as memory. It has a similar relationship to the Causal body as the *ātmic* plane has to the Monad, the "Thinker" on

---

11 *John 6:51-56.*

the plane *anupādaka*. A clearer picture of these metaphysical concepts is obtained if they are anthropomorphised, for the human frame of reference relates to that which we know about ourselves.

The plane *ātma* here relates to the Mind of Brahmā. *Buddhi* corresponds to the etheric body, with its *chakras* and *nāḍīs*. *Manas* represents the nervous system. The billions of Causal bodies of humanity signify Brahmā's blood and circulatory system (directed by the Heart). The astral plane is the Watery aspect, found mainly in the digestive system. The physical plane corresponds to the 'flesh and bones' of Brahmā. The *devas* form the substance of the cellular constitution and organs of His Body.

Sense & Plane	Base Quality	Evolved Quality
1. Hearing	Limitation	Freedom
Physical (The instinctual actions)		
2. Touch	Desire	Realisation
Astral (The energy of desire)		
3. Sight	Intelligence	Visualisation
Mental (The reasoning faculties)		
4. Taste	Right discrimination	Illumination
Buddhi (intuitive faculty)		
5. Smell	Sense of unity	Perfection
Ātma (Universal consciousness)		

Table 6: The evolved attributes of the senses

The five organs of action

The five organs of sensation are synthesised by the intellect and together with the five organs of action (making the number 10) they form the active manifest expression of Brahmā, as reflected in our constitution.

Together they constitute the means of expression and of gathering the qualities needed by a causative agent to project a purpose.

The five organs of action are:

Organs	Function
1. Mouth	Speaking
2. Hands	Grasping
3. Legs	Walking
4. Genitals	Procreation
5. Anus	Excretion

Table 7: The organs of action

The organs of action express the external associations and aspects of the personality which sustain the being. They are the means whereby the senses can receive the stimuli that will eventually make the person perfect. The organs of action are literally extensions of the senses. They are the modes of creative ability and have a similar relation to the senses as the personality does to the Soul. The *senses* are inherent within the person; they constitute the basic (psychic) equipment, whilst the *organs of action* are acquired, in that they can be trained and utilised in different ways. They can thereby help to further the differing personality attributes. For example, the speech of a Japanese person (regarding the training in the articulation of speech in the use of the mouth) is different to that of an Englishman.

The mouth is the highest of the organs of action, for our intellectual capacity is expressed by our ability to clearly articulate our thoughts as speech. It represents dominance of the physical plane, and of those contained therein – humanity is the crown of evolution, Lord of the physical domain. Though animals may be able to utter sounds, they are not able to convey images by means of those sounds or to communicate intelligently via the spoken word. (They do, however, have a form of clairvoyance by means of which images can be transmitted.) All other organs of action (apart from the hands) are primarily animal functions.

By means of the mouth the sustenance is obtained whereby the life of Deity, or humanity, is maintained. The result of eating is excretion. The result of Creation is a physical manifestation of the originating ideation. Excretion and manifestation both convey the same process of a cyclic corporeality maintained by the action of the mouth that eats and speaks at regular intervals. The mouth is predominantly related to the sense of taste *(buddhi)* and, through speech, to the sense of hearing (the physical plane). Here is seen the dual attribute of *manas* as the mediator between the higher and the lower Self. It is the mediator between Deity and humanity.

The mouth controls the sense of taste, the higher correspondence being the illumination coming via *buddhi. Buddhi* reflects the mantric Creative Word from the plane *ātma,* thereby causing physical manifestation.[12] The receptive conscious entities (humanity) within that manifestation can then respond to that Word through hearing. In its highest aspect, the Mouth can eventually sound the Words of Power that enable the emulation of the Causative functions of Deity. This comes as a consequence of walking along the path of Initiation and attaining the higher Initiations. The enlightened one will 'taste' the universality of cosmic consciousness and so be able to give spiritual food, the manna that sustains the world, to all.

Upon the *mental plane* the vibrant Word is constructed as a form. Here originates the idea, the picture-form of what 'foods' to eat. The desire to eat or speak has its source in *the astral plane.* When desire overrules the discriminatory capacity of the mind, then the lowest aspect of the mouth manifests. The person consequently normally over-consumes food (usually of the adulterated, non-*prāṇic* type). This causes the miseries of obesity, as well as the various ills that result from drugging, devitalisation and the slow poisoning of the body and its senses. When dominated by desire, then mass glamour and illusions, the emotional mental illnesses to which many are susceptible increase. Here the causative agent is engaged in a morass of petty actions that consume vital resources, but produce no lasting edifice upon which future prosperity can stand. Frivolous pursuits of mind govern many

12 The three worlds of human livingness (mental, astral and physical) are the subplanes of the cosmic dense physical. Therefore, this physical manifestation does not just refer to our dense physical, but also to what represents as 'dense physical' to a Logos.

illnesses that beset the majority of (lesser) causative agents (humanity) today.

<table>
<tr><th colspan="2">The mouth (an analogue to the higher mental plane)</th></tr>
<tr><td colspan="2">Action 1: Eating</td></tr>
<tr><td>Highest Expression</td><td>Lowest Expression</td></tr>
<tr><td>Taste of Illumination</td><td>Obesity, drugged stupor</td></tr>
<tr><td colspan="2">Related to:</td></tr>
<tr><td colspan="2">Taste: buddhic plane Desire: astral plane
Excretion of food: physical plane</td></tr>
<tr><td colspan="2">Action 2: Speaking</td></tr>
<tr><td>Highest Expression</td><td>Lowest Expression</td></tr>
<tr><td>Speaking the Word</td><td>Spite, loquacity</td></tr>
<tr><td colspan="2">Related to:</td></tr>
<tr><td colspan="2">Speaking: mental plane Hearing: physical plane</td></tr>
</table>

Table 8: The mouth

The next of the organs of action are *the hands,* whose function is to grasp. Grasping is one of the major conditioning qualities of the *astral plane.* Astral substance embodies the emotions and feelings, the desires that grasp and cling to objects. The person builds or takes an object of desire with the hands, and also gesticulates and expresses emotionality when speaking. The hands are also primarily the means by which people express their creative ability – to make, mould or mend. In this context the hands also reflect *buddhi,* but inversely, via astral substance. The hands are the prime tool of the genuinely accomplished magician in conjunction with the use of the *ājñā chakra* (the third eye). Such a one is inspired from the buddhic plane, but constructively utilises astral matter to produce the appearance of phenomena, so to materialise the 'body of action'.

In their highest aspect the hands symbolise complete control over physical matter, the wielding of the forces inherent in the five planes of

Brahmā. It can be seen therefore, for instance, why the 'laying on of the hands' for healing purposes, as mentioned in the Bible[13] can and does work. They then convey the forces of the Soul, or else of *buddhi*. Its potent radiatory energy is focussed through the *chakras* in the hands, helping to cleanse maladjusted desire or astral matter of the particular diseased organ(s). Diseases associated with the astral plane and the emotional world are by far the most numerous that afflict humanity. For this reason the 'laying on of hands' will be a potent means of healing in the coming New Age.

In many ways the hands are the most important of the organs of action, being related to the sense of touch. The Eye and the hands work in unison to direct and mould the sphere of sensation into the form desired by the creative thinker.

In their *lowest* aspect, they represent brute force – a desire for or utilisation of power, assertion, dominance, tenacity or clinging to one's self-made objects of delusion. At their worst they represent the power of a black magician or tyrant. This should be looked at in the context of the relation between the left and right hands, the eyes, the *iḍā* and *piṇgalā nāḍī,* etc. The meaning of the difference between the right hand path (the way of the white Magician) and the left hand path (the way of the Sorcerer) has been presented elsewhere.

Hands (an analogue to the astral plane)	
Action: Grasping	
Highest Expression	**Lowest Expression**
Wielding spiritual energy	Brute force, tenacity
Left hand - iḍā nāḍī, left hand path *Right hand - piṇgalā nāḍī,* right hand path	
Related to:	
Buddhic plane (right hand)	Mental Plane (left hand)

Table 9: The hands

13 *1Tim 4:14.*

The next means to action are the *legs*, which represent our locomotive ability. Through their mobilisation people get to where they wish to go. This is the prime function of the *intellect,* with which by means of reason and discrimination people can assert themselves in any direction desired. This can be towards immersion in the capriciousness of the senses, or towards definite spiritual or intellectual accomplishment. In their many fields and categories of expression, reason, wisdom and knowledge are the result of the mobilisation of the mental body. One technically walks through many scenarios of thought.

In its highest aspect, this faculty enables the person to transport consciousness to any plane of endeavour or knowledge in the formed universe, just as he/she is able to travel to wherever desired on earth by means of the feet. The feet are thus related to the sense of *sight*, because the eyes direct the feet in a given direction, thus preventing one from stumbling or losing one's way, wherever there is light. Similarly one must learn not to stumble from the pitfalls of intellectual discursion. The darkness of many forms of ignorance is the pitfall of many would-be thinkers. Thus, sight corresponds to the higher *manas* and the legs to the intellect, the lower *manas*. The legs hold one upright upon the earth, providing the balance and poise that, from a higher perspective, can be seen as the basis to true reasoning abilities.

Legs (an analogue to the intellect)	
Action: Locomotive ability	
Highest Expression	**Lowest Expression**
Conscious transference to any of the planes of perception	Sensually dominated or selfishly directed intellect
Related to:	
1. The mental body a) Sight - higher *manas* b) Legs - lower *manas* 2. The physical plane - the ability to walk on the earth	

Table 10: The legs

In its *lowest* aspect, such activity results in the domination of mind by desire, producing the evils of spite, selfishness, pride, hatred etc. The legs then have proverbially taken the person into battle or over hard and thorny ground.

Next are the *genitals,* expressing the action of procreation. This is a reflection of the Divine Creative act and is the result of desire. (The mind/Mind creates the images of what is to be, which are then clothed with the substance of desire in order to clothe it with materiality.) Procreation is related to the etheric plane, which contains the force centres *(chakras).* In most people they are primarily conditioned by the desire energy streaming from the astral plane.

Esoterically, the act of procreation is the result of the interaction between two oppositely polarised spheres of action. Their expenditure of energy (via the action of various psychic centres) causes the condensation or crystallisation of the desire (the Fiery Element) of the male into seed germs (permanent atoms). They find an ideal environment for growth within the femininely polarised sphere of action (the Waters of the Womb). Depending upon the quality of the 'genetics' of the seed germs, they are able to attract the substance needed for expansion and growth. The planetary Logos similarly expressed His Desire to create via the Ideation of the earth Scheme.

The Father impregnates primal matter with the germ or spark of consciousness. This germ then lodges itself in the Waters of the Womb (the organ of primal Causative forces) and prompts the condensation of the Waters into a form. Through nine months, aeons (or Initiations) of foetal development, a self-conscious awakened Son is eventually born. Procreation implicates the building of a form by an entity, into which the Life principle is imbued. This limits the freedom of expression of the procreative being. He/She is necessarily attached to that form until the necessary qualities have been evolved by it, and that cycle of action completed.

For a prime Causative agent the objective of 'procreation' is the birth of the Soul, Solar Fire, the Son or second aspect of Deity. People recapitulate this causative drama through their sexual act that produces our endless rounds of rebirth.

In its highest aspect this process concerns the conquering or fusion of the pairs of opposites that constitute a human being and his/her little universe. In this idea lies the concept of Tantric Yoga as exemplified in Buddhist texts, the fusion of male-female causative forces within and without the human system. This also incorporates the mantric formulae and ritualistic endeavour that allow someone to contact and work directly with the *deva* (feminine) complements to our human (masculine) selves. The highest creative actions must be accomplished via them, if the causative act is to produce effective results upon the corporeal realms.

In its lowest aspect, the sex impulse results in bestiality, which needs no comment here.

This organ of action is related to sense of touch, thus to the astral plane, and subjectively to *buddhi,* for the result of procreation is birth into another, higher (Airy) realm, producing Gnosis, wisdom. *Buddhi* contains the *chakras* of the planetary and solar Logos, through which the higher correspondences of the action of procreation are eventuated.

Genitals (an analogue to the energies of the etheric plane)	
Actions: Procreation, Touch	
Highest Expression	**Lowest Expression**
Fusion of opposite forces, birth of a Son	Bestiality
Related to:	
a) Astral plane b) Buddhic plane	

Table 11: The genitals

The last of the organs of action is *the anus.* Its function is the excretion or elimination of the waste that is the result of the metabolic processes. It eliminates what is toxic to the organism. Excretion is the inevitable reflex action, the end result of a chain of events that originated in the mouth.

In the symbolism associated with the excretory process can be seen the entire story of the process of manifestation. The two functions of the mouth (speaking and eating) relate excretion to the buddhic plane, wherein the Word is sounded and the food (the *manna* or substance of 'God') is first consumed. The substance of the Word then starts its involutionary journey in the 'mouth', towards eventual concretion upon the physical plane.

Food passes down from the mouth to the alimentary canal to the stomach and intestines. This subjectively relates to the Solar Plexus centre and the astral plane, where the Waters are contained that allow the 'digestive process' of consciousness to exist. From there the waste is eliminated, and dense matter is finally excreted. Excretion thus symbolises the dense physical plane. (The mineral realm and its constant chemical transmutations.) Putrefaction, waste, solidification or inertia are all keywords of the attributes of the physical plane.

Because it is the result of the original Will-to-Be and the instinct of self-preservation, this process is thereby related to the *ātmic plane*, to the mind of Brahmā. From here the Thought of the Food needed to sustain His entire Body of manifestation was originated. (The events of the first Outpouring.) Also, because excretion putrefies and gives off a discernible odour, it is related to the sense of smell *(ātma)*. This odour symbolises the subtle link between the highest and lowest planes, and the fact that all beings must eventually return to their originating source.

The waste that was formerly spatially restricted becomes a gas *(buddhi)*, thus spatially free. Excretion is also related to the mental plane, from which the originating discriminatory impulse of what to eat emanates. In fact excretion is related to all planes of perception, just as the physical plane contains the energies from all the other planes of perception. The physical plane is purely an automaton of those energies, of the entire causative impulse. Because of this fact our main testings for Initiation manifest via physical bodies, whose characteristics we have to master in their entirety.

When the nature of excretion, as related to the human constitution, is properly understood and regulated by right control of the intake of food, then the person can fully command the actions of the corporeal body. In its *lowest aspect* this means that the personality is completely dominated by physical nature's desires and appetites. As stated, eating the wrong food results in ill health, disease, sloth, mental and physical lethargy, and death. The state of the eliminated faeces also indicates the symptoms of such malaise.

Anus (an analogue to the energies of the physical plane)	
Action: Excretion	
Highest Expression	**Lowest Expression**
Complete control of the corporeal body by 'eating' spiritual food The body and blood of Christ	Domination by corporeality, putrefaction, sickness and death
Related to:	
1. Buddhic plane – the energy body of the food 2. Mental plane – the thought of eating 3. Astral plane – desire for food 4. Ātmic plane – the smell of the food	

Table 12: The anus

The above information concerning the organs of action and of sensation is summarised in *figure 10* below. This figure shows the relation between the senses and planes of perception. The functions of the third, or Creative Logos, termed Brahmā, are specifically depicted. These functions emanate from the third systemic plane of perception, *ātma*. The second plane, *anupādaka,* is that of the Son, and the highest plane *(ādi)* is the plane whereon the Will or Father aspects emanates.

Note that planes 1, 3, 5 and 7 constitute the line of least resistance for the first Ray (Will energy). Rays 2, 4 and 6 are the line of expression for the second Ray of Love-Wisdom. The Rays manifest in an increasingly reified manner when moving from the second to the sixth Ray.

Brahmā, the third Logos, the Mother, the Creator, is considered the third person of the triune Hindu Deity. *Shiva,* the first Logos, embodies the Father, the Destroyer principle of that trinity. *Vishnu,*[14] the second Logos is the Son or Preserver aspect.

14 With the diacritics the correct terms for Vishnu and Shiva are: Viṣṇū and Śiva.

<table>
<tr><td colspan="2">1st Plane
Ādi
1st Ray</td><td colspan="2">SEA OF FIRE
Conception of the Word</td><td>ARCHETYPAL MIND OF BRAHMĀ – SHIVA
The synthesis of all Being</td></tr>
<tr><td colspan="2">2nd Plane
Monadic
Anupādaka
2nd Ray</td><td colspan="2">MONAD
Here the Word is uttered, first differentiation of form. The downpour of the 12 Creative Hierarchies</td><td>HEART OF BRAHMĀ – VISHNU</td></tr>
<tr><td rowspan="2">3rd Plane
Ātma
3rd Ray
Aether</td><td rowspan="9">***FIVE PLANES OF BRAHMĀ***</td><td>**SENSE**</td><td colspan="2" rowspan="2">CONCRETE MIND OF BRAHMĀ – BRAHMĀ
Related to the physical plane via hearing.
Here the Logoic Word is heard, producing active Intelligent response</td></tr>
<tr><td>**Smell**
To be fully developed by the 7th Root Race</td></tr>
<tr><td>4th Plane
Buddhi
4th Ray
Air</td><td>**Taste**
To be fully developed by the 6th Root Race</td><td colspan="2">Taste reflects the Love or Word from the Monad to the astral plane. This is the line of least resistance for 2nd Ray energies. *Buddhi* is the middle of the seven planes, therefore is the plane of at-onement</td></tr>
<tr><td rowspan="2">5th Plane
Higher Mental
5th Ray
Fire</td><td rowspan="2">**Sight**
Primarily the 5th Root Race 'Aryan' development</td><td rowspan="2">*Manas* reflects the energies of the *ātmic* plane, and the 'Sea of Fire', expressed as human Will, the Mind of the Soul</td><td>**ORGANS OF ACTION**</td></tr>
<tr><td>**Mouth**
Eating, related to taste, buddhic plane. Speaking, related to hearing, physical plane</td></tr>
<tr><td>**Lower Mental Plane**
5th Ray</td><td></td><td>The Intellect</td><td>**Legs**
Locomotion, related to sight</td></tr>
<tr><td>6th Plane
Astral
6th Ray
Water</td><td>**Touch**
Fully developed during the Atlantean era</td><td>Reflects *buddhi* as human love and desire</td><td>**Hands**
Grasping, related to touch, astral plane</td></tr>
<tr><td>7th Plane
Physical
7th Ray
Ether</td><td>**Hearing**
Developed during Lemurian era</td><td>a) Four ethers</td><td>**Genitals**
Related to touch, astral plane and *buddhi* - gives birth to the Son</td></tr>
<tr><td>**Dense Subplanes Earth**</td><td></td><td>b) Three dense physical sub-planes</td><td>**Anus**
Excretion, related to smell, eating, digestion and thought</td></tr>
</table>

Figure 10: The planes of perception and the constitution of Brahmā

As depicted in this figure, *the Monadic plane (anupādaka)* represents the Heart of Brahmā. By this is meant that the attributes of Vishnu lie at the heart of the work of the Creative Logos, who brings into manifestation the entire *manvantara*. Vishnu sustains that manifestation. The plane *ādi* (known as the Sea of Fire) conveys the abstract Ideation, the Idea of the *manvantara* to be, from the archetypal Logoic Mind. From this plane Shiva also projects the Will to cause its eventual cessation. The plane *ātma* represents the Intellect, or empirical Mind (Mahat) of Brahmā. From here the Thought Construct can be projected in such a way that it can be clothed in the substance of the Logoic periodical sheaths.

The five organs of action and the five senses further exemplify why the symbol of humanity's evolutionary attainment is traditionally regarded as a pentagram. The information concerning their qualities can consequently be transposed upon the points of the pentagram shown in figure 11. The pentagram also shows that our manifest form is primarily an expression of the *third Ray* of Active Intelligence[15] that empowers the quintuple constitution of Brahmā. The number five also symbolises mind *(manas),* which is presently the focus of humanity's evolutionary development. When united with Love, the mind will allow the blossoming of Sons of Wisdom.

Counting from above down, the mental plane is the fifth sub-plane of the cosmic physical plane. Also, *manas* is qualified by the *fifth Ray* of Science, of knowledgeable acquisition. This is the predominant characteristic of the intelligentsia of the world, and of their achievements in the arts, sciences and technology.

Table 13 shows the Rays associated with the planes of perception, to which the planetary rulers associated with the Rays have also been added.

This table shows that *manas* is governed by *Venus*, the Mother of illumination, the source of the intelligent mind. She is Aphrodite, the Goddess of Love, who is concerned with the relationship between the various forces of Nature. At first for humanity this relationship is

---

15 The third Ray manifests in a similar way as the dual aspect of *manas*. Normally when considering its activity it is from the higher (enlightened) perspective, in which case I have designated its main attribute as Mathematically Exact Activity. However, when considering its manifestation in average humanity, then the main attribute can be considered as Active Intelligence, which is the way that D.K. normally depicts it.

purely sensual, governed by desire (Venus united with Mars). Later, the emergent powers of Love become manifest. The intellect is then transmuted into Wisdom, awakening the higher, abstract Mind. The divine hermaphrodite Venus-Mercury is then born.

Plane	Governing Ray	Planet
1. Ādi	*1st Ray* of Will or Power	Vulcan
2. Anupādaka	*2nd Ray* of Love-Wisdom	Jupiter
The plane of the Monad		
3. Ātma	*3rd Ray* of Active-Intelligence	Saturn
Where the Will of the Father can be contacted		
4. Buddhi	*4th Ray* of Harmony Overcoming Conflict	Mercury
Plane of at-onement		
5. Mental	*5th* Ray of Science	Venus
Plane of ideas		
6. Astral	*6th Ray* of Devotion-Aspiration	Mars
Realm of desire, feelings, emotions		
7. Physical	*7th Ray* of Ceremonial Magic	Uranus
Plane of the form, sensation		

Table 13: The Rays and the planes of perception

Within the mind, ideas, concepts and sensations are brought together, stabilised and balanced. They can then be fused into a synthesis, a working unity through the mind's reasoning faculties. Such faculties are symbolically evolved through Venus and her many lovers. This interrelationship becomes the main driving force, the key to our progressive evolution towards Deity.

The act of incarnation is motivated by desire for experience. Experience is the result of sensation, and sensation is a sensitive reaction to an external stimulus that registers in consciousness. Intelligence resolves these sensations, and on the higher mental plane the cycles of incarnation finally terminate. The influence of Venus is thus of paramount importance in this scientific age. Her rulership is however specifically effective upon the three planes of human livingness.

The hermaphrodite *(Mercury-Venus)* rules the higher mental plane wherein resides the Causal body of the Soul. *Mercury* relays buddhic influences. Through Mercury (the 'messenger of the Gods') the Soul's gaze is turned upwards, to receive impressions from the realms of the spiritual triad *(manas-buddhi-ātma).* At the same time *Venus* allows the Soul to fix its gaze downwards into the material universe, and thus to give birth to its 'child' – the human personality. Therein is stored the seed of the Christ-principle (Love-Wisdom) which is an inherent force that drives the evolutionary path of humanity towards liberation from *saṃsāra.* This force can also be considered in terms of the energy of *bodhicitta.*

From Table 13 it can be seen that *Saturn,* the lord of *karma,* heads the five planes of Brahmā. This shows that these planes of perception are dominated by the effects and emerging qualities associated with the *karma* of the past, with planetary *karma.* In particular, they are concerned with what is associated with the conflict, struggle and pain or pleasure of the lower three planes. Upon *ātma* the cycles of cause and effect are projected and then finally resolved.

The *third Ray* of Mathematically Exact Activity rules the *ātmic* plane. This pertains to the forces of the Mother aspect of Deity, the universal Womb, the matrix of expression for all the Intelligent Wills (the *devas)* that constitute this Ray. Their function is to make, mould, or manifest the sum of phenomenal appearance with mathematical precision, as directed by the primal Will of the Father. Each *deva* Life is therefore an agent of *karma,* moulding the forms according to a prearranged Plan. Saturn rules the mode of manifestation of that Plan. The inherent *karma* is accordingly woven into the construct of *saṃsāra. Karma* (as the primal cause of manifestation) is therefore virtually omnipotent, omnipresent and omniscient, as far as the lower planes are concerned. Saturn can, however, be dethroned by his Son

Jupiter (Zeus), who esoterically is the embodiment of Love-Wisdom. By his rulership of the 'Gods' Jupiter effectively governs all of the elementary forces by means of this developed Wisdom. With Love and Wisdom comes accomplished radiance. A human unit thus endowed is no longer lost in the darkness of uncontrolled actions, but rather lights his/her own path. This path manifests as a journey of glory into the vaults of the Heavens.

The third Ray is thus the primal Causative Ray that conditions the evolution of Intelligence within the Womb of Life.

The *ātmic* plane is the higher correspondence of the mental, which in its turn has a similar relationship to the dense physical plane. The mental plane acts as the facilitator between the Will-to-Be of 'God' and the resultant Creation ('Excretion'), whilst the *ātmic* plane is where that Will first finds its externalised expression. From *ātma* the Elements are called forth and moulded into all aspects of the appearing form. Later, the energies from *ātma* will produce the needed death of all aspects of *saṃsāra* and their abstraction into the Heart of Being. All *karma* is thereby brought into a resolution.

From a different perspective, if one counts the planes that the personality can contact from below upwards, then *manas* is again seen as the fifth principle.

7	Ātmic plane	Ray 3
6	Buddhic plane	Ray 4
5	Higher mental plane ***(manas)***	Ray 5
4	Lower mental plane	Ray 5
3	Astral plane	Ray 6
2	The etheric sub-planes	Ray 7
1	Dense physical sub-planes	Ray 3

Table 14: The position of *manas*

The Soul resides on this fifth plane, thus is literally the Eye or directive agent for the Causative energies from Brahmā. The pentad adequately sums up the forces governing the personality when dominated by the energies of the Soul. It shows that a person, on his/her tiny scale, embodies (or reflects) the qualities of Brahmā into the three worlds of human evolution.

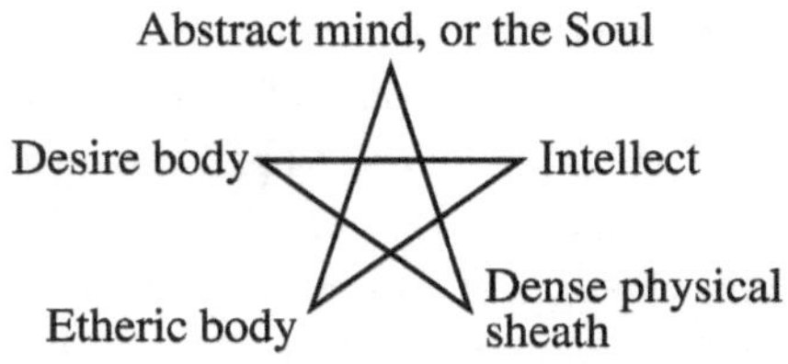

Figure 11: The pentad governing a human unit

When the pentagram is inverted, then these five sheaths become subjugated to the physical form by the person's lower nature – the base senses, organs of action and instincts. The person can then become highly sensual, separative and selfish, with an intensely materialistic and intellectual bias. The inverted pentagram therefore aptly symbolises the involutionary path, the way of the black magician.

From a higher perspective the pentagram also symbolises the attributes of the planetary Logos (Sanat Kumāra), who is the prime Causative Source for the energy of the Mind. In this case one would have to put a triangle, or the symbol of the All-Seeing Eye in the centre, to exemplify the higher functions of the Logos. This symbol shows that the planetary Logos peers into manifestation from the cosmic astral plane. Sanat Kumāra, the three Buddhas of Activity, plus the Mother of the World embody the functions of Brahmā for our planetary Scheme.[16]

It can be seen therefore that the pentagram relates to the method whereby a causative agent performs an appointed task within the realms of form, for it embodies the principles and forces that must be utilised to do so. The pentagram literally sums up the empirical attainment of humanity or Deity. It embodies the 'five-ness' of all that are demonstrating mind/Mind.

- The nature of Brahmā.
- The five instincts.
- The five senses.

---

16 This is a simplified arrangement of figure 1 given in *The Constitution of Shambhala,* Part A. Being the One that sits on the Throne, the planetary Avatar, He then synthesises the attributes of the Avatar of Synthesis and the Spirit of Peace. In figure 1 of that book, the Avatar of Synthesis and Sanat Kumāra can be interrelated, depending upon the angle of vision.

- The five organs of action and of sensation.
- The five *prāṇas*.
- The five *chakras* (when the two Head centres are esoterically taken as a unit and when the Base of the Spine and the Sacral centre are also taken as one).
- The wisdoms of the five Dhyāni Buddhas.
- The five human Root Races so far developed.

The evolutionary stages, and the basic divisions that constitute our evolving Lives, are however governed by the number *seven*. Over time there will be seven Root Races of humanity[17] that are also subdivided into seven sub-Races, and these are further divided into seven nations and then tribes, and so forth.

As a whole, humanity is progressing through its fifth cycle or stage of attainment (that of the Aryan Root Race), of which the most recent sub-Race is said to be the Indo-European class (the fifth sub-Race), though at present, the foetal sixth sub-Race is appearing. As the number five relates to the mental plane and the development of the mind, so the main emphasis of the Aryan Root Race has been the development of the intellect. The sixth sub-Race will predominantly begin to develop buddhic perception. One can look at the evolution of the Races as the way of evolution of the causative principle of Deity. Humanity presently bears the expression of the third of the five *prāṇas* coursing through His Body of manifestation. This manifests in an orange hue.

Human units also possess seven sheaths of substance. Under the Monad there are the ātmic, buddhic, higher and lower mental sheaths, the astral body, dense form, plus the Soul. Every aspect of the human form – our emotions, mind and the basic instincts, needed to be evolved and mastered by us. Everything we now take for granted (such as basic emotions, and the way the stomach operates) had to be evolved and lived through as an experiential process in a former epoch. This experiential process happened via the evolutionary journeying undergone in the sub-human kingdoms of Nature.

---

17 See Appendix two of my book *Esoteric Cosmology and Modern Physics* for elaboration of the Root Races.

The sentient qualities of all our organs had first to evolve before our consciousness could appropriate them within a bodily form. Nothing we possess is here by chance: everything associated with our personality equipment is the result of *karma,* the effect of what was earned from myriads of Lives of past unfoldment of cellular, and then organ-like consciousness. The earlier Races, or stages of the development of the human personality, were to make prime causative agents. They were thus all concerned with the process of building appropriate equipment of response to higher Causative Energies. Such was only possible once human consciousness evolved to eventually appropriate a mind that could reflect the attributes of a Logos. The development of the mind is the key to awakening the needed higher perceptions. Out of mind evolves the attributes of cosmic Mind that will truly make a human unit Divine.

Lift the Hydra high
Oh disciple.
High into the sky,
away from the lair,
the stench
and the muddy desert pool
where he resides.
Rise from your knees
and triumph.
Oh conqueror!
So you aspire
and fly arrow-like
to the mountaintop
of illumined Being.

Who sees the Vision,
who visualises the Seeing,
who, who seeing Knows,
and who knows what seeing Is?

8

The Question of Evil

A concept of evil is common to all religious teachings. Typically, the basic implications are similar, where evil is what fights against or tends to abnegate evolutionary Law. Evil can be considered as the opposition to the laws governing the progress of Nature. Therefore, evil resists the right demonstration of the *dharma,* or anything that helps humanity's evolution in any way. Obviously, evil normally leaves pain, suffering, death and destruction in it wake. But to truly understand the concept of evil one must rise above emotive concepts, to look upon the ways of those that cunningly scheme to ruthlessly manifest absolute control over whatever they deem is their right to wield power over. Evil can apply to the actions of an individual, but can also be group, national, international, planetary and cosmic in scope.

This exegesis shall endeavour to explain an esoteric viewpoint of the principal forms of evil, or the devil ('the adversary of God and tempter of man'), as found in the Bible. The information in the Bible covers the entire spectrum of understanding for what is 'evil'. This present explanation will endeavour to rectify some of the exoteric fallacies presently believed by people, such as via the textual interpretations of the theologians.

There are three principal terms that people have related evil to, as derived from the Bible. When the contexts of the symbolic meanings are interpreted esoterically, then all aspects associated with the concept of evil find their logical place. These terms are: the Serpent, Satan, and the Devil, as found in this passage:

> And the great dragon was cast out, that old serpent, called the Devil, and Satan, which deceiveth the whole world: he was cast out into earth, and his angels were cast out with him.[1]

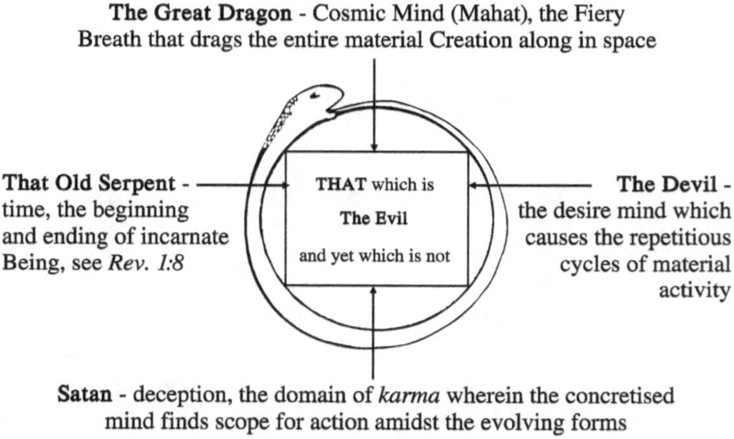
The Great Dragon - Cosmic Mind (Mahat), the Fiery Breath that drags the entire material Creation along in space
That Old Serpent - time, the beginning and ending of incarnate Being, see *Rev. 1:8*
THAT which is
The Evil
and yet which is not
The Devil - the desire mind which causes the repetitious cycles of material activity
Satan - deception, the domain of *karma* wherein the concretised mind finds scope for action amidst the evolving forms

Figure 12: The serpent, the devil and Satan

I will not here endeavour to explain the significant cosmological implications of this statement, but limit the discussion to the three above-mentioned terms. They are illustrated in figure 12 above.

The concept of a dragon here relates to a Logoic Mind, the transmuted correspondence of the fifth degree Initiate (the Master of Wisdom) who is also styled a 'Dragon of Wisdom'. We see a square at the centre of the circle of a serpent biting its own tail, symbolising the cycle of time (explained later). This represents the cosmic Seat of Power for the incarnation of the Lords of Dark Face, here depicted as 'The Evil'. This is the throne of what embodies the 'four corners' of the material domain[2] *(saṃsāra)* wherein what is designated as 'evil'

1 *Rev. 12:9.*

2 They are the mental plane, the astral domain, the etheric sub-planes and the dense

can reside. As long as manifestation *(manvantara)* exists, so there can be found that which must be overcome, hence is 'evil' in nature.

The serpent and *kuṇḍalinī*

The main consideration of the meaning of 'serpent' to take note of is that of being the *serpent of wisdom*. It was the serpent that caused Eve to pick the forbidden fruit from the 'tree of knowledge of good and evil',[3] in the garden of Eden. The serpent told Eve in relation to her stating that 'God hath said, Ye shall not eat of it, neither shall ye touch it, lest ye die'[4]:

> Ye shall not surely die: For God doth know that in the day ye eat thereof, then your eyes shall be opened, and ye shall be as gods, knowing good and evil.[5]

The serpent had the prescience to know what would happen as a consequence of eating this fruit, and thus the eventuation of the long evolutionary journey of humanity that would eventually make them 'as gods'.

Jesus provides the interpretation of the serpent relating to wisdom in His statement 'Be ye therefore wise as serpents, harmless as doves'.[6] The meaning of the word 'serpent' here suggests something good, that which is wise, not evil. The appellation, 'serpent',[7] was reserved by the ancients for those that had attained the highest wisdom, by overcoming the cycles of birth and death. These were the initiated Adepts of the ancient Mystery Schools.[8] Mircea Eliade points out the relation of serpents *(nāgas)* to wisdom:

---

physical domain.

3 *Genesis 2:17.*

4 *Genesis 3:3.*

5 *Genesis 3:4-5.*

6 *Matt. 10:16.*

7 *Nāga* in Sanskrit. In Hindu mythology they are associated with the sanctity of water, but are also custodians of the *dharma*.

8 See also H.P. Blavatsky, *The Secret Doctrine*, (Theosophical Publishing Co., London, 1888), Vol. 1, entitled 'Tree, Serpent, and Crocodile Worship', Section 10, page 403. Also, Vol. 2, entitled: 'Edens, Serpents, and Dragons', (pages 207-227).

> Now, *nāgas* are always connected with magic, yoga, and the occult sciences: and the folklore that developed around Nāgārjuna[9] shows us how living was the belief that snakes preserve a timeless "hidden doctrine," which they transmit through mysterious initiations.[10]

Jesus was not merely speaking figuratively here. He was also referring to the qualities attained by Initiates of the third degree (the gain of the wise liberation of the 'serpent power', explained later) and those of the fourth degree (esoterically symbolised by the attributes of 'doves'). Jesus was utilising a language that those amongst His disciples who were Initiated (thus had 'ears that could hear'[11]) could properly understand.

For a similar reason the Egyptian priest-kings wore the serpent (Uraeus) on their headgear (at the forehead, where the 'third eye' is centred). This is because of its connotation to wisdom and the highest spiritual powers, which aptly symbolised their exalted office. We are told in the Bible that Moses was made a 'god unto Pharaoh', and Aaron was made a prophet to Moses,[12] so that together they could entice the Pharaoh to free the children of Israel. The Pharaoh needed a miracle to convince him of the legitimacy of Moses' and Aaron's demands. Aaron was told to take his rod 'and cast it before Pharaoh and it shall become a serpent'.[13] This did not overly impress the Pharaoh, for he called forth the 'wise men and sorcerers, now the magicians of Egypt'.[14] They all cast down their rods, which instantly became serpents, 'but Aaron's rod swallowed up their rods'.[15] This stood as proof that Aaron had greater occult power than all the wise men and magicians in Egypt. He made this abundantly clear, with many catastrophes and 'miracles' wreaked upon the hapless Pharaoh and his subjects. Aaron did this with the aid of the rod under the auspices of Moses and 'the Lord'.

---

9 Nāgārjuna is a renowned Buddhist philosopher, who was the main person responsible for the formulation of the Mādhyamika philosophy.

10 Mircea Eliade, *Yoga: Immortality and Freedom.* (Arkana, London, 1989), 352.

11 *Matt. 11:15.*

12 *Exodus 7:1.*

13 *Exodus 7:9-10.*

14 *Exodus 7:11.*

15 *Exodus 7:12.*

The patriarchs of Israel and the Egyptian wise men and magicians were not the only ones with such 'rods' (or staffs). For example, staffs were one of the few possessions retained by Hindu and Buddhist *yogins* and mendicants in their wanderings. This was not only to aid their physical bodies whilst traveling, for the staff was also a major symbol of yogic prowess and austerities. Staffs symbolise the central spinal column through which the psychic energies *(prāṇas)* associated with our experiences flow, as well as the subjective energies coming from the higher planes of perception. This staff is the central support of the *yogin's* entire meditative being, externalised by the staff's physical support of their outer wanderings. Without this support, the *yogin's* attainments would not be possible.

The symbolism of the serpent is inextricably interwoven with that of the staff. In hermetic and yogic philosophy, it symbolises the Fiery energy that is released by the right meditation techniques and proper spiritual discipline. This force flows up the major psychic channel (the *suṣumṇā nāḍī)* centred in the spinal column. This Fiery energy is the energy of the Mother aspect of Deity that sustains a physical incarnation. It is the primeval causative or formative energy that lies coiled 'in potential' at the heart of every form. This central reservoir of heat that sustains the physical Life is called *kuṇḍalinī* ('serpent power').

Kuṇḍalinī can also be considered to relate to the Fires deep within the bowels of the earth, which sustain the earth's integral dynamism. It is an aspect of the 'beast' of Revelation 'that was, and is not; and shall ascend out of the bottomless pit and go into perdition'.[16] This phrase has a direct reference to the misuse of *kuṇḍalinī* by those of willful intent, the practitioners of the black arts. It is an effect of the past ('that was'), has no substantiality of its own ('is not'), and yet 'is' a potent force to be reckoned with. It is in fact the most material or concrete expression of the Will energy of Deity that sustains the phenomenal, illusory universe. It 'is' as long as this material world is sustained. The reference to the 'beast' can relate to the energy that sustains our physical (or 'bestial') selves.

The effect of *kuṇḍalinī* is seen in the spiral helix pattern of D.N.A. (deoxyribonucleic acid) found in the nucleus of cells. Deoxyribonucleic

16 *Rev. 17:8.*

acid is the major constituent of genes, which are responsible for the genetic code and thus the immense diversifications within Nature.

The animating dynamo inside a person is said to be the *chakra* situated at the base of the spine (the *mūlādhāra chakra).* The interrelation between this centre and the next one up (the Sacral centre) causes the junction for the appearance of the entire etheric web that psychically sustains Life by means of fine channels *(nāḍīs)* existing within that web. These channels roughly correspond to, and underlie, the nerve cords. The three major *nāḍīs* (*iḍā, piṇgalā* and *suṣumṇā*) are symbolised by the Caduceus – the staff of Hermes. The Grecian God Hermes was the intermediary between the Gods of Mt. Olympus and humanity. *Kuṇḍalinī* is expressed at the place of union of these three *nāḍīs*. It is liberated by the demonstration of the personal will drawing upon the energies of the Soul. The meditator evokes a mantric sound (the 'Word of God') to produce the necessary liberation. Accordingly, Hermes is styled the 'Messenger of the Gods'.

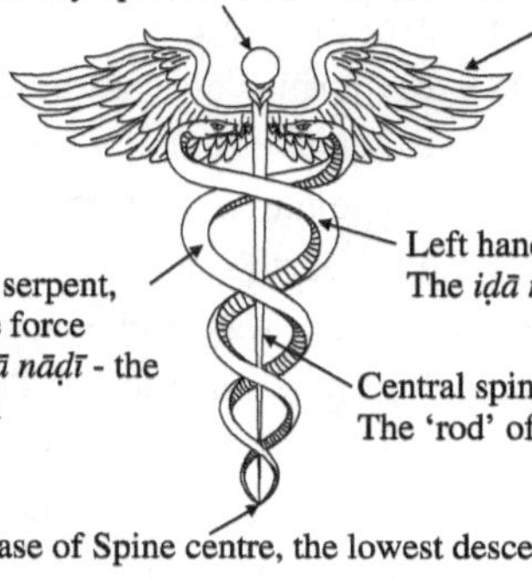

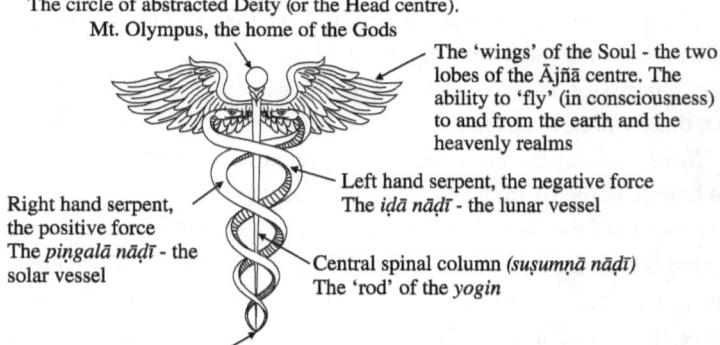

Figure 13: The Caduceus

The symbol of the serpent is seen in the spiral path of two outer *nāḍīs* surrounding the central column. One can also consider the serpentine motion of the moving *prāṇas*. One path (the *iḍā nāḍī)* is negative in polarisation, conveying the psychically receptive 'feminine' energy (an attribute of *kuṇḍalinī*). This energy sustains the corporeal form of the person and provides animal vitality to humanity.

The other *nāḍī* (the *piṅgalā nāḍī*) is positive in relation to *iḍā* (at humanity's present stage of evolution). It conveys the 'Son energy', the consciousness-engendering factor. This is the result of the experience-gathering activities of the Lives incarnate in the formed realms. The collective sharing of experiences and of energy interrelationships provides the embodied forms a wealth of experiential possibilities. The diversity seen in Nature is however but part of a unified, coherent Life. The *prāṇas* conveyed in this *nāḍī* are obtained from the outer environment, by contact or association with the holistic synergy of Nature's kingdoms. The *prāṇas* are the vitality absorbed from the air and obtained from 'food'. (Utilising that term in its broadest possible sense.)

The symbol of the *iḍā nāḍī* is the moon. Like the moon, it conveys 'reflected light', which is associated with the form nature, the energies of the personality, and those of the psychic world. The symbol of the *piṅgalā nāḍī* is the sun. The sun is called the greater luminary because it expresses the illuminating Light of Wisdom *(prajñā),* the Light of the Soul. When the sun and moon are spoken of in mystical, esoteric, alchemical, mythological, or religious texts, one can always assume that it contains veiled references to the energies associated with these *nāḍīs*.

The central channel (the *suṣumṇā nāḍī)* conveys the dynamically active 'Father energy' that impels an entity onwards in time and space. This is the energy from the Spirit-Soul that unites the highest aspect of Being to the lowest, and 'quickeneth' the life of the person, to use a meaningful Biblical expression.[17]

The *suṣumṇā nāḍī* is brought to activity through the application of the Will when the Son (consciousness) is in full expression, and the person is in deep meditation. The mind has become perfectly calmed, yet intensely receptive to the vast reaches of all-encompassing space. It has become a fully prepared and endowed womb, where the ripened ovum *(dhyāna)* as the seed of its potential sends forth its own note or sound. This note reaches out into multi-dimensional space and is embraced by a reciprocal Sound[18] consisting of the most intense type of energy. This energy reaches down into the deepest layer of matter, the base or root of manifestation, wherein our personalities reside.

---

17 *John 5:21* and *6:63.*

18 In Biblical phraseology this can be considered the 'Word of God'.

This energy fuses, or blends, with the Fires of matter (which sustain the life of every atom) and with the Fires of the evolved consciousness. The triune united Fire *(kuṇḍalinī)* will then rise up the central channel, fully vivifying the various psychic centres in the person. The 'son of man' thereby becomes a 'son of God' – fully enlightened and liberated from the throttlehold of form.

The figure of the Caduceus is but representational, as it is not possible to give an accurate picture of the nature of the 'raising of *kuṇḍalinī*' due to the immensity, subtlety, and esotericism of the subject. Therein lies hid the entire story of Creation, of evolution, and the meditative unfoldment of any being. One may endeavour to satiate one's curiosity by perusing the various meditation and occult texts on the subject, however, the reader should be warned that such information is often veiled. The facts may therefore be purposely misleading, contradictory, or cursorily treated. This is due to the potential dangers awaiting the unwise that prematurely attempt to awaken *kuṇḍalinī*.

The ability to poison and to fly

Kuṇḍalinī is many layered. It will burn and destroy the form or wreak havoc upon the psychic constitution of a person who lacks the adequate knowledge, morality and psychic purity to rightly direct it, and upon those who have utilised the force of the personal will to try to 'awaken' it. *Kuṇḍalinī's* tendency will always be to reinforce or distort any subtle uncontrolled desire or base qualities existing in the person. (For it manifests through the path of least resistance, as it allegorically seeks to unite with the Father energies.) This is symbolised by the 'burning poison' of the viper, which produces psychic madness and spiritual death.[19]

The secondary implication of the meaning of the serpent is its *ability to poison*. This happens through engendering such qualities as desire, lust, spite, hatred, enmity and vituperation. In these cases the *prāṇas* in the *nāḍīs* manifest in the form of moving serpents that bear such attributes *(saṃskāras)*. The serpent's poison thus symbolises a lifestyle associated with people that are bound to the sensual, illusion-forming material world. Such activity signifies spiritual 'death'.

19 See also my book *The 'Self' or Non-self' in Buddhism*, (Universal Dharma Publishing, Sydney, 2016), 29.

Kuṇḍalinī sustains the domain of the feminine aspect in Nature. Thus it is expressive of the Creative force, and as such is an important symbolic rendering of the term 'serpent'.

When the term serpent is found in the Bible, it can have a literal as well as symbolic meaning, but normally one must interpret its symbolism as either the ability to 'poison' or else to give wisdom. The terms 'fiery serpent' or 'flying fiery serpent' are also found, which obviously have considerable esoteric significance. These terms indicate *kuṇḍalinī* energy at differing stages of its arousal. At the beginning of its arousal the term 'serpent' can apply. When *kuṇḍalinī* has definitely begun to stimulate the higher psychic centres the term 'fiery serpent' applies. Once all major *chakras* have been fully vivified (producing liberation from the material realm, when one can travel consciously to all directions in time and space), then the 'fiery flying serpent' stage has been achieved. The following statement in *Isaiah* can be used to illustrate:

> Rejoice not thou, whole Palestina, because the rod of him that smote thee is broken: for out of the serpent's root shall come forth a cockatrice, and his fruit *shall be* a fiery flying serpent.[20]

'Palestina' is the land of the Philistines. The 'rod' represents where the serpent energy must flow. It is but a version of the *yogin's* staff. That it is 'broken' means that the prophet or man of 'God' who conveyed the energy to discipline or to seriously lecture the Philistines may have died or lost his occult power in some way.

'The serpent's root' refers to the Base of the Spine centre. From this *chakra* the serpent energy arises. This phrase therefore also signifies the fount of wisdom. The 'cockatrice' is a type of dangerous crested, winged serpent-dragon. It therefore symbolises the further awakening of *kuṇḍalinī,* as it flows through the *nāḍīs* to awaken psychic powers. Such powers can be those of dark magic (signifying the ability of the cockatrice to kill). However, here we are told that 'his fruit *shall be* a fiery flying serpent', which signifies one who shall develop the occult powers needed to become a prophet with a fully awakened vision. Such powers are needed to 'hold covenant with God'. The phrase thus tells us that a new prophet shall one day again emerge, who can give the

20 *Isaiah 14:29.*

Philistines the teachings they deserve. Then there should be a period of rejoicing.

Along this line, the book of *Numbers* states: 'the Lord sent fiery serpents among the people, and they bit the people; and much people of Israel died'.[21] This identifies these people as being involved in wrong magical practices (not condoned by the 'God' of the Israelites) that 'bit the people'. They thereby evoked negative psychic aspects associated with *kuṇḍalinī,* which killed many of them. Seeing these adverse effects, the people came to Moses and said: 'We have sinned, for we have spoken against the Lord, and against thee; pray unto the Lord, that He take the serpents from us'.[22]

Moses was instructed to make a 'fiery serpent and set it upon a pole'. Because the pole relates to the spinal column and the 'fiery serpent' to the awakened *kuṇḍalinī* energies that rose up it, so the statement informs us that he was to meditate to awaken his Head centre with this energy. This gave him – by means of the direct evocation of his spiritual Will and application of esoteric knowledge – the (occult) power to heal those that were bitten.

He then made 'a serpent of brass, and put it upon a pole', the viewing of which would allow those who were bitten to live if they saw it. This can be taken literally, however its esoteric interpretation is that Moses closed their psychic centres, thus halting the development of the psychic or clairvoyant powers that were causing them much anguish. They were thereby caused to revert to purely mundane consciousness or awareness, and thus be limited to the consciousness obtained by their five senses and intellect.

The Fiery Element was converted to 'brass' – a cold, lifeless, amalgamation of base metals (sentient qualities). It is a purely material energy (in contradistinction to being 'fiery'). Brass aptly symbolises the qualities of the intellect compared to those associated with supersensory perception. The people now lived empirically, no longer possessing the power to destroy themselves with Watery mediumistic and psychic potencies.

The importance of this story is reinforced later when Jesus alludes

---

21 See *Numbers 21:6-9.*

22 *Numbers 21:7.*

to it by stating: 'As Moses lifted up the serpent in the wilderness, even so must the son of man be lifted up'.[23]

Jesus not only refers to His actual physical death on the cross, but also emphasises the subjective means whereby the crucifixion experience could be accomplished. This is by arousing *kuṇḍalinī* (in the wilderness of material being, by overcoming the appropriate *saṃskāras*), resulting in its eventual exaltation in the Head centre. The 'son of man' will thus be completely liberated from the material world and the resultant need for further experience.[24]

Two other verses in the Bible occur where the terms 'fiery' or 'fiery flying serpents' appear: *Isaiah 30:6* and *Deuteronomy 8:15*. For the sake of completeness, a brief comment upon them should be given.

The Lord states:

> The burden of the beasts of the south: into the land of trouble and anguish, from whence *come* the young and old lion, the viper and fiery flying serpent, they will carry their riches upon the shoulders of young asses, and their treasures upon the bunches of camels, to a people *that* shall not profit *them*.[25]

The 'south' is what is down below – the bottom half of the being (wherein resides the *kuṇḍalinī* energy). The animals mentioned are the elementary forces that animate our base desires and 'beastly' nature. The 'land of trouble and anguish' refers to the material world, from any angle of vision, be it ancient Israel or modern civilisation, as well as that related to our emotional nature (the Waters).

The 'old lion' symbolises the dominant personality of one who has completely mastered the material world, becoming a lord of that domain. This is the attainment of the Initiate of the third degree, an enlightened being. A 'young lion' is therefore one who is a beginner

---

23 *John 3:14.*

24 See the chapters on Initiation in my book: *Meditation and the Initiation Process* for the true methodology that allows one (a 'son of man') to thus be able to awaken *kuṇḍalinī* in the material 'wilderness', and thereby to become liberated from *saṃsāra*. The subject of Initiation is important to properly comprehend, for much upon the spiritual path necessitates understanding what they are and how Initiation is obtained.

25 *Isaiah 30:6.*

upon the path to complete mastery. Accordingly, this symbolises the attainment of the Initiate of the first degree. The 'burden of the beasts of the south', therefore, is the 'burden' of those energies and qualities that allow this development. The direction south therefore refers to the realms of form, thus to the mass of incarnate people.

Concerning the 'viper and the fiery flying serpent' we see that the 'viper' is one whose *kuṇḍalinī* energy has been expressed to the degree that the centres *(chakras)* stimulated are those associated with the emotional desire nature (the 'Waters'). This awakens the lower psychic powers, which can quickly lead to the path of black magic. (Those who manifest the viper's poison.) The complete and appropriate control of these *chakras* is produced by the second degree Initiate.

The 'fiery flying serpent', as previously stated, symbolises one who is completely liberated from the form nature (which is the attainment of the Initiate of the fourth degree). Note that the Initiate of the fifth degree is esoterically called a Fiery Dragon of Wisdom. A dragon is thus a transformed serpent.

'Riches' and 'treasures' signify spiritual wealth, whilst 'young asses' symbolise the animal bodies of people, specifically serving disciples. (Signifying aspirants, probationary disciples and first degree Initiates.) The 'riches' that are stored upon their 'shoulders' signify the spiritual teachings gained from listening to those who have appropriately awakened *kuṇḍalinī.* Their burden then becomes the need to educate worldly humanity to the significance of these spiritual riches. Camels are mentioned because of their mastery of the need for the Watery Element (in the deserts of our material life). They therefore symbolise Initiates of the second degree that have mastered this emotional world and the related psychic proclivity. Their 'treasures' are thus the gain of the psychic powers they can rightly wield without perversion. Finally, the phrase 'a people that shall not profit them' symbolises average self-focussed humanity. They are uncomprehending of the nature of the spiritual riches brought to them by the abovementioned wise and the sages (Initiates) amongst them.

The trials and accomplishments of the aspirant in the wilderness of material being[26] also have symbolic context. This can be understood by referring to the explanations given about the temptations of Jesus in

26 *Deut. 8:15.*

the desert as a prelude to him attaining his third Initiation in my book *Meditation and the Initiation Process.*

The *chakras*

When speaking of *kuṇḍalinī* a discussion of the *chakras* (psychic centres) must be included, for they are intrinsically linked. In its simplest connotation the Sanskrit word *chakra* means wheel – the wheel of motion of the Law. The qualities of the particular *chakras,* when activated, connote the different attributes of a manifest 'son of God'. A *chakra* is literally a vortex of energy that occurs at a point of intersection of energies. There are seven major *chakras* that stem from points in the spine and are divided by means of 'spokes' of energy that have been likened to the petals of lotus blossoms in the etheric body of a person or Logos. When seen in the Bodies of planetary and solar Logoi the *chakras* convey astrological and cosmological energies.

Seen as swirling 'saucer-like depressions or vortices'[27] in a person, the *chakras* stem from various points in the spine. The seven major endocrine glands are their physiological externalisations. They are the 'wheels' mentioned in chapter one of *Ezekiel* (though depicted here in beings far more exalted than humanity). From another angle of vision, they can be perceived as 'Eyes'[28] that allow the entry of Light from one dimension of being into another. They are thus doorways to and from the realms of being (depending upon the Element each *chakra* controls). Through them an Initiate can leave and enter three-dimensional space at will. What is accessed depends upon such a one's degree of spiritual attainment.

The *chakras* are effectively eddies of Fiery energy. They gradually increase in luminosity from a dull glow to a brilliant incandescence, as the person can increasingly utilise the (*kuṇḍalinī*) energies resulting from spiritual development. This happens very slowly in the course of normal evolutionary development but can be greatly hastened by means of meditative practices. (Such as following the precepts of the Buddha's Eightfold Path.[29])

---

27 C.W. Leadbeater, *The Chakras* (Theosophical Publishing House, Adyar, 1996), 4.

28 *Rev. 4:6.*

29 See my book *Maṇḍalas: Their Nature and Development,* 249-75 for a detailed

The *chakras* are described in most books on yoga-meditation. There are also many minor centres governing the well-being of organs. The seven major centres are: the Base of Spine centre, the Sacral centre, the Solar Plexus centre, the Heart centre, the Throat centre, the Ājñā centre (the 'third Eye') and the Head centre. This is a subject of obvious importance to all students of the arcane wisdom. My writings therefore present considerable explanations of their nature and qualities. Below is a tabulation of the seven major *chakras*, indicating their basic qualities.[30]

1 **The Head centre** - *sahasrāra padma*
Centred at the top of the head.
Number of petals: 1,000 (approx).
The major colouring is white and gold.
Gland: Pineal.
Comments. Unfolds fully in a Master of Wisdom and expresses the spiritual Will of the enlightened being. It allows control of the Element Aether *(ātma),* and thus the energies governing evolutionary being.
Physiological control: the head and brain.

2 **The third Eye** - *ājñā chakra*
Centred between the eyebrows.
Number of petals: 96, divided into two parts of 48 petals each. The left side is coloured predominantly purple-blue and the right is predominantly rose-yellow.
Gland: Pituitary.
Comments. It awakens through meditative focus by spiritual aspirants, mystics and occultists. It coordinates the integration of personality and Soul forces and relates the various Elements together. The potencies of all the *chakras* are controlled by it. Thus it provides the ability to vision on many levels of being (dimensions of perception) when awakened. The right and left *nāḍīs* unite here. The Head centre and the Ājñā centre are esoterically a unit. All of the Elements can come under its direction.
Physiological control: the functioning of the eyes.

---

exposé of these paths.

30 See volumes 3, 4, 5A, 5B and 6 of my *A Treatise on Mind* series. The information in Table 15 can be found elaborated in my book *Meditation and the Initiation Process,* 15-23. See also Alice Bailey's *Esoteric Healing.*

3 **The Throat centre** - *viśuddha chakra*
Situated at the back of the neck.
Number of petals: 16.
Coloured silvery-blue.
Gland: Thyroid.
Comments. It unfolds in all intelligently creative and artistic beings. It expresses the full potential of the creativity of the mind/Mind, thus the entire articulation of the intelligentsia. From here also manifests the potency of the mantra making capacity of the *yogin*. This centre provides control of the Element Fire when fully unfolded.
Physiological control: the throat, vocal cords and lungs.

4 **The Heart centre** - *anāhata chakra*
Situated between the shoulder blades.
Number of petals: 12.
Golden in colour.
Gland: Thymus.
Comments. Unfolds in all dynamically active, compassionate people who are associated with groups, or concerned with the many. The Life-energy *(sūtrātma)* is anchored here, thus it is the centre where the *guru* or Christ, is said to reside. Here the Voice of Silence can be experienced. From this centre therefore the Intuition emanates, and thus provides control of the Element Air.
Physiological control: the heart, circulatory, lymphatic and glandular systems.

5 **The Solar Plexus centre** - *maṇipūra chakra*
Situated below the diaphragm, in the navel area.
Number of petals: 10.
Rose in colour, mixed with green.
Gland: Pancreas.
Comments. It expresses the qualities associated with the emotional body, people's desires, feelings, and sense of touch. It is the abdominal brain and therefore the organ of clairvoyance, opening the entire psychic, astral world to the mystic or occultist. It gives the control of the Watery Element when fully unfolded.
Physiological control: the digestive system.

6 The Sacral centre - *svādiṣṭhāna chakra*
Located in the lower part of the lumbar region.
Number of petals: 6.
Coloured differently according to the type of *prāṇa* each petal conveys, giving an overall sun-like appearance.
Gland: Gonads.
Comments. It expresses the sexual, animal, or physically vital forces in people. It is very strongly developed in most, especially the sensual, physical types of beings. Its energies often define the personality, when they reach out to influence the attributes of the other centres. When fully unfolded it allows control of the vital energy (*prāṇa*), insight into the etheric realm, control of bio-magnetic fields and healing currents. It forms an esoteric unity with the Base of the Spine centre.
Physiological control: the reproductive system.

7 The Base of the Spine centre - *mūlādhāra chakra*
Situated at the base of the spine.
Number of petals: 4.
Coloured red-orange.
Gland: Adrenals.
Comments. It is the primal centre and expresses the forces that produce viability to the material world. *Kuṇḍalinī* is thus centred therein. This centre is directly related to the unfoldment of the Head centre. It gives complete control of the Element Earth for those in whom *kuṇḍalinī* has risen.
Physiological control: the bones and muscular system.

Table 15: The *chakras*

Other meanings of the serpent

Another rendering of the serpent is that of the cycle of time. In this context, the serpent is seen biting its own tail, thus showing the alpha and omega of all life. This idea is conveyed in many creation myths as the cosmic or World-Egg, from which came the material universe.

Figure 14: The cycle of time

All life is governed by cycles that spiral within greater spiralling cycles. This process can be illustrated by picturing the overall course of the moon revolving around the earth. This occurs whilst the earth revolves around the sun. Likewise, the sun is propelled forward through the solar system in a progressive manner, as illustrated in the figure below.

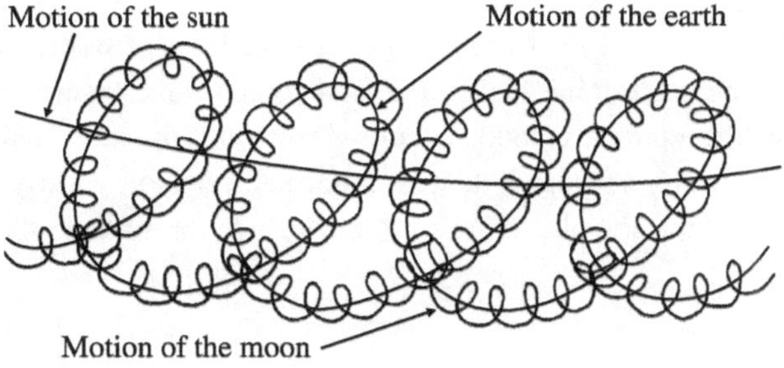

Figure 15: Planetary and solar motion

This analogy can be extended to include an understanding of the nature of the atom from an esoteric viewpoint.[31] This relates to how humanity gathers experience, and to the way the *chakras* unfold. All entities progress forward in time and space by this means – to the Heart of the Infinitude, for 'God is love'.[32] There is no conceivable beginning, nor a conceivable end. Only a timeless duration exists that is eternally conditioned by the relative beginnings and endings of lesser cycles within the greater whole. Thus the spirals progress from unity to an even greater unity, *ad infinitum*.

---

31 This idea has been developed in my book *Esoteric Cosmology and Modern Physics*, 326-49.

32 *I John 4:8.*

By its movements, the serpent symbolises all the prime types of energy qualifications that underlie the movements of all entities. This is the motion that sustains the visible universe and all in it. These motions can be depicted in the following ways:

The moving serpent symbolises the wave motion in the universe. It is also the forward propulsion that allows a being to travel from here to there.

The coiled serpent symbolises the spiral-cyclic motion (as well as potential energy), an outward expansion from a centre to the circumference of an ineffable circle that connotes the outermost field of contact, or represents motion in only one direction in space – outwards.

The moving serpent is also symbolised physiologically in the curvature of the spinal column from the base of the spine to the head.

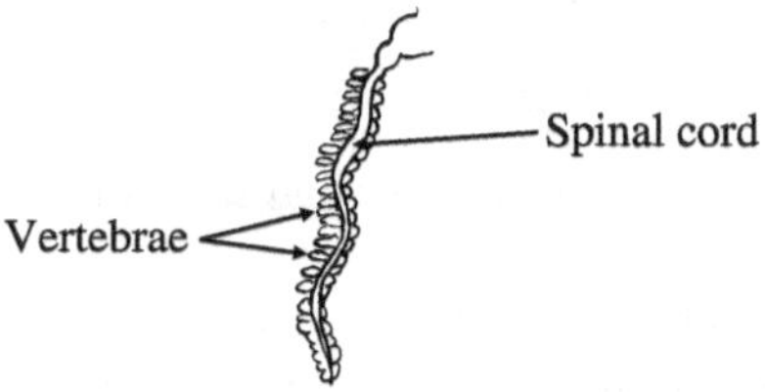

Figure 16: The spinal column

The vertebrae are placed in a ladder-like fashion. They also symbolise a spiral motion of the energies moving upwards, cycling around the central spine. The grey and white matter of the spinal cord (the physiological functions of which are analogous to those of the *iḍā* and *piṅgalā nāḍīs*) surround a central hollow tube filled with spinal fluid (which is roughly homologous to the *suṣumṇā nāḍī*). The curvature of the spinal column indicates the wave motion associated with the 'moving serpent' and the flow of *kuṇḍalinī*.

As one becomes increasingly enlightened one effectively travels up such a 'ladder' of consciousness. The grosser nature and coarser energies become increasingly refined (or 'distilled') as one works upon transforming *saṃskāras* in an increasingly subjective, sublimated, transubstantiation process. This is the changing of the 'bread and wine' of our experiences and form nature into the elixir of immortality, the Lighted substance of Life.

Such a ladder effectively symbolises 'Jacob's ladder' mentioned in *Genesis,* where it appears in the Body of Deity.

> And he dreamed, and behold a ladder set up on the earth, and the top of it reached to heaven: and behold the angels of God ascending and descending on it.[33]

As the top rung of the 'ladder' (or 'fractional distillation unit') is reached, thereon is obtained the energies of 'the Lord God', for only the most intense type of energy is left. 'The angels of God' relate to the enlightening forces that move up and down these triune *nāḍīs*. The energy contacted on the top rung of the 'ladder' can also be equated with the Electric-Fire (an expression of the Mind-nature of Deity, or the Buddha nature). It can unite with the Fiery distillate from the person. This relates to the process of liberating *kuṇḍalinī,* for once the meditator's energy has appropriately ascended to the Head centre then the combined energy descends like lightning down the *suṣumṇā nāḍī.* Now purified, it no longer contains anything antithetical to this motion. From there, it proceeds to the source of the Causative Fires that sustain the form (*kuṇḍalinī*). This sets in motion the process that liberates one's entire constitution in an infusion of Fiery Light, as *kuṇḍalinī* rises up to awaken all of the *chakras* in turn.

The transfiguration and elevation process associated with *suṣumṇā* only proceed as one develops the Mind by turning inwards towards the higher planes of perception. This is why meditation and the development of the intuition are so prominent in the religious scriptures of the East. There is also a need for the essential foundation built by developing the intellectual capacity and powers of the mind, which are the focus of attainment in the West.

33 *Gen. 28:12-16.*

The spiral motion can be extended to show the progression of consciousness in terms of the time-space continuum.

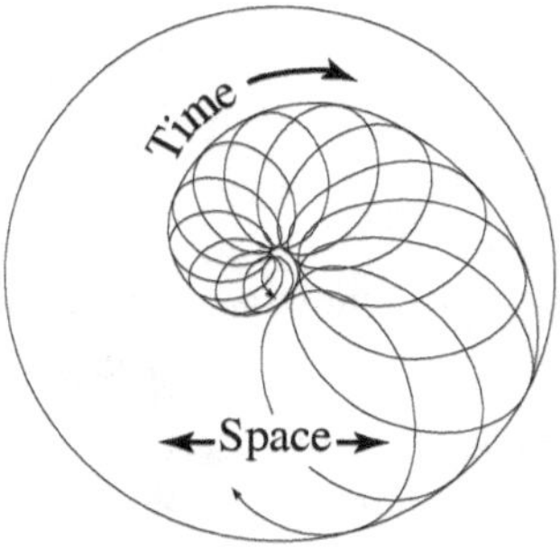

Figure 17: The spiral of the time-space continuum

This figure was published earlier in my book *Meditation and the Initiation Process,* where I stated, in part:

> When this continuum is clothed in materiality it forms a symbolic seashell, one of the major religious symbols in Eastern philosophies, often depicted in the hands of *yogins* and the major Hindu and Buddhist Deities. It can also be pictured as a *trumpet* that conveys *sound,* as also does the shell. In part it produces the esoteric interpretation of such phrases as that given in *Rev. 4:1:* 'and the first voice which I heard was as it were of a trumpet talking to me'. This means that *kuṇḍalinī* energy was effectively flowing, allowing John to listen to the 'inner Voice' produced by the resultant enlightenment.
>
> This continuum also graphically depicts the way of awakening the meditation-Mind as it builds its path in consciousness from the infinitesimal point in time and space that represents the self-conscious individual focussed upon the object of perception, the central dot *(bindu)* the seed or the focal point of meditation, to the outer limits of possible cognition or revelation, represented by the circumference.[34]

Note that nearly every ancient religion has a variation on this spiral-cyclic type of motion. It is usually a prominent element of their

34 *Meditation and the Initiation Process,* 85-6. See also *Esoteric Cosmology and Modern Physics,* 223-31, where the symbolism of this spiral is further explored. See also pages 237-42 and 261 from the book for a more detailed explanation of some of the remaining symbols related to the spiral provided in the present text.

iconography. For example, it has been depicted by the Greeks, Celts, Vikings, Hindus, Buddhists, Aztecs, Polynesians and Egyptians, etc., in the form depicted below:

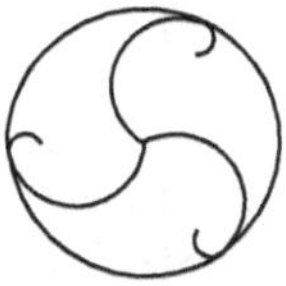

or

These versions demonstrate the three prime aspects or types of energy of Deity (Father, Son and Mother). The circles surrounding each of the symbols indicate that they have cosmological inferences, rather than just relating to humanity, in which case the circles would be omitted. The symbols thus indicate the nature of the laws associated with the projection of thought-forms and of motion.

As stated, there are four principal Elements associated with manifested space: Earth, Water, Fire, and Air. (The fifth, Aether, is all-pervasive and represents the space within which the other Elements permeate.) Together, the four Elements constitute the qualities of the manifest universe within one complete cycle or sphere of endeavour. One can also consider four such interrelated time-space continuums manifesting congruently, within each cycle of activity. This figure effectively depicts the cross-section of a *nāḍī,* which conveys the *prāṇas* of these Elements throughout the *nāḍī* system of an etheric form.

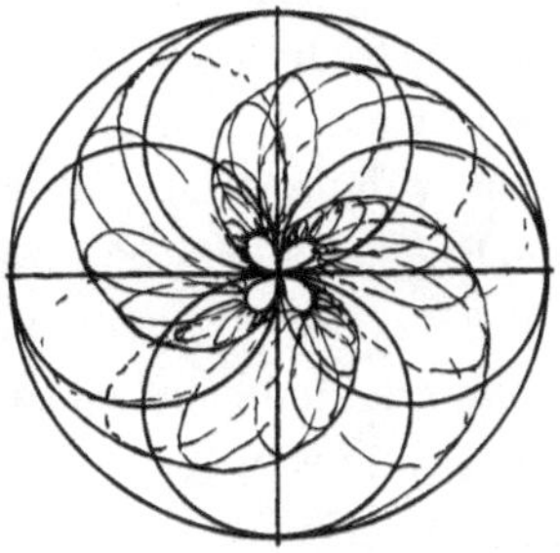

Figure 18: The cross-section of a *nāḍī*

Veiled in figure 18 is also the seed idea or foundation for the concept of the swastika, whose depiction is found in nearly all the ancient religions. Thus, we get:

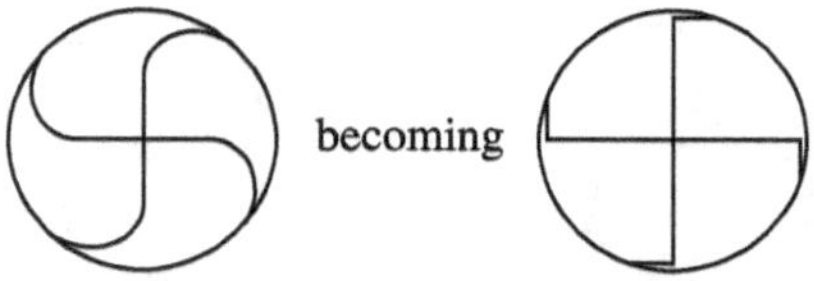

Figure 19: The swastika

These glyphs represent the four winds or forces causing and sustaining the universe. They are the four Seraphim (the four 'beasts' that support the 'throne of God'[35]). They are also known as the four Mahārājas, or guardians of the four continents (gates, or directions of the heavens) in the Buddhist and Hindu pantheon. They also share close correspondences to the analogies of many other mythologies.

There is a basic duality, a male-female polarity, in the arrangement of the *prāṇas* that constitute the swastika (symbolised by the yin-yang symbol ☯). The *prāṇas* conveying the Elements Earth and Fire assume a masculine polarity, whilst those conveying the Elements Air and Water assume a feminine polarity. At our present stage of evolution, the Element Earth is negative with regards to Fire, whilst Water, the dominant *prāṇa* in normal human consciousness, is negative with regards to Air. At the most advanced stages of evolution all the Elements become subordinate to Air *(buddhi)*. For the intellectual person, the Element Fire is dominant, and for the predominantly emotional person, the Watery Element is dominant.

A further examination of figure 18 reveals why the Base of Spine centre possesses four petals. Each of them conveys the *prāṇas* of one or other of the Elements. The increasing number and greater complexity of petals in the higher *chakras* indicates an extension of this basic pattern into all possible directions of space. This thereby allows full expression of the qualities associated with the Element embodied by any particular *chakra*.

35 *Rev. 4:6.*

Chakras form where a number of *nāḍīs* intersect. It is the spiral motion of the moving energies that causes them to function as wheels, or vortices of energetic reception and transmission. They direct *prāṇas* to the level where the *prāṇic* qualities find a positive outlet for expression. The *chakras* therefore project into the physical form qualities emanating from the dimension of perception (or kingdom of Nature) of which they are the gateways. People can be either consciously or subconsciously receptive to a *chakra's* energy.

Overall, a person's qualities are determined by the relationship between the Elements. One needs to comprehend what Elements are dominant, to what degree, and to what extent the expression of the others are retarded. These factors determine the type of *prāṇas* that flow up the *iḍā* and *piṇgalā nāḍīs*, and then to the sum of the *nāḍī* system. The energy flowing up the *iḍā nāḍī* is predominantly the Fire-Earth aspect of the various Elements, which is related to perception of the external universe. Within the *piṇgalā nāḍī* flow the Air-Water *prāṇas* that are mainly related to perception in the internal universe. The energies of the *suṣumṇā nāḍī* predominantly convey the Fire-Air aspect (Mind-Intuition), which fuses the most refined qualities of the other two *nāḍīs*.

The *suṣumṇā* path is the strait gate and narrow way that 'leadeth 'unto life'.[36] *Suṣumṇā* is the 'narrow razor-edged path' that is the essence of the Buddha's Noble Middle Way.

The energies conveyed through the *suṣumṇā nāḍī* relate to the highest possible attainment in the human form, productive of the fifth Initiation. After this Initiation one rises out of the ranks of the fourth kingdom in Nature. Such a One (a Chohan) has perfectly merged the qualities of both the human and angelic streams of consciousness. Chohans then mainly work through *chakras* external to themselves.

Finally, the symbolism of the ability of the snake to periodically shed its skin signifies the cycles of birth and death, of reincarnation. This symbol has also found its way into most creation myths in one form or another.

---

36 *Matthew 7:14*. See also *Luke 13:24*.

Satan

The meaning of the Hebrew term Satan is: 'an adversary, to obstruct', and this rendering is found throughout the Old Testament, particularly in the book of Job. There it is one of the places where Satan is used as a proper name or title.[37] In the Old Testament the concept of Satan is significantly lacking in theological embellishment, as noted in *The Interpreter's Dictionary of the Bible:*

> Nowhere in the OT does Satan appear as a distinctive demonic figure, opposed to God and responsible for all evil.[38]

Therefore, it is only in the New Testament, and by later theological assertions, that Satan begins to appear as a 'Prince of darkness' and as the leader of a host of evil entities or 'Demons'.[39]

A study of the New Testament passages where the term Satan is specifically used indicates the real esoteric significance of the term. This interpretation is that the meaning of Satan was adapted from the Pagan philosophy as a distortion of the Roman deity Saturn, the correspondence to the Greek deity Chronos. He is generally depicted wielding a scythe, to reap the experiences of life. As such, one can equate his role to the Lord of *karma.*

Equating Satan with the concept of *karma* allowed early theologians to skew esoteric philosophy into an exoteric doctrine. Thus, they turned Satan into the reaper of darkness, evil and misfortune as a reaction to those acting out their sensual, selfish and materialist tendencies. This misidentification allowed theologians to blame a host of 'evil entities' (which might be termed 'agents of *karma*') for the temptation process. Only the negative aspects of *karma* were thereby emphasised to the masses, whilst *karma's* esoteric significance was only known to Initiates.

---

37 See *Job 1:6-7,* where Satan is also considered amongst 'the sons of God'. The other places are in *Zech. 3:1-2, Psalm 109:6* and *2Cor. 2:11.*

38 George Buttrick (Dictionary Editor), *The Interpreter's Dictionary of the Bible* (Abingdon Press, Nashville, 1962), Vol. 4, 224. The term OT here means 'the Old Testament'.

39 This is a corruption of the Greek term daemon. In the Greek philosophy daemons were considered intermediaries, or messengers, between Deity and humanity, and thus were certainly not evil.

Thoroughly interwoven within the concept of *karma* are the cycles of time. Each cycle evolves from a previous one and also generates the next. Time was the prime attribute of Chronos,[40] and He was also the Father of all primeval cosmological forces (Titans).

Chronos mutilated His Father Uranus, who is absolute time. Time thus becomes finite and conditioned. In turn, Chronos is dethroned by His Son Zeus (Jupiter) after a fierce battle, who then becomes the supreme Deity. Chronos is ousted or falls from 'heaven', thus causing manifest space and all the related cycles. Zeus then sets about asserting His authority by bringing order to the universe (the realm of the mind, for Mt. Olympus symbolises the spinal column). Zeus's symbol of power is the 'thunderbolt' (lightning), thus He embodies the qualities of the Element Air.

The various allegories of Gods and Titans symbolise the various conflicts and interactions of the forces of Nature. This caused the manifestation of the solar system, or our earth sphere, whilst also referring to humanity's psychic constitution and spiritual unfoldment.

The story of the fall of Saturn can be compared with the Biblical myth of Lucifer, the 'son of the morning' (the early time of the day, or evolutionary period). Although Lucifer had 'fallen from heaven',[41] 'fallen' specifically means 'into generation'. In other words, fallen refers to material existence and the vicissitudes of a physical body. Lucifer here is symbolic of the human group-Soul that 'fell' from the spiritual realms (the Presence of 'God') into dense incarnation (which is a form of hell). Therefore, Lucifer also stands for what is limited, or conditioned by *karma,* as well as by time and its cycles. Such *karma* is what conditions all of our incarnations.

Relating this passage to those in *Luke 10:18,*[42] *Revelation 9:1-11, 12:7-9* and others, theologians evolved the concept of Satan as an adversary of 'God' (along with many ideas about the Devil). Due to their ignorance, these theologians greatly distorted the entire concept of evil contained within the scriptures. The esoteric meanings intended by the Initiated writers remained hidden.

---

40 From this, such words as chronograph and chronology are derived.

41 *Isaiah 14:12.*

42 *Luke 10:18* states: 'And he said unto them, I beheld Satan as lightning fall from heaven.'

The unsavoury ramifications of this ignorance may be witnessed in the zealous actions of the 'hell and brimstone, eternal damnation' fanatics and proselytising church ministers. The meanings of Lucifer, Satan, the Serpent, and the Devil cannot be interrelated with impunity, as we shall further see. Though they are related terms, each one also has specific and unequivocal meanings.

References to Satan in the New Testament

Here I will comment briefly on the meaning of the New Testament passages where the name Satan appears. First, we have the various permutations of the verse: 'If Satan cast out Satan, he is divided against himself; how shall then his kingdom stand?'[43] 'His kingdom' refers to the entire material world, wherein *karma* and the cycles of time rule. If what rules this kingdom is 'divided against itself', is at odds with the karmic laws that govern all being, then obviously the material world could not exist. The common rendering relates to the forces of evil (the dark brotherhood), for if they are divided amongst themselves, then obviously their power over people would be immensely weakened.

The meaning of the statement 'Get thee behind me, Satan'[44] relates to the canonical rendering of the word Satan as an 'adversary'.[45] This happened as a consequence of Jesus' days in the wilderness in order to pass his testings for the third Initiation.[46] The major perspective, however, relates to Jesus looking at Satan as the expression of being tempted with aspects of his past *karma* which is now to be eliminated, gotten 'behind him'. Where 'the devil' is involved in tempting him in the associated Biblical passages, there is a hint as to the *karma* that Jesus had from former involvement with the dark brotherhood in a cycle that literally occurred aeons ago. The ramifications of this *karma* were cleansed, for instance, in the process of his trial, scourging with whips, the crown of thorns and subsequent crucifixion. All of these happenings

---

43 *Matt. 12:26, Mark 3:23-6,* and *Luke 11:18.*

44 *Luke 4:8.* In *Matt. 4:10* the phrase is: 'get thee hence, Satan'.

45 See also *Mark 1:13.*

46 Jesus' temptations in relation to Initiation are explained in my book *Meditation and the Initiation Process,* 242-57.

were possible because of the *karma* of activities he manifested earlier, which had the chance to be cleansed in this way in that life.

The phrase 'Get thee behind me, Satan' also appears where Jesus relates Peter to Satan, for he: 'savourest not the things that be of God, but those that be of men'.[47] Here we clearly see that Jesus' concept of Satan is *not* something 'evil' in itself, but of relating to the common attributes developed by humanity, which are adverse to its spiritual development. These attributes are the *saṃskāras*[48] which perpetuate materialism in the physical plane.

It is stated in Mark that:

> The sower soweth the word. And these are they by the way side, where the word is sown; but when they have heard, Satan cometh immediately, and taketh away the word that was sown in their hearts.[49]

Here the 'sower' is the man of 'God', or the Soul, that sows the Word of wisdom, or liberation, for all who are ready to undertake the path. This 'word' was consequently 'sown in their hearts'. The heart is the source of spiritual accomplishment, the still centre and reservoir wherein the Voice of Silence resides. Those that are 'by the wayside, where the word is sown' are those on the outer periphery of the path of liberation. They listen to and perceive only superficially the context of what has been said. The fact that Satan can immediately come to take away the 'sown' word means that there is only a momentary response to the teachings. They have no in-depth comprehension.

Glamour and the related *karma* with the material world are very alluring to the average beginner on the path. There are often immediate mental-emotional conflicts (obscuration) of the spiritual truths they may have heard. Therefore, the teachings must be often repeated in many different forms and contexts before the aspirant will take determined action to properly learn.

After the seventy disciples of Jesus completed their healing work in the world, they came to tell Him 'with Joy' of their successes. They

47 *Matthew 16:23* and *Mark 8:33.*

48 Being the predilections, characteristics, developed in past lives *saṃskāras* lay the foundation for the direction of the individual's consciousness.

49 *Mark 4:14-15.*

state, 'even the devils are subject to us through thy name'. Jesus responds, 'I beheld Satan as lightning fall from heaven'.[50] Here, Satan takes on attributes of the highest energy (lightning) – conveyed by the *suṣumṇā nāḍī.* As the source of all spiritual power, this energy produces liberation. Consequently, this signified that the true beginning of their awakening happened through what they learnt upon this testing ground for them. Another concept, relating to Satan as *karma,* concerns the cleansing of some problematic *karma* of those disciples, hence Satan 'falling'.

What Jesus gave to them as a consequence was the ability 'to tread on serpents and scorpions, and over all the power of the enemy'.[51] Here, the 'enemy' symbolises what concerns the disciple's own corporeal nature and also the forces of evil in the world. Treading 'on serpents and scorpions' here refers to the 'poisons', the deadly attributes of the disciple's emotions.[52] They learnt how to master these attributes upon the path, to eventually awaken the potency of *kuṇḍalinī* (the 'serpent power'). This allowed the 'spirits' (psychic forces) to be subject to the disciples, but Jesus said:

> Notwithstanding in this rejoice not, that the spirits are subject unto you; but rather rejoice, because your names are written in heaven.[53]

'Heaven' here relates to the realm of the livingness of Hierarchy. This meant that they should rejoice that they are accepted disciples of this spiritual kingdom, rather than for the fact that they have developed some psychic powers. Being able to tread on 'serpents and scorpions' is reminiscent of sacred dances depicted in Eastern art, of such entities as Śiva, Kālī, Durgā, and the 'wrathful Deities' such as Heruka of the Buddhists. They ecstatically trample upon the bodies of the vanquished.

The description of falling 'as lightning' indicates that spiritual *karma* superseded material *karma* for the disciples as a group. They were released from attachments to what is material and transient

---

50 *Luke 10:17-18.*

51 *Luke 10:17:19.* The entire story is provided in Luke *10:17-24.*

52 'Scorpions' also relate to the zodiacal sign Scorpio, which esoterically is the sign of passing the testings for Initiation, by mastering the qualities of the nine-headed Hydra.

53 *Luke 10:20.*

(the cause of pain) so 'nothing' could 'by any means hurt' them.[54] Their (new) *karma* would be what causes 'their names to be written in heaven'. They would now manifest their lives as members of the heavenly kingdom (Hierarchy), according to its laws. Spiritual vision (supersensory perception) would be an obvious result of such 'falling'. Thus Jesus was able to 'rejoice in Spirit', and say to them privately 'Blessed are the eyes which see the things which ye see'.[55]

Next to consider is the woman, whom 'Satan hath bound, lo, for eighteen years' with an infirmity, and whom 'Jesus loosed from this bond on the sabbath day'.[56] This clearly refers to the workings of *karma. Karma* had produced both the infirmity and also the effect of its release, causing the woman to 'glorify God'. Satan, in the sense of 'adversary', is the *karma* that the woman had to bear and work out rightly if she was to be 'made straight' by the Lord.

The entering of Satan into Judas Iscariot[57] tells us plainly that Judas had to do what he was karmically impelled to do. This was to betray Jesus (which Jesus told him to 'do quickly'). Because of the consequences of this action, which Jesus plainly foresaw and which was needed for his passion play, this was essentially spiritual *karma* that was enacted. This was verified by statements following the incident, such as 'truly the Son of man goeth, as it was determined'.[58]

Immediately after Judas had left to do his Master's bidding, Jesus said: 'Now is the son of man glorified, and God is glorified in him'.[59] The only possible rendering of Satan here is *karma,* for only an incredibly foolish 'prince of evil' would cause the Plan to be set in motion, the very fulfilment of Biblical prophecy that would allow 'God' to be eternally glorified on the earth.

Later, Jesus said: 'Simon, Simon, behold, Satan hath desired to *have you,* that he may sift you as wheat'.[60] That is, Peter was always on the

---

54 *Luke 10:19.*

55 *Luke 10:23.*

56 *Luke 13:16.* See *Luke 13:11-17* for the entire section.

57 *Luke 22:3* and *John 13:27.*

58 *Luke 22:22.*

59 *John 13:31.*

60 *Luke 22:31.*

verge of falling into the power of the lord of *karma* that controls the material world. When Peter does so, however, it allows the 'chaff' (the adverse material *karma)* to be sifted out and thus eliminated from the 'wheat' – from that *karma* that leads to the 'bread of Life', to spiritual unfoldment and nourishment.

Speaking of the Gentiles, Jesus states to Paul (Saul) at the time of his conversion, that he is:

> To open their eyes, *and* to turn *them* from darkness to light, and *from* the power of Satan unto God, that they may receive forgiveness of sins, and inheritance among them which are sanctified by faith that is in me.[61]

The 'power of Satan' here is in the power of the *karma* that continually causes people to be born into the material world and sensual pursuits. (Equated with 'darkness', when compared to spiritual Light.) From this perspective, 'the forgiveness of sins' refers to the fact that one's *karma* is cleansed when one follows the teachings of Jesus, relating to the path of eventual liberation from *saṃsāra*. 'Sins' are but the actions that keep one tied to perpetual rebirth, whilst following the teachings, 'sanctified by faith' (for they are the embodiment of the living Light of Hierarchical purpose) will prevent one from so acting, thereby not creating more 'sins' *(karma)*.

Elsewhere there is the statement: 'And the God of peace shall bruise Satan under your feet shortly'.[62] This passage refers to the conquering of the material *karma* that ties one's feet to the material world. When one earnestly follows the teachings, then one's material plane *karma* is lifted, for one then is learning to enter the higher spiritual domains through elimination of attachment to what is material in nature.

The rendering of Satan as *karma* can also be applied to a statement from the book of *Corinthians* which indicates, 'lest Satan should get an advantage of us: for we are not ignorant of his devices'.[63] Earlier it is stated (in relation to the deed of fornication): 'to deliver such an

---

61 *Acts 26:18.*

62 *Romans 16:20.*

63 *II Cor. 2:11.*

one unto Satan',[64] which refers to delivering a person to the resultant *karma,* and so to suffer the consequences of their actions.

Corinthians also provides us with the theme of rendering Satan in terms of its original Hebrew meaning of 'an adversary', where it is stated for Satan or karmic opportunity (the adversary to the well-being of the marital situation) to 'tempt you not for your incontinency'.[65] A similar implication is provided in the book of Acts, wherein Peter queried to Ananias: 'why hath Satan filled thine heart to lie to the Holy Ghost, and to keep back part of the price of the land?'[66] Restated, the question that Peter was asking is: 'why has the materialistic attitude' (an effect of Satan, the adversary) of keeping back part of the price of the land, with its unsavoury karmic implications, 'filled your heart causing you to lie', thus repudiating 'the Divine Covenant (the Holy Ghost) that is within us all?'

The transformation of Satan 'into an angel of light'[67] implies the transformation of material *karma* into the manifestation of spiritual *karma* (Light). Such transformation is always the objective of the law of *karma,* for its purpose is to lead us from darkness to light, from self-centred focus, to that of the selfless service to others, that causes the liberation of all. *Karma* is also what causes the significant events or happenings (the 'occasion' that Paul speaks of) desired by the 'false apostles'.[68] In chapter five I noted that the angelic kingdom (with its various cohorts of *devas)* are the active agents of *karma.* It stands to reason that they are presided over by a *deva* 'Lord of *karma*', who is here termed Satan. (For this reason Satan is personified as an entity in the New Testament.) Paul was therefore giving to his brothers what had also been a Revelation to him – that Satan himself is transformed into an angel of Light. He therefore states: 'it is no great thing for his ministers also be transformed as the ministers of righteousness; whose end shall be according to their works'.[69]

---

64 *I Cor. 5:5.*

65 *I Cor. 7:5.*

66 *Acts 5:3.*

67 *II Cor. 11:14.*

68 *II Cor. 11:11-15.*

69 *II Cor. 11:15.*

The phrase 'his ministers' refers not only to the (angelic) entities subservient to Satan, but also to 'false apostles' and 'deceitful workers'. They demand 'signs' and 'miracles' that are essentially profane, or materialistic (which is the domain of the Lord of *karma).* The phrase 'whose end shall be according to their works' is a reiteration of the law of *karma* which Paul considered when he made these statements.

It should be noted that during translation, later theological meaning could have been interpolated into Paul's statements. Parts of the texts relating to his testimony are exoteric doctrines (not divinely inspired). We should note the fact that Paul was not initiated into the higher Mysteries for the greater part of his life. He strongly embodied the traits of a struggling, but zealously fervent disciple. Paul thus mingled both esoteric and exoteric concepts within his philosophy. On the other hand, the statements of Jesus are free from this blemish, as are also those in the *Revelation of St. John.*

Generally, it is seen that Paul's idea as to the nature of Satan seems to be directly derived from the literal Hebrew rendering of 'adversary' (as a definite entity). This is coupled with the nature of *karma* being emphasised in its most material aspect (that pertains to or exalts the material world). This is a somewhat exoteric viewpoint and is conveyed by Paul's remaining statements.[70]

Nowhere is the name Satan even vaguely depicted as a ruler of 'hell', with eternal damnation, fire and brimstone. In fact, Paul states that he had delivered 'Hymenaeus and Alexander....unto Satan, that they may learn not to blaspheme'.[71] This is exactly what would be taught by karmic purpose, but certainly not by an eternity of 'fire and brimstone'.

The statement below needs comment:

> Then shall that Wicked be revealed, whom the Lord shall consume with the spirit of his mouth, and shall destroy with the brightness of his coming: *Even him,* whose coming is after the working of Satan with all power and signs and lying wonders.[72]

'All power and signs and lying wonders', symbolises the gain of the result of humanity's intellectual or psychic prowess. This is the

---

70 *II Cor. 12:7, I Thess. 2:18, II Thess. 2:9* and *I Tim. 5:15.*

71 *I Tim. 1:20.*

72 *II Thess. 2:8-9.*

domain, or a direct result of the 'working of Satan' as the personification of *karma*. The phrase 'Even him' can refer to a member of the dark brotherhood, explained in the section concerning 'the Devil'. Interpreted literally it refers to one who, for selfish material incentives, produces great powers, signs and 'lying wonders'. Such 'wonders' can also be interpreted from a psychic perspective. Accordingly, such a one will be destroyed by the 'brightness' of the coming of the Lord. (The process concerning the reappearance of the Christ.)

In modern times the Evil to be destroyed is witnessed in the results of humanity's intellectual achievements. Clearly much good has been produced by the resultant incredible technology, in the benefits of devices such as television, radio, the Internet and newspapers. However, the potential for misuse by those who purposely purvey misleading propaganda is great. This can be interpreted as 'lying wonders' due to such media's potential to deceive and spread misinformation to the public *en masse.*

'All power' can relate to modern (nuclear) armaments, while 'signs' can correlate to the enormous unrest, political chaos and mass movements, either towards spreading light or to darkness. This present era can therefore be considered the highest point of achievement of the Lord of *karma* and of the material domain. It is a materialistic epoch that cries out for the 'brightness' of the coming of 'the Lord' to change human attitudes towards Love and Light. Such will be the achievement in this coming new Aquarian Era. When 'the Lord' comes it will spell the doom of our materialistic type of civilisation.

References from *St. John's Revelation*

First, one can look at the statement:

> I know the blasphemy of them which say they are Jews, and are not, but *are* the synagogue of Satan'.[73]

A synagogue is the place where 'God' can be worshipped and His Laws (the Mosaic code) received by the orthodox Jew. John however uses the derogatory term 'Satan' to describe what the blaspheming Jews worship. Here this term relates to what considered the 'adversary' of

73 *Rev. 2:9* and *3:9.*

'God', materialistic in its attitude, and so evil in nature. Such concepts can easily be construed as referring to a devil.

From a higher perspective the angelic kingdom residing upon the mental plane that governs the manifestation of the *karma* of the physical plane (hence ruled by Satan), can be likened to a synagogue. The reference here is to the *maṇḍala* they form as part of angelic triads in order to manifest the appearance of the phenomena wherein we reside. An interlaced hexagram is formed (Solomon's seal) ✡. The upper triad consists of the higher three groupings of the *deva* hierarchy (the Creative Hierarchies). They are the Divine Flames, the Greater Builders and the Lesser Builders. The lower triad consists of the lower three Creative Hierarchies: the fifth (Makara, the Mystery), the sixth (the Lunar Pitris), and the seventh (the Elemental Lives that embody the physical form). Together, they are the agents of the *karma* that govern the manifestation of all phenomena.

The next statement to consider is:

> These things saith he which hath the sharp sword with two edges: I know thy works, and where thou dwellest, *even* where Satan's seat *is*.[74]

A seat is a place whereupon one sits. Esoterically, it is also a term that signifies the *mūlādhāra chakra* (the Base of Spine centre). This centre governs the entire material domain *(saṃsāra),* hence the domain of the manifestation of *karma*. Therein also resides the *kuṇḍalinī* Fire that supports the sum of *saṃsāra* and its cycles. In this case Satan can signify the Lord that rules the activity of this Fire and its dissemination throughout Nature. What is implied here then is the entire process that will lead to the mastery of the material world, hence of the manifestation of *karma*. This process leads to the attainment of the third Initiation, when the Initiate is fully identified with the Sambhogakāya Flower (the Soul). This is the basis to the manifestation of divinity on earth.

Later in the chapter it is stated that:

> As many as have not this doctrine, which have not known the depths of Satan, as they speak; I will put upon you none other burden.[75]

---

74 *Rev. 2:12-13.*

75 *Rev. 2:24.*

The doctrine referred to is that of Jezebel the prophetess who teaches and seduces 'to commit fornication, and to eat things sacrificed unto idols'.[76] As Satan refers to what governs the material world, so to 'know the depths of Satan' is to have absorbed that world so thoroughly as to have descended into all aspects of material existence. This is even to the extent of manifesting the traits of the dark brotherhood, as clearly Jezebel has. The most intense (blackest) forms of *karma* are engendered thereby. The word 'depth' also indicates this, of having been completely bound by darkness.

The 'depths' can thus refer to the fear-engendering qualities, limited and circumscribed awareness and varying degrees of ignorance which people engender. From there, one slowly climbs out of the 'depths' to the fertile valleys and sunlit plains of the world. Finally, one becomes an illumined world-conqueror and ascends to the mountaintop of Initiation. Those that have not known the 'depths', therefore, have not descended into manifesting the attributes of the dark brotherhood. For them there is no specific karmic 'burden' to experience.

The following statement was depicted in figure 12 at the beginning of this chapter: 'the great dragon....that old serpent, called the Devil, and Satan, which deceiveth the whole world'. They were all said to be 'cast out into the earth'.[77] As stated, this has profound cosmological implications, relating to the formation of an earth sphere. The ability to 'deceive' the 'whole world' here is in relation to the outward appearance of the transitory material realm, the establishment of the phenomenon of *saṃsāra*. This illusory world play definitely deceives all those involved in it, for people think that it is something real. However, there is no reality to its substantiality. Such thought stems from the nature of the intellect, which classifies impressions derived from sense perceptions as real. Most people do not understand the purpose of this transience, of the nature of the path to its mastery. [78] This passage has similar

76 *Rev. 2:20.*

77 *Rev. 12:9.*

78 As stated in my book *Esoteric Cosmology and Modern Physics,* 161-2: 'Humanity have built an immense cumulative 'dweller' by means of their misplaced thought-forms and self-focussed causative streams of interrelationship. It is constituted of the myriads of glamorised images and thoughts generated by them, of everything

implications to the Greek myth of the dethronement of Chronos (Saturn).

The passage in verse 20:2 provides the same cast of characters as Revelation 12:9. Here however, the concern is with the end result of material evolution, cosmologically, after a symbolic 1,000 years.

> And I saw an angel come down from heaven, having the key of the bottomless pit and a great chain in his hand. And he laid hold on the dragon, and that old serpent, which is the Devil, and Satan, and bound him a thousand years.[79]

Christian theologians like to conflate 'the Devil' with Satan, but readers of this book now know they are two different entities. The symbolic meaning of this passage relates to the process of the ensuing of *pralaya*, the ending of a grand cycle of evolution *(manvantara)*, and incorporation into the subjective domains (symbolised by the phrase 'the bottomless pit') before later being 'Breathed' out again in another, higher cycle.[80] This means the 'sealing' or 'binding' of *karma* for the duration of the subjective cycle, or 'sleep' period *(pralaya)*. Thereafter, *karma* can again manifest. After the symbolic 1,000 year cycle is finished, Satan – *karma* 'would be loosed out of his prison',[81] thereby allowing another great cycle of Being to commence.

To better comprehend the symbolism one must consider the number 1,000 numerologically. The number 10 is considered the number of completion, of perfection, the end attainment of evolution. The number 1,000 = 10 x 10 x 10 therefore signifies the Great Perfection, signifying

---

constituting the *māyā* wherein people reside and which prevents their gaining enlightenment. It can be considered 'evil' whenever it influences the general population (as it inevitably does), preventing their right evolutionary attainment. It is effectively a thick, darkened cloud of repetitive, cancerous images of consumer items, desired ideations, commercial slogans, religious and cultural images, hallucinations concerning the world of sports and movie stars, sexual imagery of all types, political sloganism, avariciously looming wealth generating schemes, and malicious broodings surrounding us all. When it is destroyed through right thought, the demonstration of light, applied Love and goodwill to all, then humanity will receive its full endowment of divinity'.

79 *Rev. 20:1-2.*

80 The detail of this process is provided in the two volumes of my book *The Astrological and Numerological Keys to the Secret Doctrine.*

81 *Rev. 20:7.*

the annulment, etherealisation, or liberation of the material universe on three levels of expression – the mental, astral and dense physical. (The number thus signifies the completion of one major cosmological cycle.)

The Devil

The general rendering of this term is what slanders 'God' or man, being the cause of all blasphemy. Notably, the word Devil is not found at all in the Old Testament (though the term 'devils' appears four times). This is therefore another concept that gained prominence during the Christian dispensation. Esoterically, there are two renderings of this word.

A. When spelt backwards, we have the word lived.
B. If spelt D'evil, meaning 'the Evil'.

A. When spelt backwards

This conveys a very important meaning of the term – as an entity (or rather, entities, as 'devils') that once lived and yet can still exert an unpleasant psychic influence over others. These are disincarnate people that for one reason or other are confined to the grosser psychic realms and yet are still in contact with humanity. This can be the result of the aberrant base desires resulting in left hand practices, and some suicide cases.

Such beings have not yet seen what awaits them in the higher planes of experience. They are thus generally in a state of confusion or distress. Their emanations are often unpleasant in nature, but they require our compassion and help rather than fear and misunderstanding. The strong attachment to the terrestrial world of these entities may lead to them trying to enter via psychic flaws that may be found in an incarnate person's etheric body. In such a case, the person becomes obsessed by such entities.[82]

Another group of entities that can also 'obsess' a person are mischievous (astral) entities. These are nature spirits, similar to the Christian concept of 'demons'. They can be lesser angelic entities

82 This subject is explained in Alice Bailey's *Letters on Occult Meditation*, in the chapter on the dangers of meditation.

(Elementals) that embody sensual, selfish, or 'evil' thought-forms, and the like.

The average well-meaning person has nothing to fear from such entities, for flaws in their psychic constitution that would allow obsession are a relatively rare occurrence. An evolved person will have even less potential to be obsessed.

Western Kabbalistic and hermetic texts testify to such entities. Also, there are many examples within folk legends, and the various magical, mythical and traditional belief systems. Clairvoyant testimonials also provide further evidence. Examples of such entities abound in the superstitious, animistic and shamanistic teachings that are common throughout the aboriginal inhabitants of every country of the world, as well as within all traditional religious scriptures. These entities are, however, not subordinate to a 'king of evil'. Nor are they his intelligent underlings, but they do constitute part of the domain of the material world, which can be considered 'evil' in a sense. (It is the domain of *karma* – Satan.)

All such entities can definitely be utilised to do the bidding of the black magician. They are the psychic building blocks for all forms, subjective or objective. As incorporeal entities, they are evolving in their own realm of perception to eventually become people or the angelic equivalents. Thus, they must progress through stages analogous to the mineral, plant, and animal stages of consciousness in our realm.

B. If spelt D'evil

The connotation here is the sum total of what is Evil. This can be particularised as a group of entities that are known as adherents of the left hand path, the dark brotherhood (black magicians[83] and sorcerers,

83 The colour black does not relate to skin colour, rather, connotes the auric colouring they engender. This has been developed through engendering malice, hatred, extreme selfishness, psychopathic and sociopathic activities for the benefit of the self. They manifest great cunning and manipulative methodology directed for self-glorification and material or monetary power. They were practitioners of the black arts and sorcery in former lives and may still consciously do so in this life. They have made links to many sources of cosmic evil, though now many of their incarnations are unaware of such past life activity, nevertheless the accrued *saṃskāras* and psychic links dominate their lives. They are manipulated and directed from the inner realms by points of evil of vast power.

their adherents and those dominated by them). They uphold and project what pertains to the past (relating to the material realm) and which is no longer desirable to the evolutionary Plan. They are thus involved in fostering materialism, selfishness and separateness in their many forms, and generally psychically dominate those who live in *saṃsāra*.

Jesus prayed that 'God' would keep His disciples from 'the evil',[84] for this is something that fundamentally concerns the kingdom of 'God', and the Hierarchy of Light. They have the capacity to tackle the complexity of the cunning and force projections of the forces of evil. Though the conflict between the white Hierarchy (the brothers of Light) and the dark brotherhood directly affects humanity, they are oblivious to all such happenings. (Humanity, however, generate the conditions and actions that breed all aspects of the Evil.) The conflict ('war') is part of the long aeonic evolutionary journeying for control of the outcome of the manifestation of *saṃsāra*.

Those upon the Initiation path (thus disciples of the Christ) inevitably become white magicians when they learn to work with the healing effects of Light. However, the temptations of the lower psyche and lures of the left hand path are always there to entice them.

Possibly the only entities that can truly be called 'adversaries of God' are sorcerers. They have intentionally trod the path of evil. Theirs is the way of darkness and hate, the perfection of the most separative and segregative concrete attributes of mind to powerfully manifest the ability to manipulate all things. They thereby harness power in the material domain, and so deliberately combat the laws of evolution. They are thereby completely antagonistic to the forces of Light. Sorcerers subjectively (psychically) and objectively have caused much of the ignorance, wrong values and the negative aspects of human civilisations on earth, from the hoary mists of antiquity onwards.

Even though he influences the minds and actions of humanity the sorcerer is not interested in the petty wishes and desires of the average person, unless they are in a position of power over many people. By influencing the minds of such people (e.g., politicians, the super-wealthy) the sorcerer can exercise control over nations and international

---

84 *John 17:15:* 'I pray not that thou shouldest take them out of the world, but that thou shouldest keep them from the evil.

happenings. They become focal points for the sorcerer's schemes, and through them the mass of humanity can be controlled. The sorcerer's objectives and methods are, however, far too penetratingly expansive and occult to be noticed by the average (spiritual) person, or even the average psychic.

A distinction between sorcerers and black magicians should also be noted. Black magicians work completely in the realms of form, within glamour and illusion, the astral world of the psychic, and they wield power over a large number of disincarnate entities and thought constructs. They are normally completely deluded by their own exaggerated sense of individual dominance. Their method is to always try to control psychic entities and energies in an endeavour to delude the foolish and to manipulate the masses of people. A black magician will however be dominated by a sorcerer.

The basic difference between a black magician and a sorcerer is that the sorcerer is a master of yoga. He has become so through severe austerities that have completely starved out his lower psychic nature and desire principle. This allows a sorcerer to tap the potent Fiery energies of the mind (and thus of the three worlds of human livingness) for selfish and separative purposes. He aggressively utilises certain forces developed in the Soul, through many lifetimes of material evolution, in conjunction with the forced raising of *kuṇḍalinī.*

The black magician, on the other hand, actively feeds the desire principle and sensuality. Sex magic is normally their onus of operation. Psychic powers are acquired through the destruction of their own (psychic) constitution. Black magicians (like sorcerers) have emphatically developed the powers of the intellect to the utter abnegation of the principle of Love. The mind is utilised to force the development of psychic power, which is directed towards the aggrandisement of separative ends. This normally produces exaggerated facets of duality within them, and such personality characteristics become overtly dominant. Their personalities are often 'two-faced' in nature – a subtle doctor Jekyll and mister Hyde complex, rarely noticed by the casual observer. They can, therefore, hide behind the mask of being a philanthropist or healer, which veils their nefarious motives. Everything they do, however, is self-serving in its nature. Black magicians will often show petty vindictiveness toward people with whom they are acquainted. Their power may be offset if someone being 'attacked' by them appropriately resists by generating the energies of light, and by unveiling the masks the black magicians hide behind.

The more extreme the black magician the greater their driving selfish ambition. They crave power (psychic or temporal) over all sentient beings and ruthlessly use their powers to achieve their one-pointed ambitions. The words of power (mantras) and ceremonial rites of such beings are used to conjure up either very real elementary Lives *(devas),* or else phantasmic thought-forms[85] to do their bidding. The energy needed to do this comes from their personal physical and psychic constitution. This energy is used in conjunction with group energies, such as supplied by orgies and sacrifices associated with the rites and traditions of covens. The meaning of the symbolism of such things as the 'drinking of the blood' of their victims denotes the psychic 'drinking' or absorbing of the *prāṇas* (life force) of their target victims.

Not all black magicians however use magical means, many are reincarnated from former lives of such activity. The selfish *saṃskāras* and energies formerly developed now manifest to produce a life of ruthless ambitious planning to produce immense material wealth. The power of money is used to control people and organisations, to corrupt politicians, etc., and to buy whatever they want. Many are the avenues of power in our materialistic societies that they can pursue.

An overriding selfishness thus often places these black magicians in positions of great wealth and power. The psychic energy they generate greatly stimulates their desire for sensual gratification, which is projected into their rites. Their desire-nature and ego-centred attitudes gradually become more extreme from one life to the next.

Progressively, the sentience of their lower psychophysical nature begins to completely dominate the black magician. They increasingly run the risk of atrophying the Life link *(sūtrātma*[86]*)* between the Soul

---

85 These phantasms are forms of psychic power built by the desire-mind and projected to accomplish whatever is desired.

86 The *sūtrātma* can be contrasted to the *antaḥkaraṇa,* the consciousness-link, which bridges or links the empirical mind to the abstracted Mind. The *antaḥkaraṇa* is often depicted as a 'rainbow bridge' because of the Rays of energies it conveys. At a certain stage of meditative development it is consciously built through a sea of consciousness, bypassing the Soul, allowing linkage to the Monad.

and the form. Such is the result of untold lives of retrogressive emphasis that eventually may sever that link, causing the Soul to break free from that form which is lost. This leaves their corporeal entity (the personality) to wander in *saṃskāras* until its eventual doom.

This explanation gives credence to the existence of such entities as vampires. They function in the desire-mind as astral-mental entities residing in an etheric body, but possessing only a few intelligent remnants. Having lost the ability to absorb *prāṇa* from the sun and plants, they sustain themselves from the psychic bodies of others. They can thus be destructive to the psychic integrity of those receptive to their type of emanation. Their victim's *prāṇa* (subjective 'blood') is consumed as sustenance. (This is thus not the physical blood, popularised by sensationalised novels.) Eventually the vampires are destined to undergo a complete breakdown into the elements that compose their form.

A more typical path of development for a black magician, however, is to be born over and over again. They possess psychic flaws, extreme one-pointed selfish qualities, and ever-increasing insanity as a karmic result of their actions. Despite this, they will still always incarnate into situations where they could be redeemed, and often are, before the above 'vampiric' progression can happen.

Black magicians and sorcerers are effectively travelling back in (evolutionary) time instead of forwards.[87] The sorcerer's ability to subjectively manipulate and control is far greater than the black magician's because the knowledge and energies at his command are far more potent. True sorcerers are however rare, as are true white magicians (and neither are glamoured by psychic abilities).

The black magician manifests as a personality among personalities, whereas the sorcerer is rarely found incarnate. The black magician can lose the link with his Soul, whereas the sorcerer will retain this link, but the Life energy *(sūtrātmā)* between Causal body and the Monad may be severed. The black magician works from the physical and astral realms, whereas the sorcerer works from the mental and higher planes of perception. Both sorcerers and black magicians, however, manipulate

---

87 This is because they travel against the evolutionary impetus in order to sustain the conditions of *saṃsāra* and self-focussed materialism. They are consequently 'evil' because they fight against the evolutionary flow.

all entities that allow their energies and thought-forms to dominate and manifest through them.

The sorcerer represents purely separative manifest intelligence. His focus is upon the phenomenal world and works with material energies and psychic forces to keep all lives bonded to the realms of form. He works by sowing the seeds of fear, separateness, mass glamour, encourages aggressive relationships, and fosters aberrant psychological traits, philosophies and amoral values amongst humanity. Propagating lies and deceit are the modus operandi of both the sorcerer and black magician.

The white magician, by contrast, always expresses wisdom through Love, and works with the Soul of things. He/she always endeavours to liberate the Life from the imprisoning form. The left hand path is to work in darkness with matter, and the right hand path is to work in Light to progress the evolutionary Plan. Despite this distinction, black and white followers can still be seen to be 'brothers', for all are members of humanity. Even the activities of the sorcerer can be considered to form a part (of the Destroyer aspect) of the Plan of 'God'.

Exorcism and obsession by entities

The act of exorcism is not specific to Christianity and its sects. Historically, Christians may however be the most vociferous in their claims. This is likely due to their somewhat exaggerated ideas concerning the nature of evil and the devil. This seems amply backed by scriptural testimony, throughout which there are many references of exorcism. Jesus, for instance, exhorted the devils, whose 'name is Legion: for we are many', to leave the man with the 'unclean spirit' and enter a herd of swine.[88]

The names of such entities in ancient and modern religious scriptures certainly are 'legion', as many who compiled such lists have discovered. Many Buddhist, Hindu, or Shamanistic exorcists have also tried to expel such entities from the bodies of those thus obsessed. This is witnessed, for instance, by the work of such beings as Padmasambhava.

In order to bring Buddhism to Tibet, Padmasambhava could only succeed after cleansing (exhorting, subduing, or converting) much of

88 *Mark 5:7-13.*

that ancient country from the influence of indigenous 'evil spirits' or 'demons' *(pretas, rākśasas, nāgas,* etc.). This was to prepare Tibet appropriately, to receive the white *dharma*.[89]

Some people have psychic flaws and are thus susceptible to being obsessed (or possessed). Mediumistic tendencies certainly do not indicate advanced spiritual status. Animals for instance, also have psychic tendencies. Mediumship is generally not a good thing, as is frequently supposed, as a medium is often not in control of his or her vehicles, nor of the psychic entities that may possess them.

In the quest for enlightenment, psychic ailments are as much of a hindrance as mental-emotional flaws or physical disease. Psychic issues may even prove to be a greater obstacle, due to the glamour involved. Much of the Christ's work in exhortation was concerned with the healing of such beings. Psychic flaws must be rectified before a person can fully walk in the Light of the Soul.

Psychism relates to a primitive stage of development when humanity as a whole was psychic or mediumistic. Their focus of consciousness was astral-etheric and they had little control over desire, emotion or the forces manifesting through them. Intelligence, such as understood nowadays, was not developed. Humanity has evolved from that stage into a more intellectual polarisation. So also must the mediumistic person. From intellectualism we must now advance into the intuitional realm and beyond. The epoch of Love-Wisdom lies ahead of us, necessitating the advent of the rulership of the higher Mind by humanity to overcome massed desire-attachment. Wisdom involves the generation of the Will-to-Love. The onset of this epoch will avert the cyclic expression of the psychic abuse of the selfish personal will by humanity, that helped cause the sinking of Atlantis into the Watery abyss.

Symbolism of the sheep and the goats

The verses of Matthew below use the symbolism of 'the sheep and the goats' to deal with the distinction between the left hand and right hand path, therefore between black and white magic:

89 See W.Y. Evans-Wentz, *The Tibetan Book of the Great Liberation* (Oxford University Press, London) for detail concerning the life of Padmasambhava.

> When the Son of man shall come in his glory, and all the holy angels with him, then shall he sit upon the throne of his glory: And before him shall be gathered all nations: and he shall separate them one from another, as a shepherd divideth his sheep from the goats. And he shall set the sheep on his right hand, but the goats on the left.[90]

This passage deals with a time in the future when many of humanity are in the process of attaining enlightenment, as part of the externalisation process of the Hierarchy of Enlightened Being. This will allow 'the Son of man' (the Christ, the head of the Hierarchy) to 'come in his glory and all the holy angels with him'. For only then will people have developed the capacity to perceive this happening and comprehend the nature of what 'sits upon the throne' (the *mūlādhāra chakra)* 'of his glory'.[91] The four petals of this *chakra* here represent the four kingdoms of Nature that the Christ will administer to, and so to awaken the creative Fires in each according to their capacity. Such Fires manifest in differing ways for each of the kingdoms. 'The holy angels' are the members of the *deva* kingdom in their various orders, that will begin to be perceived by humanity as they regain clairvoyant vision.

The imminent coming of the Lord in the New Age signifies the beginning of the process that will eventually allow the Christ to manifest in the form of a planetary Logos for earth.[92] An obvious 'parting of the way' will come at that stage of evolution, wherein the failures of our present evolutionary period will no longer be able to reside on earth.

It should be noted that most theologians take a far too literal approach in their rendering of Biblical chronology, such as in the previously mentioned 1,000 year period that Satan is to be bound. They err just as greatly in this interpretation as when they conceived the date of the creation of the earth as being 4,004 B.C. (A symbolic truth, but according to scientific research, an erroneous concept.)

Those that are placed on the 'left hand' side, or path, are symbolised by the term 'goats'. They are not only those that have deliberately chosen separateness and darkness as their path, but also those still bound to the

---

90 *Matt. 25:31-3.* See verses *25:31-46* for the complete story.

91 The ability to thus sit is the cause of enlightenment and its all-pervasive radiance.

92 This is symbolised by the word 'King' in *Matt. 25:40.*

material world for one reason or other. They are deluded by glamour and illusion in some way, and thus are dominated or influenced by 'left hand' tendencies. Goats are renowned for their sure-footed ability to scale mountains, which can symbolise disciples climbing the mount of Initiation. However, goats can also symbolise dwelling in hard, rocky, adamantly unyielding materialism (wherein the goat finds a home). This is the mountain of *karma,* to which those of the 'left' are still tied. It is the domain of Satan. The mountain also relates to formed (as opposed to formless) space.

The 'sheep' are the flock of the 'Lamb of God, which taketh away the sin of the world'.[93] They are thus followers of the Christ and the path to Light. The 'sin of the world' refers to *karma,* which causes people to remain tied to the realms of darkness and to material objectives. What takes it away is a new major cycle of endeavour, for which the Christ-consciousness (the intuition), and not the intellect (as in this cycle) is the basis. This represents the next step in the evolutionary journeying of humanity, which the newly manifesting Aquarian Age will usher in. Humanity will then as a whole be eliminating material *karma* and not producing it. This new cycle is symbolised by the 'lamb', which will mature into Aries the ram. Aries is the first sign of the zodiac, of the twelve great constellations in the heavens, through which the sun journeys.

The shape of a goat's face, horns and beard form an inverted pentagram. The inversion symbolises what is antagonistic or adverse to the goal of evolution. The direction signifies that the mind is pointed downwards, towards dense material involvement. The upright pentagram is associated with the qualities that constitute man, the thinker. It relates to the mind/Mind, and the five Elements, or *prāṇas*, that embody the various planes of evolution wherein *karma* manifests (thus from *ātma* down). This direction indicates upwards to spirit, and the path of evolution.

The ram's predominant quality is the head, which it uses to butt and to lead. This symbolises the energies of the Mind plus the impulsive first Ray energy. This Ray expresses the Will or Power that awakens the Head centre. It is the energy that emanates from Shambhala, a

93 *John 1:29.*

direct expression of the Logoic Mind. Correspondingly, the Hierarchy of Enlightened Being is an expression of the Heart centre of the Logos, an embodiment of Love-Wisdom. The sheep therefore are those who are properly developing the attributes of the Love-Wisdom that is the mainstay of Hierarchy.

The relation between sheep and goats may also be interpreted from the point of view of the levels of attainment for Initiates of differing degrees. In Matthew it states:

> Then shall the King say unto them on his right hand, Come, ye blessed of my Father, inherit the kingdom prepared for you from the foundation of the world.[94]

The 'kingdom' is also symbolised by the term 'New Jerusalem' which the externalised Hierarchy of Light will eventually build upon earth. The 'son of man' will then have inherited this 'kingdom' from His 'Father' and will rule over His Father's domain. The Law of evolution proceeds in this manner. For when a great One vacates His Seat to take an even higher office in the ineffable universe, so another (who is well-prepared for the new role) will take that position of Power. The 'blessed' become adepts or Masters, the senior executives that administer that kingdom.

The statements following this passage: 'for I was an hungered, and ye gave me meat: I was thirsty, and ye gave me drink'[95] indicate the qualities developed by those of the right hand path. 'Meat' and 'drink' signify spiritual sustenance of varying degrees and capacities. These are equitable with the Body and Blood of the Christ, which he asked us to eat and drink in remembrance of Him.[96]

The concept of hell

The meaning of 'hell fire' was explained in chapter three but needs further comment, and also the phrases: 'everlasting fire', 'fire and brimstone' and 'everlasting punishment'. They appear a number of times in the Bible and are subject to much misconception.

94 *Matt. 25:34.*

95 *Matt. 25:35.*

96 *Mark 14:22-24.*

As noted earlier, the term hell has been used to translate the Hebrew word Shoel in the Old Testament, but nowhere in that portion of the Bible is there a description of its qualities. The concept of 'hell fire' thus arose in the later Christian dispensation. We saw also that the word is used in the New Testament to translate the Greek word Hades and the Jewish concept of Gehenna.

The esoteric position is that the term hell refers to the three planes of perception associated with human livingness – the mental, astral and physical. The capacity to suffer hell-like states in these planes is never-ending. There is a constant thirst for sentient existence for all people therein that causes them to be continuously born into a collective existence that 'groaneth and travaileth in pain together'.[97] These cycles produce never-ending bouts of pain, suffering, mental-emotional appetites, physical and psychic Fires: everything that confronts a person in the astral realms.

Note that hell is depicted as something that a person descends (incarnates) into. Each time the term is used in the book of Revelation, the word 'death' is directly related to it. *Revelation 1:18,* for instance, states 'I have the keys of hell and of death'. This means that the incarnation process has been completely mastered, therefore the entire material world and all associated illusional, ever-changing (ever-dying) experiences.

Concerning the fate of those who follow the left hand path, Jesus states:

> Then shall he say also unto them on the left hand, Depart from me, ye cursed, into everlasting fire, prepared for the devil and his angels: For I was an hungred, and ye gave me no meat: I was thirsty and ye gave me no drink.... Verily I say unto you, Inasmuch as ye did it not to one of the least of these, ye did it not to me. And these shall go away into everlasting punishment but the righteous into life eternal.[98]

This realm of 'everlasting fire' is a hell zone. For those that manifest sufficiently evil activities whilst on earth they will experience a hell state upon the astral plane after they die. They will however eventually escape from that zone to be reborn so as to continue their evolution.

---

97 *Romans 8:22.*

98 *Matt. 25:41-6.*

All major religions speak of such an experiential zone. The concept of 'everlasting' literally means cycle after cycle, and for members of the dark brotherhood the special zone into which they are cast is called the *eighth sphere* (which can last the duration between planetary, and even solar evolutions).

The phrase 'everlasting punishment' therefore refers to the seeming everlasting rounds of evolution in the material realms for the duration of the Life of one Incarnation of the solar Logos. The karmic rewards of life therein (for those on the left hand path) are punishment indeed – certainly 'everlasting' when compared to the life of a person.

What can also be implied in the phrase 'everlasting fire' is the Fire associated with the higher mental realm wherein resides the Soul. Its Solar Fire is 'everlasting' because it outlasts the births and deaths of successive incarnations of any evolving person. This Fire is 'prepared for the devil and his angels', for their fate is a seemingly never-ending succession of incarnations into the material world. The Soul works hard to adjudicate the *karma* in various ways via projecting the incarnating personalities into various hell state scenarios in such a way that hopefully they eventually learn what not to do.

There is also a subtle reference here to the esoteric fact that black magicians, or those with left hand tendencies, are able to obtain the second Initiation and related powers before the door of Initiation is closed to them.[99] They are able to draw upon certain energies from the Soul but are not able to tread upon the 'higher way' that leads away from material evolution altogether.

In Buddhism, the term for the worst (lowest) of the hells existing upon the astral domain is *avīci,* signifying 'endless torture', indicating never-ending flames of torment. It is a state of consciousness (not a locality *per se)* seen as virtual uninterrupted hell, but not without hope for final redemption. It can be viewed as a zone or residence for members of the dark brotherhood, the transgressors of the Law, in which they reside awaiting the cycle for when they are again released.[100]

---

99 See also A.A. Bailey, *The Rays and the Initiations,* 348-9.

100 See my book *An Exoteric Exposition of the Bardo Thödol,* Part A, 149-51 for a description of the various hell states. For an explanation of the eighth sphere see my books *The Constitution of Shambhala,* Part A, 248-9, and *The Astrological and Numerological Keys to The Secret Doctrine,* Vol. 2, 145-46.

The idea that hell exists as a locality below the surface of the earth is purely an exoteric notion. In actuality, hell is a state of mind that conditions a being, whether incarnate or disincarnate. Though the personality may 'descend into hell' the Soul however projects the *saṃskāras* (conditioning the hell state) that its incarnation must experience. The phrase: 'his name is death, and hell followed with him',[101] sounds an esoteric truth, for as each person dies in consciousness to an aspect of their personality (thus to the *saṃskāras),* so they are born into another aspect of the hellish material world. This is the 'hell that followed with him'. A person suffers the related *karma* until completely liberated from the three worlds of human livingness.

That hell is not a perpetual state is indicated when John describes the events that must occur before the establishment of a 'new heaven and a new earth'.[102] He states that he saw:

> (T)he dead, small and great, stand before God....and the dead were judged out of those things that were written in the books according to their works. And the sea gave up the dead which were in it; and death and hell delivered up the dead which were in them: and they were judged every man according to their works. And death and hell were cast into the lake of fire. This is the second death. And whosoever was not written in the book of life was cast into the lake of fire.[103]

The events depicted here relate to what might be described as the final day of Judgement, at the ending of the *mahāmanvantara* (great round of evolution) of our earth system. After that a new evolutionary round of evolution will commence upon a newly forming planet, the 'new heaven and a new earth'. 'The sea' that 'gave up the dead which were in it' is the astral realm, wherein exists the heaven and hell realms to which those that die eventuate.

The concept of 'death' delivering up the 'dead' that are within it can really only be thought of in terms of the ending of the evolutionary cycle, when such a thing as death will no longer exist.

---

101 *Rev. 6:8.*

102 *Rev. 21:1.*

103 *Rev. 20:10-15.*

The dead that are delivered up from 'hell' during this time of the Judgement day for our earth system refers to those who are resident in the *eighth sphere*. These members of the dark brotherhood are to be judged in accordance to the role they will be permitted to play in the newly forming planetary sphere. All beings must be given a chance to resolve their *karma*.

To 'stand before God' can only mean they were no longer in hell and, therefore, were taken from that state of existence. Also, how can they be 'judged...according to their works' if, as theologians would have us believe, they suffer eternal damnation and ceaseless punishment in hell-fire? It would, however, be possible if those 'works' were the result of the normal course of evolution in the material realms, with the resultant karmic judgement.

Next is the statement: 'And death and hell were cast into the lake of fire. This is the second death'. It is of value to realise here that whenever the term 'fire' is utilised it symbolises the energies pertaining to the mind/Mind. The dense physical realm and all associated forms and objects are a direct result of the creative energies originating in the realms of the mind. As a person (or a 'God') thinks, so thought-forms are created, which generally externalise as 'works' on the material realm. This is dependent upon the driving will of the thinker and the material at hand needed to clothe the thought. To say, therefore, that 'death and hell were cast into a lake of fire' is tantamount to stating that all was resolved back into primeval substance. One cycle of the creative impulse was therefore completed. From a Logoic perspective this entails that the originating Thought-Form (the material universe) had run its course and could be cast back into its source. In turn, this would allow a new creative urge or Thought-Form of 'God', a 'new heaven and earth' to manifest.

The 'first death' is when the residing consciousness casts aside its dense physical, corporeal form. The 'second death' then refers to when it is also able to cast aside its subtle astral, or psychic, emotional-desire body and enter the realm of pure Mind substance (Fire). This is the *devachan* of the Hindu and Buddhist philosophies.

It is precisely the ability to think (our conceptualisations in the form of memory and imagination) that produces much of our misery, –

especially when coupled with emotions and desires. Since animals are free from the Fiery impetus of the mind they do not have many of the types of suffering that afflict humanity. An example of the expression of the mind is the production and perpetuation of the firepower of modern armaments and warfare.

Intensified desire-mind is exemplified when 'the lake of fire and brimstone' is mentioned, as in the passage below:

> And the devil that deceived them was cast into the lake of fire and brimstone, where the beast and false prophet *are,* and shall be tormented day and night for ever and ever.[104]

Brimstone is a form of sulphur that melts as it burns, producing a nauseating, choking, poisonous, yellow-orange-violet flame and a thick obscuring sulfurous cloud. Brimstone thus aptly symbolises the nature of the cloud of thought-forms surrounding the 'sulfurous' minds that pervert doctrines for selfish, egotistic motives. The Fiery aspect is seen in the scorching, burning, cynical, criticising tendencies of those with strong intellects directed in a very egocentric, selfish manner. Such attributes when wilfully projected are generated by members of the dark brotherhood.

Fire and brimstone can also refer to the sum total of the irate illusions, fanaticism and aggrieved, angry war-like forms of glamour that people create with their desire-minds whilst incarnate. There can also be different degrees of jealousy, spite, malice, conceit and anger. To the Initiated this appears as a seething mass of energies, or a 'lake of fire and brimstone', coloured by the predominant hue of the mind-nature – orange, enflamed with red, signifying the intensity of the fanaticism, hatred, etc.

The 'lake of fire' is an admixture of the Watery Element (the molten sulphur), the Earthly Element (the thick smoke) and the Fiery Element, the brimstone (burning sulphur). Being a 'lake' it can be considered the hell part of the Watery astral plane. (Its lower sub-planes, though there are other sub-planes that will be more likened to a murky swamp.)

'Smoke' is productive of (or the result of) people's mass illusions and their glamour, clouding and beguiling their minds.

---

104 *Rev. 20:10.*

Here 'the beast and false prophet' can be considered attributes of the dark brotherhood residing in this 'lake'.

The saffron coloured robes that Buddhist and Hindu mendicants wear signify that controlling the energies of the Mind is a fundamental goal of their meditations and austerities. Orange-yellow can be considered the general colouring of the *prāṇas* in a person's body at this stage of evolution.

In the story of Judas, previously quoted *(Luke 22:3),* where the term Satan is used, I noted that Judas' act was essentially karmic. A paralleling statement within John has the words: 'And supper being ended, the devil having now put into the heart of Judas Iscariot, Simon's son, to betray him'.[105] Although Judas was a disciple of Jesus (and thereby included as part of His council and was Initiated into some of the Mysteries by Him) his mind was conflicted. This phrase therefore indicates that Judas was susceptible to being impressed by thought-forms from the dark brotherhood. This is actually a common occurrence for many disciples, because the forces of evil are intensely preoccupied in trying to pervert their minds, and so to try to convert them to the left hand path. This is part of the war between the white and the black hierarchies. Many are the disciples that fall victim to such thought projections, and Judas but symbolised this fact.

The connotation of 'devil' is used here to show that though Judas was karmically affiliated with the dark brotherhood, this fact was incorporated in Jesus' plans. Judas' betrayal of Jesus for 'thirty pieces of silver'[106] was also a betrayal of the energies conveyed to Judas by his Soul.

It takes considerable evolutionary time to completely transform darkened *saṃskāras (praṇās)* in the *nāḍīs* into light bearing substance. The process must be accomplished whilst the aspirant is walking the path in the material domain. Much psychic and mental-emotional 'dirt' can be accumulated in this way. It is principally for this reason that Jesus stooped to wash His disciple's feet.[107] In that moment, Jesus stated to Simon Peter:

---

105 *John 13:2.*

106 *Matt. 26:15.*

107 *John 13:4-16.*

> He that is washed needeth not save to wash his feet, but is clean every whit: and ye are clean, but not all. For he knew who should betray him, therefore said he, Ye are not all clean.[108]

'Feet', in this passage, represent the aspect of a person that is in constant contact with the material world, the Earthy Element. They enable one to travel in any direction one wishes to go. The symbolism of dirt and material activity can therefore symbolise the type of accomplishment attained by the black magician, that dominates the material world in its entirety.

We see by these statements that because Judas was an accepted disciple (due to ancient karmic affiliation), Jesus assumed with steadfast certainty the responsibility to cleanse the subjective (or psychic) dirt that clung to his feet (and of the other disciples). In all such actions Jesus truly exemplifies the paradigm of the enlightened Bodhisattva. This dirt is perpetuated by wandering in the material *saṃskāras* which have 'claimed his heart'. This karmic or psychic dirt caused Judas to betray the subjective energies of Life, Light and Love that were his inheritance from the Christ.

The fate that befalls the followers of the left hand path is indicated by the words of Mark, when referring to Judas: 'woe to that man by whom the Son of man is betrayed! good were it for the man if he had never been born'.[109] 'Woe' here means much sorrow, grief and the misfortune of having to constantly incarnate into the realm of sorrow *(saṃsāra).* It is better to not have been born rather than to follow the ways of the left hand path. The dire karmic results of actions taken by their activities will take many lives to cleanse. Ideally, on the other hand, disciples learn to change such methods and motives of their actions so as to thereby eventually conquer the need for rebirth.

The fact that Judas had repented, for he saw that he had 'betrayed the innocent blood'[110] indicates a major transformation of his consciousness. This is a complete turning about. He was bereft of what in the past had sustained him, as the future was inconceivable without the guiding Light

---

108 *John 13:10.*

109 *Mark 14:21.*

110 *Matt. 27:4.*

of the Christ. Since he had betrayed this Light, it seemed to Judas that the only possible solution was to end his life, and thus he hung himself. This act was symbolic of his resolve to lift his feet off the ground (and the dirt thereon). It was the first step in the journey back to the Christ Light. This is the way with many disciples, as they battle the powers of the darkness within them. Eventually they come to the realisation of the severe consequences of following the 'evil within' and so sincerely make the vow to follow the narrow straight path that 'leads unto life'.[111]

Accusations against Jesus

It is important to note that Jesus was often accused of being possessed by 'a devil: who goest about to kill thee'.[112] The verses following this passage are specifically concerned with this question, whilst the qualities of 'the devil' (who personifies the black magician), are exemplified. After a long dialogue with the Scribes and Pharisees, who tried to trick him into committing blasphemy so that they could arrest him, Jesus states: 'why do ye not understand my speech? even because ye cannot hear my word'.[113] This means that those that are beguiled by the adepts of the left hand path have not the ability to understand the nature of what 'proceeded forth and came from God'.

Jesus continues with the words:

> Ye are of *your* father the devil, and the lusts of your father ye will do. He was a murderer from the beginning, and abode not in the truth, because there is no truth in him. When he speaketh a lie, he speaketh of his own: for he is a liar, and the father of it. And because I tell *you* the truth, ye believe me not.[114]

In the statement 'Ye are of your father the devil, and the lusts of your father ye will do' Jesus is pointing out that the Jews (symbolising humanity in general) will automatically and unthinkingly do the bidding of (or be manipulated by) 'the devil'. The statement 'he was a murderer

111 *Matt. 7:14.*

112 *John 7:20.*

113 *John 8:42-3.*

114 *John 8:44-5.*

from the beginning, and abode not in the truth' at first may seem to implicate the slaying of Abel by his brother Cain.[115] It may also refer to the ousting of Adam and Eve from the garden of Eden. This story symbolises slaying the spiritual man (who is in communion with 'God') so that the material aspect may live (which is perpetually born in the world of form, the realm of the devil).

The concept of being 'a murderer' here more specifically refers to the fact that the dark brotherhood would not hesitate to murder if it suited their plans and they could get away with it. But often karmic law and the activities of the white Hierarchy prevent such happenings. 'Murdering' can also be extended to warfare, which the forces of evil excel at instigating.

The devil 'abode not in the truth' because lying propaganda is the *modus operandi* of the dark brotherhood. Compare this idea to the constant barrage of falsehoods, misinformation, omissions of pertinent facts and aberrant narratives constantly coming from mainstream reporters. The gullible public are presently incapable of discerning the truth from the lies. They live in a state of constant mass psychosis. Esoterically, the 'truth' is what emanates from the realms wherein reside the Hierarchy of enlightened Being. Within these domains of light the black magician (the embodiment of evil) cannot reside.

Jesus then exemplifies this statement by saying: 'because there is no truth' (enlightenment) 'in him'. There can be no enlightening 'truth' for the adept of the left hand path, for his onus is to keep people bound to the phenomenal world of illusion and glamour. Only in the material world can the objectives of such a being be achieved. Jesus thus states that 'when he speaketh a lie, he speaketh of his own', meaning that he is entirely ego-centred, 'for he is a liar'. As such, his purpose is always to delude everybody about all things, and so is 'the father of it'. It is obvious that the greatly bewildered masses that are ensnared by such lies are unable to comprehend the esoteric wisdom spoken by Jesus (or any enlightened messenger), thus he states 'because I tell you the truth, ye believe me not'. To make the point clear Jesus follows with the statement:

---

115 As related in *Genesis 4:8*.

> He that is of God heareth God's words: ye therefore hear *them not,* because ye are not of God.[116]

This statement can effectively be extended to all that follow the exoteric doctrines of orthodox Christianity. They have been lied to for millennia and have promulgated these lies in their teachings, which by now should be clear to all the readers of this book. The Jews countered: 'Say we not well that thou art a Samaritan' (at this time, this is virtually synonymous with the term 'heretic') 'and hast a devil?'[117] (That is, possessed by evil forces.) Jesus obviously denied this. He states: 'I seek not mine own glory' (which those that are influenced by the left hand path always do, in pursuit of their aims) 'there is one that seeketh and judgeth' ('God', acting also as a Lord of *karma).* 'Verily, verily, I say unto you, if a man keep my saying, he shall never see of death'.[118] This statement entirely confounded the Scribes and Pharisees. Thus they then questioned:

> Art thou greater than our Father Abraham, which is dead? and the prophets are dead: whom makest thou thyself?[119]

That which is 'greater' than Abraham is 'God'. They therefore presumed Jesus was equating Himself to God'. They saw this as sheer blasphemy and thus they sought to stone Him. In a similar sense the statements of Jesus also confound modern materialistic humanity. They symbolically 'stone' the teachings of the Christ (to 'kill' the teachings) by interpreting them in a most mundane, esoterically mediocre way. As already shown, the conquering of 'death' is a natural development of enlightenment. We see also that the Jews thought only in terms of physical death, as does modern humanity, and not of spiritual death (which is birth into the material world). At that time it appears that the Scribes and Pharisees did not conceive that 'God' would send to the Jews yet another prophet to administer to their spiritual needs, hence the statement: 'the prophets are dead: whom makest thou thyself?' In relation to this query Jesus answered:

---

116 *John 8:47.*

117 *John 8:48.*

118 *John 8:50-51.*

119 *John 8:53.*

> If I honour myself, my honour is nothing: it is my Father that honoureth me; of whom ye say that, he is your God.[120]

Here Jesus plainly says to them that he is in fact a similar prophet as were the other 'God' inspired ones that the Jews revered from their Biblical passages.

The serious debates amongst the Jews of his time concerning the nature of Jesus is revealed in this passage:

> And many of them said, He hath a devil, and is mad; why hear ye him? Others said, These are not the words of him that hath a devil. Can a devil open the eyes of the blind?[121]

Apart from the obvious effect of the healing work of Jesus, the question really asked concerning opening 'the eyes of the blind' here is: 'can a devil enlighten those that cannot spiritually see?'

Conceptions of evil and related fears

In this increasingly enlightened age many people are realising that they are often manipulated in various ways to fulfil the ambitions of a small group of selfishly orientated people. Such tyrants wield great power in the fields of world finances, politics and the mass media. This is especially evident to those who do proper research on the Internet. People must therefore learn to confront this massed tyranny within the circle of their own lives and within the bounds of society as a whole. Also, they must change their notion of what really constitutes evil.

That pertaining to evil is not so much humanity's innate desires, selfishness, lusts and wishes for material things, or the manifold aspects of people's sexuality. People can quite adequately work these out for themselves, if left to their own resources. Intuitive impressions can also come from within. Nor is evil a person's ability to think, for this has resulted in both our spiritual and scientific heights, and both the worst and best in civilisation (because of the nature of the mind as a mediator).

A person's aspirations and particular point in the ladder of evolution determines what is evil for that person. What is wrong (evil) to one person (because it prevents the attainment of their aspirational goals)

---

120 *John 8:54.*

121 *John 10:20-21.*

may not be evil for another with entirely different life goals. Therefore, what is perceived as evil to one could be a virtue to the other. Evil may be defined as the wilful hindrance, or retarding of, the emerging Life within a form from expressing its full potentialities. This also includes the forceful or seductive coercion or manipulation of others to do one's bidding, or to extort their resources for the manipulating entity's benefit.

Only a sorcerer can be truly considered evil. It is said, however, that even a brother of the left hand path will (in the unimaginably distant future), be gradually abstracted back to the Heart of 'God'. We are all at different stages of becoming a Christ or Buddha, and they are evolving themselves into what is known as 'God'.

Evil exists only in our presently developed, mental-emotional consciousness, and the empirical mind, which is conditioned to view things as separate and distinct from all other things. As self-focussed attitudes are gradually annulled, humanity will eventually merge back into the source of the One Life. Evil as such will then no longer exist. Such realisation will become more prevalent as time progresses. As humanity begins to dispel or conquer evil by compassionate means, so gradually the Hierarchy of Enlightened Being will manifest exoterically on the earth and the New Jerusalem will finally be established.

In humanity four broad statements concerning evil can be made.

First, evil is that state of mind that calls for separateness, that separates man from man, man from 'God', and humanity from all other kingdoms in Nature. This is accomplished through the perpetuation of the belief that a particular aspect of one's life (a creed, philosophy, race, religion, etc.) is superior to another person's, therefore this aspect should be imposed upon others.

For example, the assertion of the idea of a 'master race', of only one path or approach to 'God', or of the 'only possible' political doctrine. Such assertions produce tendencies towards the dissention, strife and wars that afflict humanity. The results are seen all around in this troubled world. Its perpetuation prevents the seeds of brotherly and sisterly love in all of us. It silences the commandment that the Christ gave to us, to 'love one another'.[122] Once separateness is rectified, it will create a strong foundation for the New Age lifestyle.

---

122 *John 15:12:* 'This is my commandment, That ye love one another, as I have loved you'.

The mentality of separateness strongly conditions the thoughts and actions of present day humanity. As long as this continues, no true or lasting peace can reign. If the Christ is to reappear, many forms of separateness that act as potent forces amongst us must thus no longer be present. Therefore, people need to be educated to think in terms of peace, love and brother/sisterhood. Many disciples and Initiates are working to produce such attitudes upon a worldwide scale.

Secondly, evil is also the state of mind that ever tends to narrow and cloud people's minds to the true state of Being. It perpetuates darkness and ignorance by withholding and distorting relevant information. It consequently allows people to be easily dominated by a small power-hungry elite.

More specifically in the Western world, ignorance is generally perpetuated by those controlling the mass media, the educational policies of our schooling systems, by politicians, and by such methods as business marketing and advertisements for consumer items. Above all other people stands the power of a group of super-rich individuals that have corrupted all aspects of government, and whose aims are well served by keeping people in a state of ignorance. A tight grip over the minds and actions of the majority is therefore commanded by the relative few. Selfishness, rather than loving-kindness, is the code of ethics that is generally fostered. Elsewhere, ignorance is fostered by the policies of totalitarian regimes, which could not stand if freedom of thought and the means to its expression were available to their citizens.

Despite such efforts, the world is however gradually becoming enlightened, for people are being introduced to the many differing avenues of thought through an amazing cultural efflux and interchange of ideas. Nowadays the Internet exists as the main tool as a mechanism of education. The world's demand for basic freedoms and human rights for all, cultural exchanges and international sport's events are other positive signs. The ending of the bamboo and iron curtains that segregated China and the USSR from the West, and a fuller emergence of the Third World from domination of the world's hegemon (the USA) is beginning to nurture a more inclusive consciousness in humanity as a whole. The forces of evil have, however, worked to overcome the positives through endeavouring, for instance, to control (censor) the free flow of information on the Internet, and to foster various wars on this planet.

Various methods of indoctrination are being undermined by the generally well-educated people of today, with their liberal-mindedness and co-operative spirit. Dissenters, especially in the West, have given the general public different perspectives to the prescribed orthodox presentations, within all spheres or aspects of life. Many people are reasoning things out for themselves, despite counter-reactionary efforts towards regimentation by the various propaganda machines. As an increasing number of people break free from mass indoctrinations of all forms, so increasingly the New Age will dawn.

Third, evil is also that state of mind that tends to drive people and their sense of values away from the realms of causes and into the world of effects. It drives them from the subjective and beautiful and into the concrete, the material and distorted. Evil thus fosters desire for superfluous material goods and money, driven by unmitigated selfishness. This allows people to be controlled (by their conditioned need for possessions) by the power-hungry minority in every country, who control the various national and world monetary systems with ruthless effectiveness.

This conditioning has prevented humanity from understanding, and thus expressing, the law of Love. This spiritual law, of effortlessly and spontaneously supplying increasing benefit for the greatest number, tends to produce a holistic harmony with all sentient beings. Jesus explains this law with His usual straightforwardness.

> Consider the lilies of the field, how they grow; they toil not, neither do they spin: And yet I say unto you That even Solomon in all his glory was not arrayed like one of these. Wherefore, if God so clothe the grass of the field, which today is, and to morrow is cast into the oven, *shall he* not much more *clothe* you, O ye of little faith? Therefore take no thought, saying, What shall we eat? or, What shall we drink? or, Wherewithal shall we be clothed? (For after all these things do the Gentiles seek:) for your heavenly Father knoweth that ye have need of all these things. But seek ye first the kingdom of God, and his righteousness; and all these things shall be added unto you.[123]

---

123 *Matthew 6:28-33.* This entire chapter in Matthew should also be read in context with the Beatitudes in Matthew chapter five, and the related statements in chapters six and seven.

If people take this passage into their hearts and earnestly follow through, they will see that life becomes wonderfully simpler and saner. They will begin to see through the eyes of 'a little child', like seeing the sun arise for the first time. Are excessive material encumbrances really needed (other than those which make the basic processes of life easier)? They take much effort, painful striving, and many work hours to collect and hold. It is much easier to be unburdened of the superfluous and feel free (thus also save precious natural resources). To be born anew in the Christ one needs to die to the material self. Wars, cataclysms and economic instabilities (inflations and depressions) all teach people these lessons.

Fourth, evil is that state of mind that perpetuates the doctrine of fear. These fears may be categorised under five main types:

a. Fear of death and the unknown.
b. Fear of old age, sickness and senility.[124]
c. Fear of isolation and of loneliness.
d. Fear of not being noticed, being left behind, or failure.
e. These fears produce the fear of the pains engendered by humanity itself.

a. Fear of death and the unknown

There is really no death except in a cyclical sense. Death effectively leads to a freer life, as exemplified by the words of Paul, 'I die daily'.[125] Fear of death results in a wrongly directed stimulation of the innate instinct for self-preservation (related to the instinct towards knowledge). Through such fear people are content to live and cultivate habits that do not produce spiritual gain. They are psychologically unable to experiment with and experience the new, and thus do not progress on the path. They rigidly uphold crystallised, narrow-minded attitudes in the face of advancing times, while suffering (and causing others to suffer) because of it. The instinct towards knowledge is here directed towards amassing information relating to trivia, gossip, the highly glamourised and extremely transient and irrelevant, except to others also thus engrossed. Only that relating to the mundane world and its

---

124 This is an offshoot of the fear of death.

125 *I Cor. 15:31.*

activities are deemed worthwhile. Only what is fed to them by the leaders of society is deemed real. From a broad perspective, the perpetuation of such instincts produces the attitudes of those engrossed in our present extremely materialistic civilisation.

This fear will eventually become rectified when humanity is able to assimilate truthful knowledge on all possible subjects. Such will elucidate the way life actually manifests: physically, psychically and spiritually. The conquest of this fear leads to immortality and the ability to express the wisdom from the Soul (when death itself will no longer be a mystery) and also from Hierarchy.

b. Fear of old age, sickness and senility

This fear is an offshoot of the fear of death. Sickness is really caused by the actions of humanity itself, though it is karmically induced. Our actions lay the conditions that allow the influx and growth of disease-bearing organisms, and other factors that induce the disruption of homeostasis in the body's systems. For those that have sufficient sustenance to live and who do not directly intake toxins, sickness is primarily the result of poor nutrition. This can be viewed as constant intake of under-nourishing, polluted, over-refined and chemicalised foods, coupled with aberrant projections of thought and desire energies. (Our varying emotional and mental moods.)

The food we eat feeds the cells of our bodies and brains. If we constantly malnourish, intoxicate and poison them, then disease and senility eventually ensue. Thinking about the foods that affect the physical body is the first step towards reorientating one's mental-emotional nature towards higher values.

'You are what you eat,' is a truism worth meditating on. Here the word 'eat' should be taken in its widest connotations. For example, ingesting mental or spiritual information - the symbolic 'body and blood' of the Christ. A person's entire thought life and mode of living are reflected in their choice of food and eating habits (and vice versa).

A general indication that a person may have undertaken the first Initiation is when eating habits are changed from the 'need' for gross, sensual foods, and drugs of all types, to desiring intrinsically wholesome, sun-ripened, nutritious foods. The purpose being to aid the body to master its innate urges and to control its physiology in a holistic manner.[126] This is coupled with a corresponding change in people's mental-emotional ingestion, from the desire for sensational and sensual information full of glamour, to unbiased, informative and practically relevant facts.

At this stage, a question of whether or not to eat the flesh of animals is generally raised in the aspirant's mind. One normally concludes that it would be erroneous to do so for any of the reasons mentioned below.[127] A generally accepted consensus shall be given here, as presented by the more enlightened naturopaths, herbalists, those involved in drugless healing techniques, and by those that follow various yoga-meditation disciplines. It is realised that this presentation may be somewhat partisan and that other systems of healing are valid. These precepts are, however, a framework upon which the esoteric position may be elaborated, as consistent with the philosophy of *ahimsa* (harmlessness).

First, from the physiological viewpoint, we may begin by looking at people's digestive systems and the construction of their teeth. They are patterned primarily as those of a primate. That is, they are geared to eat and digest principally fruit, vegetables, and nuts. Meat products are said to putrefy in a human digestive system, which is far longer than that of carnivorous animals who need to rapidly eliminate the toxic substances that are by-products of their digestive processes. The slow passage of partially digested and putrefying meat products through human intestines forms an ideal culture for harmful bacteria. Taken as a unity, poor nutritional habits include:

- Overconsumption of chemicalised, over-refined, and mucus-forming foods, as well as wrong food combinations.
- The ingestion of devitalised foods with poor or next to zero nutritional value, such as the 'five poisons': white sugar, white flour, white rice, non whole-wheat pasta products and potatoes with the skin cut from them.
- Wilful, excessive intake of drugs, stimulants and toxic substances, such as alcohol, caffeine, and many pharmaceutical products.

126 In the past, before foods were heavily chemicalised, the question of what food to eat was not nearly so important.

127 See my book *Meditation and the Initiation Process*, 52-66, for greater detail concerning this subject.

- What results from putrefaction of meat in the bowels produces additional toxins and wastes (e.g., uric acid) that counter optimal metabolism. The result is the overworking, breakdown and premature aging of body systems (such as the kidneys, liver, and digestive organs).

In conjunction with wrongly directed or excessive desire-emotional or mental energies (such as worry, irritation and anger), the aforementioned habits cause a general weakening of the system. The body's cells are thereby improperly fed and gradually poisoned by toxic waste. The body thus becomes easily susceptible to various diseases, germs and viruses. One may also become prone to kidney and renal failure, or various complaints associated with the digestive process (such as ulcers, gastro-enteritis, or appendicitis).

The body has many avenues to excrete impure energies, such as the alveoli and bronchial cavities, as well as the skin and kidneys. We therefore have the many bronchial and respiratory diseases (coughs, colds, flues), inflammation, skin diseases, kidney stones, etc. If the body cannot eliminate toxins fast enough, then it is forced to store them in interstitial spaces between cells. As old age advances, stored mineral substances tend to crystallise. This causes complaints such as arthritis, varicose veins and senility.

Next, one may consider the moral argument. The immense slaughterhouse of animals on the earth would not be possible if the word 'love' had real meaning within the hearts of civilised people. Immense amounts of good produce (such as corn, oats and other grains) are used to feed livestock animals, fattened-up in preparation for human consumption after they are slaughtered. (This is to say nothing about the methods used to force-feed these animals.) Instead, this excess produce could be directly used to feed those in this world that are undernourished.

One must consider the enormous tracts of land that are used to feed grazing animals for human consumption. If this land were used to directly produce vegetables, grains and nuts, the production of food to feed the world's population would be increased many times over. This food would also be of better quality. For instance, an acre of land bearing nut trees or soya beans produces ten to twenty times more usable protein per year than a similar acre of land for beef cattle. This fact needs to be realised by those responsible for feeding the world's populations.[128]

Eating as little meat as possible is a feasible option for those seeking normal health. If, however, one wishes to make the three-fold body a fit vehicle for the Christ-consciousness, one must cleanse its emanatory qualities, and so raise the general 'vibrational rate', or tone, of one's sheaths. In effect, the various psychic channels (*nāḍīs*) through which are expressed the needed potent energies must be unclogged.

Energetically speaking, other than direct poisons, animal products are the coarsest foods there are. They are consequently generally detrimental to the psychic cleansing process. People eat the crystallised fear that the animal possessed when it was slaughtered. Also, there are negative psychic effects from the elementary entities associated with breakdown of animal products. These negative effects are destructive to the subjectively developing awareness of an increasingly sensitive aspirant. They are akin to aggravating base human emotions and sensuality, which disciples must endeavour to eliminate from their constitution.

In contrast, the vegetable kingdom is bathed in the radiance of the sun. It absorbs and converts this into the foodstuffs that the animal kingdom is nourished upon. Plants act as both receivers of solar *prāṇa* (which they store), and as transmitters (as they offer up the results of their activities as food). This is the plant kingdom's means of service to the higher kingdoms. Through this process the plants evolve. As they are ingested into the animal kingdom, animal-like qualities are imbued into the plant kingdom. This is by the means of a type of empathic assimilation, on a subjective (etheric) cellular level. At death, there is a transformation of the sentience of plant life from one state of existence to the next.

The principal means to cleanse one's body (and mind) is *to fast.* Jesus fasted for forty days and forty nights in the desert, directly after His baptism. It was a definite cleansing process for his subjective life (as He had to successfully resist the resultant temptations). Fasting fully prepared Him for the difficult work that was to follow. It is of

128 The physiological and moral causes concerning this subject are adequately explained in such books as: *Food for a Future* by Jon Wynne-Tyson, or those of Shelton, Arnold Ehret, and others; therefore, only the briefest outline is given here.

such importance in the early stages of the enlightenment process that Jesus taught us how to fast:

> Moreover when ye fast, be not, as the hypocrites, of a sad countenance: for they disfigure their faces, that they may appear unto men to fast.... But thou, when thou fastest, anoint thine head, and wash thy face; That thou appear not unto men to fast, but unto thy Father which is in secret: and thy Father, which seeth in secret, shall reward thee openly.[129]

There is nothing to be gained by being outwardly pretentious, for the real objective of the fast is to cleanse the inner person. Therein resides 'the Father' and from that 'secret place' the person can be 'openly' rewarded. This plainly refers to the many benefits accrued from the fast – physiologically, psychically and spiritually. These are produced in such a way for the effects to be openly seen by all.

Jesus told us when to fast: 'when the bridegroom shall be taken from them, and then shall they fast'.[130] That is, when the Christ is not with us – when we are erring emotionally, mentally, psychically and spiritually. This is when we are not expressing the Love principle that is our heritage. Then we must fast to cleanse ourselves from these negative or coarse qualities. We thus will allow the purity of the Christ principle to manifest in their place.

From the above it is seen that fasting does not involve the physical body alone. In fact, the physical body is the least important body of our threefold constitution; it should not be irrationally or unduly dwelt upon. The first step towards rationally fasting, therefore, is to adopt a diet of cleansing foods (such as fruits and vegetables).

The animal kingdom heals itself by means of fasting. As our physical bodies are an integral part of the animal kingdom, it stands to reason that fasting should be the prime means to heal our forms. Injections and infusions of drugs (chemotherapy) often only suppress the symptoms of disease and do not get to the real sources of the cause - our wrong actions and desires.

People need to learn to heal themselves and the first step is to eat healing foods. However, it is important to learn to control one's 'diet'

---

129 *Matt. 6:16-18.*

130 *Matt. 9:15.*

of negative states of consciousness (habitual thought forms, emotional appetites, moodiness, etc.). As *kleśas*[131] arrive they should not be dwelt upon. One must instead work to develop the appropriate and beneficial counters. For example, this might include practicing the pursuit of patience instead of irritation, or focussing on understanding other people instead of criticising them.

Correct posture and breathing, right mental growth, emotional control, as well as meditation, all come under the category of right eating. This must be stressed. For it will be more damaging to the aspiring spiritual being who eats 'healthily' while espousing a critical and assertive mind, than for one who eats meat while striving to help those in need.

The rectification of this fear produces a perfectly balanced physical, emotional and mental nature that will allow all the energies of Deity (*prāṇa*, manna, ambrosia) to flow freely within the body. This eventually allows an enlightened being to etherealise a 'transfiguration body' that allows the manifestation of great *siddhis,* spiritual powers akin to what Jesus possessed.

c. Fear of isolation and of loneliness

This fear is quite prevalent despite the fact that life abounds with the livingness of 'God' everywhere. The result is the abuse of the sexual instinct and of the group or herd instinct. These are closely allied to the instinct towards self-preservation.[132] This is partially a cause of humanity's recent population explosion and an abandonment of the countryside to herd together in the cities. Overcrowding perpetuates

131 *Kleśas* are afflictive emotions coming under the umbrella of *kliṣṭamanas* (the defiled mind). They are projected in the form of *saṃskāras* when the personality is focussed upon an object of desire. When these emotional *saṃskāras* surface they immediately fuse with the mental consciousness, to produce such things as desire-mind, self-will, or forms of ego-clinging. The emotions always manifest in relation to a concept of 'self', executing the will to appropriate things desired. They thus produce attachments for all things deemed pleasurable, glamorous, or needy by the personality, and react to what they dislike. *Kleśas* are stored as *bījas* (seeds) in the *ālayavijñāna* (the storehouse of consciousness). They can be considered the Watery attributes of the five Elements.

132 These instincts and their corresponding fears are also found explained in Alice Bailey's *A Treatise on White Magic.*

the obvious evils of pollution, social frustration, unequal distribution of wealth, fostering of materialistic attitudes, and wastage of natural resources. The vicissitudes of violence and other crimes associated with life in the cities need not be elaborated. These problems compound the fostered phobias and frustrations of individuals (which become part of the problems that society as a whole must address).

The conquest of this fear in an individual leads to a realisation of the nature of the subjective life of the spiritual being. This is the Love of the Christ, which is the foundation for the reappearance of the Hierarchy and the exoteric establishment of the New Jerusalem[133] on earth. The entire universe – every galaxy, star, planet, and the incorporated uncountable streams of Life are all interrelated and interdependent. Such awareness becomes a definite part of the equipment of an enlightened Being. It provides knowledge of one's place in the universal scheme of things. Loneliness thereby ceases to have any meaning.

d. Fear of not being noticed, failing, or being left behind

This is the result of the growing awareness of the powers of the personality, of people's responses to the glamour displayed by other personalities that shine out or are exemplary in their field. People thus become prone to bolstering the illusion of self-esteem. This produces a competitive ideology, in which scruples and ethics are often abandoned to varying degrees so as to achieve the desired goals.

This fear results in abuse of the instinct for self-assertion. It causes aggressiveness, hero worship, and the banding together of groups and nations into antagonistic factions. This is especially apparent when nations are viewed as being personalities, each possessing their own particular needs, problems and fears.

The conquest of this fear eventually produces spiritual independence, thus becoming 'a spark within the flame' of Spirit. For we all convey a different aspect of Deity – of the one Life that pulsates through our veins. Manifold are the colourings that together blend into the unified Light of this Life.

Our destiny (the unfolding Life Purpose) can be defined in terms of a particular minor hue of this Light. An individual's purpose is part

---

133 This is symbolised by the events associated with the 'marriage supper of the Lamb' (*Rev. 19:9* and chapter 21).

of a group unfoldment. This would be seen as the merging of many minor hues into a shade of a major colouring. Many such groups form a national unfolding colouration, seen as its destiny, and so forth.

Each of us has an undeniable function and purpose in the scheme of things. We must work harmoniously with all other entities (aspects of Being) to fulfil that purpose. As this awareness develops in the mind of an individual, it provides the means whereby this fear may become transmuted into cooperative service, brother/sisterhood, and goodwill.

e. The fear of humanity itself

All the various fears enumerated above cumulatively produce the fear of pain engendered by people and nations upon others. This arises due to indoctrination and conditioning to accept the 'normalcy' of wars, combativeness, separateness, and various forms of aggression and violence. We are assailed by such propaganda during our upbringing – in the media, in schools, and by general normative cultural socialisation. This is reflected not only by the concrete cages of prisons, but also in the emotional jails built by individuals. Most individuals try to assuage their fear of being hurt with an attitude of unapproachability, coldness, and lack of charitable actions. Alternatively, people may focus on learning various forms of self-defence that they believe are necessary to feel safe from their fellows. Similarly, at the political level, this fear spurns constant escalations in the quantity (or technological advancement) of armaments that nations deem necessary for their protection.

By internalising this fear, various statements of Jesus in the book of Matthew[134] are completely ignored. He asks us to 'resist not evil', and to 'turn the other cheek'[135] to those that smite us. His words also find correlation in every religion. Furthermore, we are encouraged to give to those who ask from us, to love our enemies, to bless those that curse us, to help those that hate us, and pray for those that spitefully use us. Thereby, we may be as the 'children' of our 'Father', 'which is in heaven: for he maketh his sun to rise on the evil and the good'.[136]

To 'resist not evil' does not mean to apathetically allow evil to dominate in world affairs. One does not work compassionately for

134 *Matt. 5:38-48.*

135 *Matt. 5:39.*

136 *Matt. 5:45.*

the common good thereby. Not rectifying the (evil) imbalances in our own lives and society in general contradicts the entire message of the Christ's teachings. Despite this, we should not resist the means by which the force of *karma* is expressing through us – be it evil or good *karma* (for to do so would produce more *karma).* 'Evil' here therefore refers to the way that personal *karma* manifests.

Karma must manifest as it wills. The *karma* accrued from past evils (or wrongs) must be rectified by being able to express itself in the way planned by the Lords of *karma.* People therefore need to adopt an attitude of desirelessness regarding the expression of their own *karma,* personality desires and needs. They must offer themselves completely to the providence of 'God'. His Kingdom might thereby be made manifest in our hearts, and thus, by extension, on earth. When this is an accomplished fact, then the 'devil' can find no place in us, and there will be no evil to resist.

An example of this is when Jesus made no resistance to those who would crucify Him. Neither did Socrates offer a word of defence in the face of the accusations of his inquisitors, who made him take his own life by drinking hemlock. Milarepa, Tibet's great yogi, allowed himself to be poisoned by a being that despised him when he knew his time had come. Even the Buddha was said to have willingly accepted poison ('pig meat'), which resulted in his *parinirvāṇa.*

One may find many such examples of acceptance of the inevitable by our enlightened sages at the hands of their inquisitors. Martyrdom, for instance, of early Christians at the hands of Roman emperors, is common throughout history. What sets the deaths of enlightened beings apart from that of the average being is that, almost without exception, they know of the manner and time of their death beforehand. They utilise this knowledge in a manner that serves to enlighten and inspire disciples and the general public for many generations.

People should therefore learn to give charitably to those in need and to not forcibly resist those who would take. If one's *karma* confronts us with such a situation, it is much better to be free of the old *karma* while generating goodwill, rather than to produce new (evil) *karma.* We cannot take our material possessions with us when we die, so why tenaciously hold on to them (in the face of adverse conditions) while we live?

When people everywhere learn to wisely give with their hearts, minds and hands then crime as such will virtually disappear. A more gratuitous balanced distribution of the world's wealth, with right urban development, and educational attitudes will thereby be produced.

The abovementioned fears and their effects will eventually be transmuted into fearlessness in the face of all adversity. This will enable individuals to tread the narrow, razor-edge path to enlightenment. All that conditions us will gradually become revealed and all adversity must be fearlessly overcome.

People doing evil deeds condemn only themselves for their actions, for no other being can do so.[137] Jesus also demonstrated this when the Scribes and Pharisees brought a woman to Him that had committed adultery. By Mosaic law she should have been stoned, but Jesus did not judge her. Neither could the others, for they all had committed similar offences – as have all of us. Later, Jesus states:

> Ye judge after the flesh; I judge no man. And yet if I judge, my judgement is true: for I am not alone, but I and the Father that sent me.[138]

Most of us are influenced and controlled to differing degrees by the mass-mind, through public opinions, or social, religious, political, and racial conditioning. These factors affect our judgement and criticism. We are therefore not perfect; thus, when we judge others for their wrongs or 'evils', we also judge that which exists within ourselves (to varying degrees). People enmasse must also open their eyes to the subjective thoughts and emotions that condition and influence, and so refuse to be ruled by them. They must try to get a true perspective of the nature of things, and to seek actions not for one's 'own glory'[139] but for the glory of all.

However, no matter what people do, they will never be condemned to eternal punishment by a supreme Being[140] (or any other). For, we are all brothers and sisters, composed of the same Elements and susceptible

---

137 See *Matt. 7:1-5.*

138 *John 8:15-16.*

139 *John 8:50.*

140 The exception here might be the sorcerer, and the condition associated with the eighth sphere, explained earlier.

to the same entrapments and diseases. It is a person's own Soul (veiling the Christ and the 'Father' above) that judges. This is because the Soul is responsible for the karmic adjudication that is woven into the matrix of Life, to be played out in the future rebirths of the person.

Evil can even be considered to be included as part of God's Plan for evolution, as is indicated in the book of Isaiah: 'I form the light, and create darkness: I make peace, and create evil: I the Lord do all these *things'*.[141] Even one embodying the 'pits of darkness', such as a sorcerer, shall one day in the immeasurably distant future (and through much tribulation) be filled with Light. For we are all 'sons of God'[142] and shall evolve to eventually become a 'God'.

141 *Isaiah 45:7.*

142 *Phil. 2:15.*

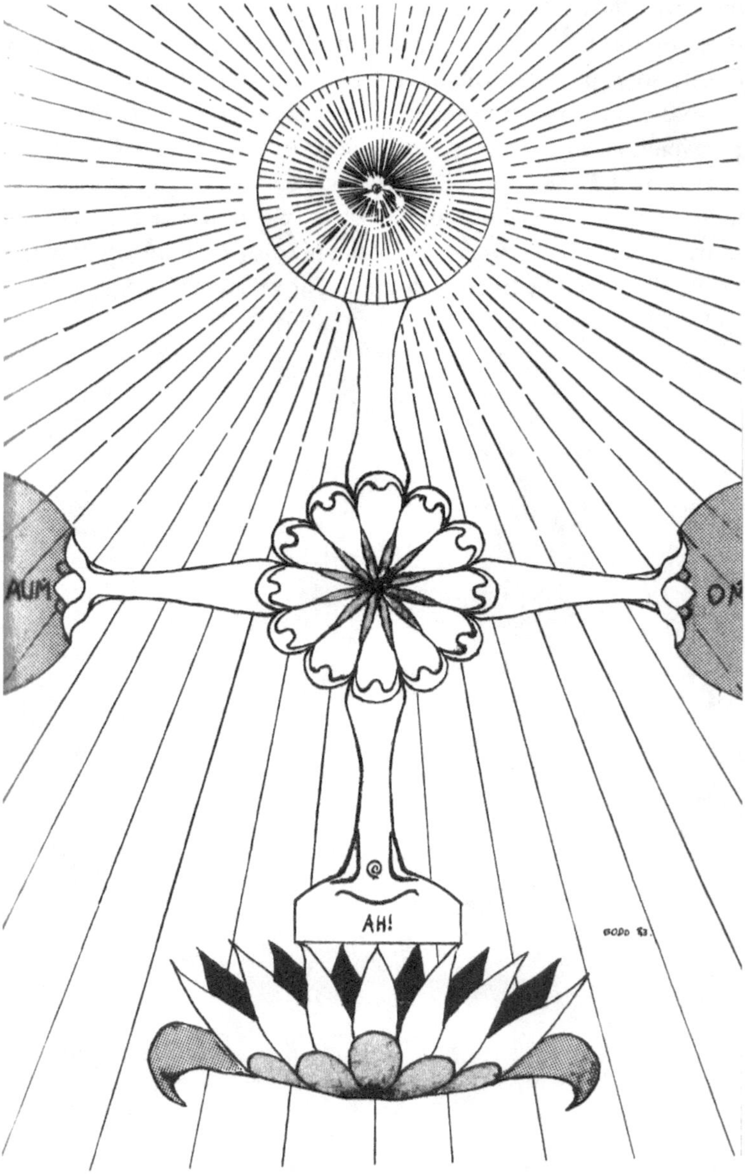

AUM
AH!
BODO '83.

Take care dear one
to not confuse intense subjective desires,
and heightened emotions to be what emanates
from the Heart's gracious bounty.

Take care to not be too attached
to forms that only veil the inner Light.

Take care to distinguish between family
or social responsibility
and the dharma's needs.
Can you follow the Light
if it means leaving all you know behind?

Take care to not let the mind's articulations
override the Heart's understandings.
Know that the evil ones may foster
your mind's self-focussed formulations
to further their machinations against
all servants of Love.

Take care to note the difference
between intuitive flashes
and heightened feeling-perceptions.

Take care not to undertake
wrong spiritual activities.
The Christ need not walk
the way that you wish to find Light.

Take care to tread carefully
upon the thin line between this and that
when tested upon the path.
Seek out the way of enlightenment
where Heart and Mind are fused as One.

My Heart is eternally bound to those
that climb the Initiation tree with me.
Forever we be in Light Supernal.
Glory be forever and ever!

9

The Five Vayūs (Prāṇas) and the Causative Process

The factor of *prāṇa*

Integral to understanding the mode of expression of the entire causative process is that most esoteric of subjects: the five *prāṇas* and the way they are conveyed through the *nāḍīs*. The entire field of evolution can be viewed in terms of the *prāṇas* and of their interrelationships. The *vayūs* (meaning winds, breaths, or airs) are concerned with the mode of expression of the five *prāṇas* in the *nāḍī* system, and consequently the effect they have in the system as a whole. The *vayūs* are *prāṇa* in motion, and this movement is causative of the vitalisation of all that is manifest.

Prāṇa is what is absorbed into our little systems, either directly via the psychic centres concerned, through the process of breathing, or indirectly via the digestion of food. As stated in chapter two, *prāṇa* is the 'breath of life' and is the name given to the energy that is drawn to the physical plane from the etheric aspect of all phenomenal life. It is the sum total of the vital energy composing a body: human, planetary, or solar, for there are many types of *prāṇa*. It is vital, active, radiatory heat – the aggregate of myriads of little *prāṇic* fires or lives, which vary in vibration or quality according to the nature of the transmitting entity. All entities in the solar system, it seems, absorb what they need and retransmit *prāṇa* after it has passed through their systems to those around them. (Therefore it is coloured by their own particular characteristics, be they malefic or beneficent.) In our solar system all *prāṇa* originally emanates from the sun.

Three prime agencies focus this energy upon humanity and thus have an important bearing on our lives, as health is directly proportional to the correct assimilation of *prāṇa* into our systems. These agencies, as well as the work of the angelic kingdom in general, should be considered here because it is the substance composing these units of intelligent energy that essentially concerns us. Indeed, the sum of the substance (and thus energy forms) constituting our bodies is angelic. It consists of angelic *(deva)* units appropriated from the reservoir of angelic substance for the duration of the incarnation of a person. The angelic kingdom is therefore the transmitter of *prāṇa,* whilst consciousness, the human mind or psyche, can be considered the assimilator and transmuter of that energy. The mind is the sublime, oft unknowing alchemist. The retorts, distillation units and other equipment of this alchemist are the component parts of our bodies.

There are *three types of devas* to be considered.[1]

a. *Solar devas.* They are golden hued and transmit *prāṇa* to the etheric counterpart of all embodied forms. They are very powerful and are of an evolutionary status higher than of humanity. Their influence is strongest in tropical areas. This energy is generally absorbed in the upper part of the body and finds its way via the Heart and diaphragm to the Splenic centre. This centre is the organ of distribution of this *prāṇic* 'food' to the various *chakras,* and acts as a reservoir for this vitality. When the etheric body functions properly and absorbs the correct amount of *prāṇa,* then it will keep the form organised. This constitutes the ABC's of healthy living. These *devas* transmit solar *prāṇa* to all Life.

b. *Planetary devas* of a violet colour. These are the *devas* of the shadows working upon the etheric levels. They are closely allied

---

1 This section is adapted from Alice Bailey's *A Treatise on Cosmic Fire.*

to humanity, particularly concerning the health and well being of our forms. They transmit the vitality or magnetism from the planetary Entity, an involutionary being that constitutes the physical shell of the planetary Logos. The vital animal health of our forms is obtained from this planetary reservoir of energy. This *prāṇa* is absorbed directly by the spleen or through the pores of the skin.

This present epoch heralds the dawning of the time when the most advanced medical practitioners will work in close cooperation with these *devas*. The indications of this are seen in the enormous growth in the demand for vegetarian and health foods, for naturopathic and alternative medical methods, and the strong orientation towards yoga, occultism and the psychic sciences. These *devas* transmit planetary *prāṇa* to all Life. This type of *prāṇa* is indigenous to the planet as a whole. It is the effect of the solar *prāṇa* that has been absorbed into the sum of all planetary Lives, coloured with their own particular qualities and then retransmitted into the general atmosphere.

c. *The devas embodying the lesser kingdoms* (the animal, vegetable and mineral kingdoms). They all exchange energy with the human system. The health and vitality of one group is closely related to that of the other groups. Their synthesis produces one vibrant interlocking of forces, from the humblest atom to the greatest cosmic Intelligence. Where this flow is restricted, there exist the causative forces of friction and strife. Disease or disorder can be found throughout, for no group is free from the effects of the qualified (tainted) *prāṇa* that has emanated from another group, or of the negative karma from past actions. What is disorder to one may however be perfection to another lower down on the scale of evolution. These devas transmit the type of *prāṇa* termed *animal magnetism*. Animal magnetism is the active radiatory vitality emitted from the etheric body of the animal unit after it has converted solar *prāṇa* into *jīva* (the individual life force).

Disease is inherent in the soil of the earth, for the soil has been so imbued by burying the sick and diseased bodies of countless generations. It is inherent in animals and plants and in the *karma* of our planetary Logos. The restricted and tainted energy flows from one to another cause epidemics, scourges, famines, etc. Humanity is not an island. It must begin to work in harmony with Nature by understanding the nature of the causative flows of *prāṇa*. Humanity's major troubles will then become rectified.

The process of causation is concerned with energy direction and the means whereby gross energies (e.g., of diseases) are transmuted into the subtle and refined. They can then penetrate, uplift and transmute the bounds of all past action. There can be no impediments to the right flow of energy if the causative agent is to be successful. The ability to know how to rightly project energies constitutes the science of meditation. This necessitates the right control of breath in relation to mental unfoldment and projection (or non-projection) of all creative factors. Where impediments exist, there are effected sickness and disease, factors that frustrate the purpose of all creative beings.

Three fundamental energies

All causative agents utilise three prime types of energy that together produce all manifest Life. They relate to the Father, Son and Mother aspect of Deity: Spirit, Soul and matter, etc. D.K. has provided the names:

A. *Dynamic electricity* – the Father aspect, related to the first Ray of Will or Power, conveyed via the *suṣumṇā nāḍī.*

B. *Prāṇa* – the Son aspect, related to the second Ray of Love-Wisdom, conveyed via the *piṇgalā* (male) *nāḍī.*

C. *Kuṇḍalinī* – the Mother aspect, related to the third Ray of Active Intelligence and to the *iḍā* (female) *nāḍī.*

A. *Dynamic electricity.* All other types of energy are aspects of this energy. It emanates from the Mind of 'God' and produces the interplay between positive and negative forces in Nature. It is positive in that it causes the desired objectivity – the magical endeavour or spiritual work accomplished by the inspired Thinker. It is the cause of that blaze of energy on the mental plane termed solar Fire. Here the dynamic energy of the Spirit (which is positive) and the energy of matter (which assumes a negative role) meet and interact, causing the Fiery formation of the Soul, and then its final consummative blaze at the fourth Initiation.

This energy flows in the *suṣumṇā nāḍī* after the etheric webs in the body have been eliminated by necessary meditative practices. These webs exist to prevent too rapid a contact with the subjective realms by people who have not refined their consciousness sufficiently to prevent psychic obsession and the rise of evil forces by uncontrolled mental-emotions. The webs also counter too rapid an expression and assimilation of this dynamic energy, for this energy inevitably causes the disintegration of the form by the liberation of the atoms of substance. The intense energies cause the atoms to etherealise. Once consciousness has done the necessary work by passing the testings associated with the third Initiation, then the dynamic electricity moves down the spinal column to the Base of Spine centre to unite with the feminine *kuṇḍalinī* energy. When rightly controlled, then the liberation of consciousness manifests. Consciousness is consequently 'lifted to heaven' by the united Fires that now radiate from every atom of the meditator's being.

This Monadic Father energy manifests as Will or Power, the Destroyer-Regenerator aspect of Deity. Physical plane electricity is the Mother aspect of this energy. The Father energy vivifies each *chakra* by means of its seed point *(bīja)* in the centre. (The Jewel in the Heart of the Lotus.) The *chakras* then qualify this central reservoir of energy according to their varying capacities and are also vitalised by it. Some understanding of this Dynamic energy can be obtained by reflecting upon the qualities of electricity, magnetism and gravity. Only an Initiate of the third degree (or greater) can consciously work with it in its relatively unveiled form. This energy manifests to form the seed-point of an idea that grows into a complete *maṇḍala* of expression.[2] The Will is needed also to project the entire idea onwards and outwards on its path to objectivity. This seed point is the point of power sustaining the integral purpose of the idea.

B. *Prāṇa*. This has been somewhat dealt with. In its totality it is the energy of the Son emanating from the sun – from the Heart of the One that continually radiates to the earth the vitality needed for the well-being of all. This is truly of the Life that is the Christ principle (the sustainer or second aspect of Deity) that we breathe, live within, eat as

2 See my book *Maṇḍalas: Their Nature and Development* for detailed information upon them.

food and directly absorb into our systems. It is the product of His Love and vitality. Our whole being bathes in the aura of the planetary and solar Christs, in the *prāṇic* vitality that is symbolised by the Blood of the last supper of the historical Christ, which He told us to drink,[3] and which can symbolically wash away the sins and stains of the earth. In its aspect as 'blood', *prāṇa* can also be equated with the energy termed *ākāśa,*[4] which manifests through *buddhi* (the cosmic etheric universe). It therefore has its correspondence on all planes of perception.

Being the *medium of consciousness, prāṇa* is thus conveyed via the right control of breath, gross and subtle, vital and psychic. Therein lies the secret of transmutation of gross substance, and the key to liberation (which necessitates the use of the Fires of the mind). Metaphorically, the *prāṇic* purification and preparation of the body allows the coiled serpent of matter and the flaming Sword of Spirit to fuse and make that person a dynamic Dragon of Wisdom. It thereby transmutes the poison of our treacherous serpent-like natures into the elixir of Life. Electric Fire is the cause of Being and *prāṇa* gives it a Soul, a Life.

Prāṇa is absorbed into our systems via the etheric body, from which it is practically indistinguishable. The densest of the four ethers is visible as a transparent (sometimes rose-bluish) band about 1/8 - 1/4 of an inch around the body. The ethers are intermediate between the astral and the dense physical plane and are a definite part of the constitution of the physical plane. The causative agent utilises *prāṇa,* in its five types or grades, to build around the seed point of the idea the vital substance that will give it a Life and help it to sustain its purpose on its (spiry) evolutionary path.

C. *Kuṇḍalinī.* This is the name given to the Mother forces of Nature. It is many layered and multidimensional, and when released it allegorically seeks union with the energies of the Father (Dynamic electricity). Unless properly directed it will burn and destroy everything in its path. It therefore liberates the wise, who through purification possess no substance that can offer resistance to it. They also possess

---

3 *John 6:54.*

4 See my book *The Astrological and Numerological Keys to the Secret Doctrine,* Vol. 1 for detail concerning *ākāśa.*

the necessary knowledge, the directive Soul energy, to guide *kuṇḍalinī* back to the all-consummating source from which the Mother has been separated for the eternity of manifestation. *Kuṇḍalinī* ('serpent power') can also destroy the foolish that seek to wield this brute force without the necessary preparation, purification or understanding.

When the union with the Dynamic electrical energy is rightly eventuated, then the person radiates the Fiery magnetic force, which now permeates the form and radiates intense energies. (When the body's substance is undergoing fourth dimensional transmutation.) The change in consciousness and the ensuing radiation is such that the person has a general stimulating effect upon people and upon their psychic constitution, if that constitution is receptive to these energies. The transmutative process concerns undertaking the fourth Initiation. This Fiery energy is utilised to bind all peripheral atomic units around the central seed point that is needed for the fulfilment of the task of a causative agent. The seeded idea thus gains a form, a means of contact and interrelation with all other similar created forms. Inherent within the idea of *kuṇḍalinī* are the qualities associated with the five instincts. Any or all of these qualities are automatically built into the created form.

Where a number of *nāḍīs* intersect there are formed the *chakras*. They act as transmitters of high vibrational forces from the subtler planes. The *chakras* regulate and control the functioning of the working mechanism and vitality of the body. Where twenty-one or more *nāḍīs* cross, there are formed the major *chakras,* of which there are seven. The minor *chakras* are formed where a lesser number of *nāḍīs* intersect.

The seven principle glands are the physical expressions of the major *chakras*. The over or under-stimulation of these glands affects the particular area of the body which they control. This largely predetermines, through the malfunctioning of the organ concerned, a tendency of the body to certain diseases. Here lies the occult basis to the understanding of the causes of diseases. When there is a dearth or oversupply of psychic energy to a particular part of the body, it will react accordingly, producing an over or under stimulation of the related glands and the hormones they secrete. This also depends upon where the consciousness of a person is polarised (mental, emotional or physical). If for instance, the person is the emotional type who reacts strongly to emotional appetites, then he/she will be subject to disorders arising from the overstimulation of the Solar Plexus centre (and its corresponding gland). This thereby lays the foundation for stomach, liver and gall bladder upsets. (For these organs also come under the general influence of this *chakra*.)[5]

All causative agents work principally through one or other of the major or minor *chakras,* which colour the seeded ideas appropriately. The *chakras* are the agents whereby all ideas *must* be propelled into objectivity in the arena of concern associated with that *chakra.* One literally *thinks* with these dynamic centres of active resolve, provided of course one has developed the centre concerned. It is not possible to underestimate their value in this respect. The *chakras* therefore are primarily agents of the Fiery energy during this present epoch that is governed by scientific materialism.

Further notes concerning the *chakras*

The Head centre transmits energies from the *ātmic plane* via the Soul. It corresponds to the Central Spiritual Sun and is brought into functioning activity during the process associated with the third Initiation. This centre is composed of matter of the highest ether and therefore is the organ of synthesis, an expression of the dynamic Will (the first Ray aspect of Deity). The Head centre's energies are externalised through the pineal gland that is said to influence the higher subconscious brain and the right eye. This gland is dormant in the average person, as is also the Head centre. This centre consists of twelve major petals coloured white and gold that organise 1056 subsidiary petals patterned by the number twelve.[6]

The Ājñā centre is really an extension of the Head centre. It is the Eye of the Soul, the third Eye centred between the eyebrows. When vivified, it gives the person spiritual vision. The left half of this centre, coloured blue and purple, relates to the synthesised energies coming from the completely integrated personality. The other half (coloured rose and yellow) channels energies directed from the Heart centre.

---

5 This whole section is adapted from Alice Bailey's *Esoteric Healing.*

6 See my book *An Esoteric Exposition of the Bardo Thödol,* pages 377-432 for a detailed explanation of the petals of the Head centre and their function.

The Ājñā centre, when developed by the spiritual aspirant coordinates the personality and Soul forces. It acts as a screen upon which can be seen the radiance and beauty of all attributes of Life and the far vistas of the past and the future. It distributes the energy of the third aspect of Deity – active Intelligence (and is therefore related to the Throat centre). It is the organ of the Creative Will and so embodies the idea lying behind active creativity, expressing imagination and desire in their highest forms – the dynamic factors behind all Creation. It is therefore the organ of focus for all causative forces, the directive Eye which projects all Seed points to fulfil their purpose. This Eye works through all other points of Power *(chakras)* in the Body Logoic, galvanising their latent forces into sources of causative action.

The energies from this centre externalise themselves through the pituitary gland. They are said to influence the lower brain, cerebro-spinal nervous system, left eye and nose.

The Heart centre corresponds to the Heart of the Sun and is the Source of Life and Love. The *sūtrātma* (Life thread) which emanates from the Spirit-Soul is anchored there. This *chakra* transmits energy from the buddhic plane and also from the Soul (Sambhogakāya Flower). It is only brought into full functioning activity after the second Initiation, when the emotions and desire have been brought under Soul control. Desire, for instance, for the benefit of the personal self has been transmuted into Love for all.

The ability to 'think with the heart' implies that the twelve-petalled lotus in the centre of the Head and the Heart centre (its lowest reflex) have reached a point of real vibratory activity and mutual interplay. Also the desire energies of the Solar Plexus centre must have been transmuted and directed to the Heart as the energy of Love *(bodhicitta)*. Only then is the Soul able to pour to the aspirant the forces from its own realms and from the spiritual Hierarchy.

The Heart centre is the instrument of the energy that produces inclusiveness. When the process of alignment is accomplished, then self-consciousness becomes superseded by group consciousness. As this centre becomes active it draws the person into the Ashram of one of the Masters of Wisdom (according to the person's Soul Ray) and into a close service relationship with humanity.

The energies of this twelve-petalled Lotus externalise through the thymus gland and the vagus nerve, and are said to influence the heart, circulatory system and blood.

From the Heart centre the energy that sustains the entire causative process emanates via the five *vayūs,* for it interrelates their various functions. This organ helps engender the expansive vistas of the causative agent, enabling vision of the completion of the Plan *in toto,* in accordance with what is accomplished by all other similar agents.

The *Throat centre* is the higher correspondence of the Sacral centre and is therefore specifically the organ of the Creative Word (expressing the third Ray of Mathematically Exact Activity). The physical-generative energy that the undeveloped person expresses through the Sacral centre is transmuted and translated via the Throat centre into mental creation. (Note that humanity must eventually channel, by the act of transmutation, the forces from the centres below the diaphragm to the four centres above it if real spiritual progress is to be made.)

The Throat centre is related to the personality by the creative thread, to the Soul by the thread of consciousness and to the Monad by the *sūtrātma* or Life thread. (These threads are further explained below.) This centre is also related to the first Initiation.

The Throat centre channels and directs all of the Fires of the mind. Thus it is the causative organ *per se,* for these Fires are causative of everything within the formed realms. Corporeality, as we understand it, is but crystallised or condensed Fire, for all forms possess latent heat. This is evidenced on a grand scale in the nuclear fission and fusion that are the mainstays of the atomic bombs now in possession of those that have mentally gained some of the secrets of the nature of these Fiery forces.

The energies of the *Throat centre* are externalised through the thyroid and carotid glands. They are also said to influence the breathing and alimentary systems.

The *Solar Plexus centre* is externalised through the pancreas and stomach. This centre is said to influence the digestive system, liver, gall bladder, and the autonomic nervous system. It is the outlet for the astral body into the phenomenal world, the instrument through which emotional energy flows. As this centre is the recipient of all emotional reactions and of desire impulses, so it is of great importance for the average person that virtually 'lives and moves' in these impulses and energies. Humanity is subject to an ever-increasing group pressure through the individual as well as the collective Solar Plexus centre. This is because powerful desires, phobias and emotional conditionings (group hype, moods, temperaments, nationalist feeling, etc.) are generated and perpetuated by them. This centre also governs the psychic (astral) life of any person, for mediumistic tendencies, most forms of telepathic rapport and psychic revelations, are conveyed via it. It is the centre therefore through which most mediums and clairvoyants function.

The Solar Plexus centre is the powerhouse of the concept of the 'I', of self-centredness and selfish attitudes, and consequently is the most separative of all the centres (except the Ājñā in the case of a black magician). It also stands midway between the centres situated above the diaphragm (the Throat and Heart centres) and those below it (the Sacral and Base of Spine centres). It is therefore the centre for the ingathering of all the lower energies and is a focal point for the direction and distribution of all those energies by transmitting them to their receptive higher centres.

The directions of the flow of energies from the lower to the higher centres are:

The energies from the Solar Plexus flow to the Heart centre.
The energies from the Sacral centre flow to the Throat centre.
The energies from the Base of the Spine flow to the Head centre.

The transference of Solar Plexus energy *per se* to the Heart centre, as well as the gradual awakening of that centre, are the tasks of all spiritual aspirants.

The Solar Plexus is the centre of the personal will. Hence a causative agent utilises this centre to build the forms desired in the realms of sensation. Here all of the forces associated with the *inner round* (the *prāṇic* circulation in the twenty-two minor centres) find their apogee of expression and point of synthesis. It is consequently the 'abdominal brain', the means of communication with the sentience associated with all embodied ideas and images from various emotive thinkers. This is a vast field of study for all students of magical endeavour. It also veils the Way of unfoldment of the Purpose of the Logoi ensconced upon the cosmic astral plane. This centre allows one to contact the *devas* of the Waters and thence to build with the substance of the Army of the Voice and all Elementary Lives.

The *Sacral centre* expresses the sexual, animal, or physically vital force in humanity, and is therefore strongly developed in most beings. The colourings of the six petals to this centre – red, orange, yellow, green, blue and violet[7] – indicate the different qualities and attributes of the vital force, the *prāṇa* that it transmits. Five of the colours relate to the colourings of the five types of *prāṇas* and one is indigenous to the Sacral centre itself, which allows the interrelation of all six. *Six* is the number governing the manifestation of form and thus the substance of the feminine *devas.*

This centre corresponds to the *physical sun,* the source of vitality, the life-giving agent to our planet. Hence it energises all forms of creative endeavour. The meditator uses this centre to direct the *prāṇic* flow rightly so that the appropriate qualities are gained in the meditative construct. The *yogin* consequently needs to be able to completely control the potent expression of this centre. D.K. states that:

> The symbolism of the Sacral Centre is concerned primarily with the gestation period prior to birth[8]...It is perhaps above everything else the centre through which the forces of IMPERSONALITY must eventually express themselves, and the whole problem of dualism must be solved.[9]

This centre and the Base of the Spine centre are seen as a unit, which form a functioning duality with the higher corresponding unit of the Ājñā and the Head centres. Between them we have the alpha and the omega of the energies that make a personality.

---

7 C.W. Leadbeater, *The Chakras: A Monograph,* (Theosophical Publishing House, Adyar, 1996), 12. Leadbeater here depicts the six petals of the Sacral centre as 'The Spleen centre', but in reality the Splenic centre is a dual centre composed of a twelve-petalled lotus superimposed over an eight-petalled one. The colour red here is really an intense pink, signifying the energy of sensual desire. The main colouring of this centre is overall sun-like, for it is the centre of vitality.

8 Alice Bailey, *Esoteric Healing, 176.* My summation is largely adapted from that book.

9 Ibid., 177.

The *Base of the Spine centre* is the primal centre. It expresses the Mother forces of matter *(kuṇḍalinī)* and is directly related to the Will energy of the Head centre. The related glands, the adrenals, are said to influence the kidneys. There are four petals that take the shape of a cross, which radiates an orange Fire.

This centre supports all the others, as well as the spinal column. Under evolutionary Law, Spirit and matter meet here, allowing Life to interrelate with matter to produce a consciously evolving form. The spinal column houses a *threefold* thread, from which the entire *nāḍī* system is extended:

a. The *creative thread* (the *iḍā nāḍī),* through which the energy that feeds matter is poured. This thread is developed by way of mind.

b. The *consciousness thread* (the *piṅgalā nāḍī).* This is related to the evolution of consciousness and sensitive psychic unfoldment. It necessitates travelling the way of unfoldment of the Heart.

c. The *Life thread* (the *suṣumṇā nāḍī).* This is related to the path of the Spirit, the gaining of enlightenment.

In the Base of the Spine centre therefore, Life, consciousness and the forces of the form are blended and uplifted to 'heaven', as the response apparatus in a person is developed and perfected. This enables one to contact the entities on all planes of perception and to work with their energies.

Kuṇḍalinī, which is centred in this *chakra,* is the result of the union of these three types of energies when they are:

> focussed by an act of the enlightened will, under the impulse of love, in the basic centre. This unified fire is then raised by the use of a Word of Power (sent forth by the Will of the Monad) and by the united authority of the Soul and the personality, integrated and alive. The human being who can do this in full consciousness is therefore an initiate who has left the third initiation behind him...the kundalini fire will be raised and carried up into heaven *when* all the centres are awakened and the channels up the spine are unimpeded.[10]

---

10 Ibid., 185.

For a prime causative agent working via meditative techniques this centre is of great importance. Without the usage of the primal Creative Fires that are held in potential in this centre the thought construct cannot actualise as a form on the physical domain. The true mode of evocation of these Fires is an esoteric secret that can only be revealed when the Heart centre is awakened.

From the above it can be seen that an understanding of the way of unfoldment of the *chakras* is most important. This is not only if the secrets of the causative process are to be gained, but also if cosmology, all methods of esoteric or psychic healing and of humanity's psycho-spiritual constitution and evolution are to be understood. These are related to the consciousness-aspect of any being. When vivified, they provide clairvoyant abilities and higher spiritual perceptions. They make us what we are.

In the average person the lower five *chakras* are generally found functioning in different Stages of unfoldment. When the Head centre is finally vivified by the dual forces of the Soul and personality (in accordance with the treading of the Initiation path) then that person will obtain mastery of the energies of the higher planes of perception.

The information provided earlier concerning the nature of spiral-cyclic motion and the serpent is needed to comprehend the nature of the awakening of the *chakras*.

The *vayūs*

The *prāṇic* energy conveyed by the *nāḍīs* constituting the subtle bodies of humanity, the planetary Schemes and the sun, is called *prāṇamayakośa,* the illusional *(māyā)* sheath *(kośa)* of energy *(prāṇa).* In this light the physical body is known as the *annamayakośa,* the illusional body (sheath) of food. This food is not only physical, but also the vital energy that permeates every iota of being. The web of *prāṇic* energies is an adamantine jewel *(maṇi),* the foundation stone underlying dense manifestation. In the human body or that of a Logos, there are five principal types of *prāṇa.* The yogic practice of *prāṇāyāma*, the science of the control and right direction of breath, is concerned with them. This relates to the in and out-breathing of all causative streams of Thought. Such is the breath of Life that was breathed into the Adam of clay by the 'God' of Genesis. A Fiery Breath also causes the changing of the seasons, of the cyclic and cataclysmic effects from Shambhala upon the face of the earth. Our solar sphere, and the fabric of the cosmos of which we are a part, are all governed by the rhythmic pulsations of Logoic Breath. The five types of *prāṇas* ('winds' – *vayūs)* are termed:

A. Prāṇa – here taken in its narrowest, most literal sense, as *the breathing in of life.* This concerns sustaining the body through breathing, the assimilation of the external Life force for internal usage. It therefore concerns the right relationship between a person and those around, involvement in the world, group interaction, and the effects of that interaction to the person concerned. *Prāṇa* is said to result in the *control of the nāḍī extending from the nose to the heart.* The colour assigned to it is yellow.

B. Samāna – *the control of the nāḍī from the heart to the solar plexus.* It concerns the right nourishing of the threefold body (physically, astrally and mentally) through the medium of food and drink. It therefore implies the integral assimilation or digestion of all the Elements of Life – those that emanate from the Soul and also from the personality. Its colour is green.

C. Apāna – *the control of the nāḍī from the solar plexus to the feet.* It therefore controls the various secretions associated with the organs of elimination and of birth (the reproductive system). It also concerns the right handling of one's external impact upon the environment, on one's circle of friends and upon society in general. The implication is that the 'child' to which one gives birth is adequately nourished and rightly directed in its path of life. *Apāna* thus involves the full use of one's discriminatory capacity. Its colour is orange-red.

D. Udāna – *the control of the nāḍī from the nose to the top of the head.* This *nāḍī* coordinates the various *prāṇas,* and when it is properly controlled, breath becomes a vehicle of the mind, of the creative Word and of artistic vision. Its colour is violet-blue.

E. Vyāna – *the sum total of the prāṇic energies as they are distributed evenly throughout the body.* This distribution is analogous to the functioning of the blood vessels (in particular) and also of the nerves. It implies the unimpeded circulation of all aspects of Life in the

Body of Deity. The control of this *nāḍī* results in the activity of the enlightened person. Its colour is rose.

It is posited here that these *prāṇas* are not just channels of vitality in the human body, but also the psycho-physiological correspondences between humanity and Deity and their respective evolutionary progress. Their right control therefore signifies the perfect coordination of all our capabilities.

Each tiny *nāḍī* carries all the five principle *prāṇas*, however in some *nāḍīs* a particular type of *prāṇa* is dominant. For example, in the Stage called Prāṇa the yellow *prāṇa* dominates. The five *prāṇas* find their correspondences in the five great states of energy called planes of perception that are related to the five Elements. These Elements are Earth (physical plane), Water (astral realm), Fire (mental plane), Air (the intuitional realm – *buddhi)* and Aether (the realm of cosmic Mind – *ātma).* These *prāṇas* constitute the medium of consciousness for the evolving human entity. They are:

The ātmic plane *(dharmakāya)* The Head and Ājñā centres	**Vyāna**	Aether (Stage 5)
The buddhic (intuitional) plane The Heart centre	**Prāṇa**	Air (Stage 1)
The mental plane The Throat centre	**Udāna**	Fire (Stage 4)
The astral plane The Solar Plexus centre	**Samāna**	Water (Stage 2)
The physical plane The Sacral and Base of Spine centres	**Apāna**	Earth (Stage 3)

Table 16: The five *vayūs*

The first three Stages are concerned with the proper control and assimilation of the vital energies needed for healthy bodily functions and reproduction. They prepare the ground by cleansing the body, therefore they are primarily related to the second Ray line of endeavour. In the last two Stages the lower energies are raised to the head, liberating the person from bondage to the material realms. They are concerned with the Will, the conscious arousing of the energies from the *chakras*. They are therefore related to the first Ray line of endeavour, with the sum of the factors making a causative agent.

In their totality the *vayūs* are concerned with divine alchemy, the transmutation and refinement of coarse physical matter to make it a suitable vehicle for Divinity to transform substance into Light, desire into Love, differentiation into Unity.

The energies flowing via *buddhi* (Air and Stage 1) are found at the heart of every atom. The energies cause the appearance of forms, which thereby become an integral aspect of the Heart of Life. The Airy Element also consequently vitalises all that exists, as it is the carrier of all the *prāṇas*. Fundamentally, all forms (be they of a physical atom, world or solar sphere) emanate from the Heart centre of 'God' and are an expression of His Love.

The five Stages of unfoldment of the *vayūs*

In this synopsis the five Stages of the unfoldment of the *vayūs* will be related particularly to humanity's psychic constitution and evolution. They can be considered to be the Stages of the evolutionary process in Nature. They are also the process of the unfoldment of the *prāṇas* in the body that come as a consequence of the practice of yoga-meditation.

> **Stage 1 – Prāṇa.** *The nāḍī from the nose to the heart.* This is related to the buddhic plane (the fourth cosmic ether) and to the Heart centre.

On the involutionary path this Stage has a general group stimulus on all forms and upon the various kingdoms of Nature. It concerns the force of Life as it is distributed through the *chakras* in any manifest body and it is an expression of the general emanative vitality from the physical sun that is absorbed by plants, animals and humanity.

This *prāṇa* is absorbed by the *prāṇic* triangle, where the Splenic centre becomes the organ of distribution of the energies. This triangle consists of the centre between the Shoulder Blades, the Diaphragm centre and the Splenic centre. The central dynamo for the absorption of *prāṇa* via this triangle is the Heart centre. It integrates the absorbed *prāṇa* with the Life force from the Soul, producing a resultant energy *(jīva)* which is the integral energy of each particular human unit. From the Splenic centre the *prāṇas* are specifically distributed to the centres existing upon the fourth ether.

- The *Solar Plexus centre.* The *prāṇas* from the animal kingdom are also absorbed here.
- The *Sacral centre.* The general distributer for plant-like *prāṇas.*
- The *Base of Spine centre.* Mineral-like *prāṇas* are expressed here.

The fourth ether is the dense correspondence of the buddhic plane and its qualities.

Prāṇa is what vitalises the myriad forms of the various kingdoms in Nature, and facilitates their sentient response to each other's external impacts. Such responses occur through radiatory emanations, so that consciousness evolves through these interactions. The attributes of a human kingdom are thereby gradually evolved. They are the causative agents in Nature and synthesise the qualities of the lesser three kingdoms. *Prāṇa* therefore has a special relationship to the human (the fourth) kingdom in Nature, for they will become an embodied sun in Nature, radiating the energies of Love-Wisdom. They are effectively the 'Son of God' to all forms in all kingdoms. (Note the correspondence to the fourth ether and the fourth plane of perception.) When they manifest so then the work of Stage 1 is completed. Here the Heart centre is also seen to have a direct relationship to humanity.

On the path of *evolution* (of humanity) the right evocation and expression of *prāṇa* results in the stimulation of the Heart centre through the right control of breath. Eventually the powers of the golden twelve-petalled Head lotus are awakened, and then all of the petals of the Sambhogakāya Flower, allowing the person to enter into the Hierarchy of Light and Love. The full accomplishment of this *prāṇic* circulation gradually replaces the atomic units of the fourth ether with etheric atoms from the second etheric sub-plane. This has a direct relationship to the second (son) aspect on all levels of expression. It also results in the translation of the group or herd instinct and its consequent fear of loneliness, into intuition. This perception is fully developed by the

Initiate of the fourth degree. (This lays the foundation to contact the Monad and then eventually become identified with it at the attainment of the sixth Initiation.)

Therefore, though Prāṇa heads the list of the *vayūs,* it is also basic to one's entire evolution and, in fact, constitutes our path in life, involving the principle of renunciation by association with the energies of Life and Light. This enables a person to become a dispassionate dispenser of these qualities, to be an all-embracing sun, so that all beings may thereby benefit. They are to be stimulated towards group unfoldment by the evocation of Love rightly applied with knowledge, so that wisdom is the gain. This implies completely following the instructions that Jesus gave:

> Ye are the Light of the world....Let your light so shine before men, that they may see your good works, and glorify your Father which is in heaven.[11]

This Stage is also responsible for the probationary Path, for the higher esoteric aspect of the group or herd instinct produces a sense of group sharing with humanity in the aspirant, bringing him/her into contact with any of the Ashrams of the Masters of Wisdom. This is the foundation of the expressed Love that is the basis for treading the path. The end result of the expression of this *vayū* is to develop the qualities of the fourth Initiation. (Complete sacrifice of the one for the all in such a way that even the Soul form is destroyed, being unable to contain the intensity of the incoming energies from the Monad.) The energy of the fourth cosmic ether *(buddhi)* becomes the domain of the Initiate, equated with *śūnyatā* or *mokṣa* of the Buddhists and Hindus.

Stage 2 – Samāna. The *nāḍī* from *the heart to the solar plexus* – related to the astral plane, the Element Water and the Solar Plexus centre.

On the *involutionary* path in Nature (the development of plant and animal life forms) the astral plane is non-existent. In Nature therefore, this Stage is particularly associated with the *devas* and their response to solar *prāṇa,* which they distribute in such a way that the intellect is stimulated in animal forms. Through much experimentation they

11 *Matt. 5:14-16.*

gradually built forms that were evolving towards what could contain the principle of mind. This necessitated animal evolution in a way that the nervous system is developed as a medium of sentient response to external impacts. This process inevitably led to Individualisation (the formation of a human kingdom). Once animal-man developed the emotions, and then the mental-emotions, what is understood as the astral plane, with its heavens and hells, came into being. The entire pageant of evolution therefore leads to this Stage. The qualities, however, associated with the (involuntary) autonomic (sympathetic) nervous system that governs the basic functions of life, are what can be considered 'astral' in functioning. This is because the *devas* that built the early forms of life projected the qualities pouring through the astral/etheric domain (reifications of the laws governing the higher domains). The various basic instincts were also developed during this time, prior to the appearance of the forms that could bear mind.

In Stage 4 (Udāna) the qualities associated with the human cerebro-spinal system are developed from the animal kingdom. (Thus what concerns the evolution of a human brain and thinking capacity.) These two Stages (two and four) were therefore woven together throughout the palaeontological record in the form of a DNA helix pattern to produce the forms of life familiar to us now.

Mother Nature works mostly via the Solar Plexus centre for the greater part of evolutionary time and has engendered the primal Stages of causative action in humanity. (The tendency to produce thought-forms, though at first purely of a desire or emotional nature.) This created much glamour and desire-images of all types that eventually built the attributes associated with the astral plane. The astral plane then progressively became a plane of residence in the afterlife for humanity. Therein the deceased experience the *karma* of their thought and desire-constructs. Emotional development also caused humanity's domestication of the animal kingdom, for the Solar Plexus centre (and the inner round *chakras)* is the organ of communication with all lesser kingdoms. Humanity works unknowingly in association with the *devas* through all such relationships.

The unfoldment of this *vayū* (Samāna) therefore also produced people's psychic powers: the clairvoyance, mediumship (etc.) related to the Solar Plexus centre and the autonomous nervous system. Once the

Throat centre was awakened through the development of intellectual faculties, more potent mental thought-forms were produced. Many mental illusions thereby came into existence, the methodology of the forces of evil, and also the path of Initiation that awakened the powers of the Soul (the radiant sun within us) became known. The Light from the Soul eventually dispels glamour and illusions. This methodology is discovered upon the path of Initiation.

The right control of this *vayū* eventually produces the *second Initiation* and the transmutation of the *instinct towards knowledge* into applied wisdom. Here the Initiate learns to rightly fuse the energy of Love with streams of thought-forms, to produce benevolent effects in the world's Watery astral sphere. Such control implies the ability to utilise the creative imagination, fully developed by the Initiate of the second degree. It helps produce the development of the intelligence aspect of the path of probation with regard to thought-form building (Stage 4).

In the earliest Stages of our evolution Samāna helps cause the fear of the unknown, and then the rectification of that situation. This fear is essentially the effect of thought-form building. It stems from the effect of primeval thought-forms (of grotesque psychic shapes, and the vampire-like effects of these forms) upon our subconscious minds and psyches. This fear will be rectified when thought-forms denoting the qualities of (white) Light are built, dispelling and destroying the effects of these ancient forms. In more modern times this fear concerns an anticipatory reaction to what is unknown or unfamiliar. This fear is completely mastered by the time the second Initiation has been undertaken. The person has then controlled the manifestation of all forms of astral plane substance.

> **Stage 3 – Apāna.** The *nāḍī from the solar plexus to the feet* – related to the physical plane, the Base of the Spine and the Sacral centres.

On the path of *involution* this Stage concerns the general effects of the massed sentience of the Elementary Lives from which the human body is appropriated. This concerns the planetary etheric body and the means by which energies are precipitated into the dense form, and then their right utilisation and appropriation by the various kingdoms in Nature (via the plant kingdom) so that their forms can be sustained.

Apāna concerns building forms that can inevitably contain *manasic* energies. The work involves the activities of the tenth, eleventh and twelfth Creative Hierarchies – Makara, the Lunar Lords and the Baskets of Nourishment[12] that embody the substance of all forms. The related energies also control the various rhythms and cycles that govern the formed realms. (The seasons, cyclic geological upheavals, the ocean's tides and so forth.) Also taken into account are the internal Fires, the heat-engendering factors sustaining the mineral kingdom, of which *kuṇḍalinī* is the focus.

On the path of *evolution* (regarding humanity) Apāna concerns sexual expression, rhythmic response to Life's forces, our impact on the external environment and everything associated with right human relations. This path therefore produces all of the experiences associated with humanity's relationships (social, family, sexual, tribal, national and international). These eventually stimulate us (by means of reaction to pain and suffering) to set our feet upon the path to liberation and thus undertake the first Initiation. This Initiation relates to the control of external as well as internal cycles by means of *hatha yoga* (bodily exercises), *prāṇāyāma* and healthy living styles. It also concerns the gradual transmutation of the effects of the sexual instinct and fear of isolation into what produces the perfection of the intellect and mastery of all life, to produce an Initiate of the third degree (the higher correspondence to the first Initiation). All the causative factors governing manifest life thus come under the control of the Initiate.

The Initiate of the first degree begins to have a proper understanding as to the effects of the sexual instinct within the precincts of his/her own psychic constitution. It is an effect of the positive and negative forces associated with the etheric body (yin-yang), the *iḍā* and *piṅgalā nāḍīs,* which one has begun to relate in a dynamic and positive manner. This produces the 'son' in terms of consciousness. The treading of this path is concerned with the ability to relate these internal energies to the external universe (of which they are a symbol). The Initiate of the first degree is initiated into this, the realm of the etheric forces that are causative of the effects in the gross body.

---

12 They are explained in Alice Bailey's *Esoteric Astrology* and my book: *The Astrological and Numerological Keys to the Secret Doctrine,* Volume 2.

The form of the devotion developed by the plant kingdom is seen in their ability to be sacrificed as food for the animal kingdom. They also produce a wonderful diversity of colour and perfume. (Their purpose is to effect liberation from the plant kingdom by developing animal-like qualities.) This is translated into aspiration by the human unit that sets foot upon the path of the Initiation process. Therefore, though this is the third Stage of the liberation process associated with the *vayūs,* it can also be considered *the first,* for here the 'turning about in the seat of consciousness' is finally effected. (This starts at the Base of Spine/ Sacral centres, which support all the others.)

The involutionary path for the Stages so far mentioned concern the *inner round,* the evolution of the qualities associated with the minor *chakras* in the body. (They are flowers of energy interrelationships within the body.) This produces the gradual transmutation of the grosser effects associated with these minor centres. At first this is an automatic or unconscious process, then a conscious response to group or massed energies is produced. In this third Stage, the energies associated with the seven major *chakras* centred in the spinal column can be properly evoked. The person can then earnestly start the process of transmutation of the base substance of his/her vehicles.

From the point of view of *the progress of the aspirant,* therefore, the five Stages can be re-ordered as below. Each Stage governs the qualities producing the related Initiation.

Stage 1	Apāna	1st Initiation
Stage 2	Sāmana	2nd Initiation
Stage 3	Udāna	3rd Initiation
Stage 4	Prāṇa	4th Initiation
Stage 5	Vyāna	5th Initiation

The next two Stages (Udāna and Vyāna) are directly related to the path of human enlightened attainment, the evolution of everything concerning the unfoldment of Mind in relation to Love, the path of aspiration and Initiation. An enlightened causative agent is the gain.

Stage 4 – Udāna. The *nāḍī from the nose to the top of the head,* related to the mental plane and the Throat centre.

Little need be said here. This Stage is associated with the qualities developed by the present Aryan (fifth Root Race) humanity. Their purpose is to wisely utilise the mind and then develop the Will by means of meditation, and so to use the skilful means that will enlighten that person, awakening the higher Mind. The process facilitates conscious contact with the *devas* to produce a direct working relationship. The individual will also die to the concept of personal 'self', by means of integrating with the Soul (the Sambhogakāya Flower), and so to embody its powers. Everything concerning the attainment of the third Initiation (the *ālayavijñāna* enlightenment), explained in my previous books, comes into play here. The activities that produce the awakening of the *kuṇḍalinī* Fire and its vivification of the Head centre are therefore produced in this Stage. The complete expression of this allows the person to build into his/her constitution the matter of the third ether. It brings the person into enlightened awareness of the planetary centre termed Humanity. The third Initiation is the first cosmic Initiation, hence the first true Initiation, wherein all aspects of the personality are completely mastered. The fifth Initiation is its higher correspondence. The third Initiation produces the transmutation of the instinct of self-assertion, with its consequent fear of failure of not being recognised.

Stage 5 – Vyāna. The *sum total of all prāṇic energies,* related to the ātmic plane and the combined Head centres.

The right application of this *vayū* leads eventually to the development of reception to cosmic Mind *(dharmakāya).* This necessitates following all of the precepts of the path that drive the *prāṇas* from below the diaphragm to the higher centres, and then to fully awaken the combined Ājñā and Head centres. The process produces the complete awakening of the Head centre gained by the Initiate of the fifth degree.[13] The transmutation of the instinct of self-preservation manifests, with the consequent fear of death. Vyāna allows the Master to build into his

13 See chapter 6 of my book *Meditation and the Initiation Process* for detail concerning the third to fifth Initiations, and *The Constitution of Shambhala,* Volume 1 for explanation of the Ashrams presided over by the Masters of Wisdom, as well as many other facts concerning the attributes of Hierarchy.

constitution matter of the first ether (the atomic sub-plane). This lays the foundation to eventually gain the potency of the seventh degree Initiate.

The information presented so far can be tabulated thus:

Stage 1 **Prāṇa**
Instinct. Group or herd (animal kingdom).
Expression. Buddhic plane, Heart centre, fourth Initiation. Love aspect of the path of probation.
Transmuted quality. Sixth Initiation.

Stage 2 **Samāna**
Instinct. Towards knowledge (human kingdom).
Expression. Astral plane, Solar Plexus centre, second Initiation. Knowledge aspect of the path of probation.
Transmuted quality. Fourth Initiation.

Stage 3 **Apāna**
Instinct. Sexual (plant kingdom).
Expression. Physical/etheric plane, Sacral/Base of Spine centres, first Initiation.
Transmuted quality. Third Initiation.

Stage 4 **Udāna**
Instinct. Self-assertion (kingdom of Souls).
Expression. Mental plane, Throat centre, third Initiation.
Transmuted quality. Fifth Initiation.

Stage 5 **Vyāna**
Instinct. Self-preservation (mineral kingdom).
Expression. Ātmic plane, Head centres, fifth Initiation.
Transmuted quality. Seventh Initiation.

Table 17: The five *vayūs* and the Initiations

The *vayūs*, the Instincts and Initiation

An esoteric objective of the Stages of the *prāṇic* circulation is the betrothal, marriage and then eventual fusion of the activities of the human and angelic kingdoms. The *devas* represent the *iḍā nāḍī,* and humans are the *piṇgalā nāḍī* in the Body of Deity. There is therefore a higher circulation of the five Stages within the Body of the planetary Logos that incorporates these parallel evolutionary streams.

Humanity learns the causative art concerning the manipulation of substance (embodied by the *devas)* through the use of the hands and the development of the mind. Intelligent application of the creative will presently dominates our society. Later will come demonstrable *siddhis* (psychic powers) to produce similar results by the right control of breath in conjunction with mantric Sound. Human thought processes will eventually become so much a conscious extension of 'breath' that it will no longer be a question of manipulation, but rather an identification with the subtle forces that cause the appearance of phenomena. The *devas* reside in a universe of Sound and of sound intonations. Apart from the noises created by our materialistic civilisation, the human unit learns to live in a world of silence once the meditative path is undertaken. Understanding the laws of Sound therefore concerns the ability to creatively work with the *devas.*

The major step towards integration between the human and *deva* attributes happens at the fourth Initiation and is completed at the sixth, when the Initiate exits out of the ranks of the human kingdom altogether. (He then enters the *suṣumṇā nāḍī* in the Body of Deity.)

The first step in this marriage process begins with Apāna, wherein the person's internal and external sexual expressions are related. One learns to control internal energies so that the first Initiation can be undertaken. This is specifically in relation to the physical form and its powers. Conscious control of the potency of the *deva* forces and Elementals who embody the form nature is begun, plus the regulation of the Initiate's own *karma.* (This is a main objective of the tests in the sign Scorpio.) The first degree Initiate learns to work with the *devas* of the shadows and other *deva* entities. (The Elemental Life manifesting via the etheric domain.) This produces an appreciation of the quality of Life associated with the vegetable kingdom and its right utilisation in the maintenance of bodily health.

The next Stage (Samāna) can be considered somewhat of a respite from active outwardly focussed activity. The *instinct towards knowledge* is directed towards learning about the laws of Life, specifically that concerning the psychic world and the nature of mental integration.

All tendencies to glamour are to be overcome in order to take the second Initiation. The rules of conduct necessary to prepare for the third Initiation (enlightenment) are also followed. Obtaining inner quietude is an objective at this Stage. This is necessary if the desire forms and glamour-making tendencies are to be completely eliminated. The Initiate is often confronted with psychic delusions (attacks from the dark brotherhood). High energisations are experienced, which can intensify mental-emotional problems, necessitating much meditative quietude and observation of psychic perturbations. The betrothal process with the *deva* kingdom happens at the second Initiation, for the Initiate must learn much about working with Elementals and cooperation with the greater *devas,* the angels who come to instruct. The Initiate thereby learns to become a true causative agent.

The next Stage (Udāna) associated with *the instinct of self-assertion* and the third Initiation, is an outward-going meditation where the Initiate learns to work in conjunction with the fifth Creative Hierarchy (the Agnishvattas, also called Makara the Mystery) who embody the substance of the mental plane. They form the substance built into the kingdom of Souls, with which the third Degree Initiate is now a conscious member. The Initiate is learning to direct *karma* in the three worlds of human perception, and thus to project the energies (hence the *deva* entities) that produce outer tangible results in the realms of form. Such Initiates become spiritual teachers and are often found to be profoundly influencing human affairs in one form or another, according to Ray disposition.

It should be noted that those who took Initiations in former lives will generally not remember their Initiation status when they reincarnate. Nevertheless, they will manifest service arenas proportionate to their spiritual status and will often discover the teacher that has the capacity to lead them towards their next Initiation Stage.

The Stage termed Prāṇa, when fully expressed is productive of the Initiate of the fourth degree. The experience here is of *śūnyatā* (the Void). This represents a type of interlude between cycles of outward activity. This does not mean that Bodhisattvic service work is diminished, for great are the demands of the 'cries of suffering' that reach the Initiate's inner ears. Rather, it means that inner contemplative awareness is a constant focus of the Initiate's life. The Will aspect of

Deity now manifests its potency and drives the Initiate to obtain great pre-ordained heights of revelation and service arena. Life in the world of form is renounced, and the focus is upon *buddhi* (the fourth cosmic ether), whereon the Ashrams of the Hierarchy of Love and Light are externalised. The qualities of the Logoic Heart centre are thereby expressed. At this Stage there is a marriage with the Initiate's *deva* compliment, and much integrated service work ensues.

Primarily, the Initiate is concerned with the means of occultly directing all the energies that emanate from Shambhala and the various Creative Hierarchies. He/she now lives in a sea of energies – planetary, inter-planetary and even cosmic. These must be identified in order to be properly directed. The motive is to play an appropriate part as an organ of Light and Love within Hierarchy, in accordance with their collective Plan.

After the Initiate has mastered the various techniques associated with energy direction in our planetary Scheme, learnt the Words of Power that control the Lives in the realms of form, and mastered the next Stage (Vyāna), then a Master of Wisdom has arisen. This Stage can be considered *outward-going.* The Master controls all energies associated with dense incarnation and can direct the creative flow of large groups of entities, human and *deva* alike, according to the Vision of the Plan of 'God' of which the Master is a part, according to the domain of the sub-Ray Ashram the Master oversees.

Eventually a sixth degree Initiate appears, the Chohan of a Ray line that has consciously Identified with the Spirit-Monad. The Chohan has totally fused with His/Her *deva* compliment, and so rises out of the human kingdom altogether. The proper appellation given to such a one is Dhyān Chohan (a divine Being of meditation substance). The Chohan must inevitably choose one of the cosmic Paths that lead out of the confines of our solar system altogether. If He stays upon the earth, then an intense (internal) meditation and spiritual tuition ensues associated with planetary occultism, as instructed by the Lords of Shambhala. He works to build the externalising Temple of the Lord as a high executive member of Hierarchy, and also plays a direct role in Shambhala.

Those that attain the seventh Initiation upon the earth Scheme are effectively *outward-going,* being involved in planet-wide energy distribution. Cosmic *prāṇa (ākāśa)* is distributed via our seven planes of perception. Seventh degree Initiates, for instance, work through one of the three great Departments of Life. They are the field of Civilisation (the third Ray line governing the Mahāchohan's department), the Teaching Ray (the second Ray Christ's department), and that of world Government (the first Ray Manu's department).

Figure 20 effectively depicts the expression of the meditation process of Deity. His In and Out-breathing produces concrete effects in His Body (incorporating the various planes of perception and the Chains and globes of a planetary Scheme). This cyclic Breath produces a corresponding circulation of the respective *vayūs* within our planet. There are many different levels of this cyclic Breathing process during the sum total of our planetary evolution. The Initiation process for a human kingdom, as explained above, can be considered to be Stage 4 (Prāṇa) of the overall schema. The earlier Stages therefore relate to the evolution of the Life forms upon our planet prior to the appearance of humanity, as is shown in the paleontological record. There is consequently one Stage remaining, which concerns the final evolutionary development of humanity, and then consequent planetary dissolution *(pralaya).*

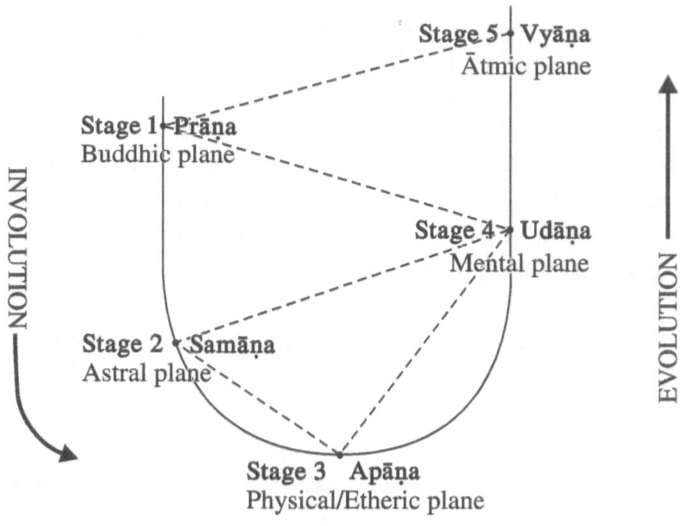

Figure 20: The Stages of *prāṇic* circulation

The entire Life process, therefore, is an effect of the Breathing process of the planetary Logos. Each in and out-Breath is accompanied by a corresponding mantric Sound (song or stanza) that energises the Creative Hierarchies of *deva* Lives to produce the needed changes for the appearing and disappearing phenomena they embody. Initiates learn to play their role in this process according to the degree of Initiation and the specialisation of the Ray line they embody.

It is seen here that the fourth Stage (Udāna) holds the key to the unfoldment of all the others. This Stage is effective after the process of involution has been accomplished. The person then no longer automatically responds to massed consciousness or to purely emotive forces, but is beginning to master life. This is because once the mind has been developed the meditation process associated with the right direction of breath and the means to liberation can proceed with certainty.

The Table below summarises the breathing process with respect to the Initiations.

Inbreathing	First Initiation	Apāna
Interlude	Second Initiation	Samāna
Outbreath	Third Initiation	Udāna
Interlude	Fourth Initiation	Prāṇa
Inbreathing	Fifth Initiation	Vyāna
Interlude	Sixth Initiation	
Outbreath	Seventh Initiation	

Table 18: The Stages of Initiation and Breath

On the path of evolution Udāna relates Stage two to Stage three, and Stage one to five. This is depicted below in figure 21.

It is seen here that Stages three to five are related to the development of the Will (the first Ray line) needed to be developed by a causative agent. It concerns the ability of the person to project the *antaḥkaraṇa* through a gap in consciousness (between the empirical mind and the abstract Mind) to a sea of consciousness. Such a 'gap' also exists between the physical brain and the etheric brain, and from the mental unit to the mental permanent atom.[14] These Stages eventually relate the highest and lowest centres (the Head and the Base of Spine) by means of a 'flux' as it were. This 'flux' is the second Ray (Love-Wisdom) line of development. When the Watery energies of Stage two are evoked, this line of development produces the *creative imagination*. This allows the created idea (thought-form) to be projected into objective expression. The thinker imagines something as if it were accomplished fact. It is visualised in consciousness and then made a reality with the application of the Will.

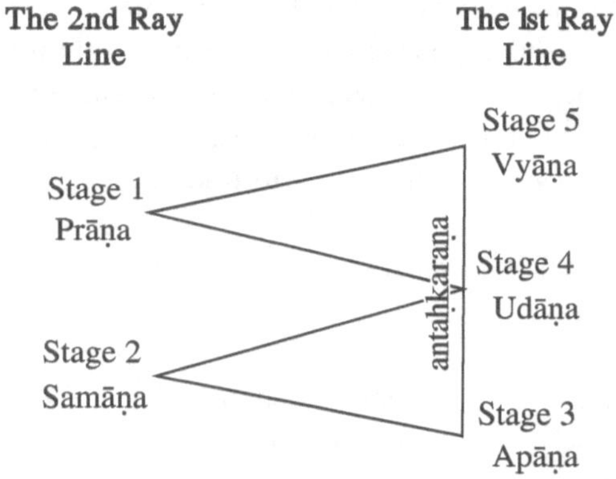

Figure 21: The Ray lines for the *vayūs*

What is desired is imagined, and the object of that desire (as aspiration) forms the seed point of the meditation. This happens in Stage three (Apāna) via the dense form. (This is the place wherein all Stages and planes can be found interpenetrated and interrelated.) On this plane, therefore, the straight and narrow path that relates the one to the other can be found and travelled upon. Eventually this becomes the *suṣumṇā* path. This is the reason why possession of a dense physical body is deemed so valuable in Buddhist philosophy. (Only in such a form can the enlightenment process be undertaken and Buddhahood obtained.)

The actual meditation concerns focussing the Light of Revelation into the sphere of consciousness (which is lighted substance) and

14 See my book *Esoteric Cosmology and Modern Physics,* and Alice Bailey's *A Treatise on Cosmic Fire* for an explanation of them.

extending this from the Heart of one's life to the outer periphery of one's entire sphere of contacts. All is expressed as embodied Light. First there is the Light of consciousness, and then enlightenment, the clear cold Light, which is all-embracive and omnipotent.

The Light of the mind associated with Stage four (Udāna) is the field wherein all this is enacted. The mind relates the Light of the Spirit (Stage five) with the light of matter (Stage three) and is fuelled by the quality of the Airy flux of Stage one (Prāṇa) by the energies of the fourth cosmic ether *(buddhi)*. This allows the person to revel in the Hierarchical aura by visioning in Light. The visual impressions must then be made a reality through the application of the Will (Vyāna) and applied to the dense physical realm (Stage three).

The Airy quality *(prāṇa)* directed by the combined effect of Stages four and five (the directive Mind), with which it forms a triad, produces the Word that is both the cause of manifestation, and then the final abstraction of all Being.

Concluding explanations concerning the *vayūs*

The information presented so far is depicted in figure 22. The Stages marked 1a, 2a, 3a and 4a in this figure concern by far the greater part of the evolutionary process – up to the development of the intellect as a functioning expression in a person. Then comes the complete integration of all aspects of a personality (Stage 5a) as the sum of everything making one a self-centred individual. The development of the abstract Mind comes as a consequence of such personality integration. Once the perceptions from the Soul begin to properly manifest in relation to self-motivated service work in the world, then Stage 1b has commenced. This path of probation to attain Initiation necessitates a developing expression of compassion and of the wisdom needed to rightly serve. This is necessary if knowledge concerning esoteric matters, as gained in meditative unfoldment and Initiation, is not to be abused by the over-zealous, self-centred or fanatical aspirant.

The second Stage of the probationary path (Stage 2b) commences with the necessary thought-form building and meditative unfoldment regarding the service work that will lead to attaining the first Initiation (Stage 3b). Proper wisdom needs to be accomplished to thus serve. A 'turning about in the seat of consciousness' then ensues, leading up the leg of the pentagram to thoroughly awaken the powers of critical thinking and analytical deduction in Stage 4a. Finally the enlightenment represented by attaining the third Initiation (Soul identification – Stage 4b) is gained after the needed testings are passed. Before this accomplishment however, the aspirant has many lives of character building, mental accomplishment, spiritual activity and service work to undertake. The attributes of the first and second Initiations must be attained. This process is indicated by the lines at the feet of the pentagram that contain the arrows facing each other. Stages 2b and 3b therefore signify the bulk of the treading of the path wherein many unruly *saṃskāras* and *kleśas* must be cleansed out of the aspirant's psyche. Disciples must live out the related *karma* and transform the attributes of darkness into arenas of Light and Love.

In the figure, the line from Stage 2b to Stage 4b is bolded because this indicates that most of the work concerning the transforming process is accomplished in relation to undertaking the second Initiation. There the disciple must battle with the sum of the nine-headed Hydra[15] that lurks in the swamp of *saṃsāra,* and deal with the worst of the psychic and emotional *karma* developed in former lives. The techniques of overcoming the attacks and beguiling thought projections from the dark brotherhood must be mastered. This lays the path clear for the third Initiation. The testings for the second Initiation are often so difficult for the disciple that often much of the work for the third and fourth Initiations have been done before the second is properly mastered.

Stage 4b represents the completion of the integral harmony of the minor system that is the corporeal person, the mastery of one's personal involvement with *saṃsāra.* The third Initiation signifies the purpose of the repetitive incarnations of the Soul. Revelation is gained from the store of information obtained out of the myriads of incarnations of the Soul and from the realms of divinity it has access to. After this, the next series of incarnations relate to the process that will eventually lead to the death of the Soul and attainment of buddhic perception at the

15 See my book *The Constitution of Shambhala,* Parts B and C for detail concerning the nine-headed Hydra in relation to Initiation testings. For a general summary of the heads of the Hydra refer also to the figure: https://www.universaldharma.com/ud_downloads/files/the_nine_headed_hydra.pdf.

fourth Initiation. The conditioned, aeon-long cycling is thus terminated at the fourth Initiation (Stage 1c). The Initiate then enters into another cycle of endeavour associated with eventually travelling into cosmic space (esoterically signified by the term *nirvāṇa).*

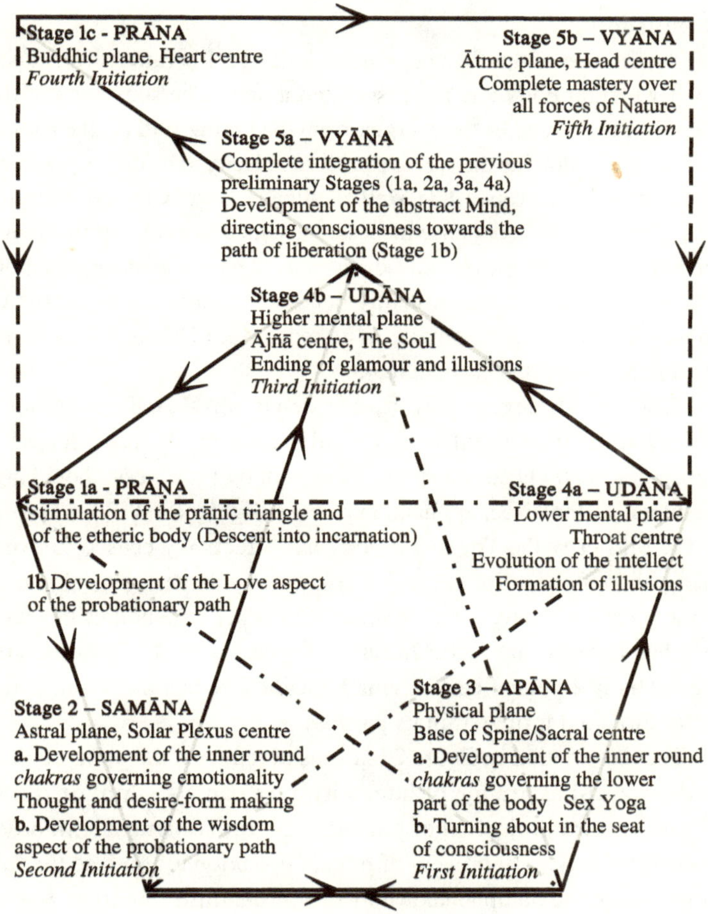

Figure 22: The five Stages to liberation and the pentagram

The Initiate of the fourth degree is able to vivify his/her etheric body directly with the Light from the Heart of the Spiritual Sun, to produce a radiant healing aura. It becomes a transformation Body by the time the fifth Initiation is reached. The radiant energy fields produced by these Initiates allow them to perform the types of miracles attributed to our greatest saints. The radiance producing the etherealisation (liberation) of the dense atoms of the form is indicated by the dotted line from Stage 1c to 1a.

The Initiate of the fifth degree has a similar liberating effect upon his/her mental body and the associated atoms. The substance of the Mind is transformed by the energies from the Living Will of 'the Father' (the Monad), allowing the creative process of Deity to be directly applied to the material universe. The Mathematically Exact Creative energies from the ātmic plane organise manasic substance so as to imprint upon it the Master's part of the overall Logoic *maṇḍala* for planetary evolution. The intellect per se consequently becomes 'below the threshold of consciousness', thus automatic in its response. (This is indicated by the dotted line from Stage 5b to 4a.)

To the fifth degree Initiate the dense physical form is but a *māyāvirūpa* (illusional body) in all respects. It has become a transmutation body, an illusional form built on the etheric mould and sustained by the direct application of the enlightened Will for as long as the Master wills. The astral body has effectively ceased to exist, being absolutely refined, long devoid of any tendency to glamour. Some great Ones have therefore been said to keep the bodies in which they had attained their fifth Initiation for centuries. Their expression is essentially a single line of Living Monadic Fire that incorporates the entire threefold form within its purpose.

The information in figure 22 is considered from the point of view of the upward aspiration of humanity. One can also think in terms of a downward projection of the energies from Shambhala in order to energise the entire process of human evolution to produce the full flowering of the Sambhogakāya Flower at the third Initiation. In this case there is an inverted pentagram, where Stages 5b and 1c represent the feet of the energisation process. They direct the energies from the Logoic Mind to the higher mental plane in order to liberate these enlightened Souls from the bondage of form altogether. All Life is thereby to be abstracted into the cosmic ethers, bringing with it the gain of the entire evolutionary process.

What is effectively produced are two arms of a swastika composed of pentads of energies. In this case a north-south direction is indicated (see figure 23), whereby cosmic Fire is directed to the domain of crystallised Fire that represents the three worlds of human livingness. There is a process hinted at here concerning the liberation of planetary *kuṇḍalinī.* This is effected upon a large scale when the epoch of group, and then mass Initiation, is to occur, such as will eventuate in the New Age. This will be heralded by a large number of disciples taking their first Initiation simultaneously. With them will be a sprinkling of Initiates of higher degree that will also take their Initiations. Such is the process that will produce the externalisation of the Hierarchy proper, and the eventual building of the New Jerusalem on earth.

There would also be another similar pair of pentads to consider that is oriented in and east-west direction, whose purpose concerns the externalisation of the energies from the cosmic Christ needed to awaken the Love-Wisdom principle in humanity, and its consequent service arena.

The manifestation of the arms and legs of these pentads are in continuous motion, moving the swastikas accordingly. The overall picture is quite complicated because the 'arms and legs' are not of equal size in terms of energy qualifications. Much depends upon humanity's ability to handle the input of energies and to their response to the associated qualities. The dark brotherhood also have their opposing swastikas trying to counter the main thrust of the incoming energies.

What is presented in figure 23 is part of the esoteric explanation of the nature and qualities of the pentagram, which is but an elaboration of the constitution of Brahmā. The five planes of Brahmā are from the ātmic plane downwards. They are concerned with the creative process in Nature, as part of the Mother's department. These planes direct the reified attributes of the Logoic Mind into manifestation.

The information given earlier concerning the *organs of sensation and of action* can also be added to complete the information concerning these *vayūs*. Prāṇic circulation is illustrated in figure 24 and given further information in Table 19.

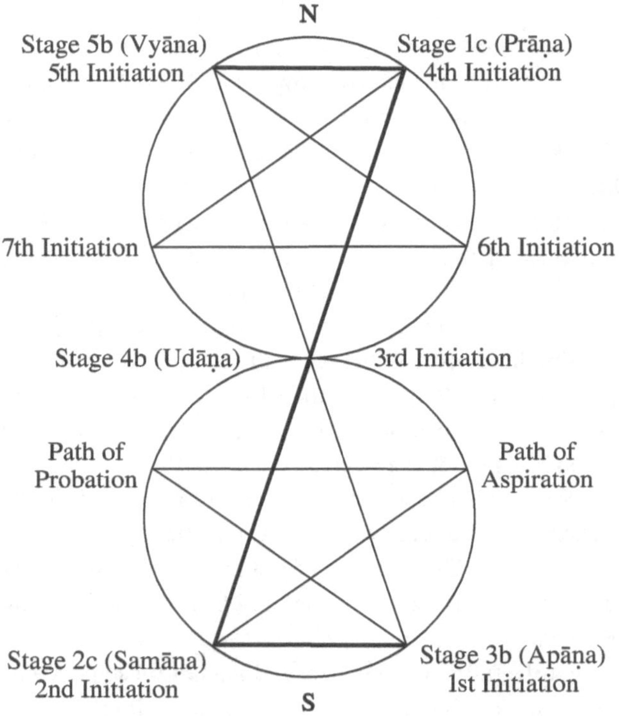

Figure 23: The interrelated pentads

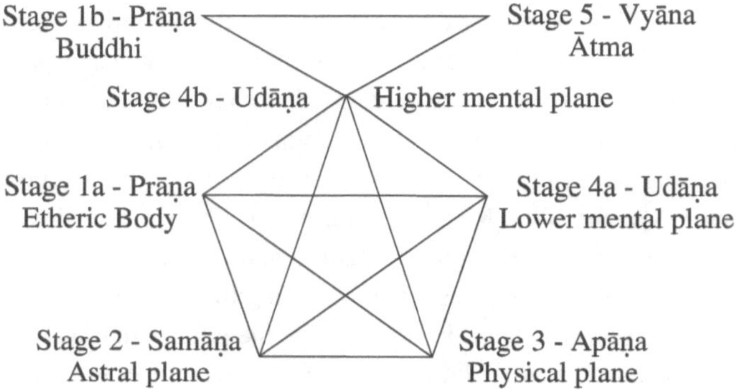

Figure 24: The summary of the *prāṇic* circulation

Stage 1a – Prāṇa

Organ of Action: Genitals – related to touch, astral plane and *buddhi.*
Gives birth to Son.
The etheric body.

Stage 1b – Prāṇa

Sense: Taste – to be fully developed by sixth Root Race.
Buddhic plane.

Stage 2 – Samāna

Organ of Action: Hands – grasping, related to touch.
Sense: Touch, fully developed during Atlantean era.
Astral plane.

Stage 3 – Apāna

Organ of Action: Anus – excretion, related to:
1 – smell, 2 – eating, 3 – digestion, 4 – Thought.
Sense: Hearing, fully developed during Lemurian era.
Dense physical plane.

Stage 4a – Udāna

Organ of Action: Legs – locomotion, related to sight.
Lower mental plane.

Stage 4b – Udāna

Organ of action: 1. Mouth – eating, related to taste.
2. *Speaking* – related to hearing.
Sense. Sight, primarily a fifth Root Race development.
Higher mental plane.

Stage 5 – Vyāna

Sense. Smell, to be fully developed by the seventh Root Race.
Ātmic plane.

Table 19: Notes to figure 24

All light comes
from the golden Orb
in the Heart of Life,
veiled by the cross
fixed in space,
and in the skull
sumptuously crowned
with thorns –
a laurel of honour,
glorifying the sacrifice
of the Son of man
in the earthly realm.
Appraise, applaud, salute
the victorious One.
Come and greet Him.
He is the resurrected Christ,
the anointed Saviour,
the coming Buddha,
and the enlightened man.

10

The Nature of the Christ

The gospel of John tells us plainly that Christ-Jesus was the bearer of the Light of the spiritual Sun that is the source of illumination for all Life on this earth. Jesus states:

> I am the light of the world: he that followeth me shall not walk in darkness, but shall have the light of life.[1]

Light is seen as the illumination that is the light of knowledge, conscious awareness of all knowable things, or enquiry into what is unknown. Esoterically, light also refers to the transmutative energy that resides at the heart of every atom. The destructive potency of nuclear fusion or fission and its constructive potency when it is controlled in our nuclear reactors are also revealed in light. This indicates the power of this energy on a purely material level, but the effects of Light are found on all planes of perception.

Light is the radiance of inner achievement (of which humanity's harnessing of the energy of the atom is the outer symbol). It is the demonstration of the glory – the magnetic potency of an enlightened person's aura that heals the diseased, stimulates the depressed, and gives

1 *John 8:12*. See also *John 9:5*.

succour to all forms. Light (and its Rays) is the energy that emanates from the Fiery furnace of every sun, both in the objective and subjective universes. When visioned by the illumined seer it is said to be 'brighter than a thousand suns', the intensity of which puts to shade all other forms of light. The darkness of the night sky thus but veils the intensity of the Light from abstract space. Space here can be considered an Entity, the auric sphere of an absolute Logos.

That all people are expressions of Light is provided by a statement in Matthew, where Jesus told His audience that: 'Ye are the light of the world...Let your light so shine before men, that they may see your good works, and glorify your Father which is in heaven'.[2] The Christ embodies the collective expression, and highest pinnacle, of this Light 'of the world'. He is the illuminating Sun of humanity's radiance, expressed in the kingdom of Souls and by all illumined light bearers (Hierarchy) upon this planet. The Divinity within each person can be considered a Ray of this Sun. Humanity thus have the capacity to demonstrate the potency of its glory, but most people live in the shade of the darkened light of their desires, attachments and mental-emotions. Such collective darkness is not pleasant to perceive, nevertheless the potential is there for great radiance.

When a seer receives a vision of this Sun, it therefore comes complete with a compassionate understanding of the qualities demonstrated by the various Rays of the collective Soul of humanity. The seer also sees the resultant world-picture of the needed task at hand to factually demonstrate this Sun's potency. Therein the past's dark attributes, the present opportunity and the future glory are seen in perspective.

Jesus' discourse with the Scribes and Pharisees

In His discourse with the Scribes and Pharisees[3] Jesus tells them: 'Ye are from beneath; I am from above: ye are of this world; I am not of this world'[4] (and its conditionings). The question that arises here is, *'beneath'* and *'above'* what?

---

2 Matt. *5:14-16.*

3 This section explains further aspects of the dialogue originally presented under the heading entitled: 'Accusations against Jesus' in chapter eight.

4 *John 8:23.*

He earlier said to them 'I go my way, and ye shall seek me, and shall die in your sins: whither I go, ye cannot come'.[5] If they seek Him then they are aspirants to the Mysteries, though the Christ-Nature is not yet born in them, thus they do not and cannot yet recognise Him, or His 'Father'. To 'die in your sins' means to 'die' in *karma* by the perpetuation of the actions that keep one tied to the realm of birth and death – to the dense physical, astral and mental worlds that are ruled by 'that old serpent, called the devil, and Satan'.[6] These realms thus constitute the world that is 'beneath'. The Christ resides in the higher, exalted, realms of perception that are completely free from material *karma* and of 'death'. This is the world 'above', to which the aspirants cannot yet go.

What stands between these worlds is the domain of the abstract Mind, wherein resides the Souls that are the radiant suns within humanity. The kingdom of Souls is but an expression of the 'light of the world'. They are thus energised by the radiant aura of the Christ. He moulds this kingdom like a potter utilising the great wheel of the heavens as it cycles through time. The energies from the Heart of the Sun pour through Him, empowering the potency of His compassion. He thus 'stands above' the domain of earthy Life but works with it and through it. As a high degree Initiate directly overshadowed by the Christ, Jesus also shares in the 'moulding process'. The Scribes and Pharisees, on the other hand, had not even gained a perception of this process and hence were 'beneath it'. They were bound to *karma* – their 'sins' prevented their light to 'shine before men' in such a way as to glorify their 'Father which is in heaven'.[7] To 'glorify the Father' necessitates doing service activities along the Initiation path that increases the brilliance and potency of their subjective Suns. Their Souls then become 'supernovas' at the attainment of the fourth Initiation.

The Scribes and Pharisees (who symbolise the world's religious aspirants) could not comprehend the meaning of the Master's statements, thus they asked Him directly 'who art thou?'[8] He answered this question

---

5 *John 8:21.*

6 *Rev. 12:9.*

7 This 'Father' can here signify their Souls, Monads, or the planetary Logos.

8 *John 8:25.*

somewhat cryptically – 'Even *the same* that I said unto you from the beginning'. 'The beginning' does not only refer to His earlier statements, such as, 'I am the light of the world', but also to the statement:

> In the beginning was the Word, and the Word was with God, and the Word was God.[9]

The phrase 'the Word' here is a translation of the Greek term Logos, which is what expresses a thought, as well as the thought itself. It is generally interpreted as the rational principal of the universe – Divine Reason, and theologically, it is seen as the second person in the Trinity, the 'Son of God'.

The Word

Esoterically, 'the Word' is the Sound of Creation – the emanatory reverberation of wave patterns of mantric harmonies, chords, songs and stanzas that sustain all Being. Later, first Ray mantras will be intoned that will abstract all into what was before 'the foundation of the world'. In meditation texts the significance of 'the Word' is of prime importance, taking three major attributes, each with different though interrelated connotations. They are *Aūṁ, Oṁ* and the *nameless Sound.* Each symbolises a different attribute of the triune Deity.

The *Aūṁ* symbolises the energies of the *Mother,* of procreation, producing the manifestation of the corporeal world. It indicates the energies pertaining to the *past,* and therefore is 'the Word' that 'in the beginning was'. It summarises the qualities of the archetypal Mind (conceived of as a trinity) that are reflected into manifested space, thus forming the seal of Solomon (the hexagram). It is thus the Word of the creative Logos that caused the precipitation of the manifest universe. When sounded, it leads to bondage in matter or it helps mould or control material forms. All of Nature resonates with this sound in its myriad combinations or intonations. It is thereby specifically the Word that is embodied by the *deva* kingdom. Thus it relates to *activity* (the third Ray aspect) in the material world that eventually causes the appearance of the intellect in the forms that can express it.

---

9 *John 1:1.*

The *Oṁ* symbolises the forces of the Son, of consciousness, therefore that associated with the evolution of Love-Wisdom. It initiates what pertains to and sustains the present, and also the resolve back to 'the Father'. It is effectively the Word that 'was with God', the direct expression of the qualities of the Christ-Nature. Oṁ is therefore a Word of transcendence. It empowers the objective of the evolutionary process. When rightly sounded by a person who is attuned and aligned with his/her higher self it is able to release that person from the bondage of matter. As it is the Word of the Son in incarnation, it resides eternally in the hearts of all enlightened beings and resounds in all their thoughts, words and deeds. Even the act of breathing is said to be the unconscious voicing of this mantra. The Hindus give it the name *prāṇava,* the vehicle of the vital energy *(prāṇa)* or breath of the various 'winds' *(vayū),* the Elements constituting the consciousness-aspect of Being, the energy of the Rays of Light.

The *Oṁ* can be considered the vehicle of the Mind, for the Mind and *prāṇa* are said to be extensions of each other. It is the Word that specifically governs the development of humanity. Humans therefore can be considered purveyors of the Logoic Breath once they manifest their enlightened attributes. It can be symbolised thus: Ⓜ becoming ⨀.

The *nameless Sound* conveys the Will or Power of the Father aspect of Deity. It is the forward-projecting energy and also destroyer of the form that is only known by those that have attained the higher Initiations. It is the Word that is given by the Spirit/Soul, and relates to the future – the complete Identification with, or Absorption into, 'God'. This provides the meaning of the statement: 'and the Word was God'.[10]

Exoterically, it is the syllable 'A', which is said to synthesise all the elements of the other letters. Mahāyāna Buddhists state that the major context of their philosophy is contained in the symbolic 100,000 stanzas of the Prajñāpāramitā Sūtra (meaning 'Transcendental Wisdom'), and this can be condensed into one stanza, and then finally into the letter 'A'. Note also that in Hebrew, the first letter of their alphabet (aleph) symbolises the nameless Sound.

10 *John 1:1.*

The Christ therefore specifically embodies the second letter of the sacred Word. There are numerous other mantras used as invocations to Deities, other Elemental forces in Nature, or to invoke any of the Powers latent in us. The triple Word is, however, what precipitates the conceived Creation, sustains it, and then resolves it back to its emanating Source.

Such esoteric implications were incomprehensible to the Scribes and Pharisees, nevertheless, Jesus strove to indicate the method by which they could come to understand. Thus He stated:

> When ye have lifted up the Son of man, then shall ye know that I am *he,* and *that* I do nothing of myself; but as my Father hath taught me, I speak these things.[11]

This statement does not specifically refer to his future crucifixion, nor does it give the Jews of that time the awareness that Jesus was the Christ. Specifically, it implicates the *elevation* of consciousness, the Love-Wisdom principle (via the *piṅgalā nāḍī),* until it is crucified on the cross of compassionate understanding. (As explained previously regarding the phrase: 'As Moses lifted up the serpent in the wilderness, even so must the Son of man be lifted up'.[12] The Love-Wisdom principle is 'the Son of man' for it is the result of humanity's evolutionary attainment.[13] Only then can the Christ be known for what He is, for those that undergo this 'lifting up' process will assume the attitude of all Bodhisattvas, who can say with sincerity: 'I do nothing of myself; but as my Father hath taught me'. ('The Father' here is the *guru* or Master.) In the awakened Bodhisattva the concept of personal self no longer exists, for all is seen as a continuum of divine energies. The Bodhisattva becomes a purified vehicle of that energy, which is an ocean of Bliss poured into, and emanating from, the emptied receptacle of the Bodhisattva's Heart and Mind. The Christ is the premier Bodhisattva example that all others follow.

---

11 *John 8:28.*

12 *John 3:14.*

13 Further implications of this statement will be discussed in chapter 11, in relation to the phrase 'the sign of the Son of man'.

The Son (the Love-Wisdom aspect, as exemplified by the Oṁ) will therefore free people from of their material *karma* when 'lifted up' in the manner that Christ-Jesus implied. Therefore, He could say to those that 'believed on him': 'If ye continue in my word, *then* are ye my disciples indeed; and ye shall know the truth, and the truth shall make you free'.[14] The *'word'* is the mantra that resonates in the Hearts of all His disciples. It is what makes them disciples, indeed, and allows them to *know* the Truth. Such Truth is something that cannot be known by merely listening to His sayings. (This was demonstrated by the 'deafness' of the Scribes and Pharisees, causing Jesus to say: 'He that is of God heareth God's words: ye therefore hear them not, because ye are not of God'.[15])

The sanctity of the Word (the silent Voice within[16]) and the cultivation of the ability to listen to it can only be known by actual internal experience, wrought within the crucible of the transmutative process by the divine alchemy that can be accomplished by us all. It is the result of the sublimation of our base natures by its infusion with the elixir of Life, and the elevation of the resultant 'essence' by means of a spiritual fractional distillation, into the 'secret place' wherein resides the Christ. (The fount of all Love and Wisdom.) The result is ambrosia, 'the hidden manna'.[17] This fount of Truth eliminates all sin because all actions become thereby transmuted into compassionate undertakings, as there is naught in the material world that can oppose the 'Word of the Lord' residing in the Bodhisattva's Heart. 'The Word' is transcendence itself, also residing in the heart of all forms.

In its triple connotation, the Word can thus be expressed as shown in figure 25.

---

14 *John 8:31-32.*

15 *John 8:47.*

16 *Pratyakṣa,* subjective perception.

17 *Rev. 2:17* – He that hath an ear, let him hear what the Spirit saith unto the churches; To him that overcometh will I give to eat of the hidden manna, and will give him a white stone, and in the stone a new name written, which no man knoweth saving he that receiveth *it.*

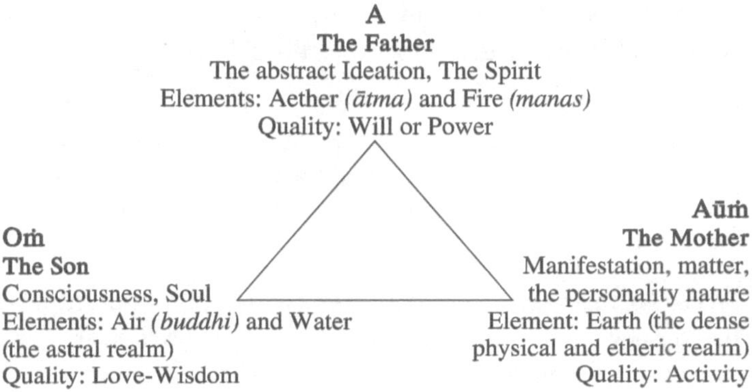

Figure 25: The attributes of Father-Son-Mother

The significance of Abraham

The dialogue between Christ-Jesus and the uncomprehending Jews continued, until eventually Jesus stated:

> Your father Abraham rejoiced to see my day: and he saw it, and was glad.[18]

The name Abraham means 'father of a multitude'. He was literally father of all the Jews, and helped bring into fruition the characteristics of the fifth Root Race. Abraham is the effective symbol of the Soul of the present intellectually polarised humanity.[19] This is implied by the fact that 'the Lord' asked Abraham to 'Lift up now thine eyes; and look from the place where thou art northward, and southward, and eastward, and westward'.[20] Esoterically, these four directions signify the directions: upwards to the 'kingdom of God', downwards to the domain of the little ones, eastwards to the Heart of Life, and westwards to the field of service that represents humanity. The directions can also be

18 *John 8:56.*

19 Here humanity is symbolised by the character traits of the Jewish nation. This is also implied by the term 'generation' that Jesus uses throughout the Gospels in reference to them, the meaning of which will be explained later.

20 *Gen. 13:14.*

related to the four Elements conveyed by a *nāḍī,* as depicted in figure 18. It is the place where these 'four directions' intersect.

'God' continues, saying:

> For all the land which thou seest, to thee will I give it, and to thy seed forever. And I will make thy seed as the dust of the earth: so that if a man can number the dust of the earth, *then* shall thy seed also be numbered.[21]

What Abraham saw was the vast extent of the realm of the Mind (as well as the obvious terrestrial realm) which humanity was entering into, the use of which would eventually allow humanity to (mathematically) 'number the dust of the earth' if they willed it.

Later, the Lord asked Abraham to: 'Look now toward heaven, and tell the stars, if thou be able to number them: and he said unto him, So shall thy seed be'.[22] 'Stars' can also symbolise the Souls in heaven, for many ancient religions thought of the deceased incarnating amongst or as them.[23] Note that in both accounts we have the idea of 'numbering' – of the 'dust of the earth', and the 'stars in heaven'. This is important, for it has reference to one of the major keys (the numerical key) possessed by Initiates to comprehend Divine providence and the laws of Being. That Abraham could do so ('And he believed in the LORD; and he counted it to him for righteousness'[24]) indicates the degree of his Initiate understanding. From a purely literal viewpoint the difference between the number of stars in 'heaven' that are observable to the naked eye and the number of dust particles are seemingly irreconcilable; there are about 6,000 of the former (for they have been counted) and countless trillions of the latter. The phrases therefore must be interpreted from an esoteric viewpoint. Counting the stars also implies that Abraham learnt the astrological science, which was well established in the Middle East when Abraham is purported to have lived.

Abraham was also asked by 'the Almighty God' to 'walk before me, and be thou perfect',[25] which only an enlightened being can do,

---

21 *Gen. 13:15-16.*

22 *Gen. 15:5.*

23 Egyptian Pharaohs, for instance, were said to become one of them after they died.

24 *Gen. 15:6.*

25 *Gen. 17:1.*

after passing testings for Initiation. This allowed Abraham to be as stated: 'a father of many nations...and kings shall come out of thee. And I will establish my covenant between me and thee and thy seed after thee in their generations for an everlasting covenant'.[26] Here the term 'kings' refers not only to temporal rulers, but spiritual ones also. They are Masters of Wisdom, 'perfected' men, with their Head centre (the 'crown of glory') fully vibrant, pulsating with radiant golden light. Note however, that the qualifications needed to attain Initiation in those days were considerably less than now. Also, the degree of attainment attained by Abraham would not have exceeded the third Initiation.

The 'seeds' are the generations of the 'sons of men' that are to follow Abraham by incarnating into the world, as part of the Soul-Group of which he is the 'father'. By being an enlightened member of the kingdom of Souls he is able to consciously 'walk before' (the kingdom of) 'God', and thus become 'perfect' by becoming receptive to the exalted energies from 'God'. Because Abraham had such an intimate communion with 'God', the Jews gave him the title 'friend of God', as in *Isaiah 41:8* and *II Chron. 20:7.* This also implies that Abraham was able to directly bear the first Ray (Will energy from Shambhala) and to wield it so that he could rightly lead the chosen people according to the dictates from 'God'.[27]

When Jesus told the Jews that Abraham rejoiced to see the day when He was incarnate, He was referring to something that could be understood by a perusal of the scriptures. It refers to Abraham's son *Isaac,* who was promised to Abraham even though his wife (Sarah) was barren and 'well stricken' with age. Hence it was something that Abraham long looked forward to, and he certainly rejoiced when he saw that day.

> And God said, Sarah thy wife shall bear thee a son indeed; and thou shalt call his name Isaac: and I will establish my covenant with him for an everlasting covenant, *and* with his seed after him.[28]

---

26 *Gen. 17:5-7.*

27 Abraham was consequently a member of the Manu's department (explained in my book *The Constitution of Shambhala,* Vol. 1) within Hierarchy.

28 *Gen. 17:19.*

Isaac was therefore to inherit his father's direct covenant with 'God'. In a sense, Isaac was destined to replace his father Abraham as the Soul of 'many nations'. Significantly, Isaac was born when Abraham was a symbolic 100 years old and when Sarah was 90. The number 100 refers to the ending of one major cycle of activity. It is the number signifying great perfection, whilst the number 90 is that of Initiation.[29] At 90, it was of course near physically impossible for Sarah to have borne a child, but the symbolism of the number is appropriate because it signified that this couple had passed the needed Initiation testings allowing 'God' to intercede in this way. The 'son' symbolises the second Ray purpose manifesting. This was the next stage of evolution for the Israelites, an attribute for Isaac to foster amongst them.

The most prominent incident in Isaac's life occurred in the twenty-second chapter of Genesis, where Abraham was told to offer Isaac as a 'burnt offering' upon a mountain that was to be chosen for him by the Lord. As explained in my former book,[30] a 'mountain' refers to the attainment of the third Initiation, or of absorption into the abstract awareness of the higher Mind (the Soul). It is important to note in this context that the mountain in question was called *Jehovah-jireh,* the 'mount of the Lord'.[31] On the symbolic mount of Abraham's spirituality (his Soul therefore) the Lord asked Abraham (who was to be the 'father of many nations') to make a sacrifice that would allow this Initiation to be accomplished. The sacrifice was to be his son Issac, who was the seed that would produce many 'kings of people'.[32] The seed of the Love-Wisdom principle is the result of the symbolic 100 years of development and expression of Abraham's life, of his exemplary covenant with 'God'. Isaac as such, was literally a 'son of God', as is implied by the words:

---

29 See my book *The Astrological and Numerological Keys to the Secret Doctrine,* Vol. 1 for an explanation of this numerological code.

30 *Meditation and the Initiation Process.*

31 *Gen. 22:14.*

32 *Gen. 17:16.* The term 'kings' here does not just refer to Masters, but also to those who appropriately develop their minds, and consequently begin to awaken their Head centres.

> And the LORD visited Sarah as he had said, and the LORD did unto Sarah as he had spoken. For Sarah conceived, and bare Abraham a son in his old age.[33]

Hence we see that 'the Lord' effectively procreated the son that was to be attributed to Abraham (as also happened to Mary, Jesus' mother). That son was later to be offered up in place of the sacrificial lamb, to atone for the sins of humanity. The Lord, however, sent an angel from 'out of heaven' in time to save Isaac, and presented 'a ram caught in a thicket by his horns'[34] in Isaac's place. The development of Love-Wisdom is necessary if the Head centre is to properly awaken via the way of the Heart's expression. (The *piṅgalā nāḍī* flow of energies.)

In this story much symbolism is seen that was later to be embodied by the dispensation of Jesus. For instance, when Jesus first appears on the world-stage as an adult, John the Baptist introduces Jesus by the words: 'Behold the Lamb of God, which taketh away the sin of the world'.[35] This thereby immediately refers to the story of Isaac and Abraham, in that Jesus was to fulfil the task that Abraham's intended sacrifice could only symbolically express. The 'son of man' (Abraham's son) that was also the 'son of God' could not at that time be sacrificed for the atonement of the *karma,* the 'sin of the world'. This, the advent of Jesus would later allow. However, in Abraham's time the Wisdom principle had yet to evolve in people's hearts (as was explained in chapter two) before the Love aspect that the Christ would bring could fully manifest and begin to cleanse the world of much of its materialistic *karma*. (This is the gain of the resultant compassionate-understanding of the world's disciples.)

Because Abraham was willing to sacrifice his 'only son'[36] for the Lord, he could be blessed.

> I will bless thee, and in multiplying I will multiply thy seed as the stars of the heaven, and as the sand that is upon the sea shore...And

---

33 *Gen. 21:1-2.*

34 *Gen. 22:13.*

35 *John 1:29.*

36 *Gen. 22:16.*

> in thy seed shall all the nations of the earth be blessed; because thou hast obeyed my voice.[37]

Such 'blessing', as a consequence of obeying the Voice from the Lord, is in fact an Initiation into the Mysteries that 'God' could then reveal to him. Paul refers to this incident when he states that 'By faith Abraham, when he was tried, offered up Isaac...his only begotten son, Of whom it was said, That in Isaac shall thy seed be called: Accounting that God was able to raise him up, even from the dead'.[38] Here is seen a subtle reference to the idea that what Abraham conceived in Spirit, Jesus actually embodied in form, in His resurrection 'from the dead'. His bodily appearance after his crucifixion, as exemplified by the story of 'doubting Thomas'[39] who could touch Him, is one of the keynotes of the aftermath of Jesus' life.

When Jesus stated that 'your father Abraham rejoiced to see my day',[40] He was also referring to a *previous incarnation of His, as Isaac*, and the related karmic implications. Christ-Jesus was indeed from the 'seed' of Abraham, whose actions would eventually allow 'all of the nations of the earth' to 'be blessed'. Jesus indicated that even in Abraham's time the seed of the future work of the Christ was sown and the general gist of His work established in symbolic form with the blessing of 'the Lord'. It also implied that, like all beings, He also had to evolve (by means of rebirth and the Initiation process) the necessary equipment to transmit and apply constructively such a potent energy as the 'Love of God'. What was formerly a symbolic enactment on the mountaintop had to be later expressed openly on the cross of Life, whereon Jesus was crucified. Abraham's willingness to sacrifice his only son was thereby materially fulfilled by this act at the time when it was appropriate.

Again demonstrating their blindness to the esoteric nature of His doctrine, the Scribes and Pharisees asked 'Thou art not yet fifty years

---

37 *Gen. 22:17-18.*

38 *Hebrews 11:17-20.*

39 *John 20:27.*

40 *John 8:56.*

old, and hast thou seen Abraham?'[41] Their materialistic view was that it is obviously physically impossible for Jesus to have witnessed this event. Christ-Jesus, however, in the manner of all Masters, was not concerned with directly answering the questions of those that queried Him. Rather, He presented seeds that had the capability of stimulating the esoteric insight of His disciples. The seeds would then allow them to develop their own awareness via the validity of the truths presented. In answering this question He therefore presented a new line of investigation regarding the nature of His essential divinity and its relation to Abraham. Thus He said:

> Verily, verily, I say unto you, Before Abraham was, I am.[42]

The ability to say 'I am' implies a self-assertion of individuality, an expression of the powers of the intellect. It is what allows the person to circumscribe a sphere or limit of possible attainment, which makes him a definite corporeal entity, as was shown in figure 4. This is the statement of a Creative Deity, of that aspect that can commune with humanity or any other incarnate self-conscious group of entities.

I am That I am

In stating 'Before Abraham was, I am' Christ-Jesus conveyed an esoteric truth: that before the time of Abraham He had already evolved His consciousness to the point wherein the intellect was dominant. This also implies that he was effectively the father of that principle for humanity, in a similar sense that Abraham was the father of the nations that were to bear it. The Christ is the foremost of the human collective-Soul, the flower of its evolution. At any stage of evolution He embodies the aspect that humanity in general is still striving to attain.

This statement also has a reference to the 'God' that appeared before Moses, Who stated 'I AM THAT I AM',[43] and Who told Moses in the same passage to tell the children of Israel that 'I AM hath sent me unto you'.

---

41 *John 8:57.*

42 *John 8:58.*

43 *Exodus 3:14.*

The statement I AM THAT I AM, which is an adaptation of the information presented in figure 1, can be depicted thus:

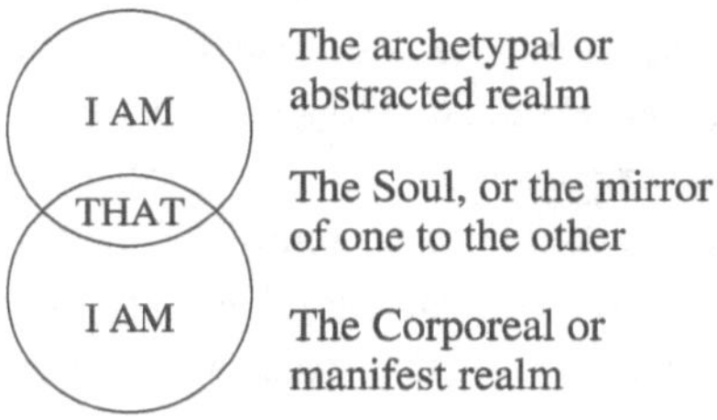

Figure 26: I am That I am

Here the I AM energy (or the Being-ness of 'God') can be seen to be projected in two directions (up or down) via the phrases I AM THAT and THAT I AM. The phrase I AM THAT as a downward projection indicates the Creative potency of the Logoic Mind. The THAT represents the limit of the Logoic descent of Mind, for the mental plane (whereon resides the human Soul) is the cosmic dense physical plane, the higher correspondence of our mineral kingdom. The further downward projection comes from the domain of the Soul, where this kingdom manifests as the THAT for the evolving personalities in *saṃsāra*.

The upward phrase I AM THAT represents the aspiration of humanity to gain enlightened Consciousness (i.e., knowledge of 'God'). The THAT can at first be considered the kingdom of Souls, then Hierarchy, and finally the Logoic Seat of Power in Shambhala. From another perspective, it can be considered as neither one nor the other, the 'golden mean' of the expression of the All. THAT then represents the Buddhist *śūnyatā* or Void. Humanity effectively aspires to this state of Beingness, for the plane *buddhi* (the domain of *śūnyatā)* is their true esoteric home. This Seat of Power is an energy field that is an open Door to Identification with the Logoic Mind *(dharmakāya).*

When the Logos stated: 'I AM THAT I AM...this is my name for ever, and this is my memorial unto all generations'[44] He therefore indicated that His Consciousness was inclusive of the Minds of all beings, of what is 'above' and what is 'below' – the THAT. What is

44 *Exodus 3:14-15.*

'below' is therefore viewed via the kingdom of Souls, or via Hierarchy. Those beings residing 'below' can only extend their conscious awareness into the THAT in terms of group consciousness, for the THAT represents universal Awareness. (The levels of transformation of consciousness into Identification with the All that is cosmos.) Paradoxically, in doing so the Initiate inevitably establishes a focal point for such Awareness (the I AM) that represents a Logoic dispensation, which distinguishes that One from all other such spheres of Activity (such as are suns).

One should note that a universe, world sphere or solar system manifests because Deity is 'imperfect', in the sense that the material world and its entities (which Deity embodies) are imperfect. The seeds of the Divine in the world must be nurtured and exalted, and so to give birth to THAT which is productive of the higher I AM. For this reason a Logos sends into incarnation His 'Son', the Christ principle, which accomplishes Divine Purpose by engendering Light and Love within those units of consciousness that have developed self-awareness. They can then evolve an understanding of the nature of That which is not the self, and to wholeheartedly embrace It.

One should here also look to the statement:

> I am Alpha and Omega, the beginning and the ending, saith the Lord, which is, and which was, and which is to come, the Almighty.[45]

When the 'beginning and the ending' is viewed diagrammatically then it implies the 'cycle of time' ('which is, and which was, and which is to come'), which was depicted in figure 14 by the serpent biting its own tail. The beginning of evolution, when Deity said I AM, was therefore synonymous with the emanation of the serpent energy *(kuṇḍalinī),* the creative potency that needs to be evoked to manifest the entire world-sphere. (This is the higher correspondence of a *yogin* using *kuṇḍalinī* to manifest *siddhis).* The ending will also result in the sounding of the I AM, but this time by the self-conscious entities that have evolved on that world sphere. The I AM sound (which is but a way of denoting sounding out the Aūṁ) therefore sparks a release of the serpent energy, which symbolically causes the cosmic serpent to swallow its own tail. The cycle is complete. Eventually the serpent

45 *Rev. 1:8.*

sheds its skin, thus regenerating itself, though on a higher turn of the spiral. The serpent eventually evolves into a Fiery Dragon of Wisdom.

When THAT is placed into figure 14 (the cycle of time) it incorporates the space that is enclosed by the serpent. This space is symbolised by the *square*, which denotes matter, the formed world, the Seat or Throne of 'God'. This Seat is the base or support of His Power and Being. It manifests as the *mūlādhāra chakra,* thus:

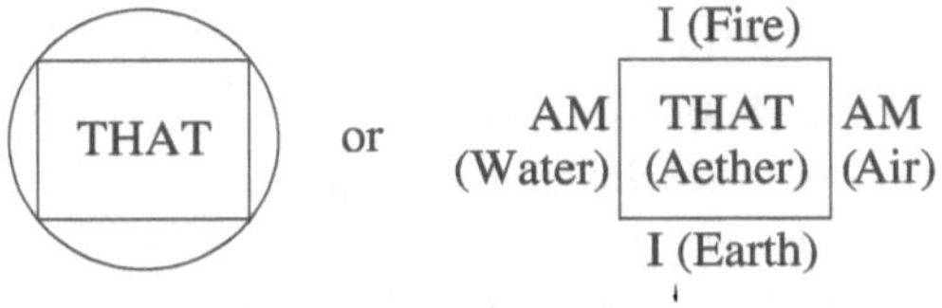

Figure 27: The THAT

The four sides of the square signify the manifestation of the four Elements: Earth, Water, Fire and Air, which are synthesised by the fifth Element (Aether/*ātma).* This produces a further elaboration of the mantra 'I AM THAT I AM'. Establishing this Throne is the cause and result of spiritual or cosmic *karma*. Logoic Mind (the I AM) is the Door veiling the Mysteries of Being, whilst comprehending THAT is the key that can be utilised to unlock that Door.

This sphere of evolution (the cycle of time) can also be symbolised by: ⊙, where the THAT manifests as the central point, the seed of Power for the entire expression of Being. This symbol signifies the nature of an atom, a cell, a planetary sphere, or a blazing sun, for the sphere is the result of the expression of individuality. The I AM becomes the circumference. It is therefore what binds, circumscribes, giving form to what is formless. The sphere inevitably becomes a source of Light that will irradiate a world sphere with its illumination. The I AM then becomes expressive of the whole, extending to the THAT, which becomes the mantra I AM THAT (which is another form of the Oṁ). Later the experience of THAT I AM manifests, which is but a version of the *nameless Sound,* the expression of the essential Integrity of the liberated being with the Logos. The phrase 'I AM THAT I AM' relates therefore to the completed Word of the Creative Deity (the Aūṁ) within which this entire world play is enacted.

What integrates the two versions of the THAT is the Christ-energy by means of which: 'All things were made....In him was life; and the life was the light of men'. This is the light of consciousness. The passage continues: 'And the light shineth in darkness; and the darkness comprehended it not'.[46] The darkness signifies *saṃsāra,* humanity's own corporeal nature, and more specifically the astral realm created by people's desire-imaginations over the millennia of human evolution.

When Christ-Jesus identified with the I AM, He essentially stated that He was Deity. This was sheer blasphemy to the Jews, so 'they took up stones to cast at him: but Jesus hid himself, and went out of the temple'[47] and thus escaped their wrath. Even though they were standing in 'God's' temple they could not understand the basic esoteric truth that Jesus was endeavouring to convey.

By His previous statement ('Ye are from beneath; I am from above'[48]) we see that He specifically identifies with the I AM as it exists 'above' (in the archetypal or abstracted realms). The objective of the Christ, Who is the Word that 'was made flesh',[49] is to bring down (from the THAT) and anchor this I AM in the material world ('Satan's seat') and thus finally claim it for Deity. It is the beginning of the process that will result in the perfection of manifestation by the exaltation, the uplifting of those who are 'below' and who govern the material world. The mantra THAT I AM then incorporates the all that is manifestation, from above-down. When Christ-Jesus stated that His objective was: 'And I, if I be lifted up from the earth, will draw all men unto me',[50] then He signified that I AM THAT will manifest from below upwards.

The I AM principle thus became completely embodied 'in the flesh' of Jesus, so to begin to fully incarnate in the material realms. His purpose therefore was to reveal to humanity the meaning of THAT, and consequently the I AM that it veils. Such a descent of the Divine principle did not manifest at the time of Moses. The children of Israel could then only commune with it indirectly, through the mediation

46 *John 1:3-5.*

47 *John 8:59.*

48 *John 8:23.*

49 *John 1:14.*

50 *John 12:32.*

of Moses, who could not see 'His face'. It hovered above the earth in a symbolic 'burning bush' and was thus abstracted from humanity. By the time of Jesus, humanity had generally evolved their intellects. This allowed the development of the Love-Wisdom that would impel humanity from the stage where they could assertively pronounce I AM,[51] to when they would be able to unequivocally say I AM THAT. The Light within a form (the I AM), fanned by the energy of Love, allows one's consciousness to escape the confines of that form to embrace all beings – as a blazing sun. This is what produces the expression of THAT.

All of the major religions, past and present, provide teachings concerning Deity as embodied Light. This is often exemplified by a clash between Light and darkness as the major aspect of their ontological or soteriological doctrines. For instance, we have the teachings of the Parsees (Zoroastrians), with their concept of Ahura Mazda (Ormazd) who embodied Light itself; those concerning Apollo, the Greek god of wisdom who daily conveyed the sun disc across the skies in his chariot; and the Mithraic cult of the Persian, Greek, and Roman empires, with its emphasis on celestial Light. (It was once a major rival of Christianity.) There is also the Pleroma of the various Gnostic schools; Ra (or Amun-Ra), the sun god and major Deity of the Egyptians (of whom the Pharaohs were said to be the earthly embodiments); the Ādityas and Surya of the Hindus; Amitābha, the Buddha of ineffable Light of the Buddhists. South America provided the all-important sun gods of the Aztecs, Mayans, and Incas – Tezecatlipoca, Kinebaham, and Inti. The teachings were either in preparation for, or expressions of, the time when 'light would be made flesh' and the 'light of the world' thereby made manifest amongst humanity.

Covenant with 'God'

Light is an emanation of the third aspect of Deity. Love is an embodiment of the second aspect. Light can be considered the radiance from the interrelation between Love and Mind. Together they manifest as the Blood that flows through the Veins *(nāḍīs)* of a Logos, whilst the Son

51 Such self-identity, in its most separative form, is exemplified by our present materialistic civilisation, with its existentially focussed philosophy.

distributes this Blood flow to the sum of the generations of cellular Lives that can be nourished by it. The Son therefore is the Heart of Life, the pump for the Love that sustains all beings. The four directions in space are the ventricles and auricles of the entire system.

The symbolism of blood is profound, as the reader by now well knows. This symbolism and all related rites was an integral part of the Covenant with 'God'. We have, for instance, the idea that the people of Israel shall not be able to lie down (and rest) until they have drunk 'the blood of the slain'.[52] All rites depicted in the Bible (and their versions in many other religions) concerning the unethical ritual slaying of animals is now superseded through more wholesome forms of ritual. The 'Son of God' that was sacrificed on the cross is an exalted form of the slaying of the Paschal lamb during Easter. It was a form of atonement before 'God' for the sins of the many, and symbolically supplanted the need for sacrificial animals. Jesus eliminated some of his worst *karma* in such a way whereby the blood that He shed could serve as an example for all upon the Initiation path. The cup of the Holy Grail (said to contain this blood) signified the methodology. Through Christ-like, Bodhisattvic activity, those who find the Grail could experience the Logoic Blood in the form of the highest spiritual ecstasy.

In the New Testament what had formerly a ritualistic and symbolic import has become transformed into 'the blood of the new testament, which is shed for many for the remission of sins'.[53] It is the same blood with which we must atone:

> the blood of all the prophets, which was shed from the foundation of the world, may be required of this generation.[54]

The phrase 'the blood of all the prophets' does not only refer to the actual killing of the prophets (which this 'generation' must karmically atone for), it also relates to the attainment of the Christ-consciousness by them, for that is the blood that was common to the prophets. They all spilled their blood for humanity, as did Jesus on the cross. A similar

52 *Numbers 23:24.*

53 *Matt. 26:28.*

54 *Luke 11:50.* See also *Matthew 23:30-39.*

spilling of spiritual blood *(buddhi)* is what is required of this present 'generation'. They will thereby atone for the sin of 'killing' the present version of the 'prophets': the truth speakers, especially in the political arena, who endeavour to educate humanity concerning the lying propaganda of the mass media. We also find a similar conception where Peter states that men are 'not redeemed with corruptible things... But with the precious blood of Christ, as of a lamb without blemish and without spot: Who verily was foreordained before the foundation of the world'.[55] Many are the mediators that work for humanity to attain a Covenant with the Divinity within and outside of their beings, but whom are not listened to by the common people.

The term *generation,* stated above, is here viewed as an entire group of beings that have evolved from an originating seed, as did the twelve tribes of Israel (with respect to Abraham) or all of humanity (with respect to Adam). It can also be viewed in terms of an originating seed thought that perpetuates many streams of realisation. More specifically, the term is normally viewed in association with a particular racial unfoldment, such as those seeded by a patriarch or originating leader bearing specialised characteristics for the 'generation'.

A psychically receptive, deeply felt attunement to and rapport with such originating patriarchs was the basis to the intensely gregarious tribal and racial feelings of our ancestors. For them, the life of one person was effectively only of importance to the degree that it served the common good of the tribe or nation. The character traits of the tribes were later embodied by a king or patriarch. A feeling of kinship was expressed in terms of blood – 'blood relations'. Even the 'blue blood' of our present European aristocracy comes under this guise. From this concept, when relegated to Biblical passages, comes the idea of the divine right of kings. This concept had validity until the time when general humanity could assertively state I AM, thereby becoming kings unto themselves. Then was seen the rapid demise of monarchies.

The dispensation of the Christ in the New Age will again lead people to a concept of tribal or group-awareness, and to the idea of relationship by means of 'blood'. However, this will occur on a higher turn of the spiral, thus upon a more transcendent level. The 'blood'

55 *Peter 1:18-20.*

will be that of the seven major and forty-nine minor Ray categories associated with the Hierarchy of Enlightened Being. They will become the externalised Ray Ashrams of the Lord. When related to the twelve zodiacal constellations they will possess a similar covenant with 'God' as the twelve tribes of Israel had in ancient times. There will, however, be a far more occult application, as the Face of His Presence will now become known and not remain hid as before.

The nature of the earlier Covenant is hinted at in the statement:

> And he did that which was right in the sight of the LORD...and turned not aside to the right hand or the left.[56]

Spiritually, to walk on a path that was neither of 'the left' or 'the right' means that the Israelites[57] were not to be involved in either black or white magical practices in the form of psychic unfoldment, as did their contemporaries in practicing the worship of Baal, Asherah etc. They were to walk the tightrope of the unfoldment of the development of intellectual faculties that would eventually awaken the Mind. This leads away from psychic practices and experiences. The specially trained prophets who could hold direct Covenant with 'God' were, however, exceptions. The intellect is sufficient unto itself, it is the 'I am' in action. Concurrent with this is the foetal development of first Ray qualities (Will or Power), as symbolised by the use of the sword, with which the Israelites would smite their enemies when the Lord was with them. When fused with Love-Wisdom, these qualities would allow the sons of Israel to become, as prophesied by Isaiah, 'a crown of glory in the hand of the LORD'.[58] Such was the then expectation, but historical events manifested in a different direction. Over time the separative powers of the intellect dominated and suppressed the awakening of the principle of Love, and so when the Jewish Messiah appeared they crucified him.

The embryonic will that the Israelites were to develop must grow into a definite receptivity to the 'Will of God' by the time the Hierarchy externalises (in this new Era), for the first Israelites were an earlier

---

56 *2Kings 22:2.*

57 Veiled by King Josiah who ruled them at that time, and to whom these words referred. The more exoteric interpretation is that he ruled even-handedly.

58 *Isaiah 62:3.*

incarnation of our present Hierarchy of Light and Love. Hierarchy instigated the earlier stages of the Jewish history, but later moved to play other roles in the world sphere. Thus we find the degeneration and abatement of this Covenant with 'God', which was evident in Jesus' time. Many members of Hierarchy incarnated with Him then to play their roles up to the crucifixion and its aftermath. Jesus' crucifixion signified the ending of the 'special Covenant'. The 'Son of God' was martyred and spilt His blood on earth for all of humanity, to whom the Covenant was thenceforth thoroughly transferred.

The reappearance of the Christ (the most senior executive of that Hierarchy) thus concerns the coming of age of the Israelites (Hierarchy), having become receptive to the direct empowerment of Divinity. For this reason, the arrival of the first Ray of Will combined with the second Ray of Love-Wisdom will herald the Aquarian Age and the new world government that will arise from it.[59] Biblical history is a fascinating codification of the evolutionary journeying of our present Hierarchy of Love throughout the various stages of its development. In the above we can see quite clearly why Christ-Jesus was styled the 'King of the Jews'.[60]

The Israelites were chosen to develop the qualities that would allow them to become a focal point for Logoic Purpose. (In a similar sense, Moses was made 'a god to Pharaoh: and Aaron thy brother shall be thy prophet'.[61]) They would become empowered by the right Hand of 'God'.[62] The hand is what one touches, grasps, manipulates (all emotional qualities) with. In this case it bequeaths saving power or providence. The Hand allows Deity to manifest a world sphere and to imbue the evolving entities with the evolutionary characteristics and qualities needed for the various stages of their development. The right Hand conveys the 'Emotional' energies of the Logos that find their outpouring through the field of *buddhi*. Receptivity to this energy necessitates a developed Mind and an awakened Heart centre. The

59 The nature of this Ray combination and detail of the externalising Ashrams is elaborated in the two volumes of my book *The Constitution of Shambhala*.

60 *Matt. 2:2, 27:29, 27:37, etc.*

61 *Exodus 7:1.*

62 See *Psalms 17:7, 20:6* and *44:3.*

twelve tribes of Israel (the twelve petals of a Heart centre or those of the crown of Glory – the Head centre, related to the twelve signs of the zodiac) are the mechanism of transmission of the energy from this right Hand. The twelve apostles of Jesus also served this function. Now we look to the present Chohans and Masters, who stand as the first twelve points in the Hierarchy[63] that have evolved to become focal points for the dissemination of this Energy from the planetary Logos.

The first stage of the Covenant with 'God' concerned the ability of the Jews to develop and bear this (new) force and type of experience by denying certain psychic practices and experiences (that they would then be so naturally involved with, as were their contemporaries). Deity would then grant them full material prosperity (a 'land flowing with milk and honey'[64]). These practices involved the various gods and goddesses that the Jews were prohibited from associating with or worshipping. The Logos would assure them of spiritual direction by means of His Presence *external* to themselves in the ark of the testimony.[65] They had thus to develop a *faith* in the surety of His Presence. It was a faith that would 'move mountains' (the mountains upon which the worshippers of the various god's practiced their rites) and place in its stead the 'Temple of God' in Jerusalem which was to house the ark.

They had also to develop the patience to practice His Commandments and wait for the benefits that such practice and the developed mind would accrue. The lure of the lower psychic nature was however too great; they continued to revert to the practices of their contemporaries. Many later prophets thus scolded them and they invited the consequent misfortunes for not eliminating such worship in their lives. The most predominant of such deities were the Sumerian fertility goddess (Asherah) and Canaanite gods (such as Baal).[66] The development of the 'I am' principle (intellectual activity) also produced its own problems, by preventing the receptivity of the

63 See figure 9, 'The Hierarchical Heart centre', in *The Constitution of Shambhala*, Part A, 122.

64 See *Exodus 3:17-18.*

65 *Exodus* chapter 25 goes into the detail of the construction of this ark that would become: a 'sanctuary; that I may dwell among them' *(Ex. 25:8.).*

66 See *Hosea 11:2.*

divinity within, which Jesus tried to show them. Thus 'a faithless and perverse generation'[67] was the result.

In this experiment with the generations of the sons of Jacob, it is probable that the planetary Logos had hoped to offset the worst effects of certain actions of the past (such as those which caused the great flood, hidden in the Mystery of the earth-moon relationship). The hope would have been to forestall the actions of the Lords of Dark Face on the earth, who amassed immense power through people's psychic misuse of certain religious practices. The 'I am' principle was the next step forward for humanity, despite the serious danger of the naturally separative attributes of the mind. What was hoped was that if a special group were educated to develop this principle correctly (in accordance with divine directions), then a successful outcome would produce a rapid pace of spiritual gain both for humanity and for Logoic Purpose.

Christ-Jesus' dispensation was a direct product of that Covenant, the result of God's promise to the Jews. He was the focus of the second main stage of this Covenant and laid the foundation that would allow the 'chosen' to embody this 'Emotional Energy' *(buddhi),* to thus effectively wield the 'crown of glory' in the right Hand of Deity. The quality Jesus embodied could only imperfectly flow to the Jewish nation as a whole, for they had repeatedly broken the Covenant. Thus they could not bear the 'Son of God' *(buddhi)* at the appointed time. They crucified this principle, as they had effectively done many times in the past by transgressing into idolatry etc., as mentioned throughout the Old Testament. The 'I am' development thereby moved into a different path, finding a receptacle in the Greek philosophers that evolved into the Western materialism which manifests today. The Christ's dispensation therefore found its outpouring through the twelve apostles, and then to the gentiles, rather than via the Jews, per se.

One wonders how different the world would be if the sons and daughters of Abraham, Isaac and Jacob had kept their Covenant throughout the generations and infused into their development a widespread Love of the Lord and understanding of His way. This was the onus of the Christ to expound. As progenitors of this type of civilisation, 'milk and honey' would certainly have flowed spiritually

---

67 *Matt. 17:17.*

and materially in abundance for the tribes of Israel. Much that is presently ordained for the future of humanity may by now have already manifested. Nevertheless, the esoteric bearers of that Covenant, the Spiritual Hierarchy, have kept it. Their energies and teachings sustain the aspirational zeal of many; they will flow in superabundance as the externalisation process ensues. This will bring about the *third main stage* of this most ancient Covenant, involving the externalisation of the Hierarchy upon the world sphere.

This exegesis is obviously concerned with the Western line of spiritual development, relating to the proper development of the intellect, and of the methods that Deity tried, in order to offset the inherent dangers of its development. The Eastern line, manifesting through Hinduism and Buddhism, concerns the development of internal meditative faculties, which was more successful. Consequently, the main effort of Hierarchy and the 'kingdom of God' has been to try to offset the machinations of the forces of evil that have largely incarnated as Lords of Western materialism.

The twelve apostles

It should be of value to list the names of the twelve apostles,[68] giving their astrological signs and briefly providing the reasons why they are thus assigned. Readers with sufficient astrological background can relate these to the twelve sons of Jacob (as given in *Genesis* chapter 49). The tribe and related sign will be listed below with the reasons for thus assigning them. The esoteric qualities of these signs will however not be delved into in any depth, as my other works will detail such information.[69] The key phrases for the signs of the zodiac governing the twelve tribes of Israel are:

Genesis 49:3. 'Reuben, thou art my first born, my might and the beginning of my strength'. This relates to the first of the signs of the zodiac, Aries the ram, and signifies the proverbial will and determination of the ram.

---

68 As given in *Matt. 10:2-3, Mark 3:14-19* and *Luke 6:12-16.*

69 See also Alice Bailey's *Esoteric Astrology.*

Genesis 49:14. 'Issachar *is* a strong ass crouching down between two burdens'. This relates to the sign Taurus the bull, who is similarly a beast of burden.

Genesis 49:5. 'Simeon and Levi are brethren; instruments of cruelty *are in* their habitations'. This refers to the sign Gemini the twins at a stage when they are busy fighting. They must learn to join their hands in service to humanity in order to overcome 'the separative relation which exists for so long between them'.[70]

Genesis 49:13. 'Zebulon shall dwell at the haven of the sea', which refers to the sign Cancer the crab, whose habitat is the shoreline between an ocean or sea and the land.

Genesis 49:9. 'Judah is a lion's whelp', which clearly refers to the sign Leo the lion.

Genesis 49:20. 'Out of Asher his bread *shall be* fat, and he shall yield royal dainties'. This relates to the sign Virgo the virgin, who, as the mother, provides the 'royal dainties' that sustains her progeny.

Genesis 49:16. 'Dan shall judge his people', which clearly refers to the sign Libra the balances, the sign of judgement and meditative interludes. As Dan spans two signs of the zodiac (to compensate for Simeon and Levi embodying one sign) I shall call this Dan (a) and the Dan governing the next sign as Dan (b).

Genesis 49:17. 'Dan shall be a serpent by the way, an adder in the path' refers to the sign Scorpio the scorpion, who like the adder, is a poisonous creature of the desert. Overcoming such poison (the results of the mental-emotions) constitutes the testings of discipleship.

Genesis 49:22-3. 'Joseph *is* a fruitful bough...the archers have sorely grieved him and shot *at him*' refers to the sign Sagittarius the archer, hence one-pointed ambition or aspiration.

Genesis 49:27. 'Benjamin shall ravin *as* a wolf: in the morning he shall devour the prey, and at night he shall divide the spoil'. This statement relates to the sign Capricorn the goat. It is the sign of accomplishment (of the mount of selfish striving, or of aspiration). The 'spoil' is the gain from such striving. (The results from 'mountain climbing'.)

Genesis 49:21. 'Naphthali *is* a hind let loose: he giveth goodly words'. This passage relates to the sign Aquarius the water bearer, which

70 Alice Bailey, *Esoteric Astrology*, 366.

is a sign governing the fluid mutability of thoughts and actions (signified by the wavy bands of its glyph). This is similar to the movements of 'a hind let loose'. Aquarius is also the sign of the accomplished Bodhisattva, who gives 'goodly words'.

Genesis 49:19. 'Gad, a troop shall overcome him: but he shall overcome at the last'. This statement refers to the sign Pisces the fishes, the last sign of the zodiac. Here the 'troop' that overcomes him for the next turning of the zodiacal wheel are the other signs of the zodiac. He 'shall overcome at the last' because this is the sign of completion, of the ending of the cycles of evolution, hence the onset of *pralaya.*

Before choosing the twelve ('whom also he named apostles') from all His disciples, Jesus 'went out into a mountain to pray, and continued all night in prayer to God'.[71] The parallel symbolism of the act of Moses going to the mountain to receive the Tablets of the Law should also be noted. After He chose His apostles, He:

> came down with them, and stood in the plain, and the company of his disciples, and a great multitude of people out of all Judaea and Jerusalem, and from the sea coast of Tyre and Sidon, which came to hear him, and to be healed of their diseases.[72]

Note also, the close parallel with Moses' action when he went down from the mountain with the Tablets from 'God', with whom he had made a Covenant, to all the Israelites encamped on the plain. The difference was that most of the Israelites gave themselves to licentiousness and idolatry, whereas those who approached Jesus came to hear Him and to be healed of their diseases.[73] Moses nevertheless 'healed' the Israelites of their 'diseases' in a wrathful way, and gave them the testimony of the Law, as written throughout the rest of Exodus and Leviticus. Jesus similarly gave the Beatitudes[74] in the rest of *Luke* (chapter six) and

71 *Luke 6:12-13.*

72 *Luke 6:17.*

73 One can speculate here that the diseases of the multitude that Jesus healed are the karmic consequences of the likelihood of these people being the reincarnations of those that manifested the licentiousness and idolatry of Moses' time.

74 See my book *Meditation and the Initiation Process,* 314-36, for an esoteric explanation of the Beatitudes.

Matthew (chapters five and six). This would henceforth become the 'testimony of the Law' for the new Covenant with 'God' (or stage two of the old Covenant).

The twelve apostles thus effectively took the attributes of the leaders of the twelve tribes and embodied the traits of the new Covenant given to them. We thus have:

1 Andrew Reuben Aries.

Andrew has the distinction of being the first of the apostles who was called. He was one of the two disciples of John who were present when Jesus came to be baptised in the Jordan. When Andrew and the other disciple heard Jesus speak they followed Him. After spending a day with Jesus, Andrew went to his brother Simon (Peter) and said 'We have found the Messias'.[75] He then brought Simon to Jesus, 'And when Jesus beheld him, he said, Thou art Simon the son of Jona: thou shalt be called Cephas, which is by interpretation, A Stone'.[76]

By this sequence of events Andrew aptly symbolises the qualities of Aries the ram, who sets the wheel of the Law, of the zodiac, in motion. (Aries being the first sign therein.) Being the first chosen, Andrew thus manifests a special relation to Jesus. He is destined to become the herald of the New Age dispensation that will manifest as the third stage of the Covenant with 'God'. From this point of view Andrew is the 'first' or 'oldest' of the twelve.

Andrew and Peter, being brothers (Aries-Capricorn) represent the dominant signs ruling the Jewish nation as a whole, as previously mentioned. By being brought together in the presence of the Christ, the entire ancient Covenant of the Jews with the Lord could be re-enacted and redefined according to the agenda of its second stage. The Covenant was symbolically re-established, with the rock or cornerstone of the new church or temple (Peter) being put into its place, brought thereto by the Ram of God (Andrew) symbolising the tribes of Israel.

Note that Andrew was also one of the apostles (with Peter, James and John) who asked Jesus privately: '*what shall be* the sign when all these things shall be fulfilled?'[77] This referred to the destruction of

---

75 *John 1:41.*

76 For the entire sequence of events see *John 1:37-42.*

77 *Mark 13: 1-4.*

the temple of Jerusalem, and later to the future reappearance of the Christ.[78] This question also implied that Andrew was part of the inner council of Christ's disciples, by possessing sufficient spiritual acumen to esoterically inquire about this knowledge. (His placing is either second or fourth in the various lists of the apostles.)

2 *Philip* *Issachar* *Taurus.*

Very little is said in the Bible concerning Philip, except in *John 1:43-5*, wherein the day following the meeting with Simon Peter, Jesus went forth to Galilee. There He found Philip, to whom He said 'follow me'. There is additional information that Philip was of Bethsaida (meaning 'place of fishing'), the city of Andrew and Peter. There 'he found Nathanael and said unto him, we have found him, of whom Moses in the Law and the prophets did write, Jesus of Nazareth, the son of Joseph'.

We see from this that Philip most probably embodied the characteristics of *Taurus the bull.* It is the sign that follows directly after Aries (thus implying also that Nathanael embodies the qualities of Gemini, which follows after Taurus). The specific citing of Philip's hometown also indicates the qualities of Taurus, which rules the comforts of home and surroundings. Another clue is his immediate response to the words 'follow me'. A major Taurean trait is to follow, often with onrushing blindness and determined faithfulness the edicts and precepts of religious scriptures, of the 'Word of God'. The Taurean often works with steadfast earnestness upon the temple of the Lord to build substance into the conceived spiritual form.

3 *Nathanael (Bartholomew)* *Simeon* and *Levi* *Gemini.*

Normally Nathanael and Bartholomew are considered the same person because the lists of the twelve apostles in the synoptic gospels (Matthew, Mark and Luke) speak of Bartholomew, not Nathanael. The gospel of John however does not mention Bartholomew but mentions

---

78 The events associated with His reappearance are portrayed in the long, much misunderstood prophetic passage from *Mark 13:7* ('when ye shall hear of wars and rumours of wars...') through to *Mark 13: 26:* 'then shall they see the Son of man coming in the clouds with great power and glory', and concluding with the words in *Mark 13: 37* 'And what I say unto you I say all, Watch'.

Nathanael twice. There is also a possibility that Nathanael was the proper name and Bartholomew the surname. The confusion of the name indicates that Nathanael-Bartholomew takes the function of Gemini the twins in this listing. From this perspective, Nathanael represents the 'immortal brother' and Bartholomew the 'mortal brother'. This is signified by the fact that Nathanael is depicted as an Initiate of the third degree in the John gospel, whereas Bartholomew is only mentioned in lists of the apostles.

This story of Nathanael is given in relation to the 'fig tree' in *John 1:45-51,* and the explanation of him being a third degree Initiate is detailed in my earlier book.[79] In speaking to Nathanael, however, Jesus presents additional information. This concerns the duality associated with the sign Gemini the twins (the heaven-earth, Spirit-form interrelations) in the statement 'Hereafter ye shall see heaven open, and the angels of God ascending and descending upon the Son of man'.[80]

4	*James, the son of Zebedee*	*Zebulon*	*Cancer.*
5	*John, the brother of James*	*Judah*	*Leo.*

Jesus 'surnamed them Boanerges, which is, The sons of thunder'.[81] The 'sons of thunder' refer to the two signs *Cancer* and *Leo.* An ancient symbol for the sign Cancer is that of herds of horses running over plains – causing the sound of thunder. Meanwhile, Leo has his roar which can be heard over a large distance. The natives from these two signs (ruled by the moon and sun, the Watery and Fiery Elements, together making the desire-mind) are said to be more emotional than all the others. The concept of thunder here relates to their fiery zeal and emotive power with reference to their abilities to spread the Word.

From the above it is seen that Andrew (Aries), Philip (Taurus) and Nathanael (Gemini) represent an important quadrant of the zodiac (the first three houses). This allows the dispensation of the Christ to be effectively born through the advent of the next two signs – James and John (Cancer-Leo), the 'sons of thunder'. Thus:

---

79 *Meditation and the Initiation Process,* 195-97.

80 *John 1:51.*

81 *Mark 3:17.*

- Aries represents primal inception, the conception of the thought-construct.
- Taurus represents the clothing of the initial thought-form with the element of desire.
- Gemini represents the vivification of the etheric form, the vitalisation of the Temple of the Lord.
- Cancer represents the actual physical incarnation, the concrete establishment of the thought form.
- Leo represents the evolutionary impetus of the thought-form or the Covenant's actual maturation (as the 'king of the beasts'). Hence James and John are the 'sons of thunder', the symbolic means whereby the thought-form or 'Word of God' (the thunder of 'a voice from heaven'[82]) can be made manifest and broadcast on the earth. As 'sons', they are the means of reverberating the message of the divine Voice to all. The remaining signs represent the qualities that consolidate and refine the process of spreading the Word.

6 Matthew Asher Virgo.

Matthew is called a 'publican',[83] and earlier it is stated that when Jesus 'saw a man, named Matthew, sitting at the receipt of custom' He said 'Follow me' and Matthew instantly arose and followed Him.[84] Matthew thus had the rather contemptible profession in those days as a tax gatherer (for Caesar), reaping the harvests and produce of those around him. In this guise he embodied the qualities of *Virgo the virgin,* who holds ears of wheat, and thus symbolises the result of the harvest of the land (of the Lord). Virgo is the 'virgin' (Mary) who bears the Christ child and gives birth to it. In relation to this Virgoan stage in His disposition Jesus could say at the end of chapter nine of Matthew that the 'harvest truly is plenteous, but the labourers are few; Pray ye therefore the Lord of the harvest, that he will send forth labourers into his harvest'.[85]

---

82 *John 12:28-29.* See also *Psalm 29:3* and *Job 37:4-5.*

83 *Matt. 10:3.*

84 *Matt. 9:9.*

85 *Matt. 9:37-8.*

The intellectual astuteness attributed to the Virgoan is what helped Matthew write his gospel.

7 Thomas Didymus Dan (a) Libra.

Thomas is mainly remembered as 'doubting Thomas' from the gospels because of his need to actually see and touch the wounds of Jesus before he would believe He was risen from the dead.[86] He thus embodied the character traits of *Libra the balances,* which must weigh and judge, and have actual tangible proof as to the validity of any hearsay evidence before accepting it.

8 Simon Zelotes Dan (b) Scorpio.

He is called Simon Zelotes in *Luke 6:15* and *Acts 1:13,* and 'the Canaanite' in *Matthew 10:4* and *Mark 3:18.* Zelotes means *Zealot.* As one of the major traits of a Scorpio personality is a tendency towards zealotry and fanaticism, producing the related tests and trials, so Simon symbolises the qualities of this sign. (Note that the Zealots were a fanatical religious sect in Israel at this time. They were a major driving force behind the Jews that produced the war against the Romans that led to the destruction of the temple of Jerusalem in 70 A.D.)

9 Judas, James' brother Joseph Sagittarius.

He is called Judas the brother of James in *Luke 6:16* and *Acts 1:13,* and 'Lebbeus, whose surname was Thaddeus' in the other gospels. (Some Biblical scholars also name him as the author of the Jude Epistle.) There is little in the scriptures concerning him, but as there is only one sign left *(Sagittarius the archer)* after analysing the others, one can safely assign the qualities of this sign to him.

10 *Peter The tribe of Benjamin Capricorn .*

Capricorn qualifies Peter because:

a. Peter was told that he was the rock upon which the Church of the Lord would be built.[87] Capricorn is governed by the element Earth and its qualities. It represents the Mount of the Lord and the transfiguration experience (the third Initiation) which Peter was Initiated into by the Christ.

86 *John 20:24-29.*

87 *Matt. 16:16-19.*

b. Jesus told Peter to 'Get thee behind me, Satan'.[88] Satan (or Saturn) is the exoteric and esoteric ruler of Capricorn and relates to the mount of *karma* (the things that peter 'savourest...that be of men'[89]). The mountain is made of rock and Peter was the 'rock' of Christ's Church. The injunction therefore is partly in the form of a pun, where Peter was called by the name of his ruling sign in the guise of Satan. Jesus represents the spiritual Sun (the Soul), thus it was natural for Peter (the embodiment of the mount of *karma)* to 'get behind' Him. Jesus was also essentially Aquarian by nature, dispensing the Waters of Life to those around Him (being thus a world server). Capricorn therefore stands behind him on the rectified wheel of the zodiac. In many ways Peter represents the *karma* of the Jewish nation as a whole – which was ruled by the Mosaic code, thus by Capricorn. He was therefore told to 'get behind' the Lord so as to allow a new dispensation that would inevitably be ruled by Aquarian qualities in the New Era.

The orthodox rendering of this phrase is that as 'Satan' Peter was (temporarily) an adversary to the Lord. This was indeed so, as the mountain load of material *karma* must be eliminated, overcome, before the Church of Christ can be built on the 'rock' of spiritual Truth, in the form of manifest Love-Wisdom.

Note that Jesus is traditionally assigned the sign Capricorn the goat, because He is said to have been born on December twenty-fifth. This is, however, an arbitrary date,[90] as it is not known when he was born. The qualities of His dispensation (the rising sign) were however Aquarian, whilst He heralded the traits of Pisces in the symbolism of relating to fishes displayed in His acts. This is important, as Pisces was the astrological epoch the sun had then earlier entered. Jesus thus effectively embodied the traits of the northern quadrant of the zodiac. It may be said that Capricorn was the moon sign (His inheritance from the past Covenant with the Lord), Pisces the sun sign (His immediate life unfoldment, as a

---

88 *Matt. 16:23.*

89 *Matt. 16:23.*

90 The date appears to have been chosen to supplant the popular pagan festival of Saturnalia (which was celebrated from the seventeenth December onwards) with a Christian alternative. Alternatively, the date relates to the winter solstice, and also is the date of the celebrations of the important Roman sun god, Sol Invictus.

world saviour), and Aquarius, the rising sign of His spiritual disposition (which expresses the long-term purpose for His teachings).

11 James, Alpheus' son Naphthali Aquarius.

The only mention in the gospels, apart from the lists of the apostles is a possible reference in *Mark 15:40,* which states that 'Mary Magdalene and Mary the mother of James the less and of Joses, and Salome' were at the crucifixion. From this information we can infer that 'James the less' (in stature) refers to the sign Aquarius, the sign of a man (the water bearer). As Jesus embodied the qualities of this sign, the appellation 'less' can also refer to the esoteric fact that James was smaller in stature than Jesus regarding the bearing of Aquarian energies. (It also distinguishes him from James the son of Zebedee.)

12 Judas Iscariot Gad Pisces.

Judas Iscariot, who betrayed Jesus, embodied the character traits of the sign *Pisces the fishes* (which are yoked together and swimming in the water of sensation). This sign is effectively the one that betrays the light of the spiritual Sun, for it binds, or puts into bondage, the Waters of Life so freely dispensed in the previous sign Aquarius. On the reversed wheel, it also instantly binds into a form the originating impulses and ideas conceived in the sign Aries.

The Piscean era has effectively betrayed the work and Words of the Christ, because those of this era have, for instance, distorted and dogmatised His Words into attributes of the mental-emotions, often to justify cruel perversions, as evidenced in the Inquisitional period in Europe. Obviously, such was never intended by the Lord of Love.

Also found in the gospel story is the symbolism of the 'sop' that Jesus dipped and gave to Judas Iscariot as a sign that he would be the one to betray Him.[91] A 'sop' immersed in the waters can here be taken as a symbol of Pisces the fishes.

Note that the transfiguration experience on the mountain, the attainment of Jesus' third Initiation[92] (where Jesus stood with Peter,

---

91 *John 13:26-27.*

92 *Matthew 17:1, Mark 9:2.* The significance of this experience is explained in my book *Meditation and the Initiation Process,* 234-37.

James and John) zodiacally dictates the four Elements, whereby the Light of the Lord could find the focus of its expression to humanity.

- *Jesus* (Aquarius) represents the Airy quality – the Spirit of the Lord.
- *Peter* (Capricorn) represents the Earthy quality – the 'rock' or foundation upon which Jesus' dispensation was to be established.
- *James* (Cancer) represents the Watery quality, signifying the massed consciousness into which the Spirit must manifest.
- *John* (Leo) represents the Fiery quality – the Soul form that must become the purified vehicle allowing the Law to be expressed throughout the form. (Leo rules the Soul form and is also the ruler of the jungle of our material lives.)

Aquarius (Jesus) and Leo (John, the beloved) are polar opposites in the zodiac (thus they have a special relationship), as also are Capricorn (Peter) and Cancer (James).

The apostolic lists in the Matthew, Mark and Luke gospels provide some important clues as to the relationship between the apostles. The order of the listing in *Mark 3:16-19* differs a little from that of the other two. It starts with Simon (Peter) in verse 16, then James and John in verse 17. Verse 18 lists eight of the apostles, headed by Andrew, followed by Judas in verse 19. This arrangement is depicted in figure 28. Here Peter, James and John symbolise the spiritual triad that is directly receptive to the attributes of the triune Logos. They are followed by the apostles that manifest the arms of the eight-pointed cross that signify direction in space. They are the eight spokes of the wheel of the Law. This cross also awakens the petals of the Heart lotus. The square under this cross signifies the sum of the forces constituting the material world, and of the people that rejected or crucified Jesus.

The twelve apostles were in fact an externalised Heart centre, and as Andrew heads the eight-pointed cross (which signifies this centre in figure 28), so he was in fact the esoteric head of the disciples under Jesus. This also relates to him having been the first chosen. This esoteric fact is also indicated in other lists where he is paired with Peter. In the work of disseminating the esoteric doctrine, Andrew is directly assisted by James, John and Bartholomew. (Who represents the eastern gate of the eight-armed cross). Peter's Capricornian role made him the head exoterically, and his mind nature (in the form of 'Satan') was attuned to the orthodoxy of the mainstream Jewish religion that his ministry mainly catered for.

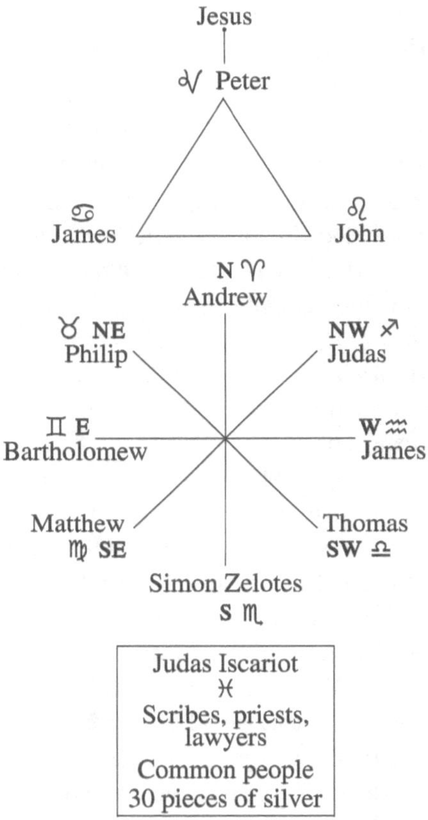

Figure 28: The twelve apostles

Simon Zelotes and Judas Iscariot had much in common, a certain zealotry in beliefs. This caused Simon to identify with an extreme religious dispensation of the Jews, and Judas to crucify Jesus. They are therefore linked to each other in this figure. Other than this, the order of the apostles in the figure is as presented in Mark's listing.

The attributes of the eight-armed cross *(aṣṭadiśas)* are explained throughout my books,[93] hence I need not repeat the detail here. Andrew

93 See for instance *Maṇḍalas: Their Nature and development,* 244-49. Also, Alice

holds the position of upwards to the 'kingdom of God', to which the will aspect of his Arian disposition provides direct access. Philip's Taurean disposition as the home builder facilitates his northeast position of 'unity'. He thus unifies the attributes of the apostles into one grouping, following the laws of group evolution.[94]

Bartholomew's position at the eastern gate ('inwards to the Heart of Life') signifies that his Gemini disposition facilitated his ability to incorporate the second Ray energies of Love-Wisdom from the Christ into the *maṇḍala* of the 'temple' established by the apostles. This function is also facilitated by Jesus' acknowledgement that Bartholomew had passed the third Initiation by the time that he met Jesus.

Andrew, Philip, Bartholomew, James and John also manifest as an esoteric pentad conveying (or fixing) the five *prāṇas* of the Christ into this *maṇḍala* that energises the rest of the dispensation of the apostles after Jesus' crucifixion. (Andrew conveys the Aetheric *praṇās,* Philip the Earthy, Bartholomew the Airy, James the Watery and John the Fiery.)

Matthew wields the southeast gate of 'expression', where his Virgoan disposition births the ramifications of the doctrine in published form that could be disseminated far and wide. His gospel might not have been the first actually written, but posterity saw that it became the first of the four gospels printed in the Bible.

The southern position of Simon Zelotes of downward towards the little ones and his Scorpio disposition facilitated his involvement with the exoteric political happenings in Jerusalem at the time. As stated, there is therefore a symbolic link to the activities of Judas Iscariot and the events that caused him to eventually hang himself.[95]

Thomas' Libran disposition and southwest position of 'understanding' is what caused him to doubt that Jesus had indeed been resurrected, unless he touched his wounds. His mind could then come to an understanding of the reality of the situation. This also implied that Thomas was the most empirically minded of the apostles, hence was also studious with respect to the study of the Judaic law, and of the other religious dispensations he encountered in his later mission to India.

Bailey's *Discipleship in the New Age,* Volume II, 176-96.

94 See my book *Meditation and the Initiation Process,* 336-97 for an explanation of these laws.

95 *Matt. 27:5.*

James western position of 'outwards to the field of service' and Aquarian disposition made him an ideal proselytiser for Jesus' dispensation.

Judas' (James' brother) Sagittarian disposition and northwest position of 'goodwill' indicates that he assisted James to fervently preach (with one-pointed determination) to the populace concerning Jesus' teachings.

Judas Iscariot of course stands in a class on his own, having betrayed Jesus in accordance with the karmic role that he had to play.

The lists in *Matthew 10:2-5* and *Luke 6:14-17* arrange the apostles in pairs with complementary attributes (though they give a slightly different ordering). These are based on the qualities of the Heart centre, allowing the pairs of apostles to be sent out to 'preach...heal the sick, raise the dead, cast out devils' etc., as explained in *Matthew chapter 10.*

In the lists of these two gospels, the foundation of Jesus' church is represented by Peter (thus the sign Capricorn), signifying the mount of Initiation which all must strive to climb. Capricorn has largely conditioned the empirical orthodox (exoteric) interpretation of the scriptures until now. Capricornian striving is followed by the Arian impetus of Andrew, who therefore signifies the will to do so.

James and John (Cancer and Leo) then signify the birthing of Jesus' dispensation (Cancer) and the Leonine Fiery presentation of the gospels. This is shown in John's gospel, which is sometimes called the Gnostic gospel because of the high esotericism presented throughout it. It starts with the memorial opening statement:

> In the beginning was the Word, and the Word was with God, and the Word was God.[96]

Philip then works to fill the mental expression with further substance so that its proper house or 'church' can be built (Taurus). Bartholomew's purpose is to help outfit the Temple of the Lord in such a way that it becomes a fit habitation for divinity on earth (Gemini). His effort therefore assists the esoteric or subjective truths to be discovered by those that earnestly seek. Those that do seek must however strive to seek out the immortal brother (the hidden Christ) in the temple, rather than be content to merely seek out the outer trappings (the mortal brother) of its symbolism (as was done by the Christian dispensation).

---

96 *John 1:1.*

Matthew and Thomas further codify the Word made flesh in the form of the gospels in written form. This is evident in the gospel under Matthew's name. *The Gospel According to Thomas,* found in the Nag Hammadi library, also contains numerous sayings of Jesus and must have been one of the earliest gospels written.

The Sagittarian impetus of Judas, James' brother helps to promulgate the doctrine far and wide, assisted by the Aquarian energies of James, Alpheus' son. Sagittarius fires the arrows of the teachings to seek their intended target, whilst Aquarius the water bearer pours the teachings of Love and Wisdom to a large audience that have the capacity to sup from this fount.

Simon Zelotes projects the true testings of the new church via his zealotry (Scorpio). In relation to this, via those he was associated with, came the effective destruction of the temple. Then came all of the religious strife that hounded the Christian church. This was especially so regarding its problems concerning the factors of sex, celibacy and inquisitional attitudes. Judas Iscariot signifies the betrayal of the true doctrines of the Christ – first of Jesus himself, and later came the many distortions of his teachings. As the cycles of centuries passed so these distortions represent the abnegation of His message, 'That ye love one another'[97] (etc.). This culminated in the dogmatic attitudes that governed Christianity throughout the Piscean era.

The next stage of the then Covenant would be forthcoming with the advent of the Christ's reappearance. This would happen properly at the beginning of the Aquarian epoch. The appearance of Jesus, however (in the room where the apostles were huddled after his crucifixion, and where Thomas touched his wounds), signified the earlier symbolic precursor to this. As a consequence Jesus said:

> Thomas, because thou hast seen me thou hast believed: blessed *are* they that have not seen, and yet have believed.[98]

So it is for the world disciple that incarnated later and could understand the esoteric teachings that underlined the fact of his reappearance. They need to develop the knowledge of the 'many other

---

97 *John 13:34.*

98 *John 20:29.*

signs', the way of the manifestation of such phenomena that Jesus did 'in the presence of his disciples'.[99] The mechanism of appearing in a 'resurrection body' (etheric form) that could be concretised by means of the power of thought is now known through the broadcasting of Hindu and Buddhist yoga doctrines to the West.[100]

The climax of the then Covenant came at the time of the Pentecost when the apostles were given the gift of tongues, so that when they spoke 'every man heard them speak in his own language'.[101] This is a precursor to the present time, because of the Internet, where it is relatively easy for people to translate one language into another. After this, groups of disciples and apostles expressing the energies of the twelve petals of the Heart centre were sent out to preach, heal etc. Next is the conversion of Saul (Paul),[102] whose ministry opened Jesus' dispensation to the gentiles, hence the world at large.

Predestination

The Voice from heaven at the time of Jesus' Baptism stated 'This is my beloved Son, in whom I am well pleased'.[103] This could only be said because the Son had been active in preparing the groundwork for the descent of the dove (or Light-Love principle) since the 'foundation of the world'. Not only was the Christ thus foreordained, but also *humanity itself,* as Paul succinctly phrases it:

> Blessed *be* the God and Father of our Lord Jesus Christ...According as he hath chosen us in him before the foundation of the world, that we should be holy and without blame before him in love: Having predestinated us unto the adoption of children by Jesus Christ to himself.[104]

---

99 *John 20:30.*

100 My books explain this philosophy and the methodology is detailed in my book *Esoteric Cosmology and Modern Physics.*

101 *Acts 2:6.*

102 *Acts 9:1-16.*

103 *Matt. 3:17.*

104 *Eph. 1:3-5.*

The concept of predestination is but an iteration of the doctrine of *karma,* for the Lords of *karma* weave the script of what must be. This is according to the *karma* that was created in the past by the actors upon the world stage. This is arranged according to a pattern decreed by the Lords of Shambhala.

In the light of the information presented so far the seventeenth chapter of *John's gospel* is most illuminating. It presents some of the most esoteric statements given to the world by the Christ. He states for instance:

> Neither pray I for these alone, but for them also which shall believe on me through their word; That they all may be one; as thou, Father, *art* in me, and I in thee, that they also might be one in us....I in them, and thou in me, that they may be made perfect in one;....Father, I will that they also, whom thou hast given me, be with me where I am; that they may behold my glory, which thou hast given me: for thou lovedst me before the foundation of the world....And I have declared unto them thy name, and will declare *it;* that the love wherewith thou hast loved me may be in them, and I in them.[105]

Those that are able to 'believe on' the Christ by means of 'their word' (that particular Sound or mantra manifesting in their Heart that is the keynote of their entire being[106]) shall therefore be formed into a unity, as 'one'. In a similar sense the Christ is in 'the Father' (the planetary Logos) and 'the Father' is in Him. ('I in them, and thou in me, that they may be perfect in one.')

If the earlier concepts given in chapter five are referred to, where it was stated that the human entity can be considered a 'cell' in the Body of Deity, so this Deity, embodying a planetary or solar system, can be said to constitute a 'cell' in the Body of an ineffable cosmic Deity 'about whom naught can be said'. Then also the implications concerning the meaning of 'all' being 'made perfect in one' must stand in proper perspective.

---

105 *John 17:20-26.*

106 This is an integral aspect of the eternal Sound, which becomes the *dharma,* the integral spiritual teachings they give to all others.

From this passage we thus see that if the historical Christ embodied the energy of the Love of 'God', even 'before the foundation of the world', then He (as the foremost and most evolved representative or embodiment of the human group-Soul[107]) could also be Impregnated with the energy of a cosmic Christ. It is an energy that He will eventually properly anchor on the earth, to make us all 'perfect in one'. (Such activity is thus also a predestined event.) In a unique way He can therefore be considered the 'Son of God' (as Souls, we are also, but not at such an exalted level, for human Souls are still at a foetal stage of spiritual development). This force first permeated the earth when the Blood of Jesus flowed from His wounds in the Garden of Gethsemane (where it fell as 'drops of sweat') and on the cross, especially when His Heart was pierced by a human hand (in the guise of a soldier).

The crucifixion was the exoteric symbol of the Divine Sacrifice and Compassion of a (cosmic) Deity, a 'Sacrifice' that will eventually transmute and infuse with Light the substance of the earth itself. (The Lives upon it are destined thereby to empower the sun of a future solar system.) This is exactly what will enable those that 'God' has 'given' the Christ, who were chosen 'before the foundation of the world' to behold the full extent of His *glory,* if He is to ascend to the Throne of His Father.

The above provides the esoteric meaning of the statement that concludes the Matthew gospel: 'lo, I am with you alway, *even* unto the end of the world. Amen'.[108] The 'Amen' can be considered a permutation or corruption of the Aūṁ, and may be an adaptation from the title of the Egyptian sun god *Amun-Ra.* In reference to the I AM principle, the Christ therefore implied here that He was 'the beginning and the ending, the first and the last' as far as the evolution of the earth and the Lives thereon are concerned. It was thus His destiny to embody the attributes of a Logos, as a future potent sun – Amen. Literally meaning 'so be it'. (The orthodox rendering of Amen.) The statement 'the end of the world' signifies the ending of an age, era or world period.

---

107 The genealogy of the Luke gospel *(Luke 3:23-38)* testifies to this by tracing the parentage of Jesus back, as the 'Son aspect' (of Deity), through to Adam and thence to 'God'.

108 *Matt. 28:20.*

Christ-Jesus was therefore predestined to embody a Divine principle. To do so, He evolved a Consciousness that is inclusive of all things associated with the earth and the kingdoms of Nature upon it. He experienced the mode of the evolution of the consciousness principle, from the hoary past to the prospective future, in a way that allowed Him to Know what is needed for the advancement of Divine Love. He was therefore the 'Son of man' born amongst us, and He evolved as all people do, by means of reincarnation and the Initiation process. However, he advanced very quickly to the exalted Initiation status that allowed Him to fulfil the role presented in the Bible.

Christ-Jesus was the most evolved representative of the collective human Soul, thus He could draw to the earth the energies of the Power and great Glory of Divinity. (Because of their great potency these energies can only be transmitted to humanity as a unit, or to Initiated groups.) These oncoming energies will eventually produce a synthesis of all aspects and approaches to the Divine, to produce world good will. Inevitably radical, transformations via the energy of Love will manifest upon the fabric of Life and human civilisation on earth. Such is the unfolding Plan of the originating Thought-Form of 'God'.

The above becomes more meaningful if it is realised that everything is Divine: every atom or sun, and all other forms. All are expressive of an embodied Life. The planets, for instance, are but the observable forms of planetary Logoi that contain within their Bodies many other subjective globes or realms, and various Hierarchies of Lives, human and angelic. All entities are either evolving towards self-consciousness or have transcended that stage, and all are embraced by the Consciousness of the Christ.

Space is but an Entity. If humanity's eyes were opened then they would be able to see the immense cosmos pulsating with the living Light of the Fiery Lives. This is the 'life....more abundantly'[109] that Jesus mentioned, and which will be slowly revealed to us as the New Age progresses. The nature of such Life is definitely part of the Revelation the Christ is to bring upon His reappearance. The potency of the rhythm in living styles, and the purified (psychic) atmosphere of the earth that will eventually be manifest, will enable people to contact and see what was formerly veiled.

109 *John 10:10.*

General summary

It can be said that a being whose reasoning facilities are developed is self-conscious, aware of the isolated self (or 'point' in the immensity of space) and all the things that objectively influence that self. That one can affirm I AM, and thus respond to planetary influences – the interaction between all other points of consciousness, or forms, within the planetary sphere of influence.

Someone that has developed intuitive capabilities, thus is illumined, is in tune with the collective-Mind that constitutes his/her subjective group, so therefore can affirm the I AM THAT. The illumined one responds to planetary and interplanetary influences and is aware of the interaction between the Hierarchies of conscious Lives within that interrelated sphere.

The Initiate that can Identify with the Spirit-aspect (the Monad), as distinct from the Soul, is universally Conscious. That One can affirm the I AM THAT I AM, and thus respond to planetary, interplanetary and inter-solar influences – to the myriad interrelated streams of energy from cosmos.

It should be emphasised that Christ-Jesus was not the first custodian of the Love energy on the earth (for 'God' has always expressed His Love to humanity). Others in the unfathomed past have done so and have long since gained their release, as *nirvāṇees* (Buddhas) that have evolved out of our world-system altogether. (Thus as One ascends, so another is equipped to take that One's former office.) The Christ was however unique in that He was the first of our present humanity to do so. He also anchored this force on the earth at a time when humanity could be receptive to it, not only as a dictum imposed from above but also coming from within. He taught humanity how the Love of 'God' could be expressed as a positive force. He is therefore the Divine embodiment of the Word for humanity, the 'Son of God', though the full implication of this will not be fully understood until after His reappearance.

Before Jesus died on the cross He told the 'disciple whom he loved' that Mary was henceforth his mother:

> he saith unto his mother, Woman, behold thy son! Then saith he to the disciple, Behold thy mother! And from that hour that disciple took her

> unto his own *home*. After this, Jesus knowing that all things were now accomplished, that the scripture might be fulfilled, saith, I thirst.[110]

He was then given vinegar to drink, and 'he bowed his head, and gave up the ghost'.[111] The implication of the symbolism here is of importance. We see that in the manner of all divine Teachers, Christ-Jesus passed on the spiritual succession of His dispensation by means of this act to His foremost disciple. That disciple was thus to attain the status of a Christ after the Christ had ascended to the Throne of 'His Father'.

Earlier, Peter was stated to be 'the rock' upon which the Christ would build His church ('and the gates of hell shall not prevail against it'[112]). For this reason Peter was given the 'keys of the kingdom of heaven',[113] thereby allowing him to unlock its Mysteries and to release the associated energies with which to build this Church. The Church in question here, however, was what was to be made manifest in the corporeal or dense physical realm (symbolised by the 'rock'), and which would later allow the definite manifestation of the New Jerusalem on the earth. What was given to the 'disciple whom he loved' by the act of offering His mother, was not so much the 'keys' of the 'kingdom of heaven', but to inherit the kingdom of Enlightened Being, which was His spiritual Church. In Buddhist tantric terminology concerning the succession of the spiritual lineage of the *guru,* Peter would be the 'Son with moonlike qualities', and the other disciple, the 'Son with sun-like qualities'.

The virgin Mary and the story of the immaculate conception symbolises the sea of virgin primeval substance from which consciousness (the Christ-principle) evolved. It relates to s*aṃsāra* wherein humanity gathers its experiences and furthers its evolution. When the one who was to be 'proxy' of the Christ could take the symbolic Mother of all forms 'unto his own home' (the stable reservoir of his spirituality), then this implies that henceforth the substance of the earth would be glorified by

110 *John 19:26-8.*

111 *John 19:29-30.*

112 *Matt. 16:16-20.*

113 *Matt. 16:19.*

the Christ energy. Effectively, it signified that the spiritualisation of all the kingdoms of Nature, including the dense physical world, was upon its upward arc and could be imbued with the spirit of the living Christ. This is the process that would make earth become a sacred planet. Such a task was specifically attributed to the disciple 'whom he loved', who could do so because he was destined to eventually take the rank and qualities of the Christ's former office.

When Christ ascends to 'His Father', He will be trained in the 'kingdom of God' for an even more exalted office – to eventually wield the 'power and great glory' of the planetary Logos. (Thus becoming the Regent of a 'new heaven and a new earth'.[114]) Jesus was therefore able to 'give up the ghost', for He knew that because a disciple had appeared that could take 'His Mother' into his place of spiritual residence, and thus appropriately look after her, so: 'all things might now be accomplished, and the scriptures might be fulfilled'. 'All things' means just that: 'all things' in Heaven and earth (of the past, present and future, which are written in the Book of Life).[115] Contained in this Book is the 'gospel of the kingdom' that 'shall be preached in all the world for a witness unto all nations'.[116]

When Jesus stated 'I thirst', He was not only referring to physical thirst (and being forced to drink vinegar, which literally killed Him), but also to the spiritual 'thirst' or desire to see the outcome of what was yet to be, and of His ascension to 'the Father'.

The disciple to care for Jesus' mother was *Lazarus*. He was beloved by Jesus,[117] possessed a home (that was also occupied by his sisters Mary and Martha) and was sufficiently wealthy to be able to afford to take Mary into his home. John 'the other disciple, whom Jesus loved'[118] could not do so, for he had given up all of his possessions to follow Jesus, being one of the twelve apostles, and was hiding at that time with them for fear of the Jews. The story of the entombment in the crypt was in

114 *Rev. 21:1.*

115 *Rev. 5:1* – 'I saw in the right hand of him that sat on the throne a book written within and on the backside, sealed with seven seals.'

116 *Matt. 24:14.*

117 *John 11:5* and *11:36.*

118 *John 20:2.*

fact that of Lazarus taking his fourth Initiation, as is properly explained in my book *Meditation and the Initiation Process*.[119] As such, Lazarus was a very high-ranking member of Hierarchy, who later evolved to become the second Ray Chohan[120] (an Initiate of the sixth degree).

119 *Meditation and the Initiation Process*, 293-96.

120 See my book *The Constitution of Shambhala*, Part A, 114 for further explanation.

BODO '83.

I care not if you see not my dream.
My lover has died,
and in dying has given birth
to the Great Awakening.
Awake! My dear friend,
arise and greet the risen one.
Arise!
The subjective
has become objective.
The objective is becoming subjective.
The crucified is resurrected.
The resurrected crucifies.
For all must ascend and
be transfixed on the fixed
cross of the heavens.
For lo!
The Christ has come
because the New Age awakens.

Glory be to 'God' in the highest,
on earth peace.
Good will to all men.

11

The Reappearance of the Christ

The doctrine of Avatars

The idea of an imminent world Saviour is not particular to Christianity. In Judaism, for instance (which is decidedly monotheistic, as is also Islam), there is the idea of a Messiah, meaning 'the anointed one'. He is the ultimate redeemer – a descendant of king David, who would come to deliver Israel from foreign bondage and lead the Jews into a definite covenant with 'God', as existed in ancient times. Christians believe that Jesus was that being, and there are many Biblical passages verifying this. The word 'Christ' is derived from the Greek rendering of Messiah – Christos.

In the Shi'ah sect of Islam the idea of the final 'restorer of the faith' gradually developed. He is called a Mahdi, the 'divinely guided one', who would either be a descendant of the prophet Mohammed or the reappearing Jesus ('Isa). He is expected to be the last of a succession of religious leaders (Imams) to reappear from His celestial place of concealment.

The Parsi philosophy also teaches of a succession of saviours (Soshyans) who will follow each other at intervals of 1,000 years after the 3,000 year period associated with Zoroaster's ministry (6th century B.C.) has run its course. The task of the last Soshyan (Astvat-ereta, 'Justice incarnate', or simply 'saviour'), who will appear at the end of our present world period, will be to restore the primal state of peace by vanquishing evil and also to rehabilitate humanity. (Evil is personified by Ahriman, the Lord of darkness.) This will occur by people abstaining firstly from meat, then milk, then plant life, to be finally sustained by only 'water'. What is known as hell will then cease to exist, thus the reign of Light would again be manifest on earth.

Hinduism presents the doctrine of the Avataras[1] of Vishnu, the second person of the Hindu Trimūrti (trinity of deities). He is the sustainer of the universe and in many ways has similar characteristics to the Christ, especially in His Avatara as Krishna (Kṛṣṇa) as depicted in the Bhagavad Gita. In the Kalki-Purāṇa we are told that the tenth and final Avatara of Vishnu (Kalki) will appear at the end of this present materialistic era (the *kali yuga,* or 'iron age') in the form of a giant with a horse's head (the symbol of courage and wisdom). He is to bring a beneficent end to the present era of suffering, licentiousness, and evil, thereby bringing forth a new golden age of prosperity and peace. In relation to this, Krishna says to his charioteer Arjuna in *The Bhagavad Gita:*

> Many births of Mine have passed as well as of thine, O Arjuna; I know them all but thou knowest not, O Parantapa (scorcher of foes).
>
> Though I am unborn, of imperishable nature, and though I am the Lord of all beings, yet, governing My own Nature, I am born by my own Maya.
>
> Whenever there is a decline of righteousness, O Arjuna, and rise of unrighteousness, then I manifest Myself.
>
> For the protection of the good, for the destruction of the wicked and for the establishment of righteousness, I am born in every age.

1 From the root *av,* meaning 'above', and *atara,* which means 'to descend'. An Avatara is therefore a direct incarnation, or an embodied aspect, of Deity. There are ten major Avatars of Vishnu: Matsya the fish, Kurma the tortoise, Varha the boar, Narasimbha the lion-man, Vamana the dwarf, Parashurāma, Rāma with the axe, Rāma, Krishna, Buddha (Balarama is sometimes substituted here) and Kalki. As such they relate to the empowerment of the ten petals of the Solar Plexus centre for humanity.

> He who thus knows, in their true light, My divine birth and action, having abandoned the body, is not born again, he comes to Me, O Arjuna.
>
> Freed from attachment, fear and anger, absorbed in Me, taking refuge in Me, purified by the fire of knowledge, many have attained to My Being.[2]

Such a period is now definitely with us, thus it is time for the fulfilment of this injunction. The divine Personalities of the past (whose works fill the pages of our religious scriptures) were born to present the doctrines that would lead to the advent of the reappearance of the 'Son of God'.

The similarity between the symbolism of the story of Krishna and Jesus (as related in various texts) should here be noted.

a. Krishna, whose birth was heralded by a star, was said to have been born of the virgin Devaki. Jesus was born to the virgin Mary, and His birth was also heralded by a star.[3]

b. Both Krishna and Jesus were of royal lineage, and both were born in a cave.[4]

c. At Krishna's birth the cave was illumined by bright light, as also related in the *Gospel of Protevangelion* regarding Jesus.[5]

d. Krishna spoke to his mother soon after his birth. According to chapter 1:2-3 of the *Gospel of Infancy* Jesus also so spoke whilst he was in the cradle.

e. Krishna was born while his foster father Nanda was in the city to pay his tax to the governor, similar to Jesus regarding his foster father Joseph.[6]

f. Krishna was adored by cowherds, whilst Jesus was adored by shepherds.[7]

---

2 Swami Sivananda, *The Bhagavad Gita,* (Divine Life Society, Shivanandanagar, 2003), 82-4. This extract is from the fourth Discourse, 5-10.

3 *Matt. 2:9.*

4 See the apocryphal *Gospel of Protevangelion* in Jesus' case. See *Matt.1:1, 12:2-3, 22:42,* etc., for Jesus being born of the line of king David.

5 See, Rutherford H. Platt, Jr., *The Lost Books of the Bible,* (Alpha House, N.Y., 1926), 'Gospel of Protevangelion' chapter 14:10-12. All of the books of the Apocrypha mentioned in this section can be found here.

6 *Luke 2:3-4.*

7 *Luke 2:15-16.*

g. King Kansa sought to kill Krishna by ordering the massacre of all male children born the same night as Krishna. This is an almost identical story to the 'slaughter of the innocents' ordered by Herod.[8]

h. Nanda fled to another country with the baby Krishna to escape the wrath of King Kansa after being warned by a heavenly Voice. In a similar manner, Joseph was warned by a Voice in a dream to flee to Egypt.[9]

i. Both Krishna and Jesus were said to have performed many miracles.

j. Krishna is sometimes depicted in Indian art as crucified with extended arms on a cross. He was also pierced by an arrow while hanging thereon, while Jesus was pierced by a spear.

k. The light of the sun was blotted out at noon during Krishna's death, whilst the sun was darkened from the sixth to the ninth hour during Jesus' crucifixion.[10]

l. Krishna went to the realm of the dead to liberate them before he ascended to heaven. The Apostle's Creed and the Gospel of Nicodemus depict Jesus doing a similar act.

m. When Krishna rose from the grave he ascended to heaven in the presence of many spectators, as also did Jesus.[11]

The patterning of the mythology is very similar because they both portray the incarnation of the same Divine Principle, the Christ Nature, as expressed both to the Western and Eastern worlds.

The advent of Maitreya

The Buddhist philosophy teaches of a succession of Buddhas, each of whom become dispensers of the Law *(dharma)* in a particular era. The future Buddha is called Maitreya, meaning 'the compassionate One'. He can therefore be considered the most advanced of all Bodhisattvas, personifying the compassionate understanding and other traits that

---

8 *Matt. 2:16.*

9 *Matt. 2:13.*

10 *Matt. 27:45.*

11 *Matt. 28:9-10.*

exemplify that Path.[12] This is also the major quality of the Christ, as has been formerly posited, and who thus could be considered to be Maitreya. The role of the one that incarnates amongst humanity to suffer the vicissitudes of *karma* (as humanity does) to gain Buddha-like liberation from *saṃsāra,* will however be played by another senior executive member of Hierarchy. This one is well prepared to embody Maitreya's function as the future Buddha. Much concerning this Initiate is presented in my book *The Constitution of Shambhala.*[13] He will come to manifest the stage of the forerunner to prepare humanity for the advent of the Christ's appearance, thus to lay the groundwork doctrines for the New Age. The Christ will seal the fact of the complete externalisation of the Hierarchy on earth. After His reappearance Hierarchy will gradually take over world governance via a totally reformed United Nations. The Christ's *karma* with *saṃsāric* involvement has ceased some time ago, which prevents him from directly playing a Buddha role.[14]

Maitreya is said to reside in His celestial abode, the highest of all the heavens, called Tushita (Tuṣita), from which he can serve all beings on the lesser realms. However, Tuṣita is not the highest of all the obtainable realms, and for many sincere devotees it is said to be quite accessible. Many pray to be born there after their deaths, as noted below:

> Moreover, Maitreya is of this world even now, dwelling in a realm that is much closer to us than is obvious to the Western observer with a rather different concept of what a heaven is. Heaven, Maitreya's abode until he is born once again among humans as a Buddha, is no remote, transcendent paradise. It is very much a part of this world system, one of a series of connected levels of existence, and not even the highest of those levels at that. In Buddhist cosmography these realms are so interconnected, in fact, that the skilled meditator moves easily among them in the exercise of yogic techniques. Much of the attractiveness of Maitreya as a cult figure stems from the fact that he is accessible to the aspirant, through meditative trance and through rebirth - even

12 How one would actually rank Bodhisattvas from a purely textual perspective is a moot point.

13 See *The Constitution of Shambhala,* Part A, 52-3, 58, 63, 65, 388-9.

14 Most high Initiates that gain the Initiation level that the Buddha did do so as the head of Ray lines that prevent them from becoming a Mānuṣa Buddha, the incarnate Teacher for a particular epoch, as was Gautama.

> now, long before his awaited advent as the next Buddha. Even more than Sakyamuni, Maitreya has been seen, in this sense, as a Buddha for the present, for those of this world and for those in even the most desperate of times.[15]

Maitreya is often depicted adorned with the ornaments of a prince (thus symbolically making Him the Son of a King[16]) seated on a chair with his legs down (in the manner of westerners) and also teaching the *dharma*. (This is in contradistinction to the usual lotus position in which Buddhas and Bodhisattvas are depicted.) The symbolism here is important. Seen in it is the forthcoming Buddha's innate affinity with the means of realisation associated with the West (which supports Him via His manner of sitting), as well as the inwards form of realisation associated with the East. (Meditative absorption is of course His intrinsic nature.) This western affinity befits Maitreya's forthcoming role in the cosmopolitan, egalitarian, international world we all now reside in.

Maitreya, however, will not repeat the same teachings or manifest the severe asceticism of His predecessor Gautama. Buddhism must be reformed, as well as the exoteric Christian doctrines. A new esoteric overlay must be given, as a new world religion must arise. The Buddhist world must therefore be prepared to discover that the outer lifestyle of Maitreya will differ significantly from what they idealistically expect. They must expect the unexpected.

Buddhists believe that Maitreya will appear as Buddha during a time when there will be innumerable inhabitants on earth who will be living in a state of peace, harmony, and cooperative good will. They will then be 'without any blemishes, moral offences are unknown among them, and they are full of zest and joy.'[17] This equates with a time when 'the holy city, new Jerusalem' will be seen 'coming down from God out of heaven, prepared as a bride adorned for her husband',[18] when there

---

15 Alan Sponberg and Helen Hardcore (editors), *Maitreya, the Future Buddha* (Cambridge University Press, N.Y., 1988), 288.

16 The King here being the Lord of the world, Sanat Kumāra.

17 Edward Conze, *Buddhist Scriptures* (Penguin Books, N.Y., 1959). See pages 238-42 for the prophecies concerning Maitreya's reappearance.

18 *Rev. 21:2.*

will be no more death, sorrow, nor pain. We see therefore, that both the Buddhist and Christian accounts of this future are similar.

The accounts concerning His appearance provide a time far in the distant future (such as 30,000, or even millions of years hence). Such time reckoning in Buddhism is generally quite symbolic, relating to meditative considerations and not to physical plane reality. When dealing with oriental mythology then numbers are nearly always highly exaggerated (with noughts added almost at whim). They are rarely literal, but are symbolic of subjective reality. Similarly is the mythos of whether he will be a Messianic figure or not. The meaning of the various exoteric doctrines concerning Him are thus open to speculation. There is a difference between the Theravādin expectations and the Mahāyāna views. My concern here, as per usual, is not to promote the exoteric accountings, but rather to present the esoteric view.

What is really symbolised in the myth of the golden era when He comes is not so much a particular incarnation of Maitreya. Rather, the appearance of an entire epoch or era and the related civilisation, which is the embodied Maitreya in a patronymic sense. His name and quality will sustain and be the father of that era. The imminent reappearance of the Christ however (with which this book is concerned), is also interwoven with that future patronym. The myths therefore relate to the period concerning Hierarchical externalisation, as a consequence of the reappearance of the Christ. Therefore, there is a process of the eventuation of that period which can be considered as the epoch of Christ-Maitreya,[19] when all of the heads of Hierarchy are externalised.

That at least one Buddhist saint has actively strived for the (imminent) reappearance of the Christ-Maitreya is provided by Lama Anagarika Govinda in his autobiography *The Way of the White Clouds*. There he states that his *guru* Tomo Géshé Rinpoché erected in the monastery of the White Conch:

> a gigantic golden statue of Buddha Maitreya, the Coming One, as a symbol of the spiritual future and rebirth of the Eternal Truth of the

19 Christ-Maitreya signifies integration of the functions of the Christ and the new Mahāchohan. The functions of both of these great Ones are explained in the two volumes of my book *The Constitution of Shambhala*.

> Dharma, which is reincarnated in every Enlightened One and is to be rediscovered in every human heart.
>
> Tomo Géshé, however, did not content himself with the success of his work at Dungkar. He erected statues of Maitreya in many other places and made the followers of the Buddha-Dharma conscious of the fact that it was not sufficient to bask in the glories of the past, but that one must take active part in the shaping of the future, and thus make it possible for the coming Buddha to reappear in this world by preparing our minds for his reception.[20]

In the Vagrakkhedikā (the *Diamond Sutra)* the question was put to the Buddha concerning whether in the most corrupt era there will be anyone that can understand the *dharma*. The Buddha answered that: 'there will always be some excellent Bodhisattvas who, even in the age of corruption, can understand the preaching of the Law'.[21] In the accompanying passage we have the statement:

> It is stated in the fifty-first section of the Mahâsannipâta-sûtra, that Buddha said: 'After my Nirvâna, in the first 500 years, all the Bhikshus and others will be strong in deliberation of my corrective Law. (Those who first obtain the 'holy fruit', i.e. the Srota-âpannas, are called who have obtained deliberation.) In the next or second 500 years, they will be strong in meditation. In the next or third 500 years, they will be strong in 'much learning,' i.e. bahusruta, religious knowledge. In the next or fourth 500 years, they will be strong in founding monasteries, &c. In the last or fifth 500 years, they will be strong in fighting and reproving. The pure (lit. white) Law will then become invisible.'[22]

When it is reckoned that approximately 2,500 years have passed since the *parinirvāṇa* of Gautama (600-500 B.C.), then we are most definitely in the age of 'fighting and reproving' when the 'pure Law' has become 'invisible' (i.e., secret). The need for the incarnation of the personification of the Divine that will allow humanity to again be strong in the deliberation of the 'corrective Law' is therefore great. It

---

20 Lama Anagarika Govinda, *The Way of the White Clouds,* (Rider and Co., London, 1972), 9.

21 E.B. Cowell, The Vagrakkhedikâ, from *Buddhist Mahayâna Texts,* (Motilal Banarsidass, Delhi, 1997), f/n, page, 116.

22 Ibid.

must certainly happen if the statement of Krishna that has been quoted is valid, for the embodiment of Compassion cannot ignore the massed cry of those that seek Light – to help when there is need.

The Aquarian epoch

The abovementioned 2,500 year period is also roughly the time of one great zodiacal year, including the intermediate period of the cusp between one sign to the next. The Buddha gained His *parinirvāṇa* near the end of the age of Aries, Jesus was born just after the beginning of the Piscean era, and we are now entering the age of Aquarius.[23] Christ-Jesus was referring to His forthcoming role in the Aquarian epoch when He asked two of His disciples to go into the city where they would meet 'a man bearing a pitcher of water', for Aquarius is the sign of the water bearer.

> Go ye into the city, and there shall meet you a man bearing a pitcher of water: follow him. And whatsoever he shall go in, say ye to the goodman of the house, The Master saith, Where is the guestchamber, where I shall eat the Passover with my disciples? And he will shew you a large upper room furnished and prepared: there make ready for us.[24]

The symbolic content of this statement is that Jesus asked His disciples to seek out that which bore the promise and qualities of the forthcoming age in the city. The city represents the type of urban civilisation that Pisces has bequeathed us.

The disciples were then to 'follow him', that is, they were to follow all that Aquarius conveys and thereby gain Aquarian qualities. The 'house' symbolises the physical body, and the 'goodman', the 'good' or spiritual person therein. To 'go in' therefore, is to enter into one's inner being. The 'guest chamber' is the lotus of the Heart, which greets openly and gives shelter to the Master and all His disciples – in fact to all sentient beings that are in need.

---

23 Dane Rudhyar presents many interesting well thought out astrological conjectures in his book *ASTROLOGICAL TIMING: The Transition into the New Age* (Harper and Row, N.Y., 1972). His thesis posits that the end of the Piscean era should be somewhere around 2062.

24 *Mark 14:13-15.* See also *Luke 22:10-13.*

The statement is 'The Master saith', for only the Voice of the Master, the 'voiceless Voice', can open the door to that chamber. The disciple must effectively become an expression of the Master to do so.

The Passover commemorates the deliverance of the Jews from bondage in Egypt, when the Hebrew nation properly came into being. To partake of the Passover supper with the Lord therefore implies that one was freed from the bondage of the material self. He/she is freed from the ties of slavery to the will of 'the Pharaoh' who rules the material world. The spiritual-self can then be said to have come into coherent activity in the physical realm.

The 'large upper room' signifies the Soul that has evolved to the degree that it is furnished and prepared with the necessary qualities to allow the Christ and His twelve disciples (the twelve signs of the zodiac and related energies) to dine therein. The entire story of the last supper thus symbolises the nature of the Aquarian dispensation, when humanity will be able to actively partake of the 'Body and Blood of the Christ'. Many will then have obtained the illumination that will allow them to stand consciously in the upper rooms of the houses of their spiritual Selves.

The 'pitcher of water' carried by the Aquarian symbolises the totality of the energies and capabilities possessed when integrated and aligned. 'Water' becomes the Blood of the Christ after one gains the visions and awareness that the mountaintop experience affords. This energy empowers all our capabilities, latent or spiritual, and what is objectivised. The developed Aquarian is the bringer of Divinity: the Wisdom, Love and the transcendental qualities that quench the thirst for spiritual knowledge. (In the undeveloped, Aquarian thirst is quenched for the sensual, the material and the transitory.) The Aquarian has effectively put all goods into his/her 'water pot', where the activities of that entire life are stored and offered for service to everyone. This is given freely to the needy, the distressed and sick, and nothing is asked for in return. Aquarians are truly universal in their embrace and are sensitive to the needs of their group that they serve with their hearts. The superficiality of the undeveloped Aquarian is transformed into deep-seated realisation and intention. Selfishness has become selflessness and personal service becomes selfless service to all beings.

The symbol of Aquarius (♒) is dual, denoting the mutual embrace of two parallel streams of energy (symbolised by two wavy lines, one above the other). The upper stream signifies the Soul (enlightenment), and the lower stream the forces of the personality. The Soul is the source of all inspiration, high ideals, and creative aspirations. It is the storehouse of all the knowledge gained through many epochs of evolutionary growth and experience. These higher, aesthetic qualities are embraced or exactly paralleled by those of the material world (the sensual, the corporeal, symbolised by the lower line). There is a vibratory mutual interplay, a balance of forces between Soul and matter that has the ability to evoke the highest in us – the most visionary, constructive, artistic, or creative amplitude that we are capable of. The undeveloped Aquarian will be fully involved in the vicissitudes of the *māyā*, the phenomenal world. In both cases however, the personality will be responsive to Aquarian influences through participation in group activities, for the wavy lines indicate that he/she is open to the polarised influences from all embracing energies. On a higher cycle, the two wavy lines symbolise the relation between Spirit and matter.

The symbol indicates that Aquarius is a fluid sign, one of constant movement, periodic cyclic activities and recurrent mutations. In Aquarius the various cycles of life are acknowledged and worked. This is seen on the earth today in humanity's intensely active (and sometimes chaotic) mass transportation systems, modes of communication, and rapid efflux and interchange of ideas. In this idea lies the fact that Aquarius is part of the Airy triplicity, with Gemini and Libra. The qualities first developed in Gemini and Libra find their fruition in Aquarius. Aquarius embodies the energy of Life, whilst Gemini is the *nāḍī* system that conveys that energy, and Libra embodies the clockwork mechanism (wheels or lotus petals) that cyclically direct these energies from one sphere of influence to the next. The mutability that orthodox astrologers assign to Gemini is an effect of the subjective influence of Aquarius.

Aquarius is part of the fixed cross, here representing the one-pointed attitude of the crucified Christ (or Initiate) who manifests the compassionate resolve of a world server, replete with the mutability needed to adequately meet ever-changing world needs.

The Element assigned to this sign is Air, corresponding to *buddhi* the realm of enlightenment. Humanity's inevitable spiritual or subjective conquest of, and receptivity to, impressions from the buddhic realms was symbolised as the physical conquest of the air by the airplane. (Such receptivity allows people to be 'born anew' into the measure of the stature of the fullness of Christ.) There is even a relation to space exploration; people have landed on the moon[25] and have sent probes to the outermost planets of the solar system and beyond. Note that buddhic perception is literally interplanetary awareness in a subjective, directly perceptive sense. Much later a touch of cosmic consciousness will be within the grasp of humanity.

The moon symbolises the energies pertaining to the form and to the personality. The feat of landing on the moon therefore finds its analogy in the integration and control of the integrated personality by the Mind. Up to the present era, however, humanity's onus has been to conquer the seas and to explore the continents of the earth. This symbolises the eventual control of the energies of the Watery and Earthy Elements.

In the previous sign, Pisces the fishes (governed by the Watery Element), Soul and form are yoked by a common bond and immersed in the waters of sensation. The keynote of the Aquarian dispensation on the other hand is freedom. In Aquarius the Piscean bond is separated, though interrelated. Therefore, we see many people rebelling against the old order – against the old Piscean, authoritarian, socio-political and religious systems. Many of the bonds that tied people to regimented, fixed ideas and modes of action are being broken by a new permissiveness, a new exploration of human livingness. There is also an amazingly rapid expansion of consciousness, producing a revelatory understanding of the nature of the cosmos.

The Aquarian dispensation will facilitate peoples' ability to access the potency of their Souls (veiled by Leo, the polar opposite of Aquarius). The Soul's energies will be able to fully embrace the material world fecundating it with the seeds of the aesthetic, the Divine. Such activity will increasingly manifest via groups of Soul-infused people. The potency of the lotus of the Soul becomes the vibrant womb of

25 Many have cast doubt concerning the possibility of this actually having happened then. One reason being that this feat has never been repeated since.

enlightenment from which the Christ-child will be born. The symbolism here also brings to light the esoteric meaning of *sukhāvatī,* the paradise realm of the Dhyāni Buddha Amitābha. The attributes of this realm will therefore increasingly manifest outwardly on earth as the Aquarian epoch progresses.

When a sufficient number of people have developed the needed sensitivity and warm-hearted response to the force of Love and universality, as indicated by Aquarius, then Christ can reappear amongst us. He will help flood the Airy propensity of this energy on earth.

Aquarius directs the Blood circulation (the 'Blood of the Christ') that distributes the energy of *buddhi* (the Air dissolved in the Blood) as the Waters of Life, to all the various cells in the Body of 'God'. Air thereby sustains their health and well being, as well as eliminating toxic substances and waste products. Esoterically, blood is *prāṇa.* Our blood stream (or its etheric counterpart) therefore transmits solar *prāṇa* to the entire form. Aquarius is thus the sign of the world server, for the bloodstream serves all aspects of the corporeal body with equanimity.

The esoteric concept of Blood circulation is viewed in terms of a trinity. Aquarius governs the Watery or Airy flow of energies, the vital Life-expression of the Blood. Gemini governs the etheric vehicle, through which this Blood flows. Scorpio (ruled by Mars) governs the Blood's objectivity (all testings relating to the flow of blood and of blood interrelationships).[26]

The orthodox planetary ruler of Aquarius is Uranus, which relates the highest and the lowest realms of perception, thereby prompting the evolutionary urge. It governs the seventh Ray of Ritual and Ceremonial Magic, hence the mode of control of the *chakras* and the etheric body. The prime expression of this Ray is to project subjective energies from Shambhala into manifestation. Uranian energies will facilitate people in the future to be able to utilise and see the *prāṇas.* Via the ethers Uranus governs the magical endeavour of the occultist and the prāṇic manipulation of the *yogin,* as well as all forms of natural healing and martial arts (such as Tai Chi) that rely on utilising *prāṇa* through rhythmic movement. The *devas* governing the ethers (the violet *devas* of the shadows that are the transmitters of *prāṇa*), also come under the

26 See Alice Bailey's *Esoteric Astrology,* 142, 212-13, 351-3 for further information.

auspices of Uranus. People will eventually enter into a new relationship with that angelic order, as was earlier demonstrated by the Findhorn community in Scotland. The Western world's present (scientific) discovery of the ethers is largely due to the subjective influx of the energies from Uranus. Inevitably many radical changes in people's understanding of the nature of Life (especially in relation to medicine) will come as a consequence. That there is life after death, for instance, will become a demonstrable fact.

Uranus is said to stimulate the organisational trend in people towards amalgamation and the formation of communal units. Much of humanity's activities in the future will therefore be organised towards a more receptive approach to world needs. The influence of Jupiter (and the second Ray of Love-Wisdom), the esoteric ruler of Aquarius, is prevalent here. It helps Uranus in its work of amalgamating people and various groups, by giving them a sense of world good will and communal Love.

Messianic sects and Christ's reappearance

A brief mention should be made of the many Eastern sects that have been gaining popularity in the West, which perpetuate in their doctrines the theme of the Reappearance of the Christ (in one form or another). The Divine Light Mission for instance, advocated that their leader, Guru Maharaji, is the actual reappeared Christ, quoting Biblical passages in an endeavour to prove their assertions. The Bahais, quoting from the writing of their founder Baha'u'llah, also believe that he (and his father 'the Bab') fulfilled the Biblical prophecy of the 'coming again of the Christ'.[27] Meher Baba, who had many followers in the West, has also stated that he was the Ancient One, the Christ, the Avatar for the New Age. Others, such as Sant Kirpal Singh (a modern Sikh saint) have also advocated the reappearance of the Christ in their writings.

Also many modern esoteric authors and movements, such as the Anthroposophical Society, the Theosophical Society (which even presented Krishnamurti as the Christ in the 1920's), the Coptic

27 See the book by J.E. Esslemont, *Baha'u'llah and the New Era* (Baha'i Publishing Trust, Illinois, 1970), 226.

fellowship, the Rosicrucians, the Findhorn community, Unity, and A.A. Bailey, all teach the imminence of the Christ in the New Age.

The presented list could be greatly extended if we also look at various 'doomsday prophets', specific Christian sects, or cults that believe their guru or Master is the direct representative or embodiment of the Divine for all people in this age. All this serves to illustrate the widespread expectancy of such an entity as the Christ amongst many religious followers in the world. The demand is great, and surely this is part of the signs of the times 'when all these things shall be fulfilled'[28] that will produce the appearance of the Christ. One can also look to the fulfilment of the part of the prophecy where Jesus asked us to 'Take heed that no man deceive you. For many shall come in my name, saying, I am Christ; and shall deceive many'.[29]

The objective here is not to point out what is right or wrong in the teachings of these schools. One must look at every religious, occult, or spiritual presentation objectively, and always be ready to sift out the kernels of truth, the substance of real worth, from what is 'chaff'. All teachings have some basis of truth, thus they attract earnest seekers, whilst many are also glamorised, offering erroneous concepts and sensationalised speculations. People must formulate what is right or wrong, truth or untruth for themselves. For in this manner, one develops one's spiritual perception, hopefully to grow in wisdom and Love, and thus evolve.

The aspirant to the Mysteries of Being must always realise that the Christ (or the *guru)* will come when the disciple 'looketh not for *him,* and in an hour that he is not aware of'.[30] For the 'kingdom of God cometh not with observation: Neither shall they say, Lo here! or, lo there! for, behold, the kingdom of God is within you'.[31] The Teacher must therefore be sought within. The Christ within must be known before the Master without can be recognised. This is a point needing reiteration because of its importance. All the outer Teacher can do is to open the awareness of the disciple by one means or another (and

28 *Mark 13:4.*

29 *Matt. 24:4-5.*

30 *Matt. 24:50.*

31 *Luke 17:20-21.*

the devices used to do this are innumerable) so that the inner Teacher, Light, the Christ, 'God', the Void, or the 'kingdom of God', can be revealed in its entirety.

It should also be noted that the theologians of many sects would have us believe many erroneous ideas concerning the second coming of the Christ. These are similar to the views that the Jews had of their expected Messiah, who would lead them to rule all the nations of the world. Jesus in fact entirely rejected such an idea in His third and last temptation in the desert – that of having temporal power over all the kingdoms of the earth. This had naught to do with serving 'the Lord thy God', thus 'Satan left him'[32] for he saw that Jesus could not be tempted with this, the most powerful of all earthly temptations.

When the Christ does come it will be because peace and good will have already been fostered amongst us and in our civilisation to a large extent. A large number of people will then have the ability to recognise what represents Divinity in their hearts. He will only come after the 'Gospel of the kingdom has been preached in all the world for a witness unto all nations',[33] as explained in chapter four. Everyone will thereby be given the opportunity to comprehend. Only then will they have the ability to recognise Him outside themselves, though not amongst the many clamouring voices that effectively say 'I am He'. The Christ will come at a time when the world's disciples will be so busy with their service work in the world that they will not be engaged in constant speculative assertions concerning this coming.

Also, it is not feasible for all 'good Christians' to be whisked away from the earth in their physical bodies by a Christ coming in the 'clouds of heaven'.[34] That He will come in this way is feasible, for many do so – by airplane. (There are however other esoteric interpretations of this verse.) The wishful expectations of the orthodoxy for (inane) miracle making, of 'great signs and wonders; insomuch that, if *it were* possible, they shall deceive the very elect'[35] (as proof of the resurrected Christ or as a reward for the faithful), will not produce His reappearance. This

---

32 See *Matt. 4:8-11.*

33 *Matt. 23:14.*

34 *Matt. 24:30.*

35 *Matt. 24:24.*

is effectively a perpetuation of the demand of an 'evil and adulterous generation' that 'seeketh after a sign',[36] which Paul also reviled against.[37]

That there will be many signs concerning Christ's reappearance, as for instance those given in Matthew chapter 24, is true. Understanding the symbolism given in that chapter and that associated with the 'signs' can however only be known by the 'elect',[38] by those that are Initiated into the symbolism of the Mysteries of the 'kingdom of God'. All others (possessing only the literal key of interpretation) can only err in their interpretations. This is especially so for that which is directly associated with the subjective domains, the conditionings concerning the future and the true nature of the Christ (and of 'God').

To 'the elect' the 'signs and wonders' are the phenomenal appearances of what they know so well from practical, internal experience. They concern the manifestation of the Real (the result of law, cyclic and karmic), which often encompasses an enormous expanse of time. Therefore, it is not possible to deceive 'the elect' (the Initiates of the higher degrees) with grandiose talk and naive expectations of miraculous happenings. Nor will they be deceived by unfounded talk of such things as: 'This is what is desired by the Christ', or 'He', or 'that', who is the 'direct representative or embodiment of the Christ, the only authority', and so forth. Through their inner visions they are able to see the Divinity in all, and the signs of its true appearance. This will be specifically so for third and fourth degree Initiates, who are to be gathered together: 'from the four winds, from one end of heaven to another'.[39]

These 'winds' refer to the four directions in the space that is the buddhic realm (of which 'wind', or Air, is the symbol of the associated energies). The 'winds' are also the cosmic *prāṇas,* from which are derived the Elements Earth, Water, Fire and Air. The phrase 'from one end of heaven to the other' can relate initially to the astral plane, but more specifically to the higher mental plane, wherein resides the Soul, and the Initiate of the third degree. Next one can consider the

---

36 *Matt. 12:39.*

37 See *2Cor. 11:14-15.*

38 See *Matt. 24:22, 24* and *31.*

39 *Matt. 24:31.*

entire domain of the Hierarchy of Love and Light. This phrase thus has a general reference to Initiates of all degrees.

The statement concerning those who would try to deceive all, even 'the very elect', needs comment:

> Wherefore if they shall say unto you, Behold, he is in the desert; go not forth: behold, he is in the secret chambers; believe it not.[40]

The 'secret chambers' refer to the various (lower) *chakras* and the powers associated with them. We are therefore asked not to believe those who would tell us that the Christ is found through awakening the powers *(siddhis)* of the lower psychic centres. Attaining such powers may or may not concern the development of enlightenment. Often they lead to the attributes of the deluded psychic. Furthermore, if developed with the wrong, selfish or egotistic motivation, then a black magician or sorcerer may become the eventual result. Such beings have the power to deceive the many. The 'guest chamber' wherein Jesus and his disciples ate the last supper is, however, a place where the Christ can be found, for it represents the 'chamber' that is the lotus *(chakra)* of the Heart.

The 'desert', where many would say He can be found, represents the battlefield of desire and the wilderness of the emotions that confronts all earnest disciples in the (spiritual) wastelands of our civilisations. It symbolises the tests and trials that the disciple must successfully overcome (as did Jesus in the desert) before he/she can be Initiated into the Mysteries and come to know the Christ. Jesus asked us therefore not to believe and follow the zealous, fanatical types in the beginning stages of their discipleship, who are still battling their material selves, and still possess much desire, glamour and illusion. They are still in the 'desert'. They are apt to try to exhibit or demand 'great signs and wonders'. They look for psychic and mediumistic types that are easily deluded by the phenomena they perceive, and who possess much egotism (the glamour of self-importance). Such people understand little about the powers that they have developed or the nature of the entities they might contact. (Many are the gullible that are fooled through the manifestation of their base *siddhis*.) The quoted passage therefore

40 *Matt. 24:26.*

illustrates the two major classes of beings that would tend to be 'false Christs and false prophets'.

In reference to this the phrase: 'For wheresoever the carcase is, there will the eagles be gathered together'[41] implies that whenever there exists the carcass of an old, outmoded, no longer viable, erroneous, or distorted doctrine or belief (what is putrid and decaying), there will always be those that profit (are nourished) by it. The term 'eagles' normally refers to Initiates of the higher degrees. Here however, the reference is to the aspirants, disciples and Initiates of the lower degrees that are still yoked to material perceptions (spiritual death and decay). They are thus illusion bound despite the Airy Element that can at times support them and allow them to soar high in the 'sky' of higher dimensional perception. Those who have a degree of illumined perception therefore, and yet whose minds are still clouded by materialistic attitudes or glamour, are effectively the cause of the greatest obstacles concerning the manifestation of the New Age. This is because of their oft fervent, zealously proselytising attitudes and ravenous intake of what is putrid and decaying – the 'carcase' of a doctrine from which the animating life has long since departed.

Other erroneous Christian doctrines

Regarding the churches, some of the (erroneous) doctrines that they have perpetuated throughout the centuries perhaps need comment.

1. Probably the most obvious is the idea of being rewarded for eternity in a heaven for all the adherents of their dogmas, and eternal damnation for all others, by a supposed 'God of Love'. This has kept millions of lives tied to the dictates of particular religious organisations through *fear* of the consequences if they turned their focus of attention elsewhere. This has also led the churches to send out missionaries to 'heathen' countries to convert them (by might and by right) into following those dogmas, with the idea of saving them from a mind-conceived eternal hell. The freedom of expression of many groups of 'primitive' people has thus been limited by forcing 'Christian ethics' and western social mores and ideals upon them.

41 *Matt. 24:28.*

Nowadays, such theological indoctrination has lost much of its persuasive power. This role has however been taken over by the materialism of the major capitalistic powers. In many ways the underdeveloped and 'backward' nations have been forced to compete materialistically with western greed in a very competitive world, when the need to was virtually non-existent.

Such indoctrinations have caused the less powerful countries of the world to choose sides in the many wars of the past century, wars in the name of a particular religion or ideology. There is very little effective difference between religious, social, or political indoctrinations. They generally result in undue friction, strife, and also enforced ignorance. It is good when people, groups and nations find out things for themselves and follow them (being fully aware of and able to choose alternatives). But if forced to follow any doctrine through the misrepresentation or banning of any other philosophy, then that is but an expression of evil. This happens one way or another to most people on the earth. That many have realised this and then reacted against such conditionings is a good and necessary sign, even though it causes much temporary strife. People who have acquired significant wealth and power through such fostered ignorance will seldom give it up without a fight.

2. Next is the concept of *original sin* (which is but a distorted form of the teaching of *karma),* that humanity is inherently wicked (instead of the opposite). Our progenitors simply followed their natural instincts, as explained earlier.
3. They also presented the concept that Jesus was the *only* 'Son of God': that all other saints, illumined and 'God-inspired' (outside of the Hebrew tradition), such as Lao Tze, the Buddha and Muhammad were deluded. They were considered advocates of Satan or of the Devil. The Christian view does not accommodate the fact that the evolution of consciousness happens via a succession of Sons of 'God', as explained in chapter two.
4. Next is presented a theism seemingly devoted to the building of stone temples and the amassing of money and material goods, instead of living the principles and maxims of the Christ. If the enormous wealth of our churches were used to truly help people, then much

of the prevalent poverty and its attendant evils would no longer exist. This is a generalised statement, for acknowledgement must be made to the beneficial philanthropic work that has been done by conscientious individuals, and some of the groups and Christian organisations to which they belong.

5. Also, Jesus is emphasised as a being of sorrow – the 'Son of God' who suffered and died on the cross, explicitly to wipe away our (original) sins. He would redeem us from a supposed perpetual limbo or hell only if we have faith in His works as exemplified by the doctrines of the Churches. What should however be exemplified is the resurrection of a *living Christ,* and of eternal Life for all of us – when we *follow the example of Jesus,* by dying on the cross of our material selves. All of us must eventually do this, and in this way enter 'heaven', by working out our 'own salvation'.[42] The Christ cannot do it for us, no matter how much one prays and wishes Him to do so. All of us, through the Initiation process, will eventually experience the Resurrection.
6. Next there is the idea of 'mortal sin' that would certainly lead one into hell – unless that person went to a confessional, presided over by a priest (in Roman Catholicism), to whom the person would confess his/her 'sins'. Then, upon payment of a token penance, such as four Hail Marys and so forth, the person would be exonerated completely (free to 'sin' again?). One can well understand the enormous power over the masses, and financial rewards the Churches received from such baseless fear-engendering practices and doctrines. (That is, being taught that it is not by one's own 'works'[43] – but *only* by going to a priest – whereby one gets to heaven and thus escapes eternal punishment.)

Even a few centuries ago the churches could torture and condemn a person to death for believing and propagating certain heresies (most of which are accepted as facts today). The subjective conditionings of the persecution of those times are still with us, with similar effects. Many Christians still condemn (through their scriptural derivations)

42 *Phil. 2:12:* 'work out your own salvation with fear and trembling'.

43 See *Matt. 16:27, James 2:14-24* and *Rev. 20:12.*

the greater part of humanity to eternal torture and punishment in 'hell', even though these views are rapidly being undermined by the dissension of the more liberal-minded members of our ecclesiastical structures.

The educational institutions of our societies have also not succeeded in fostering right human relations (on a truly intra-social and international scale), good will to all, and peace on earth. The increasing trend towards Fascism and censorship of people's right to free speech on the Internet, and through Government edicts, is now rapidly increasing. It appears that a great deal of the dogmatists and religious thought police of the earlier centuries have reincarnated into similar contemporary positions of power. This time their chosen vehicle is not so much with religious organisations, but via the organs of corrupt corporate and government agencies, politicians and the legacy mainstream media. Materialistic ideas are now espoused with a similar voracity as the religious ones of the past. Our educational institutions have generally posited extreme materialism and also selfishness, in part as a consequence of the amazing explosion of scientific and philosophic explorations and discovery of the past. Such discovery polarised people to react against the assertions of theologians,[44] and therefore oppose any concept of spirituality or of a subjective life embodied within the human form. People have realised their place in an enormous physical universe, where the laws of physics seem to aptly explain the reasons for human existence in a mechanical world. What is subtle or unseen and undetectable by instruments finds no place in the phenomenal world of materialists.

Despite its drawbacks, the age of scientific discovery has however been a necessary prologue to the New Age, for it has brought human thinking away from the domain of the zealot, and into the realm of logic from which wisdom can grow. The understanding of the physical universe and humanity's place in it has led scientific thought into the hermetic world of the metaphysician. The material is again being spiritualised in human thought,[45] and partly by this means (as previously stated) the New Age religion is dawning.

---

44 Such as that this earth came into existence in the year 4004 B.C., which was a widely sanctified and accepted dogma during that era.

45 My book *Esoteric Cosmology and Modern Physics* shows how the two disciplines (esoteric and the physical sciences) are directly interrelated.

The inconsistencies of religious, governmental, and societal policies and values are painfully obvious to most of us. Unfortunately, many are reacting and voicing their discontent in a violent way. Much of what is stated here may therefore be familiar to the reader, yet it is important to bring into perspective information that can also be found developed elsewhere. That there are many in every nation with their 'eyes open' (or whose eyes are opening) is a wondrous thing. Though many do not yet fully realise what it is they see, they have 'knocked' and the answer must come, as explained by Jesus: 'Ask, and it shall be given you; seek, and ye shall find; knock, and it shall be opened unto you'.[46]

All religions, faiths, creeds, doctrines, philosophies and approaches to Deity, are really different aspects of the ONE religion, the one perennial philosophy, as formulated by enlightened people at different times and social climates in the history of the world. The variations are but experiments in right human relations. This is a science that people are slowly learning, first religiously, and now socio-politically, through endeavours to live harmoniously as a unified body. People have learnt to interact within different societal echelons, at first tribally, then nationally, and now internationally. Eventually individuals will become 'God-realised' thereby. The most limiting, restrictive experiments must eventually move to new expansive and all-embracing forms. This is subjectively happening to our civilisation – it is changing from within, before our eyes, despite the efforts of the Lords of materialistic evil to offset the eventuation of the New Age.

The New Age

Christianity is really a bridging religion connecting the ancient philosophies (as exemplified by the Old Testament) with the forthcoming world order, the new religion that is concomitant with the externalisation of the Hierarchy of Love and Light. The new world-religion will arise primarily through agents born into the Western world, where many who formerly had Eastern incarnations, trained in oriental systems of philosophy, are now incarnating. They thus merge both Western and Eastern types of consciousness. For this reason, and through karmic

---

46 *Matt. 7:7.*

affinity, texts and videos on the I-Ching, Buddhism, Hinduism, and the Tao have become immensely popular in the West. This is to say nothing of the immense success of many Eastern teachers in the West.

The 'advance guard' of Initiates that collectively bear the intuitive faculties signifying the massed descent of the Christ-consciousness is now among us. They are found in all departments of Life. This process started in alternative cultures, such as the cooperative communal movements that appeared from 1966 on. This was the first tentative, outward manifestation of the Aquarian age. This revolution in consciousness was by a large number of alternatively minded people reaching similar conclusions in a unified manner, manifesting in many different nations across the world. The course of Western civilisation was radically changed towards a more permissive society, often to the dismay of the established conventional views of the majority of people.

The thinking of the then youth was truly international in its scope, and revolutionary in their resultant actions to transform society. There was the general idea of living in communion with Nature and combating societal evils in general. They were antithetical to nuclear proliferation and other plans of the war mongers, such as those that produced the Vietnamese war. Much of the resistance to this and other social issues was vocalised in the then popular music, which gained a vast audience. A new freedom in all aspects of living was thereby espoused.

These 'alternatives' – the hippies, environmentalists, and 'new settlers' – were effectively a collective St John the Baptist symbolically 'crying in the wilderness' (the desolation of life in our societies) against various evils perpetuated by the ruling class, to 'Prepare ye the way of the Lord, make his paths straight'.[47]

The hopeful demonstrations of illumined and alternate living styles of this group, plus those people working in the other departments of life, must continue and increase 'in wisdom and stature, and in favour with God and man',[48] to help end this present materialistic civilisation. What is seen here was the first efflorescence of the New Group of World Servers described in the books of Alice Bailey.[49]

---

47 Both quotes are from *Matt. 3:3.*

48 *Luke 2:52.* This was the way in which the boy Jesus grew to bear the vehicle of the Christ-consciousness.

49 See Alice Bailey's *The Externalisation of the Hierarchy* and *Discipleship in the*

Other indications that the New Age is dawning are seen in the constant movement, unrest, changes and tribulations presently ravaging the world.[50] This is seen in the churches, in our societies, governments, and in their educational policies. New Life is trying to pour into the diseased body of our civilisation to try to lay bare to those who have the 'eyes to see' all aspects of its corruption needing cleansing. The foundations of misconstrued beliefs that humanity formerly used to prop up obsolete social structures are now crumbling. Changes are affecting every country of the world; however, the forces of evil are using this unrest as an opportunity to try to cement their power over all upon this planet.

In retrospect then, in the twenty-first century, it has been seen that much of the tide of youthful idealism that was earlier expounded has been eliminated by the reactionary work of the dark brotherhood. They have entrenched themselves in all avenues of power in Western governments. When the present situation is coupled with the effects of the past two World Wars, and the later conflicts instigated by the USA and NATO, then what is seen is an immense slaughter of life and property by means of the 'Fiery Element'. Consequently, the prophecy in *Matthew* may well be fulfilled:

> For then shall be great tribulation, such as was not since the beginning of the world to this time, no, nor ever shall be.[51]

The word *tribulation* implies a direct and forceful type of energy, destructive in its intent, producing suffering or distress, an affliction or trials to overcome. Tribulation is therefore directly associated with life in the material and psychic worlds, where materialism has reached its greatest height (as in the present era). There is much sickness, poverty, famine and death to overcome in the world. Tribulation also implies

---

New Age, volumes 1 and 2 for detail. Of course, it is important not to idealise too much here, for there were also attendant evils that arose, such as the 'drug culture'.

50 Esoterically, this is an effect of the interrelation between the oncoming Uranian seventh Ray (the exoteric ruler of Aquarius) and Plutonian first Ray energies (the esoteric and Hierarchical ruler of Pisces).

51 *Matt. 24:21.* Such tribulation may well lead to World War III and the threat of nuclear Armageddon.

a period of great distress and destruction of the old order or scheme of things, allowing what is new and evolutionary (such as the New Age awareness) to be initiated. Once materialistic attitudes have been vanquished from human experiences, then tribulation as such cannot exist, and will never again exist on earth.

This word has further esoteric implications in relation to the destruction of material conditionings in a world sphere, zodiacal era, or kingdom in Nature. (These are all effects of increasing first Ray energies that will manifest from Shambhala during the coming epoch.)

The nations of the earth are quickening their pace of living. More is done each day than ever before and people are in a great hurry to make, explore and manipulate things. The slow, leisurely pace of the past, when every moment of the day simply flowed along virtually unnoticed, is long gone for most. Humanity is enslaved to the concept of time, and yet, because of the multiplicity of activities constantly engendered by people, time races by. Rarely is there enough time to accomplish what needs to be done. This effectively makes the days 'shorter': 'And except those days should be shortened, there should no flesh be saved: but for the elect's sake those days shall be shortened'.[52]

The *shortening* of the day is of benefit to 'the elect' because much can be given to, and quickly developed by aspirants, disciples and Initiates in the fervent pace of life. Those residing in the 'flesh' (which is the object of 'the elect' to save) can learn in a mere lifetime, or even in a few years, what it may have taken many lifetimes in the past to develop. The attainment of higher awareness (the enlightenment that will come en masse during the New Age) can also be presented to them. Group or mass Initiation is envisioned for humanity in the future.

One should therefore not be dismissal, or lose hope, concerning the activities of the forces of evil in this epoch, for Hierarchy have devised a rectifying Plan to overcome their schemes. The machinations of the forces of evil have been factored in the Plan. There is a countering strategy that will incorporate the work of the new Mahāchohan, as explained in *The Constitution of Shambhala*.[53] The epoch of Maitreya-Christ will consequently dawn.

---

52 *Matt. 24:22.*

53 See also the section 'The Doctrine of the Avatars', in *The Constitution of Shambhala,* Vol. 1, 394-411.

The twenty-fourth chapter of Matthew

The context of some of the more difficult passages of Matthew chapter 24 that have *not* already been explained shall be dealt with here. The symbolism presents significant information relating to the reappearance of the Christ, as well to the objective of evolution on the earth. An objective here is to present the necessary information that will make right interpretation of much prophetic symbolism possible. Such an exercise should prove valuable to the reader. Firstly, the passage below needs comment:

> Immediately after the tribulation of those days shall the sun be darkened, and the moon shall not give her light, and the stars shall fall from heaven, and the powers of the heavens shall be shaken.[54]

Though this can admit of a literal interpretation (such as the darkening of the sun and the obscuration of the moon by means of clouds and smog that may be the result of this 'tribulation'), its real significance is illumined through analysis of the esoteric meaning. The phrase 'Immediately after the tribulation of those days' implies that immediately after people have mastered their material selves and have stilled their turbulent activity in *saṃsāra* (the 'tribulation'), having learned to live harmoniously and in peace in the world, then 'shall the sun be darkened'. This means that 'the sun', the radiant Solar Angel (the Soul) shall be 'darkened' (put into shadow) by the brilliance of the incoming Christ-Light *(buddhi)* on earth. (In a similar sense, sunspots are darkened areas on the face of the sun, even though their temperatures range around 3-4,000 degrees Centigrade and are actually brighter than melted tungsten.) 'The moon', which symbolises the personality-nature, will then be completely subordinated to the divinity manifesting within.

The sun relates to the *piṅgalā nāḍī* and the moon to the *iḍā nāḍī,* hence the focus is a yogic interpretation. The inference concerns the integration of these two *nāḍīs* into the central *suṣumṇā* channel, which will then dominate the consciousness of the Initiate. This produces the onset of enlightenment (the third Initiation), signified by the fall of 'the stars' (illumined perceptions). The 'powers of heaven shall be shaken'

54 *Matt. 24:29.*

because 'heaven' (the realm of enlightened Being – Hierarchy) must now accommodate the increased service arena of the newly awakened Initiate.

The fall of *'the stars...from heaven'* also refers to the 'fall' or incarnation (the descent) of the entities associated with the Hierarchy of Enlightened Being. This is now manifesting in relation to a major period of tribulation; this is associated with the wars of the past century onwards, including an impending third world war. Literally then as a consequence, 'the sun be darkened, and the moon shall not give her light', because of all of the smoke and fallout raining down. The scenario of a possible nuclear war will however be relatively limited, for the Lords of Life will not deem it necessary for humanity to be extinguished. Rather, the available materialistic *karma* will be cleansed thereby. Specifically, this is the *karma* of the *rapine* that the Western nations have committed to the rest of the world (from the period of the colonial empires and their aftermath, right to the present decade).

To an awakened vision, the descent of the members of Hierarchy are seen as 'stars falling'.[55] They embody the potent, animating radiance or spiritual Life and Light that vitalises all forms. This phrase therefore has reference to the externalisation process of the Hierarchy of Enlightened Being that will result in the formation of the New Jerusalem on the earth. The verse therefore concludes with the statement: 'and the powers of the heavens shall be shaken'. This means that the entire constitution of 'heaven' (the domain of the Hierarchy) and its energies will be altered and rearranged. The powers and energies of this and the *deva* kingdom will be 'shaken' or loosened from the bonds that held them in 'leash' for many millennia. Such a mass externalisation will produce a series of testings and problematic rearrangement and adjustments amongst the Ashrams of the Masters.

There is also a hint here in that at some distant time (probably near the end of the Aquarian age), when people have transformed all aspects of materialistic life so that 'tribulation' is not possible, then the attainment of the fourth Initiation will be a common occurrence for humanity. Groups of Initiates will pass the necessary testings in order to receive it.

---

55 The literal interpretation as that of the fall of a meteor shower is relatively meaningless, whilst scientific research has aptly demonstrated the impossibility of the literal fall of the billions of suns in the universe.

Once this externalisation process has appropriately begun:

> then shall appear the sign of the Son of man in heaven: and then shall all the tribes of the earth mourn, and they shall see the Son of man coming in the clouds of heaven with power and great glory.[56]

Jesus also states categorically 'Verily I say unto you, There shall no sign be given unto this generation'.[57] Elsewhere He states that no sign shall be given to this 'evil generation', but 'the sign of Jonas the Prophet. For as Jonas was a sign unto the Ninevites, so shall also the Son of man be to this generation'.[58] The meaning of the 'sign of Jonas' was explained in my book *Meditation and the Initiation Process,*[59] where it was shown to refer to the attainment of the third Initiation. The 'sign of the Son of man in heaven' therefore would be an extension of this idea. It thus refers to the attainment of the fourth Initiation and the subjective fixed cross upon which the Initiate of this degree is crucified 'in heaven', in the realm of enlightened Being. Those that will receive this sign therefore are no longer the 'evil generation', but rather are those who have largely overcome much of the worst of the evils of that generation, and so have moved into the New Age.

The 'Son of man' literally implies 'the Son' aspect of Deity (the second Ray of Love-Wisdom) that has evolved in humanity ('of man'). The principle of Love-Wisdom is the enlightenment-consciousness that is the 'child' of our present evolutionary attainment. The 'sign' of this attainment will therefore 'appear in heaven', thereby sounding out a note or resonance of completion – the conclusion of what began aeons ago when Eve first picked the forbidden fruit in the garden of Eden (which was 'in heaven'). By this means this sign constitutes a doorway of escape to Hierarchy and eventually away from earth evolution (the material realm) for those that can rightfully develop the Initiate path to conclusion. This path leads into cosmic space, to the 'Heart of God' from a cosmic perspective.[60]

---

56 *Matt. 24:30.*

57 *Mark 8:12.*

58 *Luke 11:29-30.*

59 *Meditation and the Initiation Process,* 294-95.

60 For those of our planetary and solar system this is the star Sirius.

Then 'shall all of the tribes of the earth mourn'. To mourn means to express sorrow, usually in relation to what has died or passed away. Here, however, the 'mourning' is over the earth, which had been the home of humanity for the entire span of their existence. The reference here is to the fourth Initiation, the Renunciation, which causes what had been an ideal 'home', serving its purpose for untold ages, to be renounced in the light of evolutionary progression. (The death of the Soul-form also occurs at the fourth Initiation.) The earth will eventually lose its substantiality, it will etherealise and consequently 'pass away'. After the period when groups of Initiates pass their fourth Initiation then many will disincarnate and prepare to leave the earth far behind. (This happens at the sixth Initiation.) 'The first earth' will then pass away, as also will the 'first heaven',[61] for a new planetary sphere will have arisen wherein the present animal kingdom will become a humanity. The graduates from our earth will become the executive members of the then Shambhala. This eventuation obviously lies far in the future for humanity.

The 'sign of the Son of man in heaven' (in the 'sky', the Airy Element) also has a direct reference to the Aquarian age, for Aquarius is the sign of a man bearing a pitcher of water. The other signs are more specifically related to various aspects of the animal kingdom, except Gemini the twins, Virgo the virgin, Libra the balances and Sagittarius the archer. Aquarius is the sign wherein the qualities that are peculiar to humanity's own development become dominant. Also, as the Element it rules is the Air *(buddhi),* so its qualities aptly symbolise what will allow the attainment of the fourth Initiation by the new 'generation' that will evolve during this sign. In a similar sense, the attainment of the third Initiation, and the related wisdom (or illumination) were the onus of the past (Piscean) era, or 'generation'.

Though explained earlier in chapter ten, the term 'generation' needs further comment here, for Jesus says:

> Verily, I say unto you, This generation shall not pass, till all these things be fulfilled.[62]

---

61 *Matt. 24:35* and *Rev. 21:1.*

62 *Matt. 24:34.*

He was obviously not referring to the generation of beings alive in Jerusalem at His time (reckoned as a thirty year interval), for those things did not come to pass during their time. What He must have been referring to therefore was a racial cycle or 'generation' that dominates any particular era. By means of cyclic rebirth they evolve the same basic character traits and together manifest the same civilisation. Eventually a time will come when a generation appears where a significant number can overcome material involvement by undergoing the fourth Initiation. Then shall those that mourn see the 'Son of man coming in the clouds of heaven with power and great glory'.[63] 'Clouds' can be thought of as what clothes the air and obscures the Light of the spiritual Sun to varying degrees. They thus symbolise the outer forms (the corporeal sheaths) of all beings that reside in 'heaven', the inner planes of perception. For the 'Son of man' to come 'in the clouds of heaven', therefore, means that the Christ will come with the externalising Hierarchy of Enlightened Being. Myriad are the *devas* that will accompany them to embody the substance of what is to manifest. This is a process that will not be seen with the physical eyes, but clairvoyantly, for large numbers of that 'generation' shall possess such vision.

Collectively, the Hierarchy embody the 'Son' or Love-Wisdom aspect for this planet. The 'kingdom of God' signifies the Will or Father aspect, and humanity represents the Activity or Mother aspect.

Hierarchy will come to externalise the planetary Heart centre on earth. In time this will evolve into a planetary Head centre, the New Jerusalem, wherein the 'Son of man' (the Christ) will eventually be established as the 'King'. This is the significance of the statement that He shall come 'with power and great glory'. The meaning of the word *glory* was also explained in chapter ten. This is in relation to the radiant energies of the Christ, though most Biblical passages refer to the 'glory of God', where it has a similar implication, though upon a much vaster arena of influence. Glory means, esoterically, to give an aura, an ineffable Radiance, to what essentially has no attributes. Glory veils the *dharmakāya,* allowing it to be registered as an omnipotent Sun, the central spiritual Dynamo of All-Being. When accompanied with Power, it is essentially an emanation or radiation from the Throne

63 *Matt. 24:30.*

or Seat of Power of a planetary or solar Logos. (Power is the first Ray energy that is the fundamental aspect of a Logos as the 'Father' of All-Being.) What is therefore implied is the triumphant expression of the energies from Shambhala that will accompany the Christ's appearance.

Such is the nature of the process that will evolve from the time of the initial reappearance of the Christ onwards. The imminent Christ that will instigate the Aquarian age, on the other hand, is more specifically symbolised by the statement likening the coming of the 'Son of man' to lightning that comes from the East and shines to the West,[64] the meaning of which has been explained at the end of chapter five.

The sounding of a *trumpet* with regard to the evolution of time and space and the production of enlightenment was explained in chapter eight. In relation to this, the following verse refers to the method whereby a new world sphere or earth and the accompanying heaven are formed:

> And he shall send his angels with a great sound of a trumpet, and they shall gather together his elect from the four winds, from one end of heaven to another.[65]

That earth will be ruled by the planetary Logos Who will establish a Seat of Power thereon. The angels are the Lords of *karma,* and they will accordingly manipulate the substance of space (the *karma* of the past) into the matter of a new dense sphere of activity and evolution by means of the 'great sound' of the 'trumpet'. Here the *elect* are Initiates of the higher degrees that will embody the powers (the 'four winds', or Elements) associated with the new heaven. They represent the entities possessing the necessary qualities for the forthcoming work and will be 'gathered together' from the ranks of those that had attained liberation in the past evolution.

The phrase 'one end of heaven to the other' refers to the highest and lowest levels of the kingdom of Enlightened Being and the exalted realms of Being or dimensions of perception wherein they reside (the buddhic, ātmic, and higher realms). Thus all Initiates from all levels of perception (associated with the four Elements) will be gathered together

64 *Matt. 24:27.*

65 *Matt. 24:31.*

to manifest the needed service work associated with the coming of the 'Son of Man'. All will work to fulfil their role in the externalisation process of the Hierarchy, and of the consequences for the sum of the Aquarian epoch. They will set their mark on this earth by projecting the needed *karma* (their vision of the new globe that will come to be).

The next verse states:

> Now learn a parable of the fig tree: When his branch is yet tender, and putteth forth leaves, ye know that summer is nigh.[66]

The 'fig tree' has similar implications as the Bodhi tree under which the Buddha gained His enlightenment. It is the tree of Initiation. The branch that 'is yet tender, and putteth forth leaves', symbolises the budding of the Initiate-consciousness in the hearts and minds of people everywhere. In Jesus' time this Initiation tree for the world disciple was still at an initial stage of its development. Now, however, that tree has had time to mature, hence a large number of Initiates have since developed. People are in the midst of a worldwide development of intelligent comprehension of the nature of the universe through scientific investigation. They are asking enlightening questions in many arenas of life. This is needed if further philosophic speculation along the Eastern way is to be added to this Western orientation, to result in more of humanity undertaking the Initiation path. (As stressed throughout this work.) Those on earth will soon be initiated further into the Mysteries, because the coming of the 'Son of man' represents the appearance of the spiritual summer and the life-giving Rays of the transcendent Sun.

Many other passages of chapter 24 of Matthew have already been explained, needing no further comment. In the presented interpretation concerning the 'final day of Judgement' I have focussed upon the most esoteric meaning. Interwoven also is the symbolism associated with the imminent reappearance of the Christ. From this point of view the meaning of the darkening of the sun and moon in *Matt. 24:29* has already been noted. The fall of the stars from heaven can refer to the mass incarnation of human Souls on earth, synonymous with our

---

66 *Matt. 24:32.*

present worldwide population explosion. The 'shaking of the powers of the heavens' then means a consequent rearrangement of the constituent energies. When the 'sign of the Son of man in heaven' refers to the appearing Aquarian age, then the 'mourning' of the 'tribes of the earth' refers to the effect that the period of tribulation ('of wars and rumours of war') will have upon them. The phrases also refer to the renunciation process (the dispersion of selfish and materialistic attitudes) that will eventually lead to many obtaining their fourth Initiation at the end of that age.

The 'coming in the clouds of heaven' can, as before noted, refer to the utilisation of the airplane by the 'Son of man'. Clouds are also composed of water droplets and vapour, and thus refer to the astral or emotional realm, whereon the Christ was 'slated' to reappear in this New Age. (As noted, the dense physical, corporeal Incarnation is also expected.) The bulk of humanity are polarised on this (emotional) realm, therefore much of the work of the Christ and His disciples during this New Age will be to cleanse the astral environment, the 'clouds', the massed, glamorised thought-forms produced by people. (These effectively block the Light of the spiritual Sun.) They must be dispersed if the higher Initiations are to be undertaken. Esoterically the 'clouds of heaven' are therefore definitely material. Here the energies of the Christ are most needed, therefore where His appearance is most viable. The 'power and great glory' represents the spiritual energies that will be at His command, with which Divine Purpose will be accomplished.

The angelic kingdom embodies the forms of all Lives, as well as being Lords of *karma*. To send the *angels* therefore means to send or express those units of consciousness that will produce the perfection of the corporeal body of the earth and all upon it. Such must be perfected if spiritual *karma* is to be adequately expressed, and evolutionary purpose fulfilled. This will allow the 'passing away' (and hence 'mourning') of the streams of Life on earth, and eventually of the earth itself. The coming of the Aquarian age will effectively sound out the first major step of the liberation process, the path of active return for all. (Unfortunately, avaricious people have manifested a materialistic version of this process through the widespread denudation of our forests and destruction of its animal life.)

The 'great sound' of the trumpet can therefore be considered to be the unified subjective sound (or mantra) of every entity on earth, as each takes what is for it the next step on the 'ladder' that is the backbone of Being. Therein is found the *kuṇḍalinī* Fire. *Kuṇḍalinī* is not just centred at the base of the spine of a person, but it finds its expression on every level of evolution of all kingdoms – of those streams of Life that relate to the *iḍā* and *piṇgalā nāḍīs* of our Logos. This will effectively stimulate the arousal of planetary *kuṇḍalinī* and will tend to liberate the Life aspect within all forms by a multitude of means. (These are often seen as catastrophes by people, but even man-made disasters are really aspects of the 'great sound'.)

The congruent, hastened evolutionary progression (Initiation) of every kingdom of Nature on earth (which are embodied by the angelic kingdom) will therefore call forth 'the elect'. This will also produce the coming of the 'Son of man'. Here 'the elect' represent the foremost elements, Lives, or units of consciousness – the most advanced or perfected examples, of any evolutionary Life stream. In this context, the phrase 'the four winds' refers not only to the four directions in time and space and to the four Elements, but also to the four kingdoms in Nature, from which 'the elect' are derived, in their varying capacities.

- The *first wind* relates to the Element Earth (the etheric realm), the Initiate of the first degree, as well as to the mineral kingdom.
- The *second wind* relates to the Element Water (the astral realm), the Initiate of the second degree, and to the vegetable kingdom.
- The *third wind* relates to the Element Fire (the mental realm), the Initiate of the third degree, and to the animal kingdom (for intelligence is that to which they aspire).
- The *fourth wind* refers to the Element Air *(buddhi),* to the human kingdom (who innately embody the quality) and to the Initiate of the fourth degree (who thereby represents the flower of human evolution).

They are winds because they are *prāṇas* that flow through the *nāḍīs* of earth to produce the evolutionary development of the various kingdoms of Nature. These winds are expressed within the human *nāḍī* system, which synthesises all that has preceded it, and also incorporates a fifth wind (Aether) that signifies the future for all. The energies (winds) of differing degrees and qualities need to be mastered to gain liberation from *saṃsāra*. The enlightenment process is thus the gain of this prāṇic flow.

The phrase 'from one end of heaven to another' regarding the Initiates of the higher degrees has been commented on, though 'heaven' here has reference to all the planes of perception wherein the liberated entities from the varying streams of evolution can be found.

'The elect' are 'gathered together' because of their needed work in laying the foundation for the eventual emergence of the New Jerusalem, the 'kingdom of God' on earth. As stated, this concerns the externalisation process of the Hierarchy of Enlightened Being that must precede the appearance of that kingdom.

Because the Initiation of all 'the tribes of the earth' is the focus of the coming Christ, so Jesus gives us the parable of the fig tree.

As stated, from a psychic or yogic perspective, the sun and moon symbolise the right and left *nāḍīs*. The terms then also relate to the *chakras* that embody and qualify these *nāḍīs*. The *piṇgalā nāḍī* moves from the Solar Plexus centre to be anchored in the Heart centre, which stands as a radiant sun that intensifies as a person overcomes all forms of tribulation. In relation to this the *iḍā nāḍī* moves from the Sacral centre to be anchored in the Throat centre. The Sacral centre embodies the energies (vitality) of the personality and effectively shines similar to the moon's reflected light. (A crescent moon is its symbol in meditation texts.) From this perspective the 'darkening of the sun' refers to the opening of the central iris or 'jewel in the heart of the lotus' (of the Heart centre). This appears as an expanding, electrical, indigo-blue disc to the inner vision of the seer. It is the aperture or door of entry into space, through which consciousness must travel if one is to be liberated from the form. The light of the personality nature that is expressed by the Sacral centre consequently becomes obscured (the 'moon' thus 'shall not give her light') as a person becomes liberated. The form of desire-based consciousness that normally dominates the integral personality then no longer rules.

An enlightened person is confronted by space in its entirety, unobstructed by the points of light that represent the sentience of innumerable beings (that relate to the material world). For such a being the 'stars' can then effectively be said to have fallen from heaven. They 'fall' below the enlightened One's normal level of awareness, once *śūnyatā* is experienced. The enlightened become masters of all the forces and powers of heaven, thus they are 'shaken', for these powers no longer dominate their activities in the world. The 'sign of the Son of man' then becomes the symbol of their attained enlightenment. The 'tribes of the earth' that shall 'mourn' are the various elements, the *saṃskāras* of the three-fold personality that have been transformed or ousted from the psyche. The liberation of all the forces *(devas)* of the corporeal form produces a resultant 'mourning' of those forces. The gross form will consequently be gradually transmuted into a body of Light-substance. When looking to the world of human livingness the vision is via 'in the clouds of heaven' (through the substance of their various sheaths), and manifests with 'power and great glory'.[67]

The transmutation process is accomplished by 'gathering together' the four winds or Elements 'from one end of heaven to another', thereby allowing the Initiate to completely master their full expression. This also incorporates the angelic forces *(devas)* which constitute the corporeal sheaths and their Elements. As one learns to master such forces with increasing effectiveness, so one climbs up the Initiation tree (the 'fig tree').

The Initiation path thus produces a radical transformation occurring in every facet of life in the world. Humanity has yet to think more intelligently concerning the underlying causes of suffering on this planet. Those who are awakened must rightly educate the ignorant and insouciant masses, to try to counteract all outstanding societal problems. The hormones (the awakened messengers) in the Body of Deity must play their proper role, if That Body is to prepare for the birth of the Christ-child. That Child must yet grow and mature. Those that are against this birth cannot prevent it, for despite the outer seeming the Plan of 'God' will inevitably cause the sweeping changes needed. The forces of darkness can only act to delay the appearance of the New Age.

The ethics of modern civilisation and its materialistic mode of action must continue to change as the New Age approaches. The state

---

67 They are the first and second Ray energies of Will and Love-Wisdom that become the Initiate's manifest radiance or aura.

of awareness, or Revelation, that will be brought with the appearing Child will inevitably emerge into the 'light of day' and enlighten all. People can be taught to live at peace with others, despite their seeming predilection for war. The prime means to achieve this is by right human relations in all aspects of Life, and between the nations that rule this world.

Everyone that believes in peace, the freedom of human thought and cooperative action, the oneness of all Being, and the factor of good will should more openly unite and demonstrate their convictions. They should unitedly voice their opinions to world leaders and those in power. The new world order cannot be accomplished by violence, by running away from society, or by the avoidance of one's responsibilities. It must be achieved by active service – by changing the system from within. This is a task focussed upon today's youth. The future is their accomplishment and they must make it liveable.

General summary

It can be said that the two greatest exponents of the universal Wisdom Religion (and who have influenced more beings than any other) during historical times are the Buddha and the Christ.

The Buddha was the outcome of a system of religious training based on introspection, the quietening of all outer functions and activities – all emotional reactions and incessant mental chattering. The resultant intensely focussed, deep inner 'point of tension' allows the Source of all Life (the 'divinity *within*', living at the heart of every atom) to be contacted. A Buddha is said to reside eternally in an unformed, uncreated, unknowable, unmodified, immutable state of Being *(nirvāṇa),* possessing what has been likened to a 'diamond-consciousness' *(cintāmaṅī).*

Because this state of Being is described by the use of negatives to show what it is not, the western intellect has interpreted it as meaning the negation of Deity, of all Life. However, as previously explained, the opposite is really the case – an absorption into the eternal duration of Being/Non-Being, though it does mean a negation of the concept of the separative self. It is symbolised by the word 'Mind' and the related properties, which the Buddha embodied. This is especially significant in Mahāyāna Buddhism, where the various aspects of the Mind are given the names of the various Deities, Buddhas and Bodhisattvas of its pantheon.

The method of Divine realisation (Initiation) that arose in the East (with its emphasis upon the observation and control of the personality and its innate inner energies) can be called the *science of evocation.* Meditation is an integral part of this system. Its objective is the attainment of wisdom: the compassionate-understanding concerning the nature of Being and the resultant complete liberation from the throttlehold of what is material in nature. Such concerns non-attachment to the concept of 'I', to the vicissitudes of the formed world (which is the cause of suffering). The example of the Buddha's life exemplifies this methodology.

The other method gave a means of 'God-realisation' from outside the human personality. It arose in the Middle East and the West – the Judaeo-Christian, Chaldean, Egyptian, Persian, Assyrian and Muslim systems. (Also that of the Inca, Mayan, and the Aztec civilisations in the Americas.) This was normally highlighted by a period of internment in a cave or crypt, as symbolised by the raising of Lazarus from the 'dead'. It allowed the person's spiritual body free access to visions and the wisdom associated with the external universe. Such awareness was retained upon awakening. The entombment process was normally preceded by careful observation and control of the external forces of Nature, psychic development, and by conformity to the Laws or Commands of a transcendent Deity. High Knowledge was often conveyed via angelic messengers from 'God', or by direct embodiments (such as the Prophets and priest-Kings). They normally worked in harmony with the laws of Nature in order to help them access Divinity.

The science of astrology, prayer, contemplation and ritualistic observation were an integral part of this system. Its objective was to evoke intuitive response to external energies by means of sound knowledge that eventually allowed the *knowing* to fall below the threshold of consciousness. Love to 'God' and to humanity was exemplified, promising a consequent 'union with' or 'abstraction into' Deity, or to a heavenly paradise. This can be called the *science of invocation,* as embodied by the dispensation of the Christ.

The Buddha refused to speculate upon the existence or non-existence of a 'God', saying that one should not confuse the issue of gaining enlightenment by attempting to rationalise the nature of Deity.[68] The

68 See my book *Considerations of Mind, a Buddhist Enquiry,* 195-203 for further

Christ taught of a transcendent, All-embracing, yet personal Deity, and that the way to enlightenment was by means of union with, or explicit obedience, to the Instructions of Deity. Also taught was the Divine Approach or Union of that Deity with humanity.

The new world religion that is evolving in our civilisation (both in the East and the West) will integrate both methods of invocation and evocation.

Many are the 'Sons of man' that have realised the goal of corporeal evolution, that have gained enlightenment in the past. The trend will speed up, producing a continuously increasing number of Initiates arising out of humanity. Group consciousness, and then universal awareness, are increasingly being awakened by the candidates for enlightenment. All who aspire to high ideals and service in one form or another have subjective links with them. In the past, when the Masters of Wisdom incarnated here and there, they produced outstanding and lasting effects upon humanity and their civilisations. Together, Initiates of all degrees constitute the Hierarchy of Enlightened Being. They are now rapidly incarnating into the world to prepare the way for the Christ, to manifest the necessary educational work that must be accomplished, allowing the prophecy that 'every eye shall see him'[69] to be fulfilled. This process necessitates the 'gospel of the kingdom' to be 'preached in all the world for a witness unto all nations'.[70] This Gospel is not the exoteric doctrines that the Christian communities have preached throughout the centuries, but the esoteric doctrines presented in my books and those of Alice Bailey. Those communities have never understood what this 'kingdom' actually represents or its true constitution.

Such incarnations are found amongst today's truth tellers, who are in conflict with the forces of materialism, crystallised assertiveness, mainstream dogmas and bigoted attitudes. They can be presented as voices 'crying in the wilderness'. They are revealing the truth of what has produced much of the chaos and unrest in the world. The authorities ruling our societies therefore endeavour to censor these voices by all the means of power at their disposal. This is a natural effect of what

---

discourse concerning the concept of a 'God' in Buddhism.

69 *Rev. 1:7.*

70 *Matt. 24:14.*

is new and innovative upon people that fear change, and who hold the reigns of power.

The Christ-force can be said to represent an immense reservoir of a type of energy termed *buddhi* that can be stored and transmitted by a capacitor (a cell) for a specific purpose. In the past, individual 'cells' ('Sons of God') were overshadowed here and there as they evolved the necessary vehicles of reception. (The 'capacitance' needed.) Today, at the dawn of a new era, an increasing number of such 'cells' will be simultaneously overshadowed. They will demonstrate (and are demonstrating) a common-Mind with common motives, conveying similar energies.

When these 'cells' (isolated though in unity) are working in synchronised fulfilment, then the Christ will be able to reappear as the seed point in a lotus blossom that is a living *maṇḍala*[71] of selfless servers. Each of these blossoms forms a seed point *(bīja)* for lesser flowers, and so forth. Each petal in a flower has a different hue or vibration than that of its neighbour. Thus there is a diversity of methods, approaches and qualities. They all share a basic similarity of purpose, for all are fed by the same reservoir and produce similar seeds. This can also be likened to the workings of a radio receiver with many components, each having different characteristics and functions, some of which form the receiver part of the set, and others the amplifier part.

There are seven principal flowers or *chakras* in the body of a person and of 'God'. The seven Ray Ashrams of Hierarchy can also be considered as *chakras* under the auspices of the Heart centre. They manifest as the seven departments of Life. Some of these will be more active than others to produce the birthing of the New Era. This activity will principally be headed by the seventh Ray Ashrams, supported by the third, second and first Ray Ashrams manifesting via the agency of the fourth Ray (which governs humanity in general). Significant detail concerning their role in the externalisation process of Hierarchy and the reappearance of the Christ has been provided in my two volumes of *The Constitution of Shambhala*. No one country, group, or religion, will be able to claim the focus of His attention, for with the development

---

71 A *maṇḍala* is a diagram of hermetic symbols that can be used to evoke highly potent forces, or entities.

of modern transportation and communications, His work will be international in scope and interplanetary in magnitude. Having said this, it should be obvious that the esoteric doctrine explained in my books will be further developed by the time of His appearance and will have a wide dissemination amongst humanity. It will become the vehicle via which He clothes His manifest Purpose.

An embodied vibrant *maṇḍala* is the method whereby Divine Rhythm can be advocated for and Divine Purpose made manifest. In the last appearance of the Christ, that *maṇḍala* was composed of twelve apostles (forming the Heart centre) and an interested 500 disciples. This time it will be groups (not individuals) that will be concerned. They will have anchored and stabilised on earth some potent forces from Shambhala by the time of the manifestation of the Aquarian age. This will produce the needed changes in human thinking that will allow His approach to humanity, and so properly awaken the New Age civilisation.

Our planet will also be overshadowed by a cosmic Christ Who will project Divine energies (cosmic Prāṇas) into our planetary etheric grid (*nāḍī* system). This is symbolised by the word Power (Electricity that feeds the receiver of the established *maṇḍala).* This energy is the combination of the first and second Ray aspects of Deity. Only a number of lesser entities composing a greater whole can bear such a force that is here posited. It concerns the controlled unleashing of energies never before known to humanity. The earth's magnetic field will intensify and its vibrational rate will be raised to begin the etherealisation process of its substance. Eventually the astral world will be cleansed of its conditionings, so that the prophecy 'and there was no more sea'[72] is accomplished. The astral and physical realms will inevitably merge.

This Divine approach will in time be signified by the earth's focus of attention being altered, which will be physically signified by the changing of the pole star. All the changes to come will obviously have a profound effect upon humanity's consciousness, and upon the substance of the earth, of which the mass destruction of its vegetable and animal

---

72 *Rev. 21:1.* The astral plane is Watery in nature, and is the 'sea' here mentioned. Its heaven and hell states will consequently eventually dissipate and be no more. This will take considerable time, for humanity has much *karma* yet to cleanse via mastery of these realms of the astral plane and their Watery proclivities.

life in the past 150 years have been indications and warnings. They have their correlation in the effects that the process of gaining enlightenment has upon the physical body of a person. The disappearance of one species of life[73] but paves the way for another one that is more adaptive to the new conditionings. So it will be for the new epoch.

It is all a question of time, of sensed opportunity, and of what humanity will do with that opportunity. The 'signs of the times' will show us, and these signs will appear with ever increasing momentum. As previously stated, the entire pace of the planet is speeding up. People are doing, achieving and consuming things faster than ever before. They are experiencing new freedoms and sensations, new common international policies and interests, despite the perpetuation of the arms race and the machinations of the dark forces that have incarnated into positions of power in our societies. In short, the collective consciousness of humanity is being stimulated, whilst their reactions to this are producing many new forms of crises. These crises are rapidly destroying old customs and motives, allowing humanity to embrace the future. This is not the bleak future of servitude and enslavement to the dictates of an ultra-wealthy elite that is presently being imposed upon humanity. (Specifically in the Western hemisphere.) That yoke is in the process of being thrown off to allow humanity to embrace, at first with uncertainty, the new freedom in all aspects of life that the Aquarian Age promises. All this is really preparatory in effect. If people meet the presented opportunity rightly, conditions will manifest in such a way that they will come to recognise what the Christ bears when He reappears. That event will be engendered by their response. The time is imminent.

Whenever a major new religion was founded (such as Christianity) it necessitated a concerted effort by all senior members of the Hierarchy, plus their disciples, to produce this. They come under the direct inspiration of the world Teacher, the current Christ. The work is thus specifically along the second Ray lines (and affiliated Ashrams). The evolution of civilisation in general (the manifestation of intelligent activity *per se)* is more specifically the concern of the Ashrams embodying the Rays of Mind – the third, fourth, fifth, sixth and seventh Ray Ashrams. They come under the auspices of the Lord of Civilisation,

---

73 They can be considered as planetary *saṃskāras*.

the Mahāchohan. The first Ray department under Morya is concerned with world politics and the esoteric war against the forces of evil.

The apostles were obviously senior members of Hierarchy. Some of the functions of the apostles were shown relation to figure 28. They have evolved in spiritual stature since those comparatively simple days. Hierarchy is composed of seven major Ray groupings, which are the Ashrams of the Chohans of the Rays. Under them are the Ashrams of the Masters, who oversee the functions of the various sub-Ray groupings of Souls and Initiates of their particular Ray line. These Ashrams are powerhouses for the dissemination of Light and beneficence to all upon our planet.

Hierarchy constitutes the Heart centre of our planetary Logos and is the inner spiritual government responsible for the evolutionary growth of all kingdoms in Nature, of which humanity is one. The great Lords at Shambhala constitute the Head centre. Humanity embody the functions of the Throat and other centres in the general planetary Body.

Jesus, Paul, John the Beloved, James, Lazarus and John the Baptist are now the Chohans of the sixth, fifth, fourth, third, second, and first Ray Ashrams respectively. They are Lords of these most purified Ray qualities, embodying attributes for which the roles they have played in their past incarnations were well befitted. Each life they lived manifested in a way that played out the karmic interrelationships to derive the characteristics needed to fulfil their present tasks as the most senior executives in the spiritual world government. The other apostles are now Masters of Wisdom or senior members of Hierarchy. Matthias, who became the twelfth apostle (replacing Judas Iscariot)[74] and Judas himself, are slightly younger members.

The lines of interrelation vivifying this second Ray Dispensation can be gained from a study of figure 29.

Here we see that Jesus (being the Chohan of the sixth Ray of Devotion) is the focal point of all these energies. This Ray is the necessary energy to feed the world's religious aspirants if they are to aspire to walk the way to enlightenment. It is a driving energy that sustains them upon this path. What is also exemplified here is a most ancient interrelation between the Christ, Jesus and Andrew.

---

74 *Acts 1:26.*

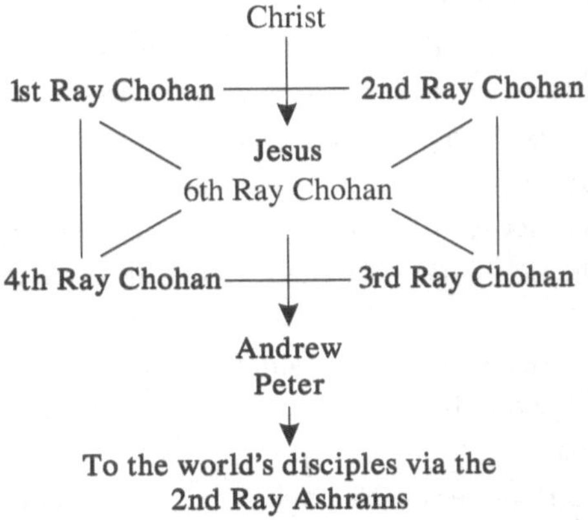

Figure 29: A line of planetary energisation

The first and second Rays always work as a unity to start all new cycles of the evocation of Love and Wisdom in humanity. The first Ray must be clothed with the Love-Wisdom Ray if abuses of Power are not to occur. Similarly, the sixth Ray must of necessity be clothed with the second Ray, if zealous aspiration is to be rightly tempered with modifying beneficent Wisdom. The development of Love-Wisdom is the overall purpose for the work of all the Ashrams in the world sphere.

The fifth and seventh Ray Chohans are noticeably absent here. They must lay the foundation in the empirical minds of people that will allow new seeds of Divinity to germinate. Such was the work of Paul, the fiery proselytiser. He came later in the gospel story, with his grouping of disciples, who were more or less upon the Rays of Mind. From this source came many of the distortions, annotations and voluminous doctrinal treatises of later Church Fathers and philosophers. These Rays of Mind had to properly flower into the type of civilisation that we now possess, before the renewed second Ray cycle can manifest upon a higher turn of the spiral, as explained in this book. The seventh Ray line (in its most concreted form as ritualised power) was influential upon the role that Pontius Pilot played, as well as on orthodox Jewry in Jesus' time: the Scribes, Pharisees, Zealots, etc. This was also so for those who were touched by Jesus' teachings, yet retained their links with orthodoxy, such as Judas and Nicodemus.

The seventh Ray (of Ceremonial or Ritualistic Purpose, Magic and Spiritual Power) is however the harbinger of the future. It will be the driving energy of the Aquarian epoch, as already stated, and will transform society in such a way that the inherent divinity of all Life on earth will be understood. A close working relationship between the *devas* and humanity will also be produced. It will give birth (under the auspices of the third Ray of Mathematically Exact Activity) to the epoch of the Mother of the World. Much further detail concerning this epoch and of the Hierarchical interrelationships is presented in my other books, especially the volumes of *The Constitution of Shambhala*. This, coupled with the writings of D.K. via Alice Bailey, presents a wealth of information that will hopefully inspire all who read to actively play an appropriate role in the externalisation process. They must open their minds to the potential of the upcoming enlightenment and awaken their Hearts to project the divinity within into their chosen field of service. We must work together to make what is imminent the divine reality. The causes of suffering must eventually become extinguished by all that work to extend streams of divine energies from the highest sources to humanity.

Peace be unto you.

Oṁ svāhā!

Bibliography

Bailey, Alice A. *A Treatise on Cosmic Fire.* NY: Lucis Publishing Company, 1951.

——. *A Treatise on White Magic.* NY: Lucis Publishing Company, 1991.

——. *Discipleship in the New Age, Volume I.* NY: Lucis Publishing Company, 1991.

——. *Esoteric Astrology.* London: Lucis Publishing Company, 1982.

——. *Esoteric Healing.* London: Lucis Publishing Company, 1998.

——. *Esoteric Psychology I,* London: Lucis Publishing Company, 1977.

——. *Esoteric Psychology II,* London: Lucis Publishing Company, 1977.

——. *Glamour: A World Problem.* NY: Lucis Publishing Company, 1998.

——. *Letters on Occult Meditation.* NY: Lucis Publishing Company, 1978.

——. *Telepathy and the Etheric Vehicle.* NY: Lucis Publishing Company, 1978.

——. *The Externalisation of the Hierarchy.* NY: Lucis Publishing Company, 1982.

——. *The Rays and the Initiations.* NY: Lucis Publishing Company, 1970.

——. *The Reappearance of the Christ.* NY: Lucis Publishing Company, 1976.

Balsys, Bodo. *A Treatise on Mind, Volume 1.* Sydney: Universal Dharma Publishing, 2016.

——. *A Treatise on Mind, Volume 2.* Sydney: Universal Dharma Publishing, 2016.

——. *A Treatise on Mind, Volume 3.* Sydney: Universal Dharma Publishing, 2016.

——. *A Treatise on Mind, Volume 4.* Sydney: Universal Dharma Publishing, 2015.

——. *A Treatise on Mind, Volume 5A.* Sydney: Universal Dharma Publishing, 2015.

——. *A Treatise on Mind, Volume 5B.* Sydney: Universal Dharma Publishing, 2015.

——. *A Treatise on Mind, Volume 6.* Sydney: Universal Dharma Publishing, 2014.

——. *A Treatise on Mind, Volume 7A.* Sydney: Universal Dharma Publishing, 2017.

——. *A Treatise on Mind, Volume 7B&C.* Sydney: Universal Dharma Publishing, 2018.

——. *Esoteric Cosmology and Modern Physics.* Sydney: Universal Dharma Publishing, 2020.

——. *The Astrological and Numerological Keys to The Secret Doctrine, Volume 1.* Sydney: Universal Dharma Publishing, 2020.

——. *The Astrological and Numerological Keys to The Secret Doctrine, Volume 2.* Sydney: Universal Dharma Publishing, 2020.

Blavatsky, Helena P. *The Secret Doctrine, Volume 1.* Adyar: Theosophical Publishing House, [1888] 2005.

——. *The Secret Doctrine, Volume 2.* Adyar: Theosophical Publishing House, [1888] 2005.

——. *The Secret Doctrine, Volume 5.* Adyar: Theosophical Publishing House, [1888] 2005.

——. *The Voice of the Silence.* Pasadena, CA: Theosophical University Press, [1889] 1992.

Bromiley, G. W. (general editor). *The International Standard Bible Dictionary, Volume 2.* Grand Rapids, Michigan: William B. Eerdmans Publishing Co., 1982.

Buttrick, George (dictionary editor). *The Interpreter's Dictionary of the Bible*. Nashville: Abingdon Press, 1962.

Capra, F. *The Tao of Physics*. Boulder, CO: Shambhala, 1975.

Conze, Edward. *Buddhist Thought in India*. Ann Arbor, MI: University of Michigan Press, 1967.

——. *Buddhist Scriptures*. NY: Penguin Books, 1959.

Cowell, E. B. *The Vagrakkhedikâ, from Buddhist Mahayâna Texts*. Delhi: Motilal Banarsidass, 1997.

David-Neel, Alexandra. *Magic and Mystery in Tibet*. NY: Dover Publications, 1971.

David-Neel, Alexandra & Lama Yongden. *The Secret Oral Teachings in Tibetan Buddhist Sects*. San Francisco: City Lights, 1972.

Eliade, Mircea. *Patterns in Comparative Religion*. NY: New American Library, 1974.

——. *Yoga: Immortality and Freedom*. London: Arkana, 1989.

Esslemont, J. E. *Baha'u'llah and the New Era*. Illinois: Baha'i Publishing Trust, 1970.

Evans-Wentz, W. Y. *The Tibetan Book of the Dead*. London: Oxford University Press, 1957.

——. *The Tibetan Book of the Great Liberation*. London: Oxford University Press, 1968.

Genno, L., Guzzon, F. & Marsigli, P. *Kirlian Photography*. London: East West Publications, 1980.

Govinda, Lama Anagarika. *Foundations of Tibetan Mysticism*. NY: E. P. Dutton, 1960.

——. *The Way of the White Clouds*. London: Ryder & Co., 1972.

Guenther, H. V. *Treasures on the Tibetan Middle Way*. Berkeley, CA: Shambhala Publications Inc., 1969.

Hall, Manly P. Man: *The Grand Symbol of the Mysteries*. LA: Philosopher Press, 1937.

Hartmann, Franz. Jacob Boehme: *Life and Doctrines*. NY: Steinerbooks, 1977.

Head, Joseph & Cranston, Silvia. *Reincarnation: The Phoenix Fire Mystery.* San Diego: Point Loma Publications, 1991.

Kingsland, William. *The Gnosis or Ancient Wisdom in the Christian Scriptures.* London: George Allen & Unwin, 1956.

Lawrence, Jodi. *Alpha Brain Waves.* NY: Avon Books, 1972.

Leadbeater, C. W. *The Chakras.* Adyar: Theosophical Publishing House, 1996.

Lovelock, James & Margulis, Lynn. *Atmospheric Homeostasis by and for the Biosphere: The Gaia Hypothesis.* Tellus, 26:1-2, 1974.

Moody, Raymond A. *Life after Life.* Harrisburg, PA: Stackpole Books, 1976.

Osis, Karlis & Haraldsson, Erlendur. *At the Hour of Death.* NY: Avon Books, 1977.

Ostrander, Sheila & Schroeder, Lynn. *Psychic Discoveries Behind the Iron Curtain.* NY: Bantam Books, 1973.

Platt, Rutherford H. Jr., *The Lost Books of the Bible.* NY: Alpha House, 1926.

Richelieu, Peter. *A Soul's Journey*, London: Thorsons, 1996.

Robinson, James M. (general editor). *The Nag Hammadi Library.* San Francisco: Harper, 1990.

Rudhyar, Dane. *Astrological Timing: The Transition Into the New Age.* NY: Harper and Row, 1972.

Sivananda, Swami. *The Bhagavad Gita.* Shivanandanagar, Rishikesh: Divine Life Society, 2003.

Sponberg, Alan & Hardacre, Helen (editors). *Maitreya, the Future Buddha.* NY: Cambridge University Press, 1988.

Talbot, Michael. *Mysticism and the New Physics.* NY: Bantam Books, 1980.

The Interpreter's Dictionary of the Bible, Volume 1. Nashville, Tennessee: Abingdon Press, 1962.

The King James Version Bible. London: Oxford University Press, 1922.

Tompkins, Peter & Bird, Christopher. *The Secret Life of Plants.* NY: Harper & Row, 1973.

Underhill, Evelyn. Mysticism: A *study in the nature and development of Man's spiritual consciousness.* Cleveland: Meridian Books, 1960.

Watson, Lyall. *The Romeo Error.* NY: Dell Publishing, 1976.

Whitman, John. *The Psychic Power of Plants.* London: Star Books, 1975.

Wynne-Tyson, Jon. *Food for a Future: The ecological priority of a Humane Diet.* London: Davis Poynter, 1975.

Zukav, Gary. *The Dancing Wu Li Masters: An Overview of the New Physics.* NY: Bantam Books, 1980.

Index

A

Aaron, 396
Abraham, 381–387, 394, 398
Adam, 347, 394, 416
Adept, xi, 71, 261
Ādityas, 392
Aether, 188
Ahriman, 425
Ahura Mazda, 392
Ākāśa, 339, 361
Akashic records, 139
Ālayavijñāna, 24, 46, 67, 357
Alchemy, 350
Alice Bailey, 438, 447, 463, 469
Alternative cultures, 447
Amen, 416
Amitābha, 392, 436
Amun-Ra, 392, 416
Andrew, 402–404, 409–411, 412, 467–468
Angel(s). *See* Devas
Anger, 211–213
Animal magnetism, 336
Annamayakośa, 347
Antaḥkaraṇa, 229, 299, 363
Anthroposophical Society, 437
Apāna, 348, 349, 354–356, 358, 359, 362, 363, 364, 370–371
Aphrodite, 250
Apollo, 392
Apostles, 399–414
Apostle's Creed, 427
Aquarius/Aquarian, 400–401, 407–408, 409, 412, 413, 433–434, 448
    Epoch/age, 59, 76, 123–124, 291, 304, 396, 413, 432–437, 447, 451, 453, 455–457, 465–466, 469
Arhat, xi, 71
Aries, 399, 402, 404–405, 408, 412, 432
Arjuna, 425–426
Ark, 397
Army of the Voice, 149, 155, 345
Aryan Root Race, 55
Asher, 400, 405
Asherah, 395, 397
Ashrams, 142, 199, 352, 357, 361, 395, 446–447, 451
Aspirants, 30
Aṣṭadiśas, 410
Astral. *See* Body/Plane
Astvat-ereta, 425
Atlantis, 71, 116, 302
Atoms, 152–154, 163, 170
Aūṁ, 377, 389, 390, 416
Aura, 40, 42, 53, 172, 210–214, 223, 365, 368
Avatara(s), 424–427

B

Baal, 395
Baha'u'llah, 437
Baptism, 94, 324, 414
Bartholomew, 403–404, 409, 410–412
Baskets of Nourishment, 355
Beatitudes, 401
Being, xii, 10, 11, 18, 20, 37, 58–59, 67
    Enlightened, 6, 11, 13, 20, 46, 55, 61, 63
Benjamin, 400, 406
Bethsaida, 403
Bīja, 40, 227, 338, 464
Black magic, 54, 70, 97, 150, 217, 226, 243, 254, 270, 296–300, 302, 344, 441
Blessing, 386
Blood, 166, 169, 185, 339, 392–395, 416, 433, 436
    Stream, 83, 168
Bodhi, 11
    Tree, 456
Bodhicitta, 4, 6, 66, 252, 342
Bodhisattva(s), xii, 11, 61, 66, 71, 94, 96, 312, 379, 380, 401, 427, 431
Body/Plane, 255
    Astral, 234, 236, 239, 241, 242, 243, 245, 246, 247, 248, 251, 253, 254, 255, 343–345, 368
    Causal, 10, 23, 47, 137, 163, 233, 238, 239, 252
    Logoic, 161, 202, 205
    Mental, 193, 206
    of Deity/God, 38, 43–44, 76, 83, 159–160, 200, 207, 234, 277, 433, 436
    Physical, 76, 89, 91, 134–135, 161, 171, 172, 432
Boehme, J, 25, 121
Brahmā, 204, 233, 239, 247–249, 252–254, 369
Brahmarandhra vidhāra, 91
Breath, 362–363, 378
Buddha, 11, 20, 25–27, 56, 59–60, 66–67, 125, 138, 159, 224, 271, 277, 281, 317, 329, 427, 428–429, 431–432, 443, 456, 461–462
Buddhi, 6, 40, 48, 83, 91, 167, 193, 204–205, 207, 208, 213, 237–238, 239, 241–243, 246, 251, 252, 339, 349, 350, 352, 361, 365, 371, 394, 396, 398, 435, 436, 450, 453, 458, 464

C

Caduceus, 264, 266
Cancer, 400, 404–405, 409, 412
Capricorn, 400, 402, 406, 407, 409, 412
Carotid gland, 343
Causation, 192, 337
Causative process, 334, 336, 341, 342, 343, 347, 353, 363
Central Spiritual Sun, 341
Centre(s). *See* Chakra(s)
Cephas, 402
Chakra(s), 26, 40, 42, 51, 91, 200, 207, 217, 227, 239, 246, 255, 270–274, 280–281, 340–347, 350, 436, 441, 464
    Ājñā, 51, 204, 242, 262, 272, 341–342, 344–345, 357
    Base of Spine, 267, 272, 280, 292, 338, 344–346, 349, 351, 356, 358, 364, 390
    Between the Shoulder Blades, 350
    Diaphragm, 350
    Hands, 243
    Head, 91, 207, 268–269, 272, 341, 344–345, 347, 349, 351, 357, 383, 385, 397, 454
    Heart, 83, 205, 207, 250, 342–344, 347, 349, 351, 361, 397, 409, 412, 441, 454, 459, 467
    Mūlādhāra. *See* Base of Spine
    Sacral, 205, 343–345, 349, 351, 459
    sahasrāra padma. *See* Head

Solar Plexus, 202, 227, 247, 341, 342, 343–345, 351, 352–353, 425, 459
Splenic centre, 335, 345, 350, 351
Third Eye. *See* Ājñā
Throat, 204, 227, 272, 273, 342, 343–344, 349, 354, 356, 358, 459
Twenty-two minor, 344
Viśuddha. *See* Throat
Chohan(s), 26, 159, 208, 281, 361, 397, 421, 467–468
Christ, xiv, xv, xvii, 5–6, 14, 19, 27, 31, 34, 40, 56, 59–60, 62, 64–69, 86–87, 98, 102, 138–139, 141, 168, 224, 228, 238, 273, 303, 327, 329, 376, 379, 387, 391, 394, 411, 412, 414–417, 418, 419, 425, 427, 428, 433, 434, 441, 444, 461–464. *See also* Jesus
Child, 46, 405, 436, 460–461
Consciousness, 4, 6, 63, 120, 168, 393, 447
Cosmic, 369, 416, 465
Light of, 70, 79, 96, 168, 225, 450
Planetary and solar, 40
Principle, 15, 31, 73, 252, 338–339, 378, 389, 419
Purpose of, 73, 183
Second coming/Reappearance of, xii, 110, 118–121, 226–227, 394, 396, 403, 413, 417, 428, 430, 432–433, 436–441, 449, 450, 454–456, 457, 459, 464–466
Christianity, 60, 63, 69, 101, 102, 212, 301, 315, 392, 413, 424, 446
Christ-Maitreya, 430–431, 449
Christos, 424
Church, 419
Cintāmaṅī, 461
Clairvoyant(s), 54, 56–57, 178, 217, 234, 273
Clouds, 186, 213, 217, 222, 439, 450, 454, 457, 460
Communal idealism, 113
Consciousness thread, 343, 346
Corporatocracy, 114, 122
Covenant, xi, 1, 27, 267, 289, 383, 384, 392–399, 401, 402, 405, 407, 413–414, 424
Covid-19, 63, 115, 122
Creation, 14, 31, 42, 48, 146, 166, 168, 266
Creative Deity, 387
Creative Hierarchies, 46, 150, 202, 204–205, 292
Creative imagination, 64, 234, 354, 364
Creative thread, 343, 346
Creative Will, 342
Crises, 466
Cross, 346
Eight-pointed, 409–410
Fixed, 222, 434, 452
of crucifixion, 53, 269, 379, 393, 416, 418, 427, 444
of Life, 386
Crucifixion, 65, 269, 284, 379, 386, 396, 408, 411, 413, 416, 427
Cycle of time, 260, 274, 389, 390
Cyclical change, 124, 434

D

Dan, 400, 406
Dark brotherhood, 115, 116, 140, 284, 291, 293, 296–297, 307, 309–311, 314, 360, 366, 369, 448
Darkness, 167, 282, 288–289, 291, 293, 297, 303, 391
David, 424
Death, 130–132, 261, 266, 281, 306–309, 315, 320–321, 329
Deity, 8, 15, 18–23, 26, 31, 38, 44–47, 58, 65, 77, 85, 103, 131, 165, 168, 198, 277, 327, 389
Delphic Oracle, 33
Desert, 212, 270–271, 324, 400, 439, 441

Desire(s), 79, 83, 105, 125, 210, 217, 222, 225, 245, 270, 323
Devachan, 184, 309
Devaki, 426
Deva(s)/Devic, 13, 50, 58, 81–82, 139, 149, 153–158, 179, 200, 204–208, 220–221, 235, 239, 246, 252, 289, 292, 299, 303, 335–336, 345, 352, 353, 357, 358–360, 363, 377, 436–437, 451, 454–455, 457, 460, 469
  Agnichaitans, 158
  Agnishvattas, 158, 200, 360
  Agnisuryans, 158
  Planetary devas, 335–336
  Solar devas, 335
Devil, 260, 284, 291, 293–296
Dharma, xi, 46, 66–67, 259, 302
Dharmakāya, 11–12, 19, 208, 349, 357, 388, 454
Dhyāna, 80, 120, 265
Dhyān Chohan, 361
Dhyāni Buddhas, 255
Dimensionality, 175, 178–179
Directions (four), 381–382, 393, 411–412
Disease(s), 336–337, 340–341
Divine Light Mission, 437
Divine (the), 10–11, 13, 19, 21, 28, 31, 38, 44, 47, 50, 72, 88, 90, 100, 103, 130, 131, 234, 238, 256, 389, 431, 435, 438
  Causation, 23, 193, 230
  Impulse, 192
  Law, xiv–xv, 23, 46, 61, 85, 116
  Love, 7, 57, 60
  Marriage, 159, 198
  Purpose, 20, 58, 63, 456, 457, 465
  Reason, 377
  Sacrifice, 416
  Will, 21, 150, 159, 204, 208, 235
D.K., 469
DNA, 353
Dogma, 2, 99
Dove, 414
Dragon of Wisdom, 260, 270, 339, 390
Duality, 200

E

Eagles, 442
Ear-whispered truths, 68, 94
Eden, 49, 51, 99, 261, 314, 452
Ego, 16, 19
Eightfold Path, 125, 127–130, 271
Eighth sphere, 307, 309, 330
Electric Fire, 277, 339
Electricity, 37, 337, 338, 339–340, 465
Elect, the, 439–440, 449, 455, 458–459
Elemental(s), 82, 206, 292, 296
Elementary Lives, 345, 354, 359
Elements, 188, 253, 272, 279–281, 304, 312, 348, 349, 382, 390, 440, 455, 460
  Aether, 188, 459
  Air(y), 48, 185–186, 273, 280, 283, 349, 350, 435, 436, 442, 453, 458
  Earth, 274, 280–281, 435, 458
  Fire(y), 45, 94, 116, 184, 186, 201, 229, 245, 263, 266–268, 270, 273, 280, 404, 448, 458
  Water(y), 116, 169, 185, 205, 273, 280, 404, 433, 435–436, 458
Emotion(s), 176, 179, 269–270, 273, 280, 285–286, 302, 306, 309, 311, 317, 321–323, 325–326, 328
Energy, 14, 18, 37, 38, 40, 45, 60, 84–85, 89, 148, 171, 185, 201. *See also* Prāṇa
Enlightenment, xvi, 37, 51, 71
Entropy, 180
Etheric body/double, 39, 41–44, 339, 351, 414, 436
Etheric webs, 338
Evil, 259–261, 282–286, 292,

294–297, 301–302, 330, 354, 446, 448–449, 467
Evocation, 462
Evolution, 13, 15, 20–21, 26, 31, 44–47, 49–52, 56, 59, 65, 70, 72, 77, 79, 81–82, 86, 97, 100, 103, 111, 116, 124, 131–132, 138, 142, 146, 147, 149, 151, 154, 157–158, 162, 165, 180, 185–186, 188, 192, 197, 199–202, 203, 204, 206–208, 217, 225, 250, 252–253, 255, 261, 280, 294, 297, 303–305, 307–308, 311, 331, 334, 339, 346–347, 349–351, 352–354, 356, 362, 368, 378–379, 387, 389–391, 396, 405, 411, 417, 434, 436, 450, 452–453, 455, 458, 467
Excretion, 166, 240, 246–248
Exorcism, 301

F

Faith, 99
Fascism, 445
Father, 19, 38, 47, 66, 68, 202, 204, 245, 265, 328, 376, 378, 379, 420
Father energy, 338
Fear, 5, 147, 173, 293, 295–296, 301, 316, 320–321, 324, 326–328, 330, 442
Fiery Breath, 348
Fig tree, 404, 456, 459, 460
Findhorn, 437, 438
Fire, cosmic, 369
Fires, Creative, 347
Four Noble Truths, 125–127

G

Gad, 401
Gaia theory, 114
Gautama, 11
Gemini, 400, 403, 404–405, 411, 412, 434, 436
Generation(s), 381, 393, 394, 398, 440, 452–454
Geometry, 31–32
Gethsemane, 66, 416
Glamour, 213–214, 225, 237, 241, 285
Glory, xiv, 52–53, 159, 253, 303, 315, 330, 374, 375, 383, 397, 398, 416–417, 454, 457, 460
God, 1, 4–5, 8, 13–18, 20–23, 25–26, 28–29, 31, 34, 37, 48–49, 52, 59, 61–62, 63, 66, 68, 95–97, 99–100, 102, 142, 152, 157, 159–161, 165–167, 185–186, 238, 253, 261, 277, 283, 285, 291, 297, 309, 315, 317, 361, 380, 382–384, 387–390, 395, 397, 452, 460, 462, 466
  Kingdom of, 6, 30, 33, 67, 70, 98, 121, 123, 192, 224, 381, 383, 399, 411, 420, 439–440, 454, 459
  Love of, 168, 275, 350, 386, 416–417, 418, 438–439, 442, 454
  Mind of, 12, 23, 47, 61, 85, 131, 138, 153, 155, 164, 167, 185, 186, 229, 337
  Realisation, 60–61, 73, 95, 388
  Son(s) of, 14, 52, 56, 98, 266, 271, 331, 351, 377, 384–385, 393, 398, 416, 418, 443–444, 464
  Word of, 2, 21, 46, 235, 265, 377–378, 405, 412
Good will, xiv, 5–6, 63, 89, 114, 116, 123, 294, 412, 417, 429, 439, 445, 461
Gospel of the kingdom, 439, 463
Great Symbol, 12, 192
Guest chamber, 432, 441
Guru, 68–71, 379, 419

H

Hand symbolism, 396, 398
Hatha yoga, 355
Heart, 4, 8, 28, 34, 50, 65, 393. *See also* Chakra(s)
Heart of the Sun, 342, 376

Heavenly realm (heaven), 12, 30, 47, 77–79, 85, 88–89, 90–91, 99–100, 105, 106, 153, 159, 166, 173, 180–181, 253, 283, 286–287, 308, 346, 353, 382, 419–420, 427–428, 439, 440, 442, 444, 450–453, 454–457, 459–460, 465
Hell, 5, 77–79, 173, 283–284, 290, 305–310, 445
Hermes/Hermetic, 14, 33–34, 263–264, 464
Herod, 427
Hierarchy, 31, 34, 46, 55, 59, 61–63, 67, 69, 157, 204–208, 225, 297, 303, 327, 351, 361, 388, 395–397, 399, 421, 428, 441, 446, 449, 451–452, 454–455, 459, 467
Holy Ghost, 46
Hormones, 157, 160, 169, 340, 460
Hydra, 286, 366

I

I AM, 387–392, 398, 416
I AM THAT, 388–392, 418
I AM THAT I AM, 387–392, 418
Imagination, 12, 106, 234
Imam Mahdi, xii
India, 411
Individualisation, 47, 202, 353
Initiate/Initiation(s), 16, 31, 59, 110, 119, 121, 141, 202, 347, 354, 356, 358, 363, 365–367, 384, 440, 442, 447, 449, 455–456, 459–460, 462–463
  1st, 270, 343, 355, 359, 366
  2nd, 270, 354, 360, 366
  3rd, 47, 194, 207, 214, 224, 262, 269, 338, 355, 357, 360, 366, 384, 406, 408, 440, 450, 452
  4th, 11, 19, 198, 208, 262, 270, 337, 352, 359, 360, 366–367, 421, 440, 453–454
  5th, 207–208, 260, 270, 281, 357, 368
  6th, 208, 281, 352, 359, 361, 421, 453
  7th, 59, 208, 362
Inner round, 344, 353, 356
Inquisition, 2
Inquisitors, 329
Instinct(s), 193, 194–201, 204–209, 247, 340, 351, 352, 353, 354, 355, 357, 358, 359
Intellect, 58, 150, 193–194, 208, 220–221, 230, 238, 244, 255, 268, 290–291, 293, 298, 302
Intelligence, 149, 152, 193–194, 197, 342
Internet, 414, 445
Intuited/Intuition, 4, 12, 60, 120, 140
Intuitive perception, 52
Invocation, 379, 462
Isaac, 383–386, 398
Israel, 32, 63, 78, 262, 263, 268, 269, 387, 391, 393–395, 399, 402, 406, 424
Israelites, 268, 384, 396, 401
Issachar, 400, 403

J

Jacob, 398, 399
Jacob's ladder, 277
James, 93, 402, 404–406, 408–409, 411–413, 467
James. Alpheus's son, 408
Jehovah-jireh, 384
Jerusalem, 397, 403, 406, 454
Jesus, 52, 57, 59–63, 65, 68, 70–72, 92–95, 97–98, 100, 123, 140, 141, 228, 261, 262, 269, 270, 284–285, 287, 290, 301, 311–316, 324, 325, 326, 328, 329, 374–376, 379, 380, 383, 385–387, 391–393, 396, 398, 401–409, 411–414, 416–420, 424, 426–427, 432, 439, 441, 443–444, 447, 456, 467
Jews, 95, 313, 315, 379, 381, 383, 391, 397, 402, 424, 433, 439
Jīva, 336, 351
Jñāna, 46
John, 278, 308, 311, 402, 404–405,

409, 411–412, 420, 467
John the Baptist, 92, 94, 97, 385, 447, 467
Jonas, 452
Joseph, 400, 426–427
Josiah, 395
Judah, 400, 404
Judas Iscariot, 287, 311–313, 408, 410–411, 412–413, 467
Judas (James' brother), 406, 412–413
Jupiter, 437

K

Kabbalah, 32
Kali yuga, 425
Kalki, 425
Kalki-Purāṇa, 425
Kāma-manas, 176, 210, 214, 221, 229
Kansa, 427
Karma/Karmic, 24, 50, 51, 58, 64, 77, 78, 79–81, 83–85, 92, 95–97, 102, 116, 120, 123, 138, 155–156, 181, 184, 187, 201, 204, 217–218, 224, 252, 256, 282–294, 296, 304, 307–309, 329, 336, 376, 385, 407, 415, 428, 443, 451
 Cosmic, 162, 390
 Lord(s) of, 315, 455, 457
Key, Physiological, 160
Kingdom(s), 296
 Angelic/devic, 20, 53, 58, 81, 149, 155–157, 220
 Animal, 47–50, 53, 102–103, 170, 194–197, 202, 269–270, 302, 310, 322–325
 Gospel of, 420
 Human, 103, 157, 159, 196
 Mineral, 49–50, 53, 170, 194–197, 205
 of God, 98, 121
 of Heaven, 31
 Plant/vegetable, 49–50, 53, 170, 194–196, 206, 218, 300, 324
Kirlian photography, 42
Kleśas, 326, 366
Kośa, 347
Krishna (Kṛṣṇa), 425–427, 432
Krishnamurti, 437
Kuṇḍalinī, 62, 110, 208, 226, 263–264, 266–270, 274, 276–277, 286, 292, 298, 337, 338, 339–340, 346, 355, 357, 369, 389, 458

L

Lama Anagarika Govinda, 430
Lamb, 385
Lao Tze, 443
Law(s), 58–59, 66, 67, 401, 402, 409, 431
 of karma. *See* Karma
 of physics, 58, 84
 of thermodynamics, 180
Lazarus, 420–421, 462
Left hand path, 243, 296–297, 301–304, 306–307, 311–315, 317
Lemurian(s), 56, 71, 371
Leo, 400, 404–405, 409, 412, 435
Levi, 400, 403
Libra, 400, 406, 411, 434
Life, 37, 38, 44, 46, 57, 59, 61, 65, 76–77, 132, 146–147, 151, 165, 263–266, 273–275, 281, 282, 296, 327, 408, 420, 458
 Force, 348, 350
Light, 38, 70, 167, 365, 374–376, 389, 392, 417, 460, 467
Logos/Logoi(c), 46, 80, 150, 168, 203–204, 303, 377, 389, 392, 396, 415
 Planetary, 21, 25–27, 44, 50, 54, 68, 116, 119, 138, 161, 199–202, 204, 245–246, 254, 336, 398, 420, 458, 467
 Solar, 44, 138, 162, 168, 199, 246, 455
Lord of Glory, 52–53
Lords of Dark Face, 260, 398
Lord, the, 384, 395

Love, 5, 7, 57, 59–61, 70, 159, 188, 226, 352, 354, 392, 417, 418, 436
of 'God', 386, 418, 462
Love-Wisdom, 38, 59, 60, 62, 86, 87, 127, 129, 132, 143, 151, 159–160, 197, 214, 224, 236, 251, 253, 302, 305, 351, 369, 378–380, 384, 385, 392, 395–396, 407, 411, 437, 452, 454, 468
Lucifer, 283–284
Lunar Lords, 205, 355
Lunar Pitris, 292

M

Magnetic, 5
Mahāchohan, 362, 449, 467
Mahāmanvantara, 308
Mahat (cosmic Mind), 204, 250, 260, 357
Mahdi, 424
Maitreya, xii, 427–432, 449
Makara, 205–206, 355, 360
Manas, 193, 244, 250. *See also* Mind/mind
Maṇḍala, 138, 175, 464–465
Manna, 238, 380
Mānuṣa Buddha, 428
Manu's department, 362, 383
Manvantara, 81, 236, 250, 261
Mars, 436
Mary, 46, 385, 405, 418–419, 426
Mary and Martha, 420
Mary Magdalene, 408
Mass media, 115, 117, 118, 394
Masters of Wisdom, xi, 32, 68, 71, 86, 207, 260, 383, 463, 467. *See also* Ashrams
Material domain, 260
Matthew, 403, 405–406, 411, 413
Matthias, 467
Māyā, 10, 347, 434
Māyāvirūpa, 368
Medium(s), 268, 302
Meher Baba, 437
Messiah, xii, 424–425, 439
Metempsychosis, 102, 104–105
Mind/mind, 8–10, 12–13, 15–16, 21, 23–26, 34, 44–47, 51–52, 70, 82, 152, 165, 197, 200, 204, 219, 233, 245, 254, 273, 357, 363, 377, 378, 418, 435, 461
Abstract, 365, 376, 384
Cosmic. *See* Mahat
Logoic, 25, 149, 204, 207–208, 229, 260, 368, 369, 388
of Deity/God, 23, 44, 47, 61, 85, 199, 229, 277
Miracle(s), 70
Mokṣa, 352
Monad(ic), 11, 19, 23, 50, 159, 198, 200, 204, 207–208, 250, 255, 299, 343, 346, 352, 361, 368, 418
Moon, 167, 168, 235, 265, 275, 398, 404, 407, 435, 450–451, 456, 459
Mortal sin, 444
Moses, 262, 268, 269, 379, 387, 391–392, 396, 401
Mother, 19, 38, 46, 58, 204, 235, 248, 250, 254, 263, 279, 337, 340, 346, 377, 454
Great, 82, 201
Nature, 153
of the World, 469
Mountain(top), 64, 72, 99, 208, 293, 304, 384, 386, 397, 400, 401, 407, 408, 433
Mourn (to), 452, 453
Muhammad, 443
Mystery(ies), 29, 30, 52, 57, 60, 64, 66, 68, 69, 71–72, 98, 110, 123, 192, 376, 398, 419, 440–441, 456
of Being, xiii, 64, 96–98, 117, 390, 438
Schools, 30, 68, 71, 261

N

Nāḍī(s), 39–40, 57, 200, 277, 279, 281, 324, 340, 346, 347, 348–349, 434, 458–459, 465
Iḍā, 208, 243, 264–265, 276, 281, 337, 346, 355, 358, 450, 458–459

Piṅgalā, 208, 243, 264–265, 276, 281, 337, 346, 355, 358, 379, 385, 450, 458–459
Suṣumṇā, 263, 276–277, 281, 286, 337–338, 346, 359, 364, 450
Nāgārjuna, 262
Nāga(s), 261
Nag Hammadi, 413
Nanda, 426–427
Naphthali, 400, 408
Nathanael, 403–404
NATO, 448
Nature, 147–149, 189, 250
Nervous system, 239, 342
autonomic, 343, 353
New Age, xii, 62, 79, 114–115, 123, 217, 303, 369, 394, 402, 417, 442, 445–450, 452, 457, 460–461, 465
New Jerusalem, 369, 429, 451, 454, 459
Nirmāṇakāya, 11–12, 19, 26
Nirvāṇa, 61, 367, 461
Nirvāṇees, 199, 418
Non-Real, 22

O

Oṁ, 377–378, 380, 390
Original sin, 443
Ormazd, 392
Outpouring(s), 45–46, 201–204

P

Pancreas, 273, 343
Paranormal, 110
Parsees, 392
Passover, 432–433
Paul, 467, 468
Pentecost, 414
Permanent atom, 137, 364
Personality, 84, 90, 207, 219–220, 234
Peter, 66, 285, 287–289, 311, 394, 402–403, 406–409, 412, 419, 468
Pharaoh, 433
Philip, 403–404, 411–412
Pineal gland, 341
Piscean age, 123, 408, 413, 432, 453
Pisces, 401, 407–408, 432, 435, 448
Pitcher, 433
Pituitary gland, 342
Plane(s), 142, 155, 193, 251–255. *See* Buddhi
Ādi, 201, 204, 250
Anupādaka, 200, 202, 204, 207, 248, 250
Astral, 77, 83, 161, 169, 173, 174, 181, 205, 214, 218, 239, 242–243, 353–354, 465
Ātma/ātmic, 16, 199, 201, 204, 207, 233, 237–239, 247, 248, 250, 251, 252, 253, 341, 349, 368
Cosmic astral, 202–204, 345
Etheric, 206, 245
Mental, 94, 184–185, 200, 206–207, 239, 241
of Divine Causaton, 193
Physical, 185, 205, 235, 239, 240
Seven systemic, 203
Planetary Entity, 336
Pleroma, 392
Pontius Pilot, 468
Power, 417
Prajñā, 265
Prajñāpāramitā Sūtra, 378
Pralaya, 81, 180, 236, 294, 362, 401
Prāṇamayakośa, 347
Prāṇa(s), 39–41, 161, 222, 228, 263–266, 274, 279–280, 299–300, 304, 311, 324, 326, 334–337, 338–339, 345, 347–348, 351, 378, 436, 458–459
as a Vayū, 348–352, 358, 360, 362, 365, 370–371
Solar, 336, 352
Prāṇava, 378
Prāṇāyāma, 347, 355
Prāṇic fires, 334–335
Prāṇic triangle, 350
Pratyakṣa, 121

Predestination, 414–417
Probationary path, 352, 365
Psychic(s), 29, 54, 57, 71, 110, 116, 178, 184, 217, 218, 224, 263, 270, 299–300, 302, 324, 397. *See* Chakra(s)
Purpose, 9, 15, 19–20, 26, 51, 63
Pyramid of Giza, 32
Pythagorean(s), 31–33

R

Ray(s), 42, 142–143, 209, 215–216, 233–234, 248–249, 250–251, 337, 375, 378, 456, 467
- 1st, 337, 341, 350, 363, 395, 448–449, 465, 468
- 2nd, 60, 349, 364, 384, 396, 411, 437, 452, 465, 467–468
- 3rd, 250, 343, 469
- 6th, 467–468
- 7th, 436, 448, 468–469
- of Mind, 233, 466, 468

Real, 10, 19–20
Rebirth, 92, 95, 100–101
Reincarnation. *See* Rebirth
Resurrection body, 414
Reuben, 399, 402
Ring-pass-not, 198–199
Rishi, xi, 71
Room symbolism, 432–433
Root Race(s), 116, 218, 255, 371
- Fifth, 357, 381

Rosicrucians, 438

S

Sagittarius, 400, 406, 412, 413, 453
Salome, 408
Samāna, 348, 349, 352–354, 370–371
Sambhogakāya, 11–12, 19
- Flower, 11, 50, 91, 102, 207, 233, 292, 342, 351, 357, 368

Saṃsāra, 9–10, 19, 235, 252–253, 260, 288, 292, 419, 428, 450, 459
Saṃskāra(s), 24, 51, 176, 184, 266, 269, 277, 285, 296, 299–300, 308, 311–312, 326, 366
Sanat Kumāra, 202, 254, 429
Sant Kirpal Singh, 437
Sarah, 383–384
Satan, 282, 284–294, 303, 304, 311, 376, 391, 407, 410, 439, 443
Satori, 8, 121
Saturn, 251, 252, 407
Saturnalia, 407
Saul, 414
Scorpio, 359, 400, 406, 411, 413, 436
Scribes and Pharisees, 313, 315, 330, 375–376, 379–380, 386
Self-centredness, 89, 215, 344
Sense Consciousnesses, 233
Sensual desire. *See* Desire
Sepher Yetzirah, 32
Serpent, 260, 261, 266, 267, 274–276, 347, 379, 389–390
Sexual expression, 236, 355, 359, 413
Shambhala, 47, 56, 67–68, 142, 207, 224, 348, 361, 368, 383, 388, 415, 436, 449, 453, 455
Shiva (Śiva), 248, 250
Siddhis, 51, 326, 359, 389, 441
Signs, 440
Silver cord, 171–172
Simeon, 400, 403
Simon (Zelotes), 402, 406, 410–411, 413
Sins, 376, 385
Sirius, 452
Smaragdine Tablet, 33
Socrates, 56, 121, 329
Solar Angel, 50, 450
Solar Fire, 38, 245, 307, 337
Solar Logos. *See* Logos
Sol Invictus, 407
Solomon's seal, 292, 377
Son(s), 15, 19, 38, 46, 98, 155, 159, 167, 200, 202, 245, 265, 279, 303, 378, 380, 381, 392–393, 398, 426, 452, 454–455, 457–458, 460, 463.

See also God, Son(s) of
Sorcerer(s), 243, 262, 296–298, 300–301, 317, 331, 441
Soshyans, 424
Soul(s), 9–11, 19, 21, 43–45, 47, 50, 56, 70, 76–77, 82, 84, 91, 102, 138, 185, 197, 204, 207, 214, 252, 264–265, 272, 285, 292, 298–299, 302, 337, 354, 376, 378, 382, 384, 388, 389, 407, 417, 434–435, 453
  Group, 49, 50, 138, 153–154, 283, 383, 416
Sound, 57, 59, 67, 71, 81, 82, 235, 377, 458
  Mantric, 21, 54, 359, 363, 415
  Nameless, 377–378, 390
Space, 8, 10, 17, 24, 25, 28, 39, 51, 72, 81, 120, 152, 155–156, 166, 175, 177, 192, 197, 200, 204, 230, 237, 265, 267, 271, 275, 278–279, 283, 367, 375, 390, 393, 417–418, 440, 452, 455, 459
Sphinx, xi
Spirit, 9, 19, 20, 22, 38, 44, 46–47, 49, 50, 66, 119, 167, 265, 327
  Sword of, 339
Square, 390
Stars, 382, 451, 456, 460
Stomach, 341, 343
Storehouse of knowledge, 70
Subjective realm(s), 96
Subtle body, 11, 19
Suffering, causes of, 125
Sukhāvatī, 436
Sun, 345, 454, 456–457
Śūnyatā, 27, 61, 164, 352, 360, 388, 460
Surya, 392
Sūtrātma, 273, 299–300, 342, 343
Swastika(s), 280, 369

T

Tablets, 14, 401
Tai Chi, 436
Taurus, 400, 403, 404–405, 412
Telepathy, 228–229
Temple(s), 32, 57, 58, 100, 361, 391, 397, 402, 403, 405, 406, 411, 412, 413, 443
Tetraktys, 32
Tezecatlipoca, 392
THAT, 21, 22, 388–392
Theosophical Society, 437
Third Eye, 341
Thomas (Didymus), 73, 237, 386, 406, 411, 413
Thought-form(s), 138, 148, 156, 193, 199, 214, 221–225, 227, 293, 296
Thread(s), 343, 346
Throne, 390, 416, 419, 454–455
Thunder, 404–405
Thymus gland, 343
Thyroid gland, 343
Tomo Géshé Rinpoché, 430–431
Transmutation, 339, 340, 460
Tree of knowledge, 51
Tribes of Israel, 394, 397, 399–401
Tribulation, 448–450
Trikāya, 11
Trimūrti, 425
Trinity, 21
Trumpet, 455, 458
Truth, xi, 2, 7, 11, 46, 61, 66–67, 380
Tushita, 428

U

Udāna, 348–349, 356–357, 358, 362–363, 364, 367, 370–371
United Nations, 428
Unreal, 10
Uranus, 167, 251, 283, 436–437, 448
USA, 448

V

Vagrakkhedikâ, 431
Vagus nerve, 343
Vayūs, 334, 343, 347–371, 378
Virgo, 400, 405, 411
Vishnu (Viṣṇū), 248, 250, 425
  Avatars of, 425

Voice, xiv, 13, 67, 273, 380, 386, 427, 433
Vyāna, 348–349, 356–358, 361, 362, 363, 364, 365, 370–371

W

War(s), 3, 451, 457
Will, 248, 251–252, 253, 263, 268, 337, 338, 341, 346, 350, 357
    of Logos, 360–361, 368, 378
    -to-Be, 149, 151, 247, 253
Winds, 238, 280, 334, 348, 378, 440, 455, 458–460
Wisdom Eye, 69
Wisdom Religion, 110
Wisdom(s), xiii, 4, 5–6, 21, 51–53, 55–57, 60, 62, 66, 70, 73, 79, 86, 91, 98, 121, 125, 159, 199, 215, 217, 219, 238, 244, 246, 251, 253, 255, 260, 261, 262, 265, 267, 272, 285, 301–302, 314, 321, 352, 354, 365, 380, 385, 392, 413, 425, 433, 438, 445, 462, 468
Word, 21, 26, 67, 235, 241, 242, 247, 264, 265, 343, 377–381, 405, 413
Worlds, 21, 160, 161, 166, 361
World Servers, 447

X

X-Force, 41

Y

Yogācāra, 24, 67
Yogin(s), 9, 61–62, 91, 212, 236, 263, 267, 273

Z

Zebulon, 400, 404
Zodiac, 32, 433
Zoroastrians, 392

About the Author

BODO BALSYS is the founder of The School of Esoteric Sciences. He is an author of many books on subjects centred on Buddhism and the Esoteric Sciences, a meditation teacher, poet, artist, spiritual scientist and healer. He has studied extensively across multiple traditions including Esoteric Science, Buddhism, Christianity, Esoteric Healing, Western Science, Art, Politics and History. His advanced esoteric insights, gained through decades of meditative contemplation, enable him to provide a rich understanding of the spiritual pathway toward enlightenment, healing and service.

Bodo's teachings can be accessed via the School of Esoteric Science's website:
http://universaldharma.com

For any other enquiries, please email
sangha@universaldharma.com

About Universal Dharma Publishing

Universal Dharma Publishing is a not for profit publisher. Our aim is make innovative, original and esoteric spiritual teachings accessible to all who genuinely aspire to awaken and serve humanity. The books published aim in part to provide an esoteric interpretation of the meaning of Buddhist *dharma* with view of reformation of the way people perceive the meaning of the related teachings. Hopefully then Buddhism can more effectively serve its principal function as a vehicle for enlightenment, and further prosper into the future. A further aim is to provide the next level of exposition of the esoteric doctrines to be revealed to humanity following on the wisdom tradition pioneered by H.P. Blavatsky and A.A. Bailey.

www.ingramcontent.com/pod-product-compliance
Lightning Source LLC
Chambersburg PA
CBHW031957220426
43664CB00005B/57
* 9 7 8 0 6 4 8 7 8 7 7 2 3 *